TRAVELS IN INDIA

BY

JEAN-BAPTISTE TAVERNIER

BARON OF AUBONNE

Jean-Baptiste Tavernier, Baron d'Aubonne, in 1676
at the age of 74

TRAVELS IN INDIA

BY

JEAN-BAPTISTE TAVERNIER

BARON OF AUBONNE

Translated from the original French Edition of 1676 with a biographical sketch of the Author, Notes, Appendices, &c.

By

V. BALL, C.B., LL.D., F.R.S., F.G.S.

SECOND EDITION

Edited by WILLIAM CROOKE, C.I.E.
Late of the Indian Civil Service

IN TWO VOLUMES

VOL. II

ATLANTIC PUBLISHERS & DISTRIBUTORS
4215/1, Ansari Road, Darya Ganj
New Delhi-110002

Published by

Atlantic Publishers & Distributors
4215/1, Ansari Road, Darya Ganj,
New Delhi-110002

Head Office :

B-2, Vishal Enclave, Najafgarh Road
New Delhi-110027
Phone : 5413460

Reprinted 1989

Printed at :

MEHRA OFFSET PRESS
1979, Chandni Mahal
DELHI-110006
Phone No. 268574

CONTENTS OF VOL. II

	PAGE
PREFACE	ix
TABLE OF THE BOOKS AND CHAPTERS	xii
TRAVELS IN INDIA—	
Book II, Chapters XII to XXVI	1–134
Book III, Chapters I to XXIX	135–326
THE KING'S LICENCE	327–8
APPENDICES I TO VI	329–71
INDEX AND GLOSSARY	373–99

V.

ILLUSTRATIONS

I. Portrait of Tavernier . . . . . *Frontispiece*

II. Figures of Large Diamonds . . . *to face page* 97

III. Figures of Diamonds sold to the King of France „ 100

IV Figures of Rubies and Topaz . . . . . „ 102

V. Figures of Pearls . . . . . . „ 104

VI. Figures of the Koh-i-Nūr . . . . . „ 342

Map showing the Position of the Diamond Rivers of Bengal . . . . . „ 355

PLATES IN THE ORIGINAL NOT REPRODUCED

Figures of three Rubies belonging to His Majesty.

The Animal which produces Musk.

Cobra di capello.

Banyan Tree and Fakīrs.

A Penitent.

Canjare (Khanjar), or Dagger.

Marks on Batavian Reales.

Note.—The Dutch Edition (see ante, p. xi) contains some additional Plates.

PREFACE BY DR. V. BALL

VOL. II

In the course of the preparation of a work of so diversified and complex a character as this, it is almost certain to be the case that, even up to the last moment before publication, matter bearing upon the subject comes to hand. The present occasion, so far from forming an exception to the rule, exemplifies it in a very remarkable degree. The subjects upon which additional information has been acquired during the progress of the printing of these volumes are many ; but there are some in particular which deserve special notice, to which it may therefore be well to call attention here.

Through the kindness of Prof. Joret I have received a pamphlet, written by himself, entitled *Le Voyageur Tavernier* (*1670–89*), in which he has pursued his investigations as to the events of the last twenty years of Tavernier's life. As some of these confirm while others modify the conclusions set forth in the Introduction to vol. i, it is desirable to notice them briefly.

Prof. Joret describes his examination of the original manuscripts of Tavernier's *Memoirs*, which are in the possession of M. Schefer at his Château of St. Alban near Chambéry. Without entering into details, it may be said that they completely confirm the view expressed in the Introduction, that the material made use of by Chappuzeau was largely documentary ; that it could have been communicated orally by dictation, the internal evidence, as it appeared to me, sufficiently disproved.

Chappuzeau's work consisted in giving a literary style, such as it was, to Tavernier's simple and rough notes ; but in this work Tavernier himself very possibly assisted. These MS. *Memoirs* contain some details not included in the *Travels*, such as personal expenses and other minor day-to-day notes. The death of M. Ardilière, a subject of some confusion (see vol. i, 25 *n.*), is fixed by the original record as having taken place on the 12th December 1652. And Tavernier's arrival at

Ispahān in 1654 was on the 9th of July, not in May as previously supposed.

It is hoped that this original text may be published, as it would seem, from the glimpse of it thus given by Prof. Joret, that it would to a great extent aid in co-ordinating various statements in the published *Travels* which are now contradictory.

The suggestion that J.-B. Tavernier had been imprisoned in the Bastille on the 13th January 1686 is now shown [1] to be a mistake, and that it was a namesake of his, a Tavernier of Villiers-le-Bel, who was so incarcerated.

Passing the important additional information obtained as to Tavernier's relations with the Elector of Brandenburg, we find that Prof. Joret has reason for concluding that the discovery of the supposed tombstone of Tavernier at Moscow is of a somewhat mythical character; but, be that as it may, an important letter from the Swedish Resident at Moscow, dated 8th March 1689, has been discovered, by which the Swedish Chancellor was informed that Tavernier had died three weeks previously, not at Moscow, but at Smolensk, when on his journey to Moscow.

When in the course of these pages reference was made to the Grand Duke of Tuscany's diamond, it was supposed that the weight given by Schrauf for this diamond, which is now in the Imperial Treasury in Austria, was to be accepted as more correct than Tavernier's; but an examination of Schrauf's original papers shows that he really confirms Tavernier's weight for the stone in a very remarkable way. The present weight is $133\frac{1}{5}$ Vienna carats, which are equal to $139\frac{1}{5}$ of the lighter Florentine carats; and as Tavernier gives the weight at $139\frac{1}{2}$ carats we are justified in concluding that in this case he used, and that in general he was probably in the habit of using, the Florentine carat = 0·1972 grams,[2] or 3·04 grs. troy, *i.e.* 4 per cent. less than the English carat. The previous estimate of the value of the pearl rati given in Appendix, vol. i, having been calculated on the basis of $\frac{7}{8}$ths of a modern

[1] M. Douen in *Bulletin de la Société du Protestantisme Français*, vol. xxxiv, 1887, p. 95.

[2] Prof. Church, *Precious Stones*, p. 50, gives the value as 0·1965 grams.

English or French carat, amounted to 2·77 grs. troy ; but as $\frac{7}{8}$ths of a Florentine carat only amounts to 2·66 grs. troy, it seems probable that that would more closely approximate to the value of the pearl rati which was used in the weightment of jewels by Tavernier. From the discussion on the weight of Bābur's diamond given in Appendix I (p. 332) of this volume, it will be seen that there is independent testimony by Ferishta in favour of the view that 2·66 approximates more closely to the true value of the rati known to Tavernier and Ferishta. Other confirmatory evidence of this having been the value of the pearl rati will be found in the same Appendix.

A partial and preliminary notice of Tavernier's work has been referred to on p. 100 as having appeared in the *Philosophical Transactions*, to which it should be added that in the same journal abstracts of the contents of the first two volumes were subsequently published.[1]

The reader's attention is invited to the curious facts brought out in Appendix VI, from which it would appear that Chappuzeau obtained access to some of Tavernier's *Memoirs* while the latter was still absent on his last voyage. So far as I can ascertain it has never before been recognized that the *Histoire des Joyaux* and the English version of it, *The History of Jewels*, were founded on Tavernier's original *Memoirs*. This work serves to clear up several points commented on in the footnotes.

During a recent visit to Holland I ascertained that, as stated in the Bibliography (see vol. I, p. iii). there is but one edition of Tavernier's Travels in the Dutch language. It was translated by J. H. Glazemaker, and published at Amsterdam in 1682. A copy of it which I obtained contains a number of engravings by Jan Luyken in addition to copies of the original plates in the French editions.

It is hoped that the present edition of Tavernier's Indian Travels, by drawing attention to the work, will hereafter lead to the further elucidation of many points of interest ; and the Editor desires to intimate here, to those who may be willing to assist, that he will gratefully acknowledge all contributions on the subject which he may receive from readers of these volumes.

[1] No. 129, Nov. 20, 1676, p. 711 ; No. 130, Dec. 14, p. 751.

TABLE OF THE BOOKS AND CHAPTERS

BOOK II (*Continued*)

Historical and Political Description of the Empire of the Great Mogul

CHAPTER XII.—Concerning the articles of merchandise yielded by the Empire of the Great Mogul, and the Kingdoms of Golkonda and Bījāpur and other neighbouring territories . . . Page 1

CHAPTER XIII.—Concerning the frauds which can be practised in manufactures, either by the roguery of the workers or the knavery of the brokers and buyers 21

CHAPTER XIV.—Concerning the methods to be observed for establishing a new Commercial Company in the East Indies . . . 26

CHAPTER XV.—Concerning diamonds and the mines and rivers where they are found; and especially of the Author's journey to the Mine of Rammalakota (Raolconda of the original) . . 41

CHAPTER XVI.—Journey of the Author to the other Mines, and concerning the method of searching for Diamonds . . . 56

CHAPTER XVII.—A continuation of the Author's journeys to the Diamond Mines 62

CHAPTER XVIII.—The different kinds of weights for weighing diamonds at the Mines; the kinds of gold and silver in circulation; the routes by which one is able to travel; and the rule in use for the estimation of the prices of diamonds 69

CHAPTER XIX.—Concerning Coloured Stones and the places where they are obtained 77

CHAPTER XX.—Concerning Pearls and the places where they are fished for 84

CHAPTER XXI.—Concerning the manner in which Pearls originate in Oysters, how they are fished for and at what seasons . . 91

CHAPTER XXII.—Remarks upon the largest and most beautiful Diamonds and Rubies which the Author has seen in Europe and Asia, the figures of which are here given, together with those of the large Stones which he sold to the Emperor on his return from his last journey to India, with a representation of a magnificent Topaz, and the largest Pearls in the world 97

CHAPTER XXIII.—Concerning Coral and Yellow Amber and the places where they are found . . . . Page 104

CHAPTER XXIV.—Concerning Musk and Bezoar and some other medicinal stones 112

CHAPTER XXV.—Concerning the places from whence gold is obtained in Asia and Africa 121

CHAPTER XXVI.—Account of a notable act of perfidy done to the Author when he was about to embark at Gombroon for Surat 128

BOOK III

Concerning the religion of the Musalmāns and that of the Idolaters of India: the voyage of the Author by sea from Surat to Batavia, and from Batavia to Holland; and of many peculiarities in different Kingdoms of the East 135

CHAPTER I.—Concerning the religion of the Musalmāns in the East Indies 137

CHAPTER II.—Concerning Fakīrs or Musalmān beggars in the East Indies 139

CHAPTER III.—Of the Religion of the Gentiles or Idolaters of India 141

CHAPTER IV.—Concerning the idolatrous Kings and Princes of Asia 147

CHAPTER V.—Concerning the belief of the Idolaters with respect to the Deity 149

CHAPTER VI.—Concerning Fakīrs, or the professional Mendicants of India, and their penances 153

CHAPTER VII.—Concerning the belief of the Idolaters touching the condition of the soul of man after death 158

CHAPTER VIII.—Concerning the Idolaters' custom of burning the bodies of the deceased 161

CHAPTER IX.—How the women burn themselves with the bodies of their deceased husbands in India 162

CHAPTER X.—Remarkable histories of several women who have been burnt after the death of their husbands 169

CHAPTER XI.—Concerning the most celebrated Pagodas of the Idolaters of India 175

CHAPTER XII.—Continuation of the description of the principal Pagodas of the Idolaters of India 186

CHAPTER XIII.—Concerning the pilgrimages of the Idolaters to their Pagodas 190

CHAPTER XIV.—Concerning various customs of the Idolaters of India . . . . Page 192

CHAPTER XV.—Concerning the Kingdom of Bhutān, from whence comes musk, good rhubarb, and some furs 201

CHAPTER XVI.—Concerning the Kingdom of Tippera . . . 214

CHAPTER XVII.—Concerning the Kingdom of Assam . . 216

CHAPTER XVIII.—Concerning the Kingdom of Siam . . 224

CHAPTER XIX.—Concerning the Kingdom of Macassar and the Dutch Embassy to China 233

CHAPTER XX.—The Author pursues his journey in the East and embarks at Vengurla for Batavia; the danger which he runs on the sea, and his arrival in the Island of Ceylon 241

CHAPTER XXI.—Departure of the Author from the Island of Ceylon, and his arrival at Batavia 250

CHAPTER XXII.—Concerning an affair which was raised unseasonably for the Author in the Council at Batavia 254

CHAPTER XXIII.—The Author goes to see the King of Bantam, and describes several adventures in connexion therewith . . 268

CHAPTER XXIV.—The Author returns to Batavia, and some days afterwards goes again to visit the King of Bantam, giving an account, in connexion therewith, of the dangerous extravagances of some Fakīrs, or pilgrims, on their return from Mecca 277

CHAPTER XXV.—Concerning the Dutch war with the Emperor of Java 284

CHAPTER XXVI.—The Author renders the last duties to his brother, who died at Batavia, and has fresh difficulties with the General and his Council 289

CHAPTER XXVII.—The Author embarks on a Dutch vessel in order to return to Europe 298

CHAPTER XXVIII.—The Dutch fleet arrives at St. Helena, and the Author gives a description of that Island . . . 308

CHAPTER XXIX.—The Dutch fleet leaves the Island of St. Helena, and the Author arrives safely with it in Holland 314

THE King's Licence 327

APPENDICES

I.—1. The Great Mogul's Diamond and the true History of the Koh-i-Nūr . . . . Page 331
2. Summary History of the Koh-i-Nūr 343
3. The Grand Duke of Tuscany's Diamond, &c., and on the absolute weights of the carat and rati as they were used by Tavernier 346
4. On the weights of some of the Diamonds, other Precious Stones, and Pearls, mentioned by Tavernier . . 347
II.—List of all the Diamond Mines in India of which there are authentic Records, arranged in Districts, etc. 348
III.—The Diamond Mines of Bengal 354
IV.—The Diamond Mines of Borneo 359
V.—1. The Ruby Mines of Upper Burma 361
2. The Sapphire Washings of Ceylon 366
VI.—1. A Review or Abstract in the *Philosophical Transactions* of Chapuzeau's (*sic*) work, entitled *Histoire des Joyaux*, published in 1665 366
2. Note on the English Edition of the same work . . 370

TRAVELS IN INDIA

CHAPTER XII[1]

Concerning the articles of merchandise yielded by the Empire of the Great Mogul and the Kingdoms of Golkonda and Bījāpur and other neighbouring territories.

I CAN easily believe that those who have previously written accounts of the condition of the Empire of the Great Mogul did not feel themselves called upon to give full lists of all the articles of merchandise which it furnishes to foreigners. This I shall endeavour to do from the information I have acquired during the many years I have passed in different journeys in these countries. The reader will, doubtless, cheerfully approve of this research which I have made with so much care, particularly if he is connected with commerce, and desires to know what curiosities art and nature produce, in different places, for the enjoyment of the human race.

It is necessary to remember here, what I have stated at the commencement of the first book, regarding the weights and measures used in India, where I have spoken of the maund and of the ser.[2] It is still necessary to say a word about the cubit.[3]

The cubit is a measure for all goods which can be measured by the ell, of which there are different kinds, as we have different kinds of ells in Europe. It is divided into 24 tasūs,[4] and as the greater part of the Indian merchandise is

[1] In the English translation by John Phillips of 1684, this chapter is numbered x, the two preceding ones having been omitted.

[2] See Appendix, vol. i.

[3] Cobit in the original. According to the figure given by Tavernier of an eighth of a cubit, overleaf, its length must have been 27½ inches. The ordinary hāth of India, measured from the top of the middle finger to the elbow, is 18 inches, but is sometimes increased by the width of the hand or of three fingers.

[4] Tassots in the original. The tasū is properly the breadth of the second and third fingers. At present the Surat gaz, or yard, known as the tailors' yard, is divided into 24 tasū, or in all 28 inches, about 31
2 tasū equalling the English yard (*Bombay Gazetteer*, ii. 209).

delivered at Surat, there is represented on the margin, a figure of the eighth part of a cubit of the town of Surat, divided into three tasūs.

I ought to commence this list of goods with the most precious of all, namely diamonds and coloured stones; but, as that subject is somewhat extensive, and is the most important of my accounts, I shall give it separate treatment, and mention is this chapter only silks, cloths, cottons, spices, and drugs, which five classes include all the kinds of merchandise obtained from India.

Concerning Silks.

Kāsimbāzār,[1] a village in the Kingdom of Bengal, can furnish about 22,000 bales of silk annually, each bale weighing 100 livres. The 22,000 bales weigh 2,200,000 livres at 16 onces to the livre. The Dutch generally took, either for Japan or for Holland, 6,000 to 7,000 bales of it, and they would have liked to get more, but the merchants of Tartary and of the whole Mogul Empire opposed their doing so, for these merchants took as much as the Dutch, and the balance remained with the people of the country for the manufacture of their own stuffs. All these silks are brought to the Kingdom of Gujarāt, and the greater part come to Ahmadābād and Surat, where they are woven into fabrics.

Firstly, carpets of silk and gold, others of silk, gold, and silver, and others altogether of silk, are made in Surat. As for the woollen carpets, they are made at Fatehpur,[2] 12 coss from Agra.

[1] Kasembazar in original, elsewhere Cosenbazar, for Kāsimbāzār. The decay of Kasimbāzār, in the Murshidābād District, Bengal, dates from the beginning of the nineteenth century, when its climate, once celebrated for its salubrity, underwent an unexplained change for the worse, so that the margin of cultivation receded and wild beasts increased (*Imperial Gazetteer*, xi. 23). The trade in Indian silk has recently declined according to the figures given by Watt (*Commercial Products*, 1024 ff.).

[2] Vettapour in the original, Fatehpur Sīkrī, which is 23 miles W.S.W. of Agra. See vol. i, p. 73. It was founded as the Metropolis of the Mogul Empire by Akbar in 1570. Previously it bore the name of Sīkrī. Its magnificence is testified by the ruins of palaces and mosques, which still attract many visitors. Its industries were numerous, including silk-spinning, weaving, and stone-cutting. At present the carpets produced there are of an inferior and coarse kind. For the building of

In the second place, satins with bands of gold and silver, some with bands of different colours, and some all uniform are made there, and it is the same with the taffetas.

Thirdly, patoles,[1] which are stuffs of silk, very soft, decorated all over with flowers of different colours, are manufactured at Ahmadābād. They vary in price from 8 to 40 rupees the piece. This is one of the profitable investments of the Dutch, who do not permit any member of their Company to engage in this private trade. They are exported to the Philippines, Borneo, Java, Sumatra, and other neighbouring countries.

As for crude silks, it should be remarked that none of them are naturally white except that of Palestine, of which even the merchants of Aleppo and Tripoli experience difficulty in obtaining but a small quantity. Thus the silk of Kāsimbāzār is yellow, as are all the crude silks which come from Persia and Sicily. But the people of Kāsimbāzār know how to bleach theirs with a lye made of the ashes of a tree which is called Adam's fig,[2] which makes it as white as the silk of Palestine. The Dutch carry their silks and the other goods they obtain in Bengal by the canal[3] which connects Kāsimbāzār with the Ganges; this canal is nearly 15 leagues long. There remains an equal distance to descend by the Ganges to Hugly, where their goods are shipped on board Dutch vessels.

Fatehpur Sīkri see Smith, *Akbar the Great Mogul*, 104 ff.: for its trade in carpets *Āīn-i-Akbarī*, ii. 181; *Imperial Gazetteer*, xii. 86.

[1] This is from the Kanarese pattuda, 'a silk cloth' (Yule, *Hobson-Jobson*, 686). Terry calls them pintadoes, and extols the art displayed in stitching together 'fresh coloured taffata and pintadoes, and taffata and satin, with cotton wool between, to make quilts'. (*A Voyage to East India*, ed. 1777, 127.) The pintado was properly a chintz. In Bombay the term patolā is applied to the robe worn by a bride (T. N. Mukharji, *Art Manufactures of India*, 360).

[2] Adam's fig is a translation of the Portuguese name for the plantain, Musa paradisiaca. The Musalmāns believe that its leaves were used by Adam and Eve to clothe themselves with in the Garden of Eden. Hence the name. The ash of the plantain resembles that of the potato, as it contains both potash and soda salts, and the percentage of phosphoric acid and magnesia is said to be about the same in both. Ashes of the leaves and roots of the plantain are still used in Bengal for this purpose (Watt, *Dict. Economic Products*, v. 296; F. Buchanan, in Martin, *Eastern India*, iii. 964).

[3] Tavernier has 'canal', probably 'channel'.

Concerning Cotton Cloths, and first of the painted fabrics called Chites.[1]

The chites or painted cotton cloths which are called calmendar,[2] that is to say, painted with a brush, are made in the Kingdom of Golkonda, and particularly in the neighbourhood of Masulipatam ; but the quantity turned out is so small that when one makes requisition on all the workers who manufacture these cotton cloths it is with difficulty that he can obtain as much as three bales. The chites made in the Empire of the Great Mogul are printed, and are of different degrees of beauty, according to the printing and the fineness of the cotton cloth. Those made at Lahore are the coarsest of all, and consequently the cheapest. They are sold by corges,[3] a corge consisting of 20 pieces, and costing from 16 to 30 rupees. The chites made at Sironj are sold at from 20 to 60 rupees the corge or thereabouts.[4] All the chites I am about to speak of are printed cotton cloths, of which bedcovers are made, and also sufras [5] or tablecloths, according to the custom of the country, pillowcases, pocket-handkerchiefs, and especially waistcoats for the use of both men and women, principally in Persia. The chites of bright colours are manufactured at Burhānpur. They are made into handkerchiefs, which are at present much used by those who take snuff, and a sort of veil called ormis,[6] which the women throughout Asia use to put on their heads and wrap about their necks.

[1] Chintzes.

[2] Properly qalamdār, derived from qalam, Hind., a pen or brush. The Persians use the form *qalamkār* (Curzon, *Persia*, ii. 525). Prof. Jadunath Sarkar notes that the correct form of the word, as used in India, is *būqalamūn*, 'of various hues, variegated'. Bernier (p. 270) describes the canopies at the Dīwān-i-ʿāmm at Delhi: 'the outside of this magnificent tent was red, and the inside lined with elegant Masulipatam chintzes, figured expressly for that very purpose with flowers so natural and colours so vivid, that the tent seemed to be encompassed with real parterres'. For an account of this work see Sir G. Watt, *Indian Art at Delhi*, 1903, p. 259 ff.

[3] Undoubtedly, Sir W. Foster writes, from kōrī, Hind., a score.

[4] The trade at Sironj in Tonk State, Rājputāna, has disappeared (*Imperial Gazetteer*, xviii. 39).

[5] Sufra means literally 'the food of the traveller'; then 'the receptacle for food', 'a tablecloth

[6] Orhnīs (see i. 43).

The bāftas,[1] or cotton cloths required to be dyed red, blue, or black, are taken uncoloured to Agra and Ahmadābād, because these two towns are near the places where indigo is made, which is used in dyeing. They cost from 2 rupees the piece up to 30 or 40 rupees, according to the fineness and the amount of gold at the ends, and in some also at the sides. The Indians know how to pass some of these cloths through a certain water which causes them to appear like a waved camlet, and these pieces are the dearest.

These kinds of cotton cloth, which cost from 2 to 12 rupees the piece, are exported to the coast of Melinde,[2] and they constitute the principal trade done by the Governor of Mozambique, who sells them to the Kafir who carry them into the country of the Abyssins and the Kingdom of Saba,[3] because these people, who do not use soap, need only simply rinse out these cloths. Those costing 12 rupees and upwards are exported to the Philippines, Borneo, Java, Sumatra, and other islands. The women of these islands have for their sole garment a piece of this cotton cloth, of which, without cutting, one end serves as a petticoat, the remainder being wound round the waist and head.

White Cotton Cloths.

White cotton cloths come partly from Agra and the vicinity of Lahore, partly from Bengal, and some from Baroda, Broach, Renonsari,[4] and other places. They come in a crude condition to Renonsari and Broach, where they have the means of bleaching them in large fields, on account of the quantity of lemons growing in the neighbourhood, for cotton cloths can never be well bleached if they are not steeped in lemon juice.

[1] Bastas in the original, for Bāftas (see vol. i. 54).

[2] Melinda, properly Malinda, an Arab town on the east coast of Africa in S. Lat. 3° 9′ (Yule, *Hobson-Jobson*, 568).

[3] Abyssinia; Saba which was probably the Saboea of Strabo, occupies a large portion of Southern Arabia (*Ency. Brit.*, xxiii. 955 ff.).

[4] With reference to this place, Sir H. Yule states that it is Navsārī or Navasārī in Baroda, and that van Twist, in his *General Description of India* (1638), says that it was 6 Dutch miles (24 English) to the south of Surat, and produced much coarse cloth (*Imperial Gazetteer*, xviii. 425 f.). Only coarse cloths are now made at Navsārī (*Bombay Gazetteer*, vii. 568).

The cotton cloths brought from Agra, Lahore, and Bengal are sold by corges, and cost from 16 up to 300 or 400 rupees and even more, according as the merchant directs them to be made. The cotton cloths from Renonsari and Broach are 21 cubits long when crude, but only 20 cubits when bleached. Those from Baroda are 20 cubits when crude, and 19½ when bleached. The cotton cloths or bāftas from these three towns are of two kinds; for there are both broad and narrow kinds; it is the narrow of which I have just spoken, and they are sold at from 2 to 6 mahmūdīs each. The broad bāftas are 1⅓ cubit wide, and the piece is 20 cubits long. They are commonly sold at from 5 to 12 mahmūdīs, but the merchant on the spot can have them made much wider and finer, up to the value of 500 mahmūdīs the piece. In my time I have seen two pieces of them sold, for each of which 1,000 mahmūdīs were paid. The English bought one and the Dutch the other, and both were 28 cubits long. Muhammad ʿAlī Beg, when returning to Persia from his embassy to India, presented Cha Sefi II [1] with a coco-nut of the size of an ostrich's egg, enriched with precious stones; and when it was opened a turban was drawn from it 60 cubits in length, of a muslin so fine that you would scarcely know what it was that you held in your hand.[2] When returning from one of my voyages, I had the curiosity to take with me an ounce of thread, of which a livre's weight cost 600 mahmūdīs,[3] and the late Queen-Dowager, with many of the ladies of the Court, was surprised at seeing a thread so delicate, which almost escaped the view.

Concerning Spun Cotton.

Both spun and unspun cotton come from the Provinces of Burhānpur and Gujarāt. The unspun cottons are not sent to

[1] Shāh Safī or Safavī II (1629–42). Tavernier describes him in the *Persian Travels*, Paris ed., 1676, p. 524. Muhammad ʿAlī Beg was treasurer of Shāh ʿAbbās and Shāh Safī (Malcolm, *Hist. of Persia*, 2nd ed., i. 365; Manucci, iv. 433).

[2] This must have been like the famous Dacca muslins, upon which such names as ābrawān, 'flowing water', were conferred (Mukharji, *Art Manufactures of India*, 318 ff.; cf. vol. i. 47). It is said that a pair of the kid gloves, formerly made at Limerick, could be enclosed in a walnut shell (*Notes and Queries*, 11th Ser., ii. 297).

[3] i.e. about £22 10*s*.

Europe, being too bulky and of too small value; they are exported only to the Red Sea, Hormuz, Bassora, and sometimes to the islands of Sonde [1] and to the Philippines. As for the spun cottons, the English and Dutch Companies export large quantities to Europe, but they are not of the finest qualities; of the kinds exported the maund weight is worth from 15 to 50 mahmūdīs.[2] These are the kinds which are used to make the wicks of candles, and stockings, and to mix with the web of silken stuffs. As for the finest qualities, they are of no use in Europe.

Concerning Indigo.

Indigo comes from different localities of the Empire of the Great Mogul, and in these different localities it is of various qualities, which increase or diminish its price.

In the first place some comes from the territory of Biānā, from Indoua, and from Corsa, one or two days' march from Agra [3]; this is considered to be the best of all. It is also made at eight days' march from Surat, and at two leagues from Ahmadābād, in a village called Sārkhej.[4] It is from thence indigo cake comes, and some of the same kind and nearly of the same price also comes from the country of the King of Golkonda. The maund of Surat, which is 42 sers, or 34½ of our livres, is sold at from 15 to 20 rupees. Some of the same quality as this last is also made at Broach. As for that from the neighbourhood of Agra, it is made in small pieces like hemispheres, and it is, as I have said, the best in India. It is sold by the maund, and the maund in these regions weighs 60 sers, which are equal to 51¾ of our livres. One generally pays for it from 36 to 40 rupees. Indigo is also produced at 36 leagues from Burhānpur on the road to Surat at a large village called Raout,[5] and other small villages in its neighbourhood;

[1] Sunda archipelago, in the Sunda straits, where the volcano of Krakatoa is situated. (See vol. i. 154.)

[2] i.e. the maund of 34 livres is worth 11*s.* 3*d.* to £1 17*s.* 6*d.* with the mahmūdi at 9*d.*

[3] Bayānā in Bharatpur State; Hindaun in Jaipur State; Khurjā in Bulandshahr District, United Provinces: cf. Mundy, ii. 222; Bernier, 292; and see W. Foster, *English Factories in India, 1651–1654*, p. 51.

[4] Sarquesse in the original. (See vol. i. 59 *n.*)

[5] Raout, identified by Sir W. Foster with Arāvad in Chopra sub-division, East Khāndesh District, Bombay: see Intro.

and the people there generally sell more than 100,000 rupees worth of it every year.

There is lastly the indigo of Bengal, which the Dutch Company conveys to Masulipatam; but this indigo and that of Burhānpur and Ahmādābād can be bought cheaper by 30 per cent. than that of Agra.

Indigo is prepared from a plant [1] which is sown every year after the rains; before preparation it much resembles hemp. It is cut three times in the year, the first cutting taking place when it is about 2 or 3 feet high; and it is then cut to within 6 inches of the ground.[2] The first leaf is certainly better than those which follow, the second yielding less by 10 or 12 per cent. than the first, and the third 20 per cent. less than the second. It is classified by the colour, determined when a morsel of the paste is broken. The colour of the indigo made from the first crop is of a violet-blue, which is more brilliant and more lively than the others, and that of the second is more lively than that of the third. But besides this difference, which causes a considerable effect on the price, the Indians manipulate the weight and quality, as I shall elsewhere explain.

After the Indians have cut the plant they throw it into tanks made of lime,[3] which become so hard that one would say that they were made of a single piece of marble. The tanks are generally from 80 to 100 paces in circuit, and when half-full of water, or a little more, they are filled up with the cut plant. The Indians mix it and stir it up with the water every day until the leaf—for the stem is of no account—becomes reduced into slime or greasy earth. This done, they allow it to rest for some days, and when they see that all has sunk to the bottom and that the water is clear above, they open the holes made round the tank to allow the water to escape. The water having been drawn off, they then fill baskets with the slime, after which, in a level field, each man sits near his basket, takes this paste in his fingers, and moulds it into

[1] The indigo plant, Indigofera tinctoria, Linn.

[2] This is known as Jarī, or 'root', indigo, because it grows from the plants sown the previous year, as contrasted with Naudhā, 'new sown', that planted annually and ploughed up after the stalks have been cut.

[3] The indigo vats are faced with chunam or lime, which, especially when made from shells, produces a marble-like surface.

pieces of the shape and size of a hen's egg cut in two—that is to say, flat below and pointed above. But the indigo of Ahmadābād is flattened and made into the shape of a small cake.[1] It is to be particularly remarked, that the merchants, in order to escape paying custom on useless weight, before sending the indigo from Asia to Europe are careful to sift it, so as to separate the dust attached to it, which they afterwards sell to the people of the country, who make use of it in their dyes. Those who are employed to sift the indigo observe great precautions, for while so occupied they hold a cloth in front of their faces, and take care that all their orifices are well closed, only leaving two small holes in the cloth for the eyes, to see what they are doing. Moreover, both those who sift the indigo and the writers of sub-merchants of the Company who watch them sifting, have to drink milk every hour, this being a preservative against the subtlety of the indigo. All these precautions do not prevent those who are occupied for eight or ten days, sifting indigo, from having all that they expectorate coloured blue for some time. I have indeed on more than one occasion observed that if an egg is placed in the morning near one of these sifters, if it is broken in the evening, it is found to be altogether blue inside, so penetrating is the dust of indigo.

As the men take the paste from the baskets with their fingers steeped in oil, and mould it in pieces, they expose them to the sun to dry. When the merchants buy the indigo they always burn some pieces in order to see if there is any sand mixed with it. For the peasants who take the paste out of the baskets to separate it into pieces, after they have dipped their hands in oil, place it in the sand, which mingles with the paste and makes it heavier; but when burnt the indigo is reduced to ashes and the sand remains entire. The Governors do all they can to stop this fraud, but there are always some who practise it.[2]

[1] For a similar account of indigo manufacture see Mundy, ii. 221 ff. It will be noticed that there is no reference to the boiling of the precipitated dye after its removal from the vats, a common practice in Northern India, but not essential (Yule, *Marco Polo*, 1st ed., ii. 312, 317; Garcia da Orta, *Simples and Drugs of India*, 51; Watt, *Dict. Economic Products*, iv. 443).

[2] Adulteration of indigo still occurs in some places (Watt, *Dict Econ. Prod.*, iv. 435).

Concerning Saltpetre.

Saltpetre comes in abundance from Agra and from Patna, a town of Bengal; that which is refined costs three times as much as that which is impure. The Dutch have established a depot at Chaprā,[1] which is 14 leagues above Patna; and the saltpetre refined there is sent by river to Hugly. The Dutch imported boilers from Holland, and employed refiners to refine the saltpetre for themselves; but have not succeeded, because the people of the country, seeing that they wished to deprive them of the profits of refining, would not supply them any longer with whey, without the aid of which the saltpetre cannot be bleached, for it is worth nothing at all if it is not very white and very transparent. A maund of saltpetre costs 7 mahmūdīs.[2]

Concerning Spices.

Cardamom, ginger, pepper, nutmegs, mace, cloves, and cinnamon are the several kinds of spices which are known to us. I place cardamom and ginger first, because cardamom grows in the Kingdom of Bījāpur and ginger in that of the Great Mogul, while the other kinds of spices are imported from abroad to Surat, where they constitute an important article of commerce.

Cardamom is the best kind of spice, but is very scarce, and as but a small quantity is grown in the place I have indicated, it is only used in Asia at the tables of the nobles. 500 livres of cardamom are sold at from 100 to 110 reals.[3]

Ginger comes in large quantities from Ahmadābād, where

[1] Choupar in the original (vol. i. 100), Bernier, 440. The crude saltpetre is obtained in India by lixiviation of the soil on deserted and even occupied village sites. It consists of the potash nitrate, and a simple explanation may be given of the chemical reaction which produces it. The nitrogenous waste of the village being brought into contact with potash derived from wood-ash, the ammonia is converted into nitric acid, which combines with the potash, and the salt so formed permeates the soil. A century ago most of the saltpetre of the world which was used for gunpowder came from India. Now there are other sources of supply. See the full account in Watt, *Commercial Products*, 972 ff.

[2] i. e. 5*s.* 3*d.* for 34 livres.

[3] i. e. with the real at 4*s.* 6*d.*, £22 10*s.* to £24 15*s.* On cardamom see Watt, *Commercial Products*, 511 ff.

it grows in greater abundance than in any other part of Asia, and it is difficult to realize the quantity which is exported in a candied condition to foreign countries.[1]

Pepper is of two kinds, one of small size, and the other much larger ; these are respectively known as small and long pepper.[2] The long kind is chiefly from Malabar, Tuticorin, and Calicut being the towns where it is purchased. Some comes also from the Kingdom of Bījāpur, and is sold at Rājāpur,[3] a small town of that kingdom. The Dutch who purchase it from the Malabaris do not pay for it in cash, but exchange for it many kinds of merchandise, such as cotton, opium, vermilion, and quicksilver, and it is this long pepper which is exported to Europe. As for the small pepper which comes from Bantam, Achīn, and other places eastwards, it is not exported from Asia, where much is consumed, especially by the Musalmāns. For in a pound of small pepper there are double the number of seeds that there are in a pound of the long ; and it is more used in the pulaos, into which it is thrown by the handful, besides which the large pepper is too hot for the mouth.[4]

This small pepper, when delivered at Surat, has in some years been sold at the rate of 13 or 14 mahmūdīs the maund ; [5] I have seen it bought at this price by the English, who export it to Hormuz, Bassora, and the Red Sea. As for the long

[1] Zingiber officinale is cultivated all over the warmer and moister parts of India ; it grows in great perfection at Kaira and Baroda, as Tavernier says (Watt, *op. cit.*, 1139 ff.). Barbosa (ed. Dames, i. 1918, 25) speaks of ginger in Madagascar, and for Southern India see Yule's note in *Marco Polo*, ii. 316 f. At Calicut 'for the propagation of ginger, they plant a piece of small fresh root, about the size of a small nut, which at the end of a month grows large : the leaf resembles that of a wild lily' (Hieronimo di Santo Stefano, *India in the Fifteenth Century*, Hakluyt Society, iv, p. 4 f.).

[2] See Watt, *Commercial Products*, 896 ff.

[3] Regapour in the original is Rājāpur in the Ratnāgirī District. As a port its importance has much diminished, it being now inaccessible for large vessels by the creek which connects it with the sea, 15 miles distant. In 1660–1 and 1670 it and the English factory were sacked by Sivajī. (See *Imperial Gazetteer*, xxi. 66 f. ; cf. vol. i. 146.)

[4] It may be remarked that the whole-pepper obtained in the bazars, and commonly used in cookery in India, is a much smaller, less pungent, and generally inferior seed to that which comes to Europe.

[5] 9*s*. 9*d*. to 10*s*. 6*d*. per 34 livres, with the mahmūdī at 9*d*.

pepper which the Hollanders fetch from the coast of Malabar, 500 livres [1] of it yield them only 38 reals, but on the merchandise which they give in exchange they gain 100 per cent. It can be bought for the equivalent in money of 28 or 30 reals cash, but to purchase it in that way would be much more costly than the Dutch method. As for long pepper, without going beyond the territories of the Great Mogul there is enough to be obtained in the Kingdom of Gujarāt ; it is generally sold at the rate of from 12 to 15 mahmūdīs the maund.[2] The wood of long pepper costs but four mahmūdīs.

Nutmeg, mace, clove, and cinnamon are the only spices which the Dutch have in their own hands.[3] The three first come from the Molucca Islands, and the fourth, i.e. cinnamon, comes from the island of Ceylon.

There is one remarkable fact about the nutmeg, namely, that the tree is never planted. This has been confirmed to me by many persons who have dwelt for many years in the country. They have assured me that when the nuts are ripe certain birds which arrive from the islands to the south swallow them whole, and reject them afterwards without having digested them, and that these nuts, being covered by a viscous and sticky substance, fall to the ground, take root, and produce trees, which would not happen if they were planted in the ordinary way.[4] I have here a remark to make upon the subject of the Bird of Paradise. These birds, which are very fond of the nutmeg, assemble in numbers in the season to gorge themselves with it, and they arrive in flocks as flights of

[1] i. e. £6 6*s.* to £6 15*s.*

[2] 9*s.* to 10*s.* 6*d.* for 34 livres.

[3] Most of the cloves of commerce now come from Zanzibar and Pemba, where the tree was introduced early in the nineteenth century: see Barbosa, ed. Dames, vol. i, 1918, p. 28.

[4] This is so far true as regards the fact that the great fruit-eating pigeons are able to swallow large fruits, the stones of which they afterwards reject. These pigeons belong to the genera Carpophaga and Myristicivora, and Ball had often been amazed at the wide gape and the mobility of the articulation of the jaws of these birds. When wounded he had seen them disgorge very large fruits. Several species occur in the Andaman and Nicobar Islands, and other allied species in the Malayan Archipelago. That these birds aid in propagating plants in remote islands by conveying the seeds cannot be doubted. But it is now raised from seed (Watt, 791).

field-fares do during the vintage. As the nut is strong it intoxicates the birds and causes them to fall dead upon the spot, and immediately the ants which abound in the country eat off their feet. It is on this account that it is commonly said that a Bird of Paradise with feet [1] has never been seen. This is, however, not precisely true, for I have seen three or four with their feet intact, upon which the ants had not had time to operate. A French merchant, named Contour, sent one which had feet, from Aleppo, to King Louis XIII, who prized it much for its beauty.

But notwithstanding all the Dutch can do to prevent it, cloves can be obtained at Macassar, in the Isle of Celebes,[1] without the spice passing through their hands, because the islanders buy in secret from the captains and soldiers of the Dutch forts at the places where the cloves grow, giving them in exchange rice and other necessaries of life, without which, being miserably paid, they would be unable to subsist. Whilst commerce was vigorously pushed by the English, they acted as though their object was to destroy that of the Dutch. Having bought a parcel of cloves at Macassar they sent them to all the places where the Dutch were accustomed to deal, and selling them at a cheap price, sometimes even at a loss, by this means they ruined the clove trade of the Dutch. For it is an established custom in India that the first who fixes the price of any article of merchandise constrains all others, by his example, to sell at the same rate during the year. It is for this reason that the Dutch established a factory at Macassar, where their officers raise the price of cloves as high as they can when the King of the Island opens the sale. They make considerable presents to the King in order to induce him to uphold the price, which neither the English nor the Portuguese, in the miserable state in which their affairs are to-day, are able to prevent.[2]

[1] As is well known, the true origin of this fable about the apodas is, that the natives who prepare the plumes of the Birds of Paradise for decorative purposes remove the feet from the skins, and as the birds were in early times only known by these dried and stitched-up skins, the idea spread that they had no feet. Tavernier's explanation shows the tenacity of the myth (*Ency. Brit.*, iii. 978; Linschoten, i. 118; Pinkerton, *Voyages*, ix. 625).

[2] See the account of cloves in Linschoten, ii. 81 ff.

Whenever the people of Macassar have any cloves they pay for the goods brought to them with that spice; payment is also made with tortoiseshell, which is in great demand in all the Empire of the Mogul and in Europe: it is also made with gold dust, by which there is 6 or 7 per cent. to be gained instead of its being lost on the money of the island, although it be gold, because the King alloys it so much. The four places where cloves grow in abundance are the land of Amboine, the land of Ellias, the land of Seram, and the land of Bouro.[1]

The islands of Banda, which are six in number, known as Nero, Lontour, Pouleay, Roseguin, Polleron, and Grenapuis,[2] yield nutmegs in great abundance. The island of Grenapuis is about 6 leagues in circuit, and culminates in a peak from whence much fire issues. The island of Damne,[3] where the nutmeg also grows in great abundance and of large size, was discovered in the year 1647 by Abel Tasman, a Dutch commander.

The prices of cloves and nutmegs, as I have seen them sold to the Dutch in Surat in certain years, were as follows: The maund of Surat is equal to 40 sers, which make 34 of our livres at 16 onces to the livre. A maund of cloves was sold for 103½ mahmūdīs. A maund of mace was sold for 157½; of nutmegs for 56½ mahmūdīs.[4] All the cinnamon comes at present from the island of Ceylon.[5] The tree which produces it closely resembles our willows and has three barks. The first

[1] Amboyna, Gilolo, Ceram, and Boeroe (or Buru), islands in the Molucca Sea.

[2] Pulo Neīrā (i.e. island of palm wine); Lontor (the name of a palm); Pulo Ai or Pulo Wai (i.e. water-island); Rosingen (Rosolanguim of De Barros); Pulo Run (or Rung, i.e. chamber island); and Gunongapi (fire-mountain or volcano). These, with four others, constitute the Banda group. (Crawfurd, *Dict.* 33 ff.; *Ency. Brit.*, iii. 310.)

[3] Tasman discovered Van Diemen's Land, but nutmegs can hardly grow there; possibly Tavernier has made some mistake. The reference is possibly to the Dama Archipelago off the west coast of Cochin-China.

[4] Equal respectively to £3 17*s.* 6*d.*, £5 18*s.* 1½*d*, and £2 2*s.* 4*d.* per 34 livres.

[5] Tennent, *Ceylon*, ii. 161 f.; Watt, *Commercial Products*, 313 ff. On the strange tale of the mode of collecting cinnamon, in Arabia, resembling the way in which Sindbad the Sailor found diamonds, see Herodotus, iii. 111; Sir R. Burton, *Book of the Thousand Nights and a Night*, ed. 1894, iv. 357 ff.

and second only are removed, the latter being considered to be much the best. As for the third, it is not touched, for if the knife cuts it the tree dies. This is an art which the natives learn from their youth. Cinnamon costs the Dutch more than is generally believed. For the King of the island of Ceylon, otherwise called the King of Kandy,[1] from the name of the capital town, being a sworn enemy of the Dutch because they did not keep their promise with him, as I have elsewhere related, sends troops every year with the intention of surprising them when they go to collect the cinnamon. It is for this reason that the Dutch are obliged to have 1500 or 1600 armed men to defend an equal number while engaged in removing the bark of the cinnamon, and they are obliged to feed these labourers for the remainder of the year in addition to the expenditure on the garrisons in several parts of the island. These great outlays enhance the price of the cinnamon; it was not so in the time of the Portuguese, who did not incur this expenditure, but placed all to profit. The cinnamon tree bears a fruit like an olive, but it is not eatable. The Portuguese used to gather quantities of it, which they placed in cauldrons with water together with the small points of the ends of the branches, and they boiled the whole till the water was evaporated; when cooled the upper portion of what remained was like a paste of white wax, and at the bottom of the cauldron there was camphor. Of this paste they made tapers, which they used in the churches during the services at the annual festivals, and as soon as the tapers were lighted the church was perfumed throughout with an odour of cinnamon. They have often been sent to Lisbon for the King's chapel. Formerly the Portuguese procured cinnamon from the countries belonging to Rājās in the neighbourhood of Cochin.[2] But since the Dutch have taken this town, and have become masters of the coast of Ceylon, where the cinnamon grows, they find that what comes from the neighbourhood of Cochin injures the trade, because, being not so good as that of Ceylon, it was sold at a low price, and they destroyed all the places where it grew; thus there is no cinnamon now but that of Ceylon,

[1] Or Candy, as in the original.

[2] Bastard cinnamon. (See vol. i, p. 187.)

which is altogether in their hands. While the Portuguese held this coast the English bought cinnamon from them and usually paid them 50 mahmūdīs for a maund.[1]

Concerning the drugs obtainable at Surat, and those imported from foreign countries, with the price of each, per maund.

Sal Ammoniac costs per maund according to the ordinary price	20	mahmūdīs.
Borax, like the preceding, is brought from Ahmadābād[2] without being refined, and costs per maund	35	,,
Gum-lac,[3] of which I shall speak below .	7½	,,
,, washed	10	,,
,, in sticks of sealing-wax . .	40	,,
Some kinds cost 50 and 60 mahmūdīs per maund, and even more when musk is added to it		
Saffron[4] of Surat, which is only used for colours	4½	,,
White Cumin[5]	8	,,
Black Cumin	3	,,
Arlet,[6] small	3	,,
Incense,[7] from the Arabian coast . .	3	,,
Mirrha.[8] The good quality called Mirrha-gilet	30	,,

[1] £1 17*s.* 6*d.*

[2] Probably brought to Ahmadābād from Tibet, but Ball had seen a statement as to its occurrence in Kāthiāwār, which, however, requires confirmation. (Vide, *Economic Geology of India*, p. 498.) There is no evidence of its discovery in Kāthiāwār, but it has been found mixed with common salt in certain lakes in the Panjāb (Watt, *Economic Dict.*, i. 505).

[3] Shellac, produced on certain trees by the Coccus lacca.

[4] Saffron consists of the stigmas of Crocus sativus, L., which was an article of trade at the time the Periplus (ch. 24) was written, and has been cultivated in the East ever since. All the Kashmīr saffron is produced at the village of Pampur, where it causes violent headaches among the people (Elliot & Dowson, *Hist.*, vi. 304 f., 375 ; *Āīn-i-Akbarī*. ii. 357).

[5] The fruit of Cuminum cyminum, L., a small annual indigenous to the Upper Nile regions, spread by cultivation to Arabia, India, China, &c. (Hanbury and Flückiger, *Pharmacographia*, 295.)

[6] Perhaps harlā, the black myrobolan.

[7] The gum resin (olibanum) of Boswellia carterii, Endl. See Barbosa, ed. Dames, 1918, vol. i, p. 65 f.

[8] The precise nature of the trees yielding myrrh is somewhat doubtful.

Mirrha-Bolti, from Arabia	15	mahmūdīs
Cassia [1]	2	,,
Sugar-Candy	18	,,
Asutinat,[2] a kind of grain which is very hot	1	,,
Fenoüil [3] (Fr.), large	3½	,,
,, small and very hot	1½	,,
Oupelote,[4] root	14	,,
Cointre,[5]	5	,,
Auzerout,[6] from Persia	120	,,
Aloës sucotrin,[7] from Arabia	28	,,
Reglisse [8] (Fr.)	4	,,
Vez-Cabouli,[9] a kind of root	12	,,
Aloe-wood,[10] in large pieces	200	,,
,, in small pieces	400	,,
There is a sort of aloe-wood which, if very oily, costs per maund	4000	,,

Two varieties from Africa are called Heera Bol (true myrrh) and Bissa Bol (an inferior variety). Arabian myrrh is obtained to the east of Aden (see Hanbury and Flückiger, *Pharmacographia*; Watt, *Commercial Products*, 401).

[1] The fruit of Cassia fistula, L. (Watt, 287).

[2] Mr. Longworth Dames, with much probability, identifies this with Persian as*bat*ān or is*bat*ān, seeds of the wild rue, still used as bazar medicine in the Panjāb (Stewart, *Punjab Plants*, Lahore, 1869, p. 381).

[3] The fruit of Pimpinella anisum, L., cultivated in India (Watt, 887).

[4] Costus or kostus, the root of Aucklandia costus.

[5] Possibly kundur, i. e. frankincense, obtained from Boswellia floribunda carterii, but that has already been enumerated.

[6] For Anzarūt, a gum-resin once known to Europeans as a drug under the name sarcocolla. According to Ainslie (*Materia Medica*, vol. i, p. 381) it is derived from Penœa mucronata, Linn., which yields it by spontaneous exudation; it is a native of Africa. It was used by the Arabs for healing wounds, and by Mesue it was believed to have cathartic properties. According to Dymock's *Vegetable Materia Medica*, 2nd ed., Bombay 1885, it is still largely used by the natives of Western India. Sir H. Yule made the two last identifications.

[7] Socotrine aloes, prepared from the juice of *Aloe perryi*, Linn. (Watt, 59), see Barbosa, ed. Dames, vol. i, 1918, p. 61.

[8] Liquorice, glycyrrhiza (Watt, *Economic Dict.*, iii. 512).

[9] Possibly for bish, Sanskrit visha, i. e. poison, Aconite root (Watt, *Commercial Products*, 20 ff.).

[10] Bois d'aloës. This is the Lignum Aloes of Latin writers and the Aloes-wood of the Bible, quite distinct from the modern aloes, being the inside of the trunk of Aquilaria ovata and A. Agallochum, which contain a fragrant resinous substance of dark colour (Watt, 72 ff.). It was formerly generally used both for incense and for medicinal purposes,
3 but is now only esteemed in the East. From the Portuguese term agila

I shall now make some special remarks about gum-lac, sugar, opium, tobacco, and coffee.

Gum-lac [1] for the most part comes from Pegu, but it also comes from the Kingdom of Bengal; and it is dearer in the latter place because the inhabitants of the country extract from it that beautiful scarlet colour [2] which they use to dye and paint their cotton cloths. Nevertheless, the Dutch buy it to export to Persia, where it is used to produce the colour which the Persians employ in their dyes. That which remains after the colour is extracted is used only to embellish toys [3] made in the lathe, of which the people are very fond, and to make sealing-wax; and be it for the one or the other purpose, they mix whatever colour they desire with it. That which comes from Pegu is the cheapest, though it is as good as that of other countries; what causes it to be sold cheaper is that the ants, making it there on the ground in heaps, which are sometimes the size of a cask,[4] mix with it a quantity of dirt.

or aguila has come the popular name 'eagle-wood'. There is an account of it in Royle's *Illustrations*, &c., and Garcia da Orta devotes his 30th Colloquy to it under the title Linaloes (251 ff.). It is described very concisely in Yule, *Hobson-Jobson*, 335. It is used in the manufacture of the incense-sticks from Burma, which are now well known in Europe. See *Ency. Biblica*, i. 120 ff.

[1] Ball has elsewhere identified the Ἤλεκτρον of Ktesias with shellac. (See 'On the Identification of the Animals and Plants of India, which were known to Early Greek Authors', *Proc. Royal Irish Academy*, 2nd series, vol. ii, No. 6, p. 331, but this is not certain; see Watt, 1054 ff.; *Ency. Biblica*, i. 134 ff. The classical references are collected by Sir J. Frazer, *Pausanias*, iii. 548 f. In the *Revue d'Ethnographie et de Sociologie*, ii. 5, de Morgan points out that electrum, a compound of gold and silver, was collected from the nuggets and dust obtained by washing, and that as the process of separating the metals was unknown, the first Greek coins contained as much as fifty per cent. of silver (Sir P. Sykes, *Hist. of Persia*, 2nd ed. i. 99, note 2) and for an account of the production and manufacture of shellac in Bengal, see Ball, *Jungle Life in India*, 308; McCrindle, *Ancient India as described by Ktesias*, 70.)

[2] The dye consists of the bodies of the female coccus which alone secretes the lac.

[3] Such as the Benares toys, nests of boxes, &c., of the present day. The coloured lac is applied in sticks to the wood surfaces as they revolve in the lathe, after which they require only to be burnished (Mukharji, *Art Manufactures*, 249; Watt, 1063).

[4] Ball suggests that this description may be due to some confusion about white ants' nests. But he failed to find any peculiarity ascribed to the Burma lac which would explain the passage.

On the other hand, in Bengal, the district whence they bring the lac being a kind of jungle full of shrubs, the ants secrete it round the ends of branches, which makes it fair and clean, and it is consequently dearer. The inhabitants of Pegu do not use it as a dye because they receive their cotton cloths ready dyed from Bengal and Masulipatam; and, moreover, they are so uncivilized that they do not engage in any art.[1] There are many women at Surat who gain their livelihood by preparing lac after the colour has been extracted. They give it whatever colour they wish, and make it into sticks like Spanish wax. The English and Dutch Companies export about 150 chests annually. Lac in sticks does not cost more than 10 sols the livre, and it is worth 10 sols the once in France, though it be half mixed with resin.

Moist sugar is exported in quantity from the Kingdom of Bengal, and there is great traffic in it at Hugly, Patna, Dacca, and in other places. During my last visit to India I penetrated very far into Bengal, even up to the frontiers of the neighbouring States. I was told a fact by many old people of the country which should be recorded. It is that sugar kept for thirty years becomes a poison, and that there is nothing more dangerous or rapid in producing this effect.[2] Loaf-sugar is made at Ahmadābād, where the people understand how to refine it; it is called on this account royal sugar. These loaves of sugar generally weigh from 8 to 10 livres.

Opium comes from Burhānpur, a good mercantile town between Surat and Agra. The Dutch buy it there and exchange it for their pepper.

Tobacco[3] also grows abundantly in the neighbourhood of

[1] Tavernier probably knew very little of Pegu, which he never visited. Had he done so he would have found certain arts flourishing there. It is used as a dye in Upper Burma (Scott & Hardiman, *Gazetteer of Upper Burma*, part i, vol. ii, p. 394).

[2] It is not unlikely that there may be still a belief to this effect in India. Ball remembered having heard something of the same kind about rice when kept beyond a certain time. Possibly they both originate in some proverbial saying having reference to storing up articles of food too long.

[3] The practice of smoking tobacco, which was first learnt by the Spaniards from the Cuban Indians in the year 1492, was introduced into Turkey, Egypt, and India about the end of the 16th century; and it spread steadily, though opposed by the severest enactments of both

Burhānpur; and in certain years I have known the people neglect harvesting it because they had too much, and they allowed half the crop to decay.

Coffee grows neither in Persia nor in India.[1] Nevertheless, as some Indian vessels load up with it on their return from Mecca, I give it place here amongst the drugs. The principal trade in it is at Hormuz and Bassora, where the Dutch, when returning empty from Mocha, load up as much as they can, as it is an article which they can sell well. From Hormuz it is exported to Persia, and even to Great Tartary; and from Bassora it is distributed in Chaldee, in Arabia along the course of the Euphrates, in Mesopotamia, and other Turkish provinces —for as for India, it is but little used there. Coffee, which means wine in the Arabian tongue, is a kind of bean which grows at eight days' journey from Mocha, on the road to Mecca. Its use was first discovered by a hermit named Shaikh Siadeli (Sayyid 'Alī), some 120 years ago or thereabouts; for before him there is no author, ancient or modern, who ha mentioned it.[2]

Christian and Muhammadan governments. (See Hanbury and Flückiger, *Pharmacographia.*) For its early use in India see Elliot & Dowson, *Hist.*, vi. 155; Smith, *Akbar the Great Mogul*, 407 f.; Watt, *Commercial Products*, 795 f.

[1] It is perhaps needless to point out that this was written two centuries before the cultivation of coffee became an important industry in Ceylon and Southern India. The history of its introduction into India is very obscure (Watt, 367).

[2] Coffee was first mentioned in European literature in 1573 by Ruwolf. Seventy years later a sample of it was brought from Constantinople to Marseilles by Thévenot. It was first brought to Aden by Shaikh Shihābuddīn Dhabhāni, who died in 1470, hence it is concluded that its introduction was about the middle of the fifteenth century. Niebuhr states that it was first brought from Kaffa in Abyssinia to Yemen by Arabs. It appears to have been cultivated principally at Jabal, whence it was conveyed to Mocha. The Arabic name is *qahwa*, pronounced *kahveh* by the Turks. The plant itself is called *bun*. As Tavernier says, the name *qahwa* was originally applied to wine. (*Vide*, Yule, *Hobson-Jobson*, 232.) Terry's account of the use of coffee in India in his time is of sufficient interest to be quoted in full: 'Many of the people there who are strict in their religion drink no wine at all; but they use a liquor, more wholesome than pleasant, they call coffee, made by a black seed boiled in water, which turns it almost into the same colour, but doth very little alter the taste of the water. Notwithstanding, it is very good

All goods arriving from Agra at Surat, for dispatch of bills of exchange at 5 per cent., for packing, carriage, and customs, according to their classes, are charged with from 15 to 20 per cent.

All gold and silver, whether in ingots or coin, pays 2 per cent. on entering Surat.[1] The merchant does what he can to avoid this charge; nevertheless, when caught, he is let off with paying double and nothing more. The Princes would like to confiscate the whole sum, but the judges are opposed, and maintain that Muhammad forbade all custom dues and interest on money.[2] I have spoken fully in the second chapter of the first book of the custom dues, the money, both gold and silver, and the weights and measures of India, to which I refer the reader.

CHAPTER XIII

Concerning the frauds which can be practised in manufactures, either by the roguery of the workers or the knavery of the brokers and buyers.

I SHALL follow in this chapter the same order as I have observed in the preceding, with the object of making plain, for the benefit of the merchant, all the frauds which can be effected in silk, cotton cloths, cotton, and indigo, for there are none in the case of spices and drugs.

Frauds in Silken Stuffs.

Silken stuffs vary in breadth, length, and quality. The length and breadth are ascertainable by measurement, the quality depends upon whether the stuffs are uniformly woven, whether the weight is right, and whether there is any cotton introduced into the web, as the Indians very often introduce it.

to help digestion, to quicken the spirits, and to cleanse the blood.' (*A Voyage to E. India*, ed. 1777, pp. 100–1.) The facts are given more fully by Watt, 364 ff.

[1] See vol. i, p. 7.

[2] 'They who swallow down usury shall arise at the Last Day only as he ariseth, whom Satan has infected by his touch' (*Korān*, ii. 276, and other texts collected by Hughes, *Dict. of Islām*, 656 f.).

The Indians, not knowing the art of gilding silver,[1] insert in their striped stuffs threads of pure gold; on this account it is necessary to count the number of threads to see if the stuff contains the requisite quantity, and the same should be done in the case of stuffs striped with silver. As for taffetas, it is only necessary to see whether they have a uniform fineness, and next to unfold some of them to see if they contain any foreign substance to increase the weight, after which each piece should be weighed separately, in order to ascertain whether it is of proper weight.

In Ahmadābād, as I have said, an abundance of these stuffs is made of gold and silk, silver and silk, and of silk alone; and carpets [2] of gold and silver and silk, but the colours of these carpets do not last so long as those of the carpets made in Persia. As for the workmanship, it is equally beautiful. It is for the eye of the broker to observe the size, beauty, and fineness of the work in the carpets worked with gold and silver, and he should judge if it is good and rich. Finally, in the case of carpets, and in other stuffs worked with gold and silver, it is necessary to withdraw some threads to prove them, and to see if they are of the standard which they ought to reach.

Frauds in Cotton Cloths, and, firstly, in White Cloths.

All cotton cloths, both fine and coarse, which the Dutch company order to be made in the Provinces of the Empire of the Great Mogul, are brought in bales to the storehouse at Surat, and delivered to the broker about the months of October and November.

The frauds commonly perpetrated are in respect of the fineness, the length, and the breadth.[3] Each bale contains

[1] The art is now well known in India. For the methods employed see Mukharji, *Art Manufactures*, 226 ff.; Baden Powell, *Handbook of Manufactures and Arts of the Punjab*, 157 ff.

[2] The word in the original here is *tapis*, which should perhaps be translated otherwise than carpet, though that is the ordinary signification of the word. Perhaps table-covers are meant. [See also Index, *s. v.*] For the Alcatifa, 'carpet with long pile', see Yule, *Hobson-Jobson*, 11.

[3] 'It must be observed that all Indian weavers, who work for common sale, make the woof of one end of the cloth coarser than that of the other, and attempt to sell it to the unwary by the fine end, although

about 200 pieces, among which five or six and up to ten pieces may be inserted of less fine quality, thinner, shorter, or narrower than the sample of the bale; this cannot be ascertained without examination piece by piece. The fineness is judged by the eye, the length and breadth by measurement. But a still greater refinement is practised in India, which is to count the number of the threads which ought to be in the breadth according to the fineness of the sample. When the number is lacking it is thinner or narrower or coarser. The difference is sometimes so imperceptible to the eye that it is difficult to discern it without counting the threads,[1] nevertheless this difference amounts to a considerable sum in the price of a large quantity, for it requires but little to abate an écu or even two écus on a piece when the price is from 15 to 20 écus the piece. Those who bleach these cloths, in order to save something for their own profit out of the quantity of lemons which are required, beat the cloths on stones, and when fine the beating does them much injury and diminishes their price.[2]

It should be remarked that the Indians, when making their cloths, if the piece is worth more than 2 écus, insert at either end threads of gold and silver, and the finer the cloth, the more of these threads do they insert, the price of which amounts to nearly as high a figure as that of the cloth itself. It is for this reason that it is necessary to forbid the workers to insert these threads of gold in cloths ordered to be made for export to France—the gold and silver, which the Indians insert as an ornament in their own cloths and garments, being of no use to the French. But for the cloths ordered for Poland and Muscovy, it is necessary to have the gold and silver in the Indian style, because the Poles and Russians will have nothing to do with the cloths if they have not got the threads of gold and silver. It is necessary also to take care that they do not

every one who deals with them is perfectly aware of the circumstance, and although in the course of his life any weaver may not ever have an opportunity of gaining by this means.' (F. Buchanan, in Martin, *Eastern India*, i. 355.)

[1] The Manchester goods of the present day are subjected to the same examination in India. It is a matter of some notoriety that fraud in connexion with them is not unknown.

[2] The destructive methods of the modern Dhobī or washerman are familiar to all Anglo-Indians.

become black, because people in these countries are unwilling to buy cloths when the gold and silver are black.

As for cloths dyed with indigo, either violet or black, it is necessary to take care that the workers do not blacken the threads of gold at the ends of the pieces, and that they do not beat the pieces too much after being folded, because, in order to make them smooth, they sometimes beat them so much that when one comes to unfold them he finds them broken at each fold.

It should also be remarked that upon the fag end of pieces of cloth the Indians print with a seal and gold leaf an Arabesque flower, which extends the whole width of the piece. But if the pieces are destined for France, it is necessary to forbid the workers to impress this flower, which costs half a piastre, in order to save this sum on the price of the piece. But if it is for exportation to the Indian islands, anywhere in Asia, or even to a certain part of America, it is necessary that the flower should be on the fag end of the pieces, and that it should be preserved entire, otherwise one is unable to sell them.

As for coloured and printed cloths, they are coloured and printed while crude, and it is necessary to take care that the work is finished before the end of the rains, because, when they are washed, the more the waters are disturbed, so much the more do the colours applied with a brush or printing block remain vivid.[1]

It is easy to distinguish the cloths which are printed from those done with a brush, and if the broker is intelligent he will distinguish the difference in the beauty of one painted cloth from another by the cleanness of the work. But for the fineness and other qualities of the stuff, they are more difficult to distinguish than in the case of white cloths, and consequently it is necessary to observe more precaution.

Frauds practised in Cottons.

Cottons are the goods which are always first to be manufactured and the earliest to be delivered in the stores of Surat, because they are all spun in the Province of Gujarāt.

[1] In vol. i, p. 46, this is differently stated, but apparently it is so through an error in the mode of expression.

The frauds possible with them are in weight and quality. The fraud in weight can be effected in two ways, the first by putting the cotton in a damp place, and by inserting in the middle of each skein some substance which increases the weight; the second in not weighing it truly when the broker[1] receives it from the worker or from the merchant who delivers it.

The fraud in the quality is accomplished in only one way, which is by inserting in every maund three or four skeins of worse quality than that at the top, and in a large quantity that may amount to something considerable, for there is a variety of cotton thread which costs up to 100 écus the maund. As these two frauds are practised very often on the Dutch Company, the precaution they are obliged to adopt is this. It is to weigh, in the presence of the Commander and his counsel, and to examine carefully, each maund, skein by skein, to see if there is any fraud in the weight or quality. When that is done the Vice-Commander and those who are appointed under him to make this examination are obliged to attach to each bale a statement of the weight and quality; and when the bale is opened in Holland, if anything is wanting in either of these respects, those who have signed the statement are obliged to pay the loss.

Frauds practised in Indigo.

I have said[2] that the natives withdraw the paste from the baskets containing the indigo, and mould it into pieces with the fingers steeped in oil, and the cakes are then exposed in the sun to dry. The Indians who wish to cheat the merchants lay the cakes on the sand to dry, so that the sand attaches itself and the indigo then weighs more. They also sometimes lay the paste on damp ground, which makes it moist and consequently heavier. But when the Governor of the place discovers these frauds, he inflicts a heavy fine. Such frauds are easily discovered by a broker and Commander experienced in the trade in this kind of merchandise by burning some morsels of indigo, after which the sand which remains becomes visible.

I have still to make a somewhat curious remark regarding

[1] Courtier in original.

[2] See p. 9, above.

the brokers of India. These brokers are commonly, as it were, chiefs of their families, for whom they hold all the joint property in trust to turn it to account. For that reason those qualified by years and experience are selected, so that they may be able to secure benefit to all the kinsmen, being both the depositaries and the guardians of their goods. Every evening, when they return from business, and, according to the custom of the Indians, who do not sup, eat some sweetmeats and drink a cup of water, the oldest of the kinsmen assemble at the house of the broker, who renders an account of what he has done during the day, and they hold counsel together as to what should be done in the future. He is especially exhorted to take care of their business, and if possible to defraud rather than be defrauded.[1]

CHAPTER XIV

Concerning the Methods to be observed for establishing a new Commercial Company in the East Indies.[2]

SHOULD any nation desire to establish a Commercial Company in the East Indies, before all things it ought to secure a good station in the country to be in a position to refit its ships, and to lay them by during the seasons when they cannot go to sea. The want of a good harbour is the reason why the English Company has not progressed so well as it might have done, because a vessel cannot last for two years without being refitted, as it is liable to be attacked by worms.

As the route from Europe to the East Indies is long, it is desirable that the Company should have some place at the Cape of Good Hope for watering and obtaining supplies of

[1] See an interesting account of the customs of the Hindu brokers at Goa by Caesar Fredericke, Marchant of Venice, in his *Voyage and Travell* (R. Hakluyt, *Principall Navigations*, Everyman's Library, iii. 206 f.). As regards rights of property mentioned above, 'the normal state of every Hindu family is Joint. Presumably every such family is Joint in food, worship, and estate' (J. D. Mayne, *Hindu Law and Usage*, 2nd ed., 242 f.).

[2] This chapter is also introduced into the supplementary volume of Tavernier's travels entitled *Recüeil de plusieurs relations et traitez singuliers et curieux*, &c., where it is somewhat modified in details.

food, both when going and returning from the Indies, especially when returning, because, the vessels being then loaded up, they cannot carry a supply of water sufficient for a long voyage. In the meantime the Dutch have put this advantage out of the reach of other nations, by means of the fort which they have built at the Cape,[1] and the English have done the same thing at St. Helena,[2] although, by the law of nations and the general consent of the people of Europe, liberty to use these two places of refreshment has been for many years free to the whole world. Nevertheless, there may still be some mouth of a river near the Cape where another fort might be constructed, and this position would be worth more than all that can be made in the island of Daufine,[3] where there is no trade except in the purchase of cattle for their hides. But this trade is so insignificant that it would quickly ruin any Company, and the French have hitherto engaged in it without any advantage to themselves.

My reason for making this suggestion is the fact that in the year 1648 two Portuguese vessels coming from Lisbon to India, desiring to touch at the Cape to take in water, made their observations incorrectly, and the sea being very high, entered a bay 18 or 20 leagues from the Cape on the western side. They found in this bay a river, the water of which is very good, and the negroes of the country brought them supplies of all kinds of river-birds, fish, and beef. They remained there about fifteen days, and before leaving took two of the inhabitants to Goa, intending to teach them Portuguese, and endeavour to draw from them some information as to the trade which could be carried on there.[4] The Dutch

[1] In 1652 Jan van Riebeck built a fort at Table Bay, and in 1671 the Dutch purchased land from the Hottentots and founded the colony: cf. *n*. 5 on p. 305 below (*Ency. Brit.*, v. 237).

[2] The English appropriated the island after the departure of the Dutch in 1651, and built a fort in 1658 (*ibid.*, xxiv. 8). [See Introd.]

[3] The 'Daufine island' of the original stands for the Fort of Dauphin, on the south-east coast of Madagascar. It was held by the French for some years, but was afterwards abandoned (*ibid.*, xvii. 276).

[4] The details in vol. i, p. 173, differ from those here given. The distance is there stated to be 30 leagues from the Cape; the only conclusion which can be drawn is that this bay was a part of, or in the vicinity of, Table Bay. Or he may mean Saldanha Bay; see Pyrard de Laval, i. 22.

Commander at Surat asked me to go to Goa, and ascertain what the Portuguese had learnt from these two negroes ; but a French engineer named Saint Amand,[1] who had the supervision of the forts at Goa, told me that they had not been able to teach them a single word of the language, and had only guessed from their signs that they knew ambergris and elephant's tusks. The Portuguese, nevertheless, did not doubt that they would find gold if they were able to trade with the interior. The revolution in Portugal and the wars with Spain [2] have prevented them from examining this coast more particularly, and it would be well that the Company should examine it carefully without giving offence to the Dutch, or allowing them to suspect its object.

Moreover, it is necessary that the Company should have a port near Surat to lay by and refit its vessels, when delayed by the rainy season. The reason is, that during this bad weather, when it is almost impossible to withstand the violence of the sea, the Mogul, for fear of danger to his fortress at Surat, does not allow any foreign vessel into the river, where otherwise, when unladen, they might remain protected from the destructive storms which last for nearly five months.[3]

The only place suitable for harbouring the vessels of the Company is the town of Diu,[4] which belongs to the Portuguese. The advantages of its position are considerable for many reasons. The area of the town includes nearly 400 houses, and is capable of affording dwellings sufficiently numerous, where the crews of the vessels would find all they required. It is situated on the coast of Gujarāt, at the point of the Gulf of Cambay, facing towards the south-east. Its shape is nearly circular, and more than half the circle is surrounded by the sea. It is not commanded by any heights, and the Portuguese have built some fortifications on the land side which might be easily completed. It has numerous wells of good water, and also a river which falls into the sea near the town, the water

[1] Called St. Amant in vol. i, p. 164, and elsewhere.

[2] 1640–88.

[3] Aurangzeb specially favoured local Musalmān interests, because he regarded Surat as the Gate of Mecca (*Bombay Gazetteer*, ii. 88).

[4] Diu, see vol. i, p. 5.

of which is better than that of Surat and of Suwālī,[1] and the shelter is very commodious for vessels.

The Portuguese, on their first establishment in India, kept a fleet at Diu composed of galleys, brigantines. and smaller vessels, with which they made themselves, for a very long time, masters of all the commerce of the places about to be enumerated, so that no one was able to trade without taking out a passport from the Governor of Diu, who franked it in the name of the Viceroy of Portugal at Goa. The revenue he obtained from these passports sufficed to support the fleet and garrison, and the Governor, who was only appointed for three years,[2] did not omit to accumulate wealth for himself during that time.

Thus, according to the force established in this place, great benefit would result. The Portuguese, feeble as they are at present, do not fail to profit by not having to pay duty for the money they convey into the Kingdoms of the Great Mogul and the King of Bījāpur, nor for the goods which they take there.

When the rainy season is over, the wind being nearly always north or north-east, one can go from Diu to Surat in light boats in three or four tides, but if large vessels are laden, it is necessary for them to coast all round. A man on foot going by land to a small borough named the Gauges,[3] and from thence crossing the end of the Gulf, can go from Diu to Surat in four or five days, but if the season prevents him from making this passage, he cannot reach Surat from Diu in less than seven to eight days, because he must then make the circuit of the Gulf.

The town does not possess any territory outside the boundaries, but it would not be difficult to arrange with the Rājā, or Governor of the Province, and obtain from him as much as may be required for the convenience of the inhabitants. The soil of the neighbourhood is not fertile, and the population around is the poorest in all the Empire of the Mogul. Never-

[1] Suwāli or Swālly, see vol. i, p. 5. No important river falls into the sea at Diu.

[2] See i. 153 above.

[3] Gogo or Gogha on the western side of the Gulf of Cambay (Barbosa, ed. Dames, i. 134 f. : *Imperial Gazetteer*, xii. 301 f.).

theless, there is an abundance of cattle in the jungles, with which the country is covered, so that a buffalo or a cow does not cost more than 2 piastres.[1] The English and Dutch use these cattle to feed their people, in order to save the provision of their vessels during their sojourn at Suwālī.

It is well to remark that experience has shown that the flesh of buffaloes [2] often causes dysentery, which is considered most injurious to crews, but cow beef never gives rise to it.

The Rājā who rules the country bears the title of Governor for life ; and this is the case with nearly all the Rājās in the Empire of the Mogul, who were the nobles of the Provinces where their descendants only have the title of Governors.[3] He treats the Portuguese well, because their position as neighbours brings him in money by the sale of his corn, rice, and vegetables, and for the same reason he treats the French still better.

After the establishment of such a position, which should be the principal basis of the trade of the Company, there is nothing more important than to select two men, marked by their wisdom, rectitude, and intelligence in trade, and there should be no regard for economy in their allowances. These two men are intended to serve the Company, one in the position of Commandant or Commander, as the Dutch entitle them, with a council of a certain number of persons for his assistance ; the other for the office of broker or merchant, who should be a native of the country, an idolater and not a Musalmān, because all the workmen with whom he will have to do are idolaters. Good manners and probity are above all things necessary in order to acquire confidence at first among these people. It is well to secure like qualities in the private brokers, who are under the direction of the Broker-General,

[1] i. e. about 9*s*.

[2] Both the flesh and milk of buffaloes are at times, if not always, considered unwholesome (Fryer, i. 296). At the present day buffalo beef is thought, and rightly, to be coarse, unpalatable, and liable to breed maggots ; it is eaten by none but the lowest classes of the population.

[3] Bernier (p. 210 f.) accurately describes the relations of the Rājās or Chiefs to the Imperial Government. From the context, Tavernier seems to refer to the numerous petty Chiefs of Gujarāt and Kāthiāwār.

in the provinces where the offices of correspondents are established.[1]

Intelligence is not less necessary for these two men, in order that they may detect any adulteration in the manufacture of the goods. It arises, as I have said, either from the trickery of the workmen and merchants or from the connivance of the sub-brokers with them. This adulteration may cause so much injury to the Company that private brokers profit by it sometimes from 10 to 12 per cent. If the Commander and the Broker-General conspire together it is very difficult for the Company to guard against this fraud, but if they are both faithful and wise it will be easy to remedy it by changing the private brokers.

The way in which these officers are able to defraud a Company is this. When a vessel arrives in port, the letters of the Company and bills of lading are handed to him who commands on shore for the particular nation. This Commander assembles his Council, and sends for the broker and gives him a copy of the bill of lading. The broker communicates it to two or three of the merchants who are in the habit of buying wholesale. If the broker and the Commander conspire together to profit, the broker, instead of expediting the sale as he ought, tells the merchants privately that they have only to keep firm and offer such a price. Then the Commander sends for the broker and the two or three merchants. He asks them in the presence of his Council what they offer for the goods mentioned in the bills of lading which have been communicated to them. If the merchants persist in saying that they will only give so much, the Commander postpones the sale for fifteen days, more or less, according as he has reason for being pressed to sell. He causes the merchants to come many times, merely for the look of the thing, and he then takes the advice of the Council in order also to save appearances, and for his own protection; after which he orders the goods to be sold at the merchants' prices.

But although the temptation is great for these two officers,

[1] Some of the contemporary writers describe the importance of the Broker to the Factory (Fryer, i. 127 f.; Ovingtón, 401; Rawlinson, *British Beginnings in Western India*, 127).

on account of their power, the frequent opportunities, and the absence of their superiors from whom it is easy to conceal the truth, a Company is able to remedy this evil, by making a careful selection of these two officers, and by removing the pretext which the Dutch Commanders and brokers urge, which is that they are constrained to sell quickly to the merchants, wholesale, to avoid the costs of delay.

The fault the Dutch make is, that their officers order all the goods they wish to export from the Mogul Empire, to be made on credit from year to year according to the instructions they have received from Batavia. The cost of this advance is sometimes 12, sometimes 15 per cent., so that as soon as their vessels, laden with merchandise, arrive at the port where they are due, the goods must be sold promptly at the price which the wholesale merchants offer to the brokers, in order to obtain immediate funds to repay the advances made for the preparation of the goods which their vessels carry away, and to obtain credit for the manufacture of the following year.

It is this which gives an opportunity for the understanding between the Commanders and their brokers with the merchants, who profit by the necessity which forces the sales, and besides, this private profit diminishes that of the Company, and a part of the clearest gain is expended in paying the interest of the loan of which we are about to speak. For this interest mounts, from time to time, more or less, according as the Commander and the broker agree to make it increase. In the event of French vessels carrying the same goods as the Dutch, they should carry in addition money for the advances to the artisans who work in the provinces, and for a part of the price of the goods which are being made for the following year. The Company by making this advance escapes payment of the high interest on the loan, namely 12 to 15 per cent., which the Dutch pay ; and it will obtain the very best goods at the lowest price. All the artisans will work more willingly for it on account of this ready money.

The cargo for the vessels should be in readiness before they arrive in port. Being quickly laden they will be able to seize the good season for their return. The Company will not be compelled by necessity to sell at a low price to three or four local wholesale merchants who have made themselves masters of the trade, but its brokers will be able to await the arrival of foreign merchants who will come to carry away its goods, or rather, because they will have the means to have them exported to the places where they will themselves be able to dispose of them.

It should be remarked, besides, that it is profitable to carry gold and silver to India in bullion rather than in coin, because gold and silver are not valued in India except by their standard, and because there is always a deduction on coined money on account of the cost of minting.[1]

Should the broker be unfaithful, he is, moreover, able to come to an understanding with the master of the Mogul's mint, established in every port in the Empire, and to value the gold or silver, coined or in bars, at a lower standard than it really is, by telling the Commander and his Council that in the assay which has been made at the mint it is found to be only of such a standard. But it is easy to prevent this fraud, provided the Commander is upright and intelligent, if he sends for one of the native refiners of gold and silver, who can easily be found, and who understand how to assay metals perfectly, and if he sees it done in his own presence.[2]

This is what the Sieur Waikenton[3] did for the Dutch Company, in whose name he managed a factory at Kāsimbāzār, where he received each year from 6,000 to 7,000 bales

[1] See vol. i, p. 7.

[2] Ball received from Mr. J. Twigg of the N. W. P. Civil Service, the following account of the operations of one of these native assayers, as witnessed by himself. The object assayed was an ornament consisting of an alloy of gold and silver, which was first hammered out thin; it was then heated in nitric acid, the vessel used being a broken glazed English tea-cup; after some time, the silver being then dissolved out, the thin plate of gold was removed and fused with borax, the furnace being an old clay potsherd, and the fuel charcoal burnt under a mouth blow-pipe. The resulting gold button was then weighed, and the silver was precipitated by means of a piece of copper thrown into the solution. The nitric acid had been prepared by distillation of a mixture of saltpetre and iron sulphide (Pyrites). See *Diary of Samuel Pepys*, ed. Wheatley, iii. 103 ff.; *Ency. Brit.*, ii. 776 ff. For modern Indian methods Sir E. D. Maclagan, *Monograph on the Gold and Silver Work of the Panjab*, p. 16 f.

[3] See vol. i. 107.

of silk. He ascertained by this test that his broker, having an understanding with the master of the mint, cheated him of $1\frac{1}{2}$ or 2 per cent. on the quality of the gold and silver which was brought to him from Japan, either in bar or in coin, and that the Company had been defrauded of considerable sums.

The broker is also able to defraud by having an understanding with the master of the mint, or with the person who weighs the gold and silver in bars, coin, or dust, by employing too heavy weights, or scales which are not true. It is easy to prevent this fraud if the Commander, assisted by his Council, has them weighed in his presence with a scale and weights proved and stamped, which he keeps by him for the purpose.

One of the most important observations that is to be made on the commerce of the proposed Company and the discipline of its factors is this :—It should forbid the merchants, sub-merchants, the scribes, and sub-scribes, who serve under the Commanders, and the brokers, and also these superior officers, from doing any trade on their own private accounts, because having communication with all the artisans, and obtaining by the correspondence from the other factories information as to the articles of merchandise which will be saleable in the following year, they do not fail to purchase them on their own account, and ship them on the vessels of the Company to the addresses of their correspondents, who share the gain.

The Commander being himself interested, either by closing his eyes, or by a too great laxity, permits them to make this profit on account of their poor salaries.[1] The captain of the vessel is in league with them, because he secretly derives some advantage for allowing them to load and unload. And inasmuch as these officers have little capital, and desire to receive the price on the return of the vessel, they direct their correspondents to sell at from 8 to 10 per cent. below market price, which they can easily do, because, as I shall explain further on, they do not pay custom dues either at Surat or at Gombroon, and because they gain by this means about 26 per cent. ; and so this causes a considerable injury to the Company, and particularly to foreign merchants.

To remedy this disorder it is requisite to profit by the mistake

[1] See p. 37.

of the Dutch, and follow the rule which they have adopted since they realized the extent of this injury after an experience of many years. For, in fine, the Commander is not ignorant of the profit which there is for officials of the house when they load the goods of foreigners on the vessels of the Company, be it for Hormuz, for Bassora, for Mocha, or other places. With respect to Mocha on the Red Sea, the merchants who trade there are allowed one bale free of customs ; it is for this reason that among their bales they have always one five or six times larger than the others, which ten or twelve men have difficulty in carrying.[1]

The freight of some vessels amounts to 60,000 rupees, and when the Commander and broker are in league, they sometimes make a third, and even as much as a half, as their profits, besides which a vessel never leaves without the Commander and his wife presenting some rewards to their most faithful servants and slaves of both sexes. To one they give permission to ship six bales, to another eight, and to another ten, more or less, and as the bales in these countries pay freight according to the value of the goods, when a merchant has any bale of great value, amounting sometimes to 20,000 rupees, he agrees for the freight at the best price he is able, and abates one half, at least, in the case of one of these servants or slaves who has received this free permission from his master or mistress.

The pursers also take part in it, but as for the merchants and sub-merchants, they generally disdain these small profits, and content themselves with their own shipments. Another trick is played, when a merchant has some bales of rich goods, such as Deccan caps, which are sometimes worth as much as 400 écus, or the ornis [2] of Burhãnpur, of which I have spoken above, which serve to make veils for the ladies of Persia, Constantinople, and other places in Asia and Europe—when, I say, a merchant has some bales of such valuable goods

[1] The early records of the East India Company abound in complaints against the Interlopers, as they are called, who interfered with the Company's monopoly (Yule, *Hobson-Jobson*, 438), and against the trickery of officials (*Court Minutes of the East India Company, 1660–1663*, Index. s. v. Trade, Private).

[2] Orhni (see vol. i. 43).

which should pay high duty to the Prince of the place where they are to be ioaded, as soon as they are on board, the purser and captain, who are in league with the merchant, place on each the Company's mark, and after reaching the store of the place where they have been landed with the goods of the Company, they are removed at night in secret to the house of the merchant.

These people are able, moreover, to employ still another artifice. If the merchant is a friend of the Commander he settles with him, and pretending to have bought the bales of merchandise from the Company, which is free from all custom, he is released by paying the 2 per cent., the same as all those who have bought goods from the Company.[1]

The following is the remedy which can check this irregularity. It is necessary to establish in the principal factory a fiscal counsellor to act in the name of the King and by his authority. He should be independent of the General of the Company, in order that he may have the right to keep an eye upon his actions as upon those of the least of the officers.

A man of position is required for this post, who will be resolute and watchful, and has under him a representative at each factory. Each of these representatives, in the exercise of his duties, should observe what is indicated in the following articles :—As soon as he sees a vessel belonging to the Company in the offing, he should go at once, or sometimes, according to the season, he should wait till it has cast anchor. Then the captain of the vessel should deliver no letter to any other person, but should place all in the hands of the representative, who will deliver those of the Company to the Commander. He should take two or three person with him, who will remain on the vessel until it is unloaded, to see that all that is landed belongs to the Company. It is especially necessary that he should take care that the people whom he takes with him do not get drunk, for it often happens on these occasions that the officers of the vessel purposely intoxicate them when they have some contraband goods to send off the vessel, and secretly convey them to the fishing boats which bring them fish and other supplies ; this is done generally at night.

[1] The preceding four paragraphs are omitted in the reprint of the *Recüeil.*

If it is a place where there are islands in the offing, as the time is approximately known when the vessels ought to arrive, the representative of the Fiscal Counsellor should send beforehand, as far out as he can, two or three small boats, to be on the look-out round these islands, and as soon as they have discovered the vessel, they should join her, to prevent any contraband goods being landed on the islands, to which bribed persons might come to carry them secretly to the person to whom they are addressed. He should confiscate all that he discovers in the vessel which does not bear the mark of the Company, or does not belong to foreign merchants. He should have power to dismiss from his post the officer to whom the goods belong, if a subaltern; but if it be one of the superiors he should give notice to the Chief of the Factory, who, with his Council, may degrade him from his office and confiscate his salary. He may order all letters of private persons to be opened to detect contraband trade and the parties engaging in it. This is why the captain of the vessel is obliged to hand letters over to him; but he may not open the Company's letters. The proceeds of this confiscation of goods should be applied, one third to the poor of the nation, another third to the Company, and the remainder to the Fiscal and his officers, as is the custom of the Dutch. He will also represent the King in all criminal and civil processes which come before the Commander and his Council, and he will be able to requisition and take part in the name of His Majesty in all kinds of actions. Provided always that this officer is vigilant and a man of integrity, he will be able to render considerable service to the Company.

If the English had established such an official in their factories, they would have had greater profit; but the officers of that nation pretend that there is no superior power capable of withdrawing the privilege from them after they have once completed their apprenticeship in London, and hold the certificate of their master of having served him well for seven years.[1]

[1] The salaries of the English Company's officials at this period, as stated by Fryer (i. 216), were so small that one would suppose that they could have hardly subsisted without having some private oppor-

This injunction against private trade cannot be too strictly imposed. It is observed to-day with so much strictness amongst the Dutch that when a vessel of that Company is ready to leave Amsterdam, a Burgomaster administers to the captain and all on board a solemn oath that they will content themselves with their wages, two months of which are given in advance, and that they will not trade on their own account; but the conduct of the Company in respect to their wages compels them, in spite of their oaths, to aid themselves by secret traffic in order they may subsist while in their employment.

This is the artifice which they make use of to satisfy their consciences. When they have arrived in India, and see a prospect of obtaining some good employment, they marry as quickly as possible, and trade secretly in their wives' names; this is not always permitted. They imagine that in this way their conscience is relieved. But they are sometimes caught, and I shall give a somewhat amusing example of it, from among many others which I could recount.

The captain of a vessel,[1] a rich man, who troubled himself little about making court to the wives of the Chiefs of the Company, became a butt for their attacks, and was one day stung by some remarks made by Madame la Générale, who was talking to him at Batavia in the presence of many ladies. Without saying a word then, and well knowing all their intrigues, he resolved to revenge himself on the first occasion, which offered itself in this manner.

tunities for trade. The writers had to serve five years at £10 per annum, factors had £20 for three years, merchants £40 during their stay in the service, besides free food and lodging. The President received £500 a year, of which half was reserved at home to be confiscated in case of misdemeanour, in addition to his bond of £5,000. On the rates of pay of the Company's officials in the early period of its operations see Ovington, *Voyage to Suratt*, 392 f.; *Diary of William Hedges*, ii. 11, iii. 189; and the summary by Rawlinson, *British Beginnings in Western India*, 125 f. But it must be remembered that they received diet and lodging gratis from the Company, were allowed profits, often large, from private trade, and to accept presents from merchants and others who had dealings with the Company.

[1] This story is also told in the *Histoire de la Conduite des Hollandois en Asie*, chap. vi, where the [Governor] General is called Matsuker [Maatsuiker, to be quite correct] and the captain or ship Lucifer!

When this captain was about to return from Pulicat to Batavia, the wife of the Governor of the former place, who was in league with Madame la Générale in some private trade, believing that the captain was one of her friends, begged him to ship secretly eight bales of very valuable goods, and to take particular care that they were not wetted, in order to convey them to Batavia ; this the captain promised to do, and he placed the bales in a separate place.

On his arrival at Batavia, he first went according to custom, to salute the General and to hand him the letters belonging to the Company. The General is in the habit of keeping the captains to dinner or to supper, according to the hour of their arrival. Some Councillors of India are always present on these occasions, to hear the news, and remain to dine with the General.

At the close of dinner the General asked the captain what news he had from Pulicat, and if the Governor and his wife had not asked for anything to be done for them. 'Nothing,' replied the captain coldly, 'except that Madame, the Governor's wife, specially charged me with eight bales of goods, articles of great value, asked me to keep a good eye on them, so that they should not get damp, and to deliver them on my arrival into the hands of Madame la Générale.' This unexpected reply much surprised the General and those of the Council who were dining with him, and still more Madame la Générale, to whom the Governor,[1] turning, asked somewhat rudely if she carried on trade with the wife of the Governor of Pulicat, which, according to the laws of the Company, would have been criminal. Madame la Générale stoutly defended herself, and protested that she knew nothing of what the captain had said. The General then told the latter that he must be mistaken, and there and then ordered the Fiscal to go and seize the bales, and expose them on the quay to see if they would be claimed by any merchant. After they had remained there for some days without any claimant appearing, they were confiscated ; and thus, without scandal, the captain had his revenge for the ill treatment he had received at the hands of Madame la Générale.[2]

[1] [-General].

[2] The previous four paragraphs are omitted in the *Recüeil*.

All the subaltern officers of the Factories should be promoted by grades, from that of the post of sub-writer to that of Commander, so that the expectation of this promotion should encourage them to live decently, and acquire all the niceties and details of the Indian trade which qualify for the highest posts.

It is of the greatest importance not to show any favour in this, and that interest should not give advancement to anyone who has not passed through all the grades; for one of the things which does most injury to the Dutch trade is that for some years back the higher classes in Holland have sent their sons to India to seek for the posts which secret trade makes so profitable. The access which they obtain to the principal officers or to their wives, whose power is great in this country, causes them to be preferred to those who have no other recommendation than that of long service when any post becomes vacant.

It is true that some years ago the General at Batavia and his Council, seeing the injury this did to the Company, wrote to the Directors that they might send people to India of any quality they please, but that they should not send any more with recommendations; that in the future these would be of no avail, but would rather injure the advancement of their friends, because it was not fair that favour should precede merit; that the General and his Council had sufficiently good eyes to recognize the fitness of those sent, and would employ them according as they were worthy and as it was considered proper.

These are all the remarks which I have been able to make in reference to the discipline of the Factories and the methods that a new Company ought to observe for its establishment in the East Indies.

But I was forgetting one thing, which is of importance for a commercial Company, and to which it should pay attention. Up to this hour the Dutch observe this precaution, that they send to India neither captain nor pilot who has not passed through all grades, from a simple ship's boy up to the most important charge, and does not know how to take observations, and is not thoroughly acquainted with the coasts. Moreover, these captains are not of delicate constitutions, and content themselves with a piece of cheese or a slice of beef which has been in pickle for two or three years. And truly they are to be imitated in that respect. It is altogether different with some other nations, who often place on vessels captains who have never seen the sea, and whom favour alone immediately elevates to this post. In addition to which, when they embark they generally require elaborate cuisine appliances, plenty of sheep, calves, fowl, and turkeys, which consume much water, and soil the vessel with their droppings. Economy is the great support of commercial Companies, and it is an article to which those who are Directors should give their particular attention.

CHAPTER XV

Concerning diamonds, and the mines and rivers where they are found; and especially of the Author's Journey to the Mine of Rammalakota.[1]

The diamond is the most precious of all stones, and it is the article of trade to which I am most devoted. In order to acquire a thorough knowledge of it I resolved to visit all the mines, and one of the two rivers where diamonds were found; and as the fear of dangers has never restrained me in any of my journeys, the terrible picture that was drawn of these mines, situated in barbarous countries to which one could not travel except by the most dangerous routes, served neither to terrify me nor to turn me from my intention. I have accordingly been at four mines,[2] of which

[1] This is Raolconda in the original; for its identification with the modern Ramulkota, properly Rammalakota, see p. 43 below.

[2] The four mines appear to have been—1, Rammalakota (Raolconda); 2, Kollūr (Coulour or Gani); 3, Soumelpour; and 4, the locality on the Kistnā between Rammalakota and Kollūr, which, as pointed out on p. 61, may have been a deserted mine near Damārapād and Malawaram. The point is not quite clear, as in chap. xviii two mines near Rammalakota are mentioned, but there cannot be said to be descriptions of more than three mines in the text. There is ample reason for believing that the diamond mines existing in India in Tavernier's time were far more numerous than he had any conception of (see *Economic Geology of India*, pp. 1–50, and Appendix to this volume). The two rivers he mentions

I am about to give descriptions, and at one of the two rivers whence diamonds are obtained, and I have encountered there neither the difficulties nor the barbarities with which those imperfectly acquainted with the country had sought to terrify me. Thus I am able to claim that I have cleared the way for others, and that I am the first European who has opened the route for the Franks[1] to these mines, which

seem to be—1, the Penner River, below Gandikota, probably in the neighbourhood of Chenūr (see vol. i, 230); and 2, the river he did not visit, which was in Borneo (see p. 359 below).

[1] Tavernier was not aware that he had been preceded by other European visitors to the mines, e.g. Cæsar Fredericke and Methold (see p. 56 *n.*), and, as stated in the previous note, he was probably mistaken as to these being the only mines in India which were known in his time; besides many in Southern India, those at Pannā in Bundelkhand, Sambalpur on the Mahānadī, and Wairāgarh—the Bairagarh of the *Āīn-i-Akbarī* (ii. 230)—were almost certainly open then. We have, too, evidence of the working of a mine by a European at an earlier date. A paper presented by the Earl Marshal of England to the Royal Society (*Phil. Trans.*, vol. xii, 1677, p. 907) states that about the commencement of the seventeenth century (say 1610) a Portuguese gentleman went to Currure, i.e. Wajrā Karūr in the Bellary District, and expended a large sum of money, namely 100,000 pagodas or £45,000 in searching for diamonds without success. He then sold everything he had with him, even to his clothes, and on the last day when he could pay the wages of the workmen he had prepared a cup of poison which he intended to take that night if no diamonds were found. In the evening a fine stone of 26 pagodas' weight was brought to him by the workmen. The figures given in the paper indicate a value of 53 troy grains for the pagoda; at that rate 26 pagodas would be equal to 1,378 troy grains, or 434·7 carats. The recognized equivalent of the pagoda is something less, namely 52·56 troy grains (Kelly, *Universal Cambist*). In the same mine, we are told, diamonds of a seize (? ser) weight, namely 9 ounces troy, or 81½ pagodas, i.e. 1362·6 carats, had been found; and as Mīr Jumla took possession of this mine, together with the Carnatic, one cannot help suggesting that it may have been here that the Great Mogul's diamond was found, although Kollūr is particularly mentioned by Tavernier as the mine which produced it. To return to the above-mentioned Portuguese, he took the stone with him to Goa, and to commemorate its discovery put up a stone tablet, on which the following lines were engraved in the Telugu language:—

> 'Your wife and children sell, sell what you have,
> Spare not your clothes, nay, make yourself a slave,
> But money get, then to Currure make haste,
> There search the mines, a prize you'll find at last.'

For further information regarding the early history of diamond mining in India see Watt, *Economic Dictionary*, iii. 93 ff.

are the only places in the world where the diamond is found.[1]

The first of the mines which I visited is situated in the territory of the King of Bījāpur in the Province of Carnatic, and the locality is called Rammalakota,[2] situated five days journey from Golkonda,[3] and eight or nine from Bījāpur. The fact that the two Kings of Golkonda and Bījāpur were formerly subject to the Mogul, and were then only Governors of the Provinces which they acquired by their revolt, caused it to be said, and to be still said by some people, that the diamonds come from the Empire of the Great Mogul. It is only about 200 years since this mine of Rammalakota was discovered, at least so far as I have been able to ascertain from the people of the country.[4]

All round the place where the diamonds are found the soil is sandy, and full of rocks and jungle, somewhat comparable to the neighbourhood of Fontainebleau. There are in these rocks many veins, some of half a finger and some of a whole finger in width; and the miners have small irons, crooked at the ends, which they thrust into the veins to draw from them the sand or earth,[5] which they place in vessels; it is in this earth that they afterwards find the

[1] He here forgets Borneo (see p. 359 f. below).

[2] Raolconda in the original. The proper form of the name, Rammalakota, means in Telugu 'precious stone hill fort'. By means of the route given on p. 73 this locality has been identified with Rammalakota, about 20 miles south of Karnūl (Kurnool), where excavations are to be seen to this day (*Economic Geology of India*, p. 15). The position is fairly indicated on the small map of India which accompanies the Revised French edition of Tavernier's Travels, published at Rouen in 1713. The identification both of it and Coulour have foiled many investigators both in this and the last century. But it is needless to refer here to the various suggestions as to their identification, as the question is now fully set at rest by the identification of the stages on the routes to these mines.

[3] On p. 73 the distance is given as being 17 gos or 68 French leagues. The true distance by the direct route is about 120 English miles.

[4] This evidence for the antiquity of the mine is of but little value, and cannot be relied on.

[5] This description and what follows indicate that the mining was carried on in the rock, not in detrital beds. It is, indeed, now known that the matrix at Rammalakota is an old pebble conglomerate belonging to the 'Karnūl' series.

diamonds. But as the veins do not always run straight, as some ascend, while others descend, they are obliged to break the rocks, always following the direction of the veins. After they have opened them out, and have removed the earth or sand which may be in them, they then commence to wash it two or three times, and search it for whatever diamonds it may contain. It is in this mine that the cleanest and whitest-watered diamonds are found; but the evil is that in order to extract the sand more easily from the rocks the miners strike such blows with a heavy iron crowbar that it fractures the diamonds, and gives rise to flaws. This is the reason why so many thin stones come from this mine, for when the miners see a stone in which there is a flaw of some size, they immediately cleave it, that is to say split it, at which they are much more accomplished than we are. These are the stones which we call thin (*foible*), which make a great show. If the stone is clean they do not do more than just touch it with the wheel above and below, and do not venture to give it any form, for fear of reducing the weight. But if it has a small flaw, or any spots, or small black or red grit, they cover the whole of the stone with facettes in order that its defects may not be seen, and if it has a very small flaw they conceal it by the edge of one of the facettes. But it should be remarked that the merchant prefers a black point in a stone to a red one. When there is a red one the stone is roasted, and the point becomes black. I learned this trick at length so well that when I examined a parcel of stones which came from this mine, and saw that there were facettes on any of them, especially small facettes, I was certain that there was some speck or flaw in the stone.

There are at this mine numerous diamond-cutters, and each has only a steel wheel of about the size of our plates. They place but one stone on each wheel, and pour water incessantly on the wheel until they have found the 'grain' of the stone.[1] The 'grain' being found, they pour on oil

[1] The word in the original is chemin, or 'way' of the stone. It refers to the discovery of the position of the lines of cleavage, which determines the method to be adopted in the treatment of the stone. For some

and do not spare diamond dust, although it is expensive, in order to make the stone run faster, and they weight it much more heavily than we do.

I have known them to weight a stone with 150 livres of lead. It is true that it was a large stone, which weighed 130 carats after it had been cut, and that the mill was like ours, the large wheel of which was turned by four blacks. The Indians do not agree with us in believing that weighting them causes flaws in the stones. If theirs do not receive any it is because they always have a small boy who holds in his hand a very thin wooden spoon, with which he anoints the wheel incessantly with oil and diamond powder. Besides this their wheel does not go so fast as ours, because the wooden wheel which causes the steel one to revolve is seldom more than 3 feet in diameter.

The Indians are unable to give the stones such a lively polish as we give them in Europe ; this, I believe, is due to the fact that their wheels do not run so smoothly as ours. For, being made of steel, in order to grind it on the emery, of which it has need every twenty-four hours, it has to be taken off the tree, and it cannot be replaced so as to run as evenly as it should do. If they possessed the iron wheel like ours, for which not emery but the file is required, it is not necessary to remove it from the tree in order to file it, and they could give the stones a better polish than they do. I have stated that it is necessary to rub the wheel with emery or to file it every twenty-four hours, and it is desirable that this should be done every twelve hours if the workman is not lazy. For when the stone has run a certain time, the part of the wheel where it has pressed becomes polished like a mirror, and if the place be not roughened by emery or the file, the powder does not stick to it. When it does adhere more work can be done in one hour than in two when there is none on the wheel.

Although a particular diamond may be by nature hard,

details of the methods of Indian lapidaries see Mukharji, *Art Manufactures of India*, 267 ff. ; Baden Powell, *Handbook of Manufactures and Arts of the Punjab*, 193 f. ; on the European methods, *Ency. Brit.*, xvi. 198 f.

having, so to speak, a kind of knot,[1] such as is seen in wood, the Indian diamond-cutters would not hesitate to cut such a stone, although our diamond-cutters in Europe would experience great difficulty in doing so, and as a general rule would be unwilling to undertake it; but the Indians are paid something extra for their trouble.

I come to the government at the mines. Business is conducted with freedom and fidelity. Two per cent. on all purchases is paid to the King, who receives also a royalty from the merchants for permission to mine. These merchants having prospected with the aid of the miners, who know the spots where the diamonds are to be found, take an area of about 200 paces in circumference, where they employ fifty miners, and sometimes a hundred if they wish the work to proceed rapidly. From the day they commence mining till they finish the merchants pay a duty of 2 pagodas[2] per diem for fifty men, and 4 pagodas when they employ a hundred men.

These poor people only earn 3 pagodas[3] per annum, although they must be men who thoroughly understand their work. As their wages are so small they do not show any scruple, when searching the sand, in concealing a stone for themselves when they can, and being naked, save for a small cloth which covers their private parts, they adroitly contrive to swallow it.[4] The chief of all the merchants who embark in mining

[1] Certain points of a stone are often found to be exceptionally hard, as, for instance, when a facet is cut on the angle where two cleavage planes meet, or, so to speak, across the grain of the stone. (See p. 44 *n.*) A difficulty of this nature is mentioned by Messrs. Garrard as having been experienced when the Koh-i-Nūr was recut. (See Professor Tennant's lecture *On Gems and Precious Stones*, Society of Arts, 1852, p. 86.)

[2] Say 16*s.*

[3] Equal to about one rupee or 27 pence per mensem, or less than a penny a day. The rupee is now (1922) worth about 1*s.* 4*d.* In some remote parts of India labour can still be obtained at about that rate, or from 3 pice to an anna, i.e. 1⅛*d.* to 1½*d.*; but wages have greatly increased in recent years.

[4] Owing to the belief which exists in India that diamond dust is a poison (Tod, *Annals of Rajasthan*, ii. 1074; *Āīn-i-Akbarī*, i. 510 note) it is thought by some persons that native miners would not swallow diamonds. I have seen several authentic records of their having done so; Garcia da Orta, (*Simples and Drugs of India*, 343) for instance,

one day pointed out to me one of these miners, who had worked for him for many years, and who had stolen a stone from him which weighed a mangelin, i. e. nearly two of our carats.[1] He had concealed it in the corner of his eye, but it was taken from him as soon as the theft was discovered. In order to prevent these knavish tricks there are always twelve to fifteen watchmen employed by the merchants to see that they are not defrauded. If by chance a stone is found which weighs above 7 to 8 mangelins, it is taken to the master of the mine, who by way of recompense gives a sarpo,[2] which is a piece of cotton cloth to make a turban, of the value of 25 to 30 sols,[3] and generally with it half a pagoda in silver, or else a pagoda,[4] when rice and a plate of sugar are not given.

The merchants who visit the mine to buy, remain in their dwellings, and every morning at from 10 to 11 o'clock the masters of the miners, after they have dined (for the Banians never leave their houses till they have washed and eaten),[5] take their diamonds to show to them. If the parcels are large, and contain many stones of the value of from 2,000 up to 15,000 or 16,000 écus,[6] they entrust them to the foreign merchant for seven or eight days or more in order that he may examine them with care. When the stones have been examined, and are returned by the merchant, if they suit him he should conclude the transaction at once, otherwise the owner of the stones wraps them in a corner of his waist-

refers to cases as evidence that the diamond is not poisonous. Once a diamond had been smuggled away from the mines, its possessor was not only safe, but if it was of large size, and he offered it to the King, either of Golkonda or of Bījāpur, he had every chance of selling it well, and being presented with a robe of honour. (See the *Account of the Diamonds, &c.*, presented to the Royal Society by the Earl Marshal of England, *Phil. Trans.*, vol. xii, 1677, p. 907.)

[1] See Appendix, vol. i.

[2] Sar-o-pā, a complete dress of honour, from head to foot. (See Yule, *Hobson-Jobson*, 808.)

[3] 1*s.* 10½*d.* to 2*s.* 3*d.*

[4] About 8*s.*, if new pagodas.

[5] This may be illustrated by the practices of the Srāvak or Jain Vāniā traders of Western India, who are careful not to eat food which may be contaminated by the presence in it of any animal life (Jagmanderlal Jaini, *Outlines of Jainism*, 69; *Bombay Gazetteer*, ix, part i, 93 ff.).

[6] £450 to £3,600.

band, his turban, or his shirt, and departs, so that one never sees the same stones again, or at least they are mixed with others, when the miner returns with another parcel. When the transaction is concluded the puchaser gives an order for payment on the Shroff or person who issues and receives bills of exchange. If you have agreed to pay in three or four days, and delay longer, you have to pay interest at the rate of 1½ per cent. per month. Most frequently, when the merchant is known to be solvent, a bill of exchange on Agra, Golkonda, or Bījāpur is preferred, but more especially one upon Surat, where, as it is the most famous port in India, the dealers desire to purchase the commodities which come in vessels from foreign countries, and are suitable for their wants.

It is very pleasant to see the young children of these merchants and of other people of the country, from the age of ten years up to the age of fifteen or sixteen, assemble every morning under a tree which is in the town square. Each has his diamond weights in a little bag suspended on one side, and on the other a purse attached to his waistband, which contains as much as 500 or 600 gold pagodas. They seat themselves there awaiting the arrival of anyone who wishes to sell diamonds, either brought from this or from some other mine. When anyone brings a stone he places it in the hands of the eldest of the children, who is, so to speak, the chief of the band ; he looks at it and passes it on to him who sits next. Thus it goes from hand to hand till it returns to the first one without anyone saying a word.

He then asks the price of the specimen, wishing to purchase, if possible ; and if by chance he buys at too high a price he is responsible. In the evening these children count up what they have purchased, and after examining the stones separate them according to their water, weight, and cleanness. Next they price each as they expect to dispose of them to strangers ,and by this they see how far the value exceeds the cost of purchase. They then carry them to the great merchants who always have a number of parcels to match, and all the profit is divided among the children, save only that their chief receives a quarter per cent. more than the others. Young as they are, they know the value of all the stones so well that if one of them has bought a stone and is willing to lose a half per cent., another gives him cash for it. You can seldom show them a parcel of a dozen stones, among which they will not discover four or five with some flaw, point, or defect at the angles.[1]

It remains to be said that these Indians have a high regard for strangers, and especially for those whom they call Franks.[2] Immediately on my arrival at the mine I went to call upon the Governor of the place, who also rules the Province on behalf of the King of Bījāpur. He is a Musalmān, who embraced me and assured me I was welcome—not doubting that I had brought gold with me—for at all the mines of Golkonda and Bījāpur they speak but of new pagodas,[3] which are golden coins—and that I had only to place it in my lodging, where it would be safe, and he would be responsible for all I had. Besides the servants I brought with me he allotted me four others, and commanded them to keep watch on my gold by day and night, and to obey all my orders. Shortly after I had left him he recalled me, and on my return: 'I sent to seek you', he said, 'in order to assure you again that you have nothing to fear—eat, drink, and sleep, and have a care for your health. I have forgotten to tell you to be careful not to defraud the King, to whom 2 per cent. is due on all your purchases. Do not attempt', he continued, 'to do as some Musalmāns did, who came to the mine and combined with the merchants and some brokers to withhold the royalties of the King—saying that they had only purchased to the value of 10,000 pagodas, while they had invested more

[1] 'The Gentoo merchants too use the same method with their children, initiating them, with the first dawn of their reason, into all the mysteries of their trade and contracts, insomuch that it is not uncommon to see boys of ten or twelve years of age so acute and expert that it would not be easy to over-reach them in a bargain.' (J. H. Grose, *A Voyage to the East Indies*, 1757, p. 238.) For the method by which children of the Bania or mercantile castes are trained in mental arithmetic see Russell, *Tribes and Castes, Central Provinces*, ii. 128.

[2] Fringuis for Franguis in the original, for Franks, i.e. Europeans. (See vol. i, 5.)

5 [3] They were worth about 8*s*., more exactly 3½ rupees. (See vol. i, p. 329.)

than 50,000.' I then commenced to purchase, and saw that there was a sufficiently large profit to be made, all being 20 per cent. cheaper than at Golkonda, in addition to which, one sometimes, by chance, met with large stones.

One evening a Banian, poorly clothed, having indeed only a band round his waist and a miserable handkerchief on his head, came towards me politely and seated himself by my side. In this country one pays no attention to dress, and a person who has but a miserable ell of calico about his loins may sometimes have a good parcel of diamonds concealed. I, on my part, treated the Banian with civility, and after he had been seated by me for some time he asked me through my interpreter [1] if I wished to buy some rubies. The interpreter told him to show them to me, upon which he drew a number of small rags from his waistband, in which he had about a score of rings mounted with rubies. After I had examined them I said that they were too small for my purpose and that I sought large stones. Nevertheless, when I remembered that I had been asked by a lady at Ispahān to bring her a ruby ring of the value of about 100 écus, I bought one of his rings which cost me nearly 400 francs. I knew well that he did not value it at more than 300 francs, but willingly risked the additional 100 francs in the belief that he had not sought me to sell the rubies only, and because I understood from his manner that he desired to be alone with me and my interpreter in order to show me something better. As the time of prayer of the Musalmāns approached, three of the servants appointed by the Governor left, and I found an excuse for getting rid of the fourth, who stayed behind to wait on me, by sending him to buy bread, where he remained a sufficiently long time. For all the people of this country being idolaters, content themselves with rice, and do not eat bread, and when a person wishes for it it is necessary to have it brought from a distance, from the fortress of the King of Bījāpur, where the Musalmāns reside. The Banian, seeing that he was alone with me and the interpreter,

[1] From this and other similar references we learn that Tavernier did not acquire a knowledge of Eastern languages. The fact is indeed referred to contemptuously by some of his critics, especially Chardin.

with a good deal of mystery, removed his headdress and untwisted his locks, which, according to the usual custom, were bound round his head. Then I observed a small rag appearing amidst his hair, in which there was concealed a diamond, weighing 48½ of our carats, of beautiful water and of cabuchon[1] shape, three-quarters of the stone clear, save for a small flaw on one side which appeared to penetrate some distance into the stone. The remaining quarter was full of flaws and red spots.

While I examined the stone, the Banian, seeing the attention which I gave to it, said, 'Do not trouble yourself now, you will see it to-morrow morning at your leisure when you are alone. When a fourth of the day has passed', it is thus that they speak,[2] 'you will find me outside the town, and if you wish for the stone you will bring the price of it with you,' and he then stated the amount he wanted for it. For it should be stated *en passant* that after this quarter of the day the Banians, both male and female, disappear into the city or town where they dwell, both to satisfy the ordinary necessities of nature and bathing, as well as to say the prayers which their priests require them to repeat. The Banian having named this hour—because he did not wish anyone to see us together—I did not fail to go in search of him, and carried with me the price he asked, less by 200 pagodas, which I kept apart, in reserve. But in the end, after we had bargained for a short time, I gave him 100 pagodas extra. On my return to Surat I sold the stone to a Dutch captain, and I earned a fair profit from the transaction.

Three days after I had bought this stone a messenger arrived from Golkonda who had been sent by an apothecary, named Boëte, whom I had left at Golkonda to receive and take care of a part of my money, and in the event of the Shroff paying in rupees, he was to change them into golden pagodas. The day after he had received payment, he was attacked by so serious a disorder in the stomach that he

[1] A cabuchon diamond is one merely polished, not cut (*New English Dict. s.v.*).

[2] The day is divided into four pahars which terminate at 9 a.m., 12 m., 3 p.m., and 6 p.m.

died in a few days. He informed me by letter of his sickness, and that he had received my money, which was all in my chamber in sealed bags ; but, as he did not believe that he would survive two days, he exhorted me to hasten my return, because he did not think that my money would be safe in the hands of the servants whom I had left with him. Immediately on receipt of this letter I waited on the Governor to take leave of him, at which he was astonished, and inquired if I had expended all my money. I replied that I had not spent half of it, and that I had still upwards of 20,000 pagodas.[1] He then said that if I wished he would afford me an opportunity of investing it, and that I should certainly not lose upon what he would enable me to buy. He further asked if I was willing to show him my purchases, although he was not ignorant of their extent, since those who sold were obliged to make a return of all to him, on account of the charge of 2 per cent. duty which is due to the King by those who buy. I showed him then what I had bought, and told him what they had cost me. This agreed with the book of the Banian who received the King's dues. At the same time, I paid him the 2 per cent. for the King's dues, on which he remarked that he perceived that the Franks were persons of good faith. He was the more persuaded of this, however, when, drawing forth the stone of 48½ carats, I said, 'Sir, this is not in the Banian's book, and there is no one in the town who knows that I have bought it, nor would you yourself had I not told you. I do not wish to defraud the King of his rights—here is what is due to him on account of the price paid by me for this stone.'[2] The Governor appeared surprised and much edified by my proceeding ; he praised me much, and said that this was an action worthy of an honest man, and that there was not another merchant in the country, either Musalmān or Hindu, who would act in the same manner if he believed that no one was aware of what he had purchased.

[1] i.e. about £8,000, which shows the extent of our author's transactions. At the same time we know that he bought largely on commission for the Dutch officials.

[2] Unlike his usual habit of giving prices, Tavernier carefully omits all mention of what he paid for this stone.

Upon this he summoned the richest merchants of the place, told them the facts, and ordered them to bring with them the best stones they possessed. This was done by three or four of them, and thus I expended my 20,000 pagodas in one or two hours. The transaction having been completed and the money paid, he told the merchants that as they had dealings with an honest man they ought to present me with a souvenir. This they did with a good grace, giving me a diamond worth nearly 100 écus.[1] As for the Governor himself, he gave me a turban and waistband.

I have to record a rather singular and curious account of the manner in which the Indians, whether they are idolaters or Musalmāns, make their sales of all kinds of commodities. All passes in complete silence and without any one speaking.[2] The seller and the buyer sit facing one another, like two tailors, and one of the two opening his waistband, the seller takes the right hand of the buyer and covers his own with his waistband, under which in the presence of many other merchants, who occupy themselves sometimes in the same manner, the sale is completed secretly without any one having cognizance of it. For the seller and buyer talk neither by means of their lips nor their eyes, but only by the hand, which they manage to do in the following manner: When the seller takes the whole hand of the buyer that means 1,000, and as many times as he presses it so many thousands of pagodas or rupees, according to the coin which may be in question. When he takes only five fingers that means 500, and when he takes only one it means 100. By taking only the half up to the middle joint, 50 is meant, and the

[1] £22 10*s*.

[2] This system of selling by means of secret signs has often been described by Indian travellers. For a recent account of it reference may be made to the *St. James's Gazette*, January 20, 1887; and for early notices see Yule, *Hobson-Jobson*, 849 f. The subject has been fully dealt with by Sir P. J. H. Grierson, *The Silent Trade*, Edinburgh, 1903. An early instance is recorded by Pliny (*Nat. Hist.*, vi. 22 (241)) for Ceylon, and by Marco Polo (ii. 416), of laying out goods and allowing the purchaser to leave the value in their place—a variant of the custom described by Tavernier. The form of bargaining noted in the text is recorded by Pyrard de Laval (ii. 179), and is familiar to all who have been present at horse or cattle fairs in India.

end of the finger up to the first signifies 10. This is the whole mystery employed by the Indians in their sales, and it often happens that, in a place where there are many people, a single parcel will change hands five or six times without those present knowing for how much it has been sold on each occasion. As for the weight of the stones, one need not be deceived if he does not buy in secret. For when one buys them in public there is a man specially employed by the King to weigh diamonds, who receives no fees from private persons. When he names the weight, both buyer and seller accept his statement, since he has no interest in favouring either party.

Having completed my business at the mine, the Governor gave me six horsemen, that I might traverse, with greater security, the tract under his authority, which extends up to a river [1] separating the Kingdom of Bījāpur from that of Golkonda. The transit of this river is very difficult, because it is wide, deep, and rapid, and there is neither bridge nor boat. In crossing it the same contrivances are used as those of which I have elsewhere spoken for the passage of certain Indian rivers, for men, for their goods, carriages, cattle, and horses. A round vessel of 10 or 12 feet in diameter made of branches of osier, like our hampers, and covered outside with ox hides, serves in place of a boat,[2] and I have described in the same place how the passengers arrange themselves. Good boats or a bridge over this river might be provided, but the Kings of Golkonda and Bījāpur do not allow this, because the river serves to separate the two Kingdoms. Every evening the boatmen on both banks are obliged to report to the two sub-governors, who reside on either side, at about a quarter of a league from the river, an exact statement of the people, beasts of burden, and merchandise which have crossed during the day.

When I arrived at Golkonda, three days had elapsed since

[1] The Kistnā with its tributary the Bhīmā, which separated the ancient Kingdoms.

[2] Coracles (see i. 235 and 239). Tavernier is probably not correct in saying that they were made of osiers or willow; more probably they were made of bamboo.

the death of Boëte, the apothecary, and the room where I had left him had been sealed with two seals—one that of the Kāzī, who corresponds to the Chief Justice, and the other that of the Shāhbandar, who is the Provost of the merchants. An officer of justice watched the door of the chamber together with the servants whom I had left with the deceased. Immediately on my arrival the fact was announced to the Kāzī and the Shāhbandar, and forthwith they sent for me

After I had saluted them, the Kāzī asked me whether the money which was in the chamber of the deceased was mine, and how I could prove it. I said I had no better proof to show him than the letters of exchange which I had given to the Shroff, and that since my departure he had by my orders paid the sum to the deceased ; that I had instructed the latter in case the Shroff paid in silver to change it into golden pagodas, and forward them to me. Upon this reply, they sent to call the two Shroffs who had paid my bills, to know if it was true, and as they agreed that it was, the Kāzī forthwith ordered his lieutenant to open the door of the room, and see if the seals were intact on all the bags. He did not leave till he had my assurance that I had found the full sum, and that nothing was wanting. I returned with him to make the same declaration to the Kāzī and the Shāhbandar, and to thank them for their trouble, and it ended by my signing a document which they had written in Persian, in which I testified my satisfaction.

The lieutenant told me that I must pay the charges of the burial of Boëte, those due to the persons who had placed the seals, and to the officer who had kept guard at the door of the chamber. These all amounted to but 9 rupees, or $4\frac{1}{2}$ écus of our money.[1] One would not have got off so easily in most places in Europe.[2]

[1] i.e. £1 0*s*. 3*d*.

[2] The story gives the impression that the affairs of the Local Government were well administered.

CHAPTER XVI

Journey of the Author to the other Mines, and concerning the method of searching for Diamonds.

SEVEN days' journey east of Golkonda there is another diamond mine, called Gani in the language of the country, and Coulour in the Persian tongue.[1]

It is close to a large town on the same river which I crossed

[1] This mine has been identified in the *Economic Geology of India*, by the routes in vol. i. 140 and vol. ii. 73 with Kollūr on the Kistnā, where, according to a MS. map by Col. Mackenzie, there was a mine in 1798. The word Gāni is equivalent to the Persian Kān-i, signifying 'mine of'. It is found in use by writers of the present century in connexion with another mine, namely Gani-Partiāl. It is the title for this mine most commonly used in works on mineralogy and precious stones, sometimes considerably modified in spelling, as Garee, &c. But it cannot be correctly used as the name of the mine where the Great Mogul or any other diamond was found. The date assigned to the discovery of this mine by Tavernier, namely about the middle of the sixteenth century, is of no value any more than the period assigned for the discovery of the Rammalakota mine. One hundred years, the native estimate, means a long time,. that is all. Somewhere about the year 1622, William Methold, together with Andreas Socory and Adolf Thomason, visited from Masulipatam certain diamond mines, which the first-named describes as being situated 'at the foot of a great mountayne, not far from a river called Christena', the mining town being 2 miles off, and distant 108 English miles, or 12 Gentine leagues (gows, or gos ?) from Masulipatam. In all respects, save as regards the distance, the description of the mines and the methods of working correspond with Tavernier's account of Coulour or Gani, i.e. Kollūr. The distance given by Tavernier is 36 coss, or 72 miles from Masulipatam—the true distance is about 100 miles. In the *Histoire générale des Voyages*, vol. xiii, p. 20, Methold is misquoted as though he said the mines were but 2 leagues from Golkonda, whereas he says 2 miles from the temporary town, containing 100,000 persons, which had grown up in connexion with the mines. He says that they were closed for a time, in consequence of a demand made by the Mogul for a vyse (i.e. 3 lb. English, Tamil Visai) of the finest diamonds. The farmer paid the King 300,000 pagodas, say £120,000, per annum for the mine, the King retaining all stones above 10 carats. This sum is possibly an exaggeration—*vide Purchas His Pilgrimage*, 1626, vol. v. 1002. There is, as already stated, an account of the diamond mines of Golkonda and Bījāpur in the *Phil. Trans.*, vol. xii, No. 136, 1677. Ruins of houses, &c., and old mines are still to be seen at Kollūr. (See *Kistna Manual*, pp. 170, 244.)

when coming from the other mine,[1] and at a league and a half from the town there are high mountains in the form of a cross. The space between the town and the mountains is a plain where the mine is situated and the diamonds are found. The nearer one searches towards the mountains the larger the stones which are found, but when one ascends too high nothing is found.[2]

It is only about 100 years since this mine was discovered when a poor man, digging a piece of ground where he purposed to sow millet, found a pointe naïve [3] weighing nearly 25 carats. This kind of stone being unknown to him, and appearing remarkable, he carried it to Golkonda, and by good luck addressed himself to one who traded in diamonds. The trader having ascertained from the peasant the place where he had found the stone, was much surprised to see a diamond of such a weight, especially because the largest that had hitherto been seen did not exceed 10 or 12 carats.[4]

The rumor of this new discovery quickly spread abroad throughout all the country, and some persons of wealth in the town commenced to mine in this land, where they found, and where they still find, large stones in greater abundance than in any other mine.[5] There are found here at

[1] i.e. the Kistnā, crossed on the route from Raolconda (i.e. Rammalakota) to Golkonda (see p. 54).

[2] The probable explanation of this is that the diamond-bearing strata do not extend far up the slope.

[3] This term (Latin *nativus*) was applied to natural octahedra and other modifications of the cube which the diamond assumes. 'In this Roca Velha [old rock], there are Diamonds founde that are callèd Nayfes ready cut, which are naturall, and are more esteemed than the rest, specially by the Indians themselves' (Linschoten, ii. 137); cf. Fryer, ii. 143.

[4] This statement is quite incorrect, as will be seen in Appendix I.

[5] In the paper in the *Phil. Trans.*, which has just been referred to, the largest diamonds are said to have been obtained at the mine of Currure, i.e. Wajrā Karūr in Bellary, where some of a seize (ser ?) weight = 9 ounces troy, or 81½ pagodas, were reported to have been discovered. This mine, though unknown to Tavernier, had been taken possession of by Mīr Jumla about the year 1640. Probably there is some mistake in the weight. In the same paper this Kollūr mine is called Quolure, and it is said to have been the first mine excavated in the Kingdom, but it was then nearly exhausted. Many of the diamonds found there were well formed and pointed, and of good lively white water, others were

present, I say, many stones from 10 up to 40 carats, and sometimes indeed much larger; among others the great diamond which weighed 900 carats before cutting, which Mīr Jumla presented to Aurangzeb,[1] as I have elsewhere related.

But if this mine of Kollūr is of importance on account of the number of large stones which are found there, it is a misfortune that, as a rule, these stones are not clear, and that their water contains indications of the quality of the soil where they are found. If the soil is marshy and humid, the stone tends to blackness; if it is reddish, it tends to red, and so with the other conditions, sometimes towards green, sometimes towards yellow, just as there is diversity of soil in the area between the town and the mountain. Upon the majority of these stones, after they are cut, there always appears a kind of grease which necessitates one always carrying a handkerchief in the hand in order to wipe them.[2]

As regards the water of the stones, it is to be remarked that instead of, as in Europe, employing daylight for the examination of stones in the rough (*brutes*), and so carefully judging their water and any flaws which they may contain, the Indians do this at night; and they place in a hole which they excavate in a wall, one foot square, a lamp with a large wick, by the light of which they judge of the water and the cleanness of the stone, as they hold it between their fingers. The water which they term 'celestial'[3] is the worst of all, and it is impossible to ascertain whether it is present while the stone is in the rough. But though it may not be apparent

yellow, brown, &c., and had a greenish transparent skin. The weights ranged from 6 to a mangelin up to 5 or 6, and even rarely 10, 15, or 20 mangelins each. In consequence of its exhaustion, the King permitted the mine at Melwillee, i.e. Mulavilly or Mulēlī, to be regularly worked in the year 1673.

[1] This statement contains two mistakes. The stone was presented by Mīr Jumla to Shāhjahān, not to Aurangzeb, and in three other places Tavernier gives its weight as 900 ratis or upwards, 787½ carats; the latter misprint has unfortunately often been quoted. (See Appendix I.)

[2] 'Diamond possesses a brilliant "adamantine" lustre, but this tends to be greasy on the surface of the natural stones and gives the rounded crystals the appearance of drops of gum' (*Ency. Brit.*, viii. 158 f.).

[3] Persian *āb-i-āsmānī*, Hind. *pānī āsmānī*.

on the mill, the never-failing test for correctly ascertaining the water is afforded by taking the stone under a leafy tree, and in the green shadow one can easily detect if it is blue.

The first time I was at this mine there were nearly 60,000 persons working there, including men, women, and children, who are employed in diverse ways, the men in digging, the women and children in carrying earth, for they search for the stones at this mine in an altogether different manner from that practised at Rammalakota.

After the miners have selected the place where they desire to work, they smooth down another spot close by, of equal or rather greater extent, round which they erect an enclosing wall of two feet in height.

At the base of this little wall they make openings, at every two feet, for the escape of the water, which they close till it is time for the water to be drawn off. This place being thus prepared, all who are about to engage in the search assemble, men, women, and children, together with their employer and a party of his relatives and friends. He brings with him a figure in stone of the god whom they worship, which is placed standing on the ground, and each person prostrates himself three times before it, their priest, however, offering up the prayer.[1] This prayer being finished, he makes a particular kind of mark upon the forehead of each one with a paste composed of saffron and gum, in order that it may sustain seven or eight grains of rice, which he places upon it.[2] Then they wash their bodies with the water which each of them carries in a vessel, and sit down in ranks to eat that which is presented at the feast given by their employer at the beginning of their work, in order to give them courage and induce them to acquit themselves faithfully. This feast merely consists of a portion of rice to each, which is distributed by the Brahman, because every idolater can eat what is

[1] The prayer is an appeal for protection from the mine spirits, which are much dreaded (Crooke, *Popular Religion and Folk-lore of Northern India*, i. 282 f.),

[2] The sectarial mark, known as tilak or nāma, of which see an illustration in Russell, *Tribes and Castes, Central Provinces*, ii. 102. (See Monier-Williams, *Brahmanism and Hinduism*, 4th ed. 66 f.; Linschoten, i. 255.)

served to him by the hands of the priests. Some among them are so superstitious that they will not eat what is prepared even by their own wives, and prefer to cook for themselves.[1] The plate upon which the rice is placed is made of the leaves of a tree pinned together ; to some extent they resemble our walnut leaves.[2] To each there is also given about a quarter of a pound of melted butter in a little cup of copper, with some sugar.

When dinner is finished, each starts work, the men to excavate the earth, and the women and children to carry it to the place which has been prepared as I have said above. They excavate to 10, 12, or 14 feet in depth, but when they reach water there is nothing more to hope for. All the earth is carried to this place, men, women, and children draw water with pitchers from the hole which they have excavated, and throw it upon the earth which they have placed there, in order to soften it, leaving it in this state for one or two days, according to the tenacity of the clay, until it becomes like soup. This done, they open the holes which they made in the wall to let off the water, then they throw on more, so that all the slime may be removed, and nothing remain but sand. It is a kind of clay which requires to be washed two or three times. They then leave it to be dried by the sun, which is quickly effected by the great heat. They have a particular kind of basket made something like a winnowing fan, in which they place the earth, which they agitate as we do when winnowing grain. The fine part is blown away, and the coarse stuff which remains is subsequently replaced on the ground.

All the earth having been thus winnowed, they spread it with a rake and make it as level as possible. Then they all stand together on the earth, each with a large baton of

[1] This is due to fear of pollution and witchcraft. In South India it is only at the marriage ceremonial eating, or confarreatio, that husband and wife eat together (J. E. Padfield, *The Hindu at Home*, 133, and compare Sir J. G. Frazer, *Pausanias*, iv. 117).

[2] In northern India and the Deccan these are the leaves of the Sāl, Shorea robusta, Gaertn., the giant creeper, Bauhinia vahlii, W. and A., or the Dhāk or Palās, Butea frondosa, Roxb. ; in Western India plantain leaves, or those of the nymphaea lotus are used (Russell, *op. cit.*, ii. 204 ; Forbes, *Oriental Memoirs*, 2nd ed., i. 52 ; Mrs. S. Stevenson, *Rites of the Twice-born*, 240).

wood like a huge pestle, half a foot wide at the base, and pound the earth, going from one end to the other, always pounding each part two or three times; they then place it again in the baskets and winnow it, as they did on the first occasion, after which they spread it out again and range themselves on one side to handle the earth and search for the diamonds, in which process they adopt the same method as at Rammalakota. Formerly, instead of using wooden pestles for pounding the earth, they pounded it with stones, and it was that method which produced so many flaws in the diamonds.

As for the royalties which are paid to the King, the annual wages to the miners for their work, and the presents which are given to them when they find any large stone which they carry to the master whom they serve, all are the same as at the Rammalakota mine.[1] No one hesitated formerly to purchase diamonds which had a green crust on the surface, because when cut they proved to be white and of very beautiful water.

About 30 or 40 years ago a mine situated between Kollūr and Rammalakota [2] was discovered, but the King ordered it to be closed on account of fraud, as I shall explain in a few words. Stones were found in it which had this green crust, beautiful and transparent, more beautiful even than the others, but when one attempted to grind them they broke in pieces. Whenever they were ground by another stone of the same quality which had been found in the same mine they submitted to the grinding without breaking, but were unable to bear the wheel, upon which they immediately flew into pieces. It is on this account that one is careful not to buy those which have been ground in this way, through fear of their breaking, and it is, as I said, on account of the deceptions which have been practised with these stones that the King ordered the mine to be closed.[3]

[1] *Vide ante*, p. 46.

[2] Ball suggests (see *Economic Geology of India*, p. 16) that this mine was situated near Damārapād and Malāwaram on the Kistnā in Lat. 16° 35′, Long. 79° 30′, where old excavations are still to be seen.

[3] A little-known but very important paper on the diamond mines of Golkonda, of which twenty-three are named, and of Visapore, i. e. Bījāpur, of which fifteen are named, is to be found in the *Phil. Trans.*, No. 136, June 25, 1677, vol. xii, p. 907. The anonymous author must have been

While the Messrs. Fremlin and Francis Breton [1] were Presidents at Surat on behalf of the English Company, a Jew named Edward Ferdinand, a free merchant, that is to say not subject to any Company, combined with these two gentlemen, a short time after the mine was discovered, to purchase a stone. This stone was clean and of good form, and weighed 42 carats.[2] Edward went to Europe, and Messrs. Fremlin and Breton placed the stone in his hands to sell to the best advantage, and render an account to them. On his arrival at Leghorn [3] he showed it to some Jew friends, who offered him 25,000 piastres [4] for it. But as he asked 30,000 he was unable to let them have it, and took it to Venice to get it cut. It was well cut, without any injury, but upon being put upon the wheel it immediately broke into nine pieces. I myself was on one occasion deceived by one of these stones, which weighed 2 carats; it broke into small pieces on the wheel when it was only half finished.

CHAPTER XVII

A continuation of the Author's Journeys to the Diamond Mines.

I NOW come to the third mine, which is the most ancient of all, and is situated in the Kingdom of Bengal. You may call it by the name Soumelpour,[5] which is a large town near

in that part of India within ten or fifteen years of Tavernier's last visit. Ball discovered this paper too late, unfortunately, to make use of it in the footnotes to his translation. It contains names, he remarks, which had long puzzled him, owing to the confused way in which they have been introduced into the literature of the subject. Full use has now been made of it in revising Ball's notes, e. g. it has been referred to on pp. 42 and 56–7 above and will be found freely cited by Ball himself in App. II to this volume.

[1] William Fremlin was President of Surat 1638–44, and was succeeded by Francis Breton, who died in 1649 (Rawlinson, *British Beginnings in Western India*, 108 ff.). For 'Ed. Ferdinand' see *Eng. Factories, 1642–1645*, p. xv.

[2] The extent to which investments in diamonds for themselves and their friends in England were made by English officials at a later period is very fully brought out in the letters published by Colonel Yule in his account of the Pitt diamond (see Hedges' *Diary*, Hakluyt Society, iii. 125 ff.).

[3] Ligorne in the original.

[4] Say £5,625.

[5] Among a host of writers of the last century, so far as known, Karl Ritter (*Erdkunde Asien*) and Francis Buchanan (in Martin's *Eastern*

to which the diamonds are found, or rather by the name Koel, which is that of the river in the sand of which they are found. The country through which this river has its course belongs to a Rājā who was formerly a tributary of the Great Mogul, but withdrew from his allegiance during the wars between Shāhjahān and Jahāngīr his father. Immediately on his coming to the throne Shāhjahān sent to demand tribute and arrears of it from this Rājā, and the Rājā, as his property was not sufficient to discharge the whole, quitted the country and took refuge with his subjects in the mountains. Upon the news of the Rājā's first refusal, Shāhjahān, who did not know that he purposed to abscond, but believed that he intended to defend himself, sent an army into his country, where he was persuaded that he would find an abundance of diamonds. It happened otherwise, however, for those who were sent into the country of the Rājā found neither diamonds, inhabitants, nor food, as the Rājā had ordered all the grain which his subjects could not carry with them to be burnt, and this was so effectually done that the greater portion of Shāhjahān's army perished of famine. The final result of the matter was, that the Rājā returned to his country on agreeing to pay a light annual tribute to the Great Mogul.[1]

India, i. 535) alone suggested that this locality was not to be identified with another diamond locality, Sambalpur on the Mahānadī, in the Central Provinces. Ball has been able to show that it was situated in the District of Lohārdagā and subdivision of Palāmau in Chota Nāgpur, and that the Gouel river, as Tavernier calls it, is identical with the Koel, which traverses that District (*Imperial Gazetteer*, xix. 335). It joins the Son not far from the fortress of Rohtās, and so its waters find their way northwards to the Ganges. It is probable that both Sambalpur and Soumelpour derive their names from the Samul tree (*Bombax malabaricum*), and about the site assigned to the latter there are the remains of an old town called Sema—Lat. 23° 35′ N., and Long. 84° 21′ E. As the available details regarding these long-forgotten mines are too long for a footnote, they will be found in an Appendix at the end of this volume. Much information on this chapter will be found in Jadunath Sarkar, *Hist. of Aurangzib*, vol. iii, especially pp. 35 ff.; *Journal, Bihar and Orissa Research Society*, vol. i.

[1] Shāhjahān came to the throne in 1628, but the reference seems to be to the campaign of 1641–2, when Shāista Khān attacked the Chero tribe in Palāmau (L. L. S. O'Malley, *Palāmau Gazetteer*, 20 ff., quoting H. Blochmann, *Journal, Asiatic Society Bengal*, xi, part i, 1871).

The following is the route to be followed from Agra to this mine: From Agra to Halabas, 130 coss; Halabas to Banarous, 33 coss; Banarous to Saseron, 4 coss.

From Agra to Sāsarām [1] you travel eastwards, but between Sāsarām and the mine you turn to the south and come first to a large town—21 coss. This town is that of the Rājā of whom I have just spoken, to whom the country belongs which is traversed by the river in which the diamonds are found.

After this town the traveller reaches a fortress called Rohtās [2]—4 coss. It is one of the strongest places in Asia, situated upon a mountain having six great bastions and twenty-seven pieces of cannon, with three trenches full of water in which there are good fish. There is but a single path by which to ascend the mountain, where there is a plain of half a league or so in area, on which corn and rice are cultivated. There are more than twenty springs which irrigate the soil, and all about the mountain from the base to the top there are precipices covered for the most part with jungle. The Rājās ordinarily held this fortress with

[1] This route is also given in vol. i, pp. 92–9, but the details are very different. Here the stages are Agra; Allahābād; Benares; Sāsarām. In the first place Sāsarām and the large town are here misplaced. The latter is probably the Gourmabad, i.e. Khurramābād or Tilothū of p. 98, but the distance, which there amounts to 27 coss, is here stated to be only 21 coss. The true distance is about 58 miles. After Khurramābād, not before it, Sāsarām comes as the next stage, distant 4 coss, the true distance being 12 miles; but after it again the distance to Rohtās is understated at 4 coss, it being really about 24 miles. These discrepancies may be explained by the fact that Tavernier does not appear to have gone to Rohtās from Sāsarām. If he visited it and the diamond mine, as is probable, he almost certainly did so from Patna, in which neighbourhood he was for some time in 1640 and again in 1665–6.

[2] Rodas in the original—Rohtāsgarh, Lat. 24° 27′ 30″, Long. 83° 55′ 50″. (See *Imperial Gazetteer*, xxi. 322 ff.; Hunter, *Statistical Account of Bengal*, xii. 209–212.) There are also detailed descriptions and plans by F. Buchanan in Montgomery Martin, *Eastern India*, i. 432 ff.; Mundy, ii. 168 f. The capture of the fortress by Mīr Jumla has not been traced. It was captured by Sher Shāh in 1539, but the present buildings were completed by Mān Singh, Viceroy of Bengal and Bihār, in 1654. In 1644 the Governor protected the family of Shāhjahān while he was in rebellion against his father. For Sher Khān's attack see Erskine, *Hist. of India*, ii. 147.

from 700 to 800 men, but at present it belongs to the Great Mogul, who acquired it by skill of that great Captain Mīr Jumla of whom I have so often had occasion to speak. The last Rājā left three sons who betrayed each other; the eldest was poisoned, the second attached himself to the court of the Great Mogul, who gave him the command of 4,000 horse, and the youngest maintains his position in the country by paying tribute like his father. All the Kings of India, successors of Tamerlane, have besieged this place without being able to take it, and indeed two of these Kings died in the city of Sasarām.[1]

From the Fortress of Rohtās to Soumelpour it is 30 coss. Soumelpour [2] is a large town with houses built only of clay, and thatched with the branches of the coco-nut tree.[3] Throughout this march of thirty coss there are jungles which are dangerous, because the thieves, who know that merchants do not visit the mine without carrying money, attack them and sometimes murder them.[4] The Rājā lives half a coss from the town, and in tents placed on an eminence. The Koel passes the fort, and it is in this river that the diamonds are found. It comes from the high mountains to the south and loses its name in the Ganges.[5]

This is the manner in which diamonds are sought for in this river. After the great rains are over, that is to say usually in the month of December, the diamond seekers

[1] Sher Shāh, killed at Kālanjar, his father Hasan Shāh Sūrī, and Islām or Salīm Shāh, son and successor of Sher Shāh, who died at Gwalior, are buried at Sāsarām.

[2] This name is left in its original form in the text, as its identification with Sema, although most probable, has not been absolutely proved.

[3] The coco-nut has been observed nearly as far inland as this locality, but it is possible that the leaves of the Tāl palm (*Borassus flabelliformis*, Linn.) are meant.

[4] Descendants of the thieves belonging to the Dom tribe, especially of the Maghaiya branch, still roam about Palāmau. Out of three occasions when Ball's camp was robbed during seventeen years' travelling in India, two were in this district and the third not very far from its limits.

[5] It joins the Son, which flows into the Ganges. It is possible that Pliny's mention of the Ganges as yielding precious stones may be connected with this fact; but the statement (*Nat. Hist.*, xxxvii. 1, 9) is vague.

await the conclusion of the month of January, when the river becomes low, because at that time, in many parts, it is not more than two feet deep, and much of the sand is left uncovered. Towards the end of January or commencement of February, from the town of Soumelpour and also from another town 20 coss higher up the same river, and from some small villages on the plain, about 8,000 persons of both sexes and of all ages capable of working assemble.

Those who are expert know that the sand contains diamonds, when they find small stones in it which resemble those we call 'thunder stones'.[1] They commence to search in the river at the town of Soumelpour and proceed up-stream to the mountains where it takes its rise, which are situated about 50 coss from the town.[2] In the places where they believe there are diamonds they excavate the sand in the following manner. They encircle these places with stakes, fascines, and clay, in order to remove the water and dry the spot, as is done when it is intended to build the pier of a bridge. They then take out the sand, but do not excavate below the depth of two feet. All this sand is carried and spread upon a large space prepared on the banks of the river and

[1] It is to be noted in reference to these 'pierres de tonnerre', which Ball takes to be ferruginous concretions (but the term is often applied to stone implements), that in the *Tuzūk-i-Jahāngīrī* as translated by Blochmann (J. A. S. B., vol. xl, p. 114) there occurs the following passage: 'When the river contains little water, tumuli and hollows are formed. The diamond diggers know from experience that those tumuli contain diamonds over which insects (?), called by the Hindus jhinga, hover.' Ball thought it just possible that the term chikā or jhīngā (shrimps) might in this instance have been applied technically to the particular kind of pebbles which Tavernier denominated as above, and that Blochmann was unaware of the technical application of the term. But this suggestion is very doubtful; see the translation in Elliot & Dowson, *Hist.*, vi. 344 f.

[2] The distance of the source of the river is here very much overstated, but by crossing the watershed, the Sānkh river is met with, and in it diamonds used to be found. (*Vide* map in Appendix III.) The sources of these rivers are close to one another, and there the diamond stratum should be looked for. Unfortunately Ball had not made this identification of Tavernier's site when traversing that part of the country, and there is, so far as he knows, no local tradition of diamonds having been found in the Koel.

surrounded by a low wall a foot and a half high, or thereabouts. They make holes at the base, and when they have filled the enclosure with as much sand as they think proper, they throw water upon it, wash it and break it, and afterwards follow the same method as is adopted at the mine which I have above described.

It is from this river that all the beautiful points come which are called pointes naïves[1] (natural points), but a large stone is rarely found there. It is now many years since these stones have been seen in Europe, in consequence of which many merchants have supposed that the mine has been lost, but it is not so; it is true, however, that a long time has elapsed since anything has been obtained in this river on account of the wars.[2]

I have spoken elsewhere of another mine of diamonds in the Province of Carnatic, which Mīr Jumla, General-in-Chief and Prime Minister of State of the King of Golkonda, commanded to be closed,[3] not wishing that it should be worked further, because the stones from it, or rather from these six mines—for there are six of them, close to one another—were all black or yellow, and not one of good water.

There is, finally, in the Island of Borneo[4] the largest of

[1] i. e. diamonds having crystalline facets and angles. (See p. 57.)

[2] From this circumstantial account it would seem probable that Tavernier visited this locality himself during his stay at Patna in 1640 or in 1666. The statement on p. 41 that he had visited the four mines which he describes and one of the two river washings is puzzling, because, if Gandikota is to be classed as one of the mines, then he describes none of the river washings, as he calls Soumelpour the third 'mine' on p. 62.

[3] This appears to be a different case from that mentioned on p. 61, where the green crust and friability of the diamonds caused the mines to be closed. It is probably the one which Mīr Jumla told Tavernier of at Gandikota (vol. i, p. 230).

[4] In 1609 Captain John Saris found a considerable trade being carried on at Soekadana in the diamonds which he says were found in great abundance there and in the river Lave. He says they were obtained, as pearls are, by diving. In a footnote to Linschoten's *Travels* (Hakluyt Society, vol. ii, p. 137 f.), Mr. Tiele gives an explanation of a statement, first made, it is believed, by Garcia da Orta (p. 343), that diamonds were found at Taniapura in Malacca. Here Malacca, it seems, means Borneo, and Taniapura stands for Tandjongpura. There is hardly a work on

all the islands in the world, a river called Succadan, in the sand of which beautiful stones are found, which have the same hardness as those of the river Koel, or of the other mines of which I have made mention.

General Vandime once sent me at Surat six of them, of 3 to 4 carats each, from Batavia, and he believed that they were not so hard as those from other mines, in which he was mistaken, because there is no difference in that respect; it was in order to ascertain the fact that he sent them to me. When I was at Batavia one of the chief officers of the Company showed me a point naive of 25½ carats, a perfect stone, obtained in this river of Succadan. But at the price which he told me it had cost him he had paid more than 50 per cent. than I should have been willing to give for it. It is true that I have always heard that these stones are very dear. The principal reason which has prevented me from going to this river of Borneo is that the Queen of the Island does not allow foreigners to carry away the stones, and there are great difficulties in conveying them thence—the insignificant number which are carried away secretly are sold at Batavia. I shall be asked, without doubt, why I only mention the Queen of Borneo, and not the King. The reason is that in this Kingdom it is the women who govern and not the men, because the people are so particular about having for their sovereign a legitimate heir to the throne that, the husband not being certain that the children which he believes he has had by his wife are his very own, and the wife being, on the contrary, quite certain that the children are hers,

precious stones which does not erroneously cite Malacca as a diamond locality. Mr. D. F. A. Hervey states that Tanjongpura is situated about 30 miles up the river Pāwan in the northern portion of the Mātang District adjoining Soekadana, according to De Carubee's Netherlands India Maps. The question of the distribution and mode of occurrence of diamonds in Borneo, though now well understood, is too large to enter upon here. Probably the best account is by Dr. Theodor Posewitz. (Vide *Mith. a. d. Jahrb. d. Kgl. Ung. Geolog. Anst.*, Bd. vii, 1885; see Appendix.) On diamonds at Soekadana see Purchas, *Pilgrimes*, ed. 1625, i. 223, 393. 'Borneo is amazingly rich in minerals, gold, silver, coal, iron, and even diamonds being won from it, mostly by the industrious Chinese' (*The Times*, 24 May, 1921).

they prefer to have a woman for their ruler, to whom they give the title of Queen, her husband being her subject, and not having more power than that which she chooses to confer upon him.[1]

CHAPTER XVIII

The different kinds of Weights for weighing Diamonds at the Mines; the kinds of Gold and Silver in circulation; the routes by which one is able to travel; and the rule in use for the estimation of the Prices of Diamonds.

I come now to some details as to the traffic in diamonds, and in order that the reader may understand this easily—believing that no one has previously written of this matter[2]—I shall speak in the first instance of the different kinds of weights which are in use, both at the mines and in other places in Asia.

At the mine of Rammalakota they weigh by mangelins, and the mangelin is equal to $1\frac{3}{4}$ carats, that is to say, 7 grains.[3] At the mine of Gani[4] or Kollūr the same weights are used. At the mine of Soumelpour in Bengal they weigh by ratis, and the rati is $\frac{7}{8}$ths of a carat, or $3\frac{1}{2}$ grains.[5] This last weight is used throughout the whole of the Empire of the Great Mogul. In the Kingdoms of Golkonda and Bījāpur mangelins are also used, but the mangelin in these places is only $1\frac{3}{8}$

[1] Descent by the mother's side obtains in some other Oriental countries, and is observed among the Nāyars of Malabar. This is one of the many incidents connected with the widely spread legends of the Kingdom of Women. The belief was current that Achīn was always ruled by a woman. On the death of the King in 1641 a Queen did reign long enough to give rise to the story: *v.* 294 below. (See Temple's note on Bowrey, i. 295; Fryer, i. 121.)

[2] In this Tavernier was mistaken, several Portuguese writers having treated of this subject before his time.

[3] Seven modern diamond grains = 5·55 grains troy, the proportion being 3·17 troy grains to the carat of 4 diamond grains.

[4] See p. 56 for meaning of Gani.

[5] This (= 2·77 troy grains) was the pearl rati, much greater than the ordinary rati, which varied from 1·75 to 1·84 grains troy, or even more. (See on this point vol. i, Appendix.)

carats.[1] The Portuguese use the same weight name in Goa, but it is then equal to only 5 grains.[2]

I come now to the kinds of money with which diamonds are purchased in India.

Firstly, in the Kingdom of Bengal, in the territories of the Rājā of whom I have spoken, as they are included in the dominion of the Great Mogul, payment is made in rupees. At the two mines[3] in the Kingdom of Bījāpur, in the neighbourhood of Rammalakota, payment is made in the new pagodas which the King, being entirely independent of the Great Mogul, coins in his own name. The new pagoda does not always bear the same value, for sometimes it is valued at 3½ rupees,[4] sometimes more and sometimes less, according as it is raised or lowered by the state of trade, and according as the moneychangers arrange matters with the Princes and Governors. At the mine of Kollūr or Gani, which belongs to the King of Golkonda, payment is made in new pagodas of equal value with those of the King of Bījāpur. But one has to buy them sometimes at from 1 to 4 per cent. premium, because they are of better gold, and because the merchants do not accept others at this mine.

These pagodas are made by the English and Dutch, who have obtained from the King, either by agreement or by force, permission to manufacture them, each in their own fortress. And those of the Dutch cost 1 or 2 per cent. more than those of the English, because they are of better quality, and the miners also much prefer them. But as the majority of the merchants are influenced by the false reports that the people at the mine are unsophisticated and almost savages, and that, moreover, the routes from Golkonda to the mines

[1] i. e. 4·36 troy grains. Mangelin in Tamil Manjādi, Telugu Manjalī, the seed of the Adenanthera pavonina, or red sandalwood (Yule, *Hobson-Jobson*, 553 ; Watt, *Economic Dict.*, i. 107 f.). These weights and their modern equivalents are discussed in vol. i, Appendix. Elsewhere Tavernier seems to imply that, Rammalakota being in Bījāpur, this mangelin was used there.

[2] i. e. 3·962 troy grains.

[3] The second mine here referred to was possibly the one mentioned as having been closed. (See p. 61 *n.*)

[4] I.e. 7*s.* 10½*d.*

are very dangerous, they generally remain at Golkonda, where those who work the mines have their correspondents to whom they send the diamonds. Payments are made there with old pagodas, well worn, and coined many centuries ago by different Princes, who reigned in India before the Musalmāns gained a footing in the country. These old pagodas are worth 4½ rupees,[1] i. e. 1 rupee more than the new, although they do not contain more gold, and consequently do not weigh more; this will be a cause of astonishment if I do not explain the reason. It is that the Shroffs or Changers, in order to induce the King not to have them recoined, pay him annually a large sum, because they themselves thereby derive a considerable profit; for the merchants never receive these pagodas without the aid of one of these Changers to examine them, some being defaced, others of low standard, others of short weight, so that if one accepted them without this examination he would lose much, and would have the trouble to return them, or perhaps lose from 1 to even 5 or 6 per cent., in addition to which he must pay the Shroffs ¼th per cent. for their trouble. When you pay the miners, they will also receive these pagodas only in presence of the Changer, who points out to them the good and bad, and again takes his ¼th per cent. But to save time, when you desire to make a payment of 1,000 or 2,000 pagodas, the Changer, when receiving his dues, encloses them in a little bag, on which he places his seal, and when you wish to pay a merchant for his diamonds you take him, with the bag, to the Changer, who, seeing his own seal intact, assures him that he has examined all the coins, and will be responsible if any do not prove good.

As for rupees, the miners take indifferently those of the Great Mogul and those of the King of Golkonda, because those coined by this King would have been the coinage of the Great Mogul if these monarchs had remained on good terms.

The natives of India have more intelligence and subtlety than one thinks. As the pagodas are small, thick pieces

[1] i. e. 10*s.* 1½*d.* Much information on the various kinds of pagodas is collected in *Madras Manual of Administration*, iii. 642 f.

of gold of the size of the nail on the little finger, and as it is impossible to clip them without it being apparent, they bore small holes in them all round, from whence they extract 3 or 4 sols value of gold dust, and they close them with such skill that there is no appearance of the coins having been touched. Moreover, if you buy anything in a village, or if when you cross a river you give the boatmen a rupee, they immediately kindle a fire and throw the rupee into it, from whence if it comes out white they accept it, but if black they return it ; for all the silver in India is of the highest quality, and that which is brought from Europe has to be taken to the mint to be recoined. I say also that those are very much deceived (as a merchant tried to make me believe on my first journey) who imagine that it answers to take to the mines spices, tobacco, mirrors, and other trifles of that kind to barter for diamonds ; for I have fully proved the contrary, and am able to assert that the merchants at the mine who sell the diamonds require good gold, and the best too.

Now let us say something as to the routes to be followed to the mines. Some modern rather fabulous accounts represent them to be, as I have said, dangerous and difficult, and frequented by tigers, lions,[1] and barbarous people ; but I have found them altogether different from what they were represented to be—without wild beasts, and the people full of good will and courtesy to strangers.

As for Golkonda, one need know but little of the map to be aware of its position ; but from Golkonda to Rammalakota, where the principal mine is, the route is less known, and this is the one which I followed. The measure of distance in this country is the gos, and a gos is equal to 4 French leagues.[2]

From Golkonda to Canapour, 1 gos ; Canapour to Parquel, 2½ ; Parquel to Cakenol, 1 ; Cakenol to Canol-Candanor, 3 ; Canol-Candanor to Setapour, 1 ; Setapour to the river, 2.[3]

[1] Lions are not likely to have occurred so far south in India in Tavernier's time (Blanford, *Mammalia of British India*, 57).

[2] i. e. to, say, about 8 miles. (See vol. i, Appendix, p. 335.)

[3] This route cannot be accurately determined. The stages possibly

This river is the boundary between the Kingdoms of Golkonda and Bījāpur.

From the river to Alpour, ¾ gos; Alpour to Canol, ¾; Canol to Raolconda, where the mine is, 2½. Thus in all it is 17 gos, or 68 French leagues from Golkonda to the mine.[1]

From Golkonda to the mine of Coulour, or Gani,[2] it is 13¾ gos, which amounts to 55 of our leagues. From Golkonda to Almaspinde, 3½ gos; Almaspinde to Kaper, 2; Kaper to Montecour, 2½; Montecour to Nazelpar, 2; Nazelpar to Eligada, 1½; Eligada to Sarvaron, 1; Sarvaron to Mellaserou, 1; Mellaserou to Ponocour,[3] 1¾.

Between Ponocour and Coulour or Gani (Kollūr) there is only the river [4] to cross.

I come now to an important subject which is little understood in Europe.

Rule for ascertaining the proper price of a Diamond of whatsoever weight it may be, from 3 up to and above 100 carats.

I do not mention diamonds below 3 carats, their price being sufficiently well known.

are: Golkonda; Konador; Burgal; Koyalconda; Kandanūl; Saidupur; the river here crossed is the Kistnā.

[1] This route is: Kistnā river to Alampur; Alampur to Karnūl; Karnūl to Rammalakota. It crossed two rivers, namely the main stream of the Kistnā and its tributary the Tungabhadra, Alampur being situated in the fork between, and Karnūl being on the south bank of the Tungabhadra. The total of these distances, as printed, is 14½ gos, which at 4 leagues to the gos would be equal to 58 leagues. The true distance by this route would be about 135 miles, which is equal to the 17 gos, or 68 leagues. Hence some of the stages must be understated.

[2] See p. 56 where it is shown that Gani (Kān-i) is only a Persian prefix signifying 'mine of', and that Coulour is identified with Kollūr on the Kistnā.

[3] The total of these distances is 15¼ (not 13¾) gos, which, as above, would be equal to 61 leagues. The distance of the first stage is evidently wrong, being in reality only about 10 miles. The distance by the route given in bk. i, ch. xi, is 76 coss. Here, again, the route is uncertain. As worked out by Ball, the stages are; Almāsguda; Munugudu, Nagulpad (Naglepar in ed. of 1678); Lingalla; Sarawaram; Mailacheru.

[4] The river here mentioned is the Kistnā, and Ponocour must have been in the position of Vellutar. Vellatoor, lower down the Kistnā, is quite distinct.

It is first necessary to ascertain the weight of the diamond, and next to see if it is perfect, whether it is a thick stone, square-shaped, and having all its angles perfect; whether it is of a beautiful white water, and bright, without points, and without flaws. If it is a stone cut into facettes, which is ordinarily called 'a rose', it is necessary to observe whether the form is truly round or oval; whether the stone is well-spread, and whether it is not a lumpy stone; and, moreover, whether it is of uniform water, and is without points and flaws, as I described the thick stone.

A stone of this quality, weighing 1 carat, is worth 150 livres [1] or more, and supposing it is required to know the value of a stone of 12 carats of the same degree of perfection, this is how it is to be ascertained: Square the 12, this amounts to 144; next multiply 144 by 150, i. e. the price of 1 carat, and it amounts to 21,600 livres—12 × 12 × 150 = 21,600.[2] This is the price of a diamond of 12 carats.

But it is not enough to know the price of only perfect diamonds, one must know also the price of those which are not so; this is ascertained by the same rule, and on the basis of the price of a stone of 1 carat. This is an example: Suppose a diamond of 15 carats which is not perfect, the water being not good, or the stone badly shaped, or full of spots or flaws. A diamond of the same nature, of the weight

[1] Say £11 5*s*., at 1*s*. 6*d*. to the livre. Thévenot gives 15 to 16 écus as the price of stones of 1 or 2 mangelins, but those of 3 mangelins were worth at the rate of 30 écus the mangelin. (*Voyages des Indes*, Paris, ed. 1684, p. 289.) As Thévenot gives the value of a mangelin at 1·6 carats, 3 would be equal to 4·8 carats, and the price of 90 écus, or £20 5*s*., while Tavernier's valuation for a stone of 4·8 carats would be 4·8× 4·8× 150 = 3,456 livres = £259 4*s*. This enormous discrepancy must be due to a mistake by Thévenot.

[2] i. e. £1,620. Whatever may have been the case, it is now apparent that no hard and fast rule can be given to determine the selling value of diamonds, as it is subject to very great variations. Among other formulae, however, the following may be mentioned:

$$\frac{m}{2}(m \times 2)\,a \text{ where } m = \text{the number of carats, and } a \text{ the value of 1.}$$

This is given in *Handbuch der Edelstein*, A. Schrauf, Vienna. A stone of 12 carats, similar in quality to that above given, so calculated, would be worth £945.

of 1 carat, would not be worth more than 60 or 80 or 100 livres at the most, according to the beauty of the diamond. You must then square the weight of the diamond, i.e. 15 carats, and next multiply the product 125 by the value of the stone of 1 carat, which may for example be 80 livres, and the product, which is 10,000 [1] livres, is the price of the diamond of 15 carats.

It is easy to see from this the great difference in value between a perfect stone and one which is not so. For if this stone of 15 carats had been perfect, the second multiplication would be by 150, which is the price of a perfect stone of 1 carat, and then it would amount not to 10,000 livres, but to 33,750 livres, i.e. to 23,750 [2] livres more than an imperfect diamond of the same weight.

According to this rule, the following is the value of the two largest among the cut stones in the world—one of them in Asia belonging to the Great Mogul, the other in Europe belonging to the Grand Duke of Tuscany—as will be seen by the subjoined figures.

The Great Mogul's diamond weighs $279\frac{9}{16}$ carats, is of perfect water, good form, and has only a small flaw which is in the edge of the basal circumference of the stone. Except for this flaw the first carat would be placed at 160 livres, but on that account I do not estimate it at more than 150, and so calculated according to the above given rule it reaches the sum of 11,723,278 livres, 14 sols, and 3 liards. If this diamond only weighed 279 carats, it would have been worth 11,676,150 livres only, and thus these $\frac{9}{16}$ths are worth 47,128 livres, 14 sols, 3 liards.[3]

[1] £750. But this calculation, though represented graphically as a sum in figures, in the original, is wholly incorrect, as $15 \times 15 = 225$, not 125, and the product of its multiplication by 80 is 18,000 instead of 10,000 livres; the value of the diamond consequently would be £1,350. In the edition of Tavernier of 1678, this sum is correctly worked out to 18,000 livres.

[2] i. e. £2,531 5*s.*, and £1,781 5*s.* The former is correctly calculated, but the latter should be 33,750 − 18,000 livres = 15,750 livres = £1,181 5*s.*

[3] These amounts are equivalent to £879,245 18*s.* 1½*d.*, £875,711 5*s.*, and £3 534 13*s.* 1½*d.*—the livre being 1*s.* 6*d.*, and the sol 0·9*d.*

The Grand Duke of Tuscany's diamond weighs 139½ carats, is clear, and of good form, cut on all sides into facettes, and as the water tends somewhat to a citron colour,[1] I estimate the first carat at only 135 livres, from which the value of the diamond ought to be 2,608,335 livres.[2]

In concluding the remarks which I have made in this chapter, I should say that in the language of the miners the diamond is called iri ;[3] that in Turkish, Persian, and Arabic it is called almās,[4] and that in all the languages of Europe it has no other name than diamond.

This, then, in a few words is all that I have been able to discover with my own eyes in regard to this subject during the several journeys which I made to the mines ; and if by chance some other has written or spoken of them before me, it can only have been from the reports which I have made of them.[5]

[1] This description and that in ch. xxii, as also the figure of the stone, correspond in all important respects with the 'Austrian yellow', once in the possession of the Emperor of Austria. Its weight is 133⅛ Vienna carats according to Schrauf, which would amount to about 134 French carats, the proportion in milligrams being 206·13 : 205·5, and not to 139½ as stated in the work quoted below. The value of the stone has been variously estimated at £40,000. £50,000, and even £155,682. (See E. Streeter, *The Great Diamonds of the World*, p. 161 ff., and Murray, *On the Diamond*, second edition, London, 1839.) The figure which the latter gives of the Mātan diamond is really of Tavernier's 'Grand Duke', not so the figure purporting to be of itself.

[2] The equivalent of 2,608,335 livres is £195,625 2*s.* 6*d.*

[3] Linschoten (ii. 136) has iraa, both are from the Sanskrit hīra, the term now used in Hindustani, and some other languages in India.

[4] Almās is believed to be closely related with the adamas of the Greeks and Romans—the latter term, however, does not appear to have been originally applied to the diamond, but to corundum or steel. (See *New English Dict.*, s. v.)

[5] It has already been shown that Methold had actually visited the mines before Tavernier. (See p. 56, *n.*) And it is probable that Caesar Fredericke had been at Rammalakota, which he describes, about the year 1570. (See Hakluyt, *Voyages*, Everyman's Library, iii. 216.)

CHAPTER XIX

Concerning Coloured Stones and the places where they are obtained.

THERE are only two places in the East where coloured stones are obtained, namely in the Kingdom of Pegu and in the island of Ceylon. The first is a mountain twelve days journey or thereabouts from Siren [1] in a north-east direction, and it is called Capelan.[2] It is the mine from whence is obtained the greatest quantity of rubies, spinelles or mothers of rubies, yellow topazes, blue and white sapphires, hyacinths, amethysts, and other stones of different colours. Among these hard stones others which are soft are found and are called bacan [3] in the language of the country. These are not considered to be valuable.

Siren is the name of the city where the King of Pegu resides, and Ava is the port of the Kingdom.[4] From Ava to Siren you ascend the river in large flat-bottomed boats, and the voyage lasts about sixty days. You cannot travel by land on account of the jungles, which abound with lions,[5] tigers, and elephants. It is one of the poorest countries in the world; nothing comes from it but rubies, and even they

[1] Siren is here a mistake for Ava. Siriam or Syriam is a port on the Pegu river 6 miles E. of Rangoon. It was famous in connexion with Portuguese dealings with Pegu, and was the site of an English factory in the seventeenth century. (See Yule, *Hobson-Jobson*, 886.) In the second reference below it would seem that the names Siren and Ava are transposed, as Ava was the capital and Syriam the port.

[2] Kyatpyen. Its distance from Ava is about 70 miles. (See Map in vol. i, and Appendix on Burma ruby mines.) 'Caplan is the place where they finde the rubies, saphires, and spinelles; it standeth six dayes iourney from Aua in the kingdome of Pegu' (R. Fitch, ed. Ryley, 172 f.; Varthema, 219).

[3] Bacan. This is possibly the Persian pākand or bākand, which signifies ruby.

[4] It is a strange statement that Ava is the port of Pegu; Barbosa (ed. Dames, ii. 1921, 159), a century and a half before, knew more of the geography.

[5] Lions here, as elsewhere, must be understood as a figure of speech, since there are none in Burma.

are not so abundant as is generally believed, seeing that the value does not amount to 100,000 écus [1] per annum.

Among all these stones you would find it difficult to meet with one of good quality, weighing 3 or 4 carats, because of the strict injunctions against allowing the removal of any which the King has not seen; and he retains all the good ones which are found among them. This is the reason why in all my journeys I have earned a sufficiently large profit from taking rubies from Europe into Asia; and I very much doubt the story of Vincent le Blanc where he says that he has seen rubies in the King's palace as large as eggs.[2]

The following is the price of some rubies which might pass as of good quality. During my several journeys I saw them sold by merchants who came from the mine, while I was at Masulipatam and Golkonda. All rubies are sold by the weight called rati, which is $3\frac{1}{2}$ grains or $\frac{7}{8}$th of a carat; [3] and payment is made in the old pagodas, of which I have spoken in the preceding chapter:

A ruby of 1 rati was sold for 20 pagodas; $2\frac{1}{8}$ ratis was sold for 85 pagodas; $3\frac{1}{4}$ ratis was sold for 185 pagodas; $4\frac{5}{8}$ ratis was sold for 450 pagodas; 5 ratis was sold for 525 pagodas; $6\frac{1}{2}$ ratis was sold for 920 [4] pagodas. When a ruby

[1] £22,500. In the year 1855 the revenue from the mines was estimated at from £12,500 to £15,000. Since the conquest of Upper Burma these mines have, as is well known, been let for a term of years to an English company. Further information will be found in an Appendix to this volume. For the Ruby Mines District see *Imperial Gazetteer*, xvi. 333 f.; Scott & Hardiman, *Gazetteer, Upper Burma*, Part ii, vol. iii. 18 ff.; *Ency. Brit.*, xxiii. 812 f.; Barbosa, ed. Dames, 1921, vol. ii. 161 f.

[2] This statement does not appear in the Paris edition of Le Blanc's *Voyages*, 1648. Sir T. Roe speaks of a ruby weighing 13 tolas, or about $5\frac{1}{4}$ oz., which was offered to Jahāngīr for 5 lakhs of rupees by the Portuguese, but he would give only one lakh for it. (See *Journal*, ed. Foster, i. 183.)

[3] Namely the pearl rati = 2·66 grains troy. (See Appendix to vol. i.)

[4] In other words, a ruby of 18 grains troy was sold for about £465 15*s.*—the rati being equal to 2·66 grains troy, and the pagoda to 10*s.* $1\frac{1}{2}$*d.* (See vol. i, Appendix.) According to Mr. Streeter (*Precious Stones*) rubies over a carat in weight vary in value from £20 to £100 per carat at present, but he adds that no definite price can be given to aid the purchaser. According to Barbosa, the King of Ceylon used to put a ruby in a fierce charcoal fire, and if it stood the test it became much more

exceeds 6 ratis, and is perfect, it is sold for whatever is asked for it.

All the other coloured stones in this country are called by the name ruby, and are only distinguished by colour.[1] Thus in the language of Pegu the sapphire is a blue ruby, the amethyst a violet ruby, the topaz a yellow ruby, and so with the other stones.

The dealers are so particular about their profit in trade that they will not show you a parcel of rubies, although they may be fine, unless you promise beforehand that in case you do not buy you will make them a small present—such as a turban or a waistband; and when you act with some liberality to them they show all their stock, and you can then transact some business with them.

The other place in the East whence rubies and other coloured stones are obtained is a river in the island of Ceylon.[2] It flows from high mountains which are in the middle of the island, and as the rains greatly increase its size—three or four months after they have fallen, and when the water is lowered, the poor people go to search the sand, where they find rubies, sapphires, and topazes. The stones from this river are generally more beautiful and cleaner than those of Pegu.

I forgot to remark that in the mountains which run from Pegu towards the Kingdom of Camboya[3] some rubies are

perfect in colour (Dames, *Book of Duarte Barbosa*, vol. ii, ed. 1921, 126).

[1] A very legitimate system of nomenclature, as they are all of the same chemical composition, viz. alumina or corundum.

[2] In Ceylon sapphire is the variety of corundum most commonly found, but rubies are also sometimes met with. The annual average value of precious stones found in Ceylon is said to be about £10,000 at present. 'Stones of inferior kinds are found in the beds of streams about Kandy, Nuwara-Eliya, Badulla, and some of the small rivers in the south; but the more precious stones, such as the ruby, sapphire, topaz, alexandrite, and catseye, must be sought within a radius of 30 or 40 miles from Ratnapura (the City of Gems), the capital of Saffragam, a district of the Western Province, though occasionally rubies are found in Uva.' (Tennent, *Ceylon*, i. 36.)

[3] The mode of occurrence of rubies in Cambodia and Siam is not very well understood, but Ball had met with some references to the fact,

found in certain places, but more balass rubies [1] than others, many spinelles, sapphires, and topazes. There are gold mines in these mountains, and rhubarb [2] also comes from these places, which is highly esteemed, because it does not spoil so quickly as that which grows in other parts of Asia.

There are also in Europe two places from whence coloured stones are obtained, viz. Bohemia and Hungary. In Bohemia there is a mine where pebbles of different sizes are obtained, some being as large as an egg, others the size of the fist, and on breaking them some of them are found to contain rubies [3] as hard and as beautiful as those of Pegu. I remember being one day at Prague with the Viceroy of Hungary, in whose service I then was, as he washed his hands with General Wallenstein, Duke of Friedland, before sitting down at table, observing on the General's hand a ruby he admired for its beauty. And he admired it much more when Wallenstein told him that these stones came from Bohemia; and, in fact, at the Viceroy's departure the General presented him with about 100 of these pebbles in a basket. When we returned to Hungary the Viceroy had them all broken, and out of the whole of the flints rubies were found only in two, one of them weighing about 5 carats and the other about 1 carat.

which appears to be undoubted. Thus Crawfurd says they are found in hills at Chan-ta-bun in Lat. 12° on the east side of the Gulf. They constitute a rigidly-guarded royal monopoly, but are much inferior in quality to the Ava stones. (*Embassy*, 4to., London, 1828, p. 419.) No recent account of rubies in Cambodia has been traced. 'Rubies are found in Siam, at several localities in the provinces of Chantabon and Krat,' and at Moung Klung (*Ency. Brit.*, xxiii. 812).

[1] The distinction made by our author between 'balass' rubies, and spinels indicates that already in his time the name had been transferred from its true original application to spinels—to rubies of a particular shade of colour, probably light, and resembling the spinel. (See vol. i, p. 303 *n.*)

[2] This was probably China rhubarb, which thus found an outlet to Europe. Afterwards it mainly came through Russia. A very interesting account of the rhubarb trade from the earliest times, though Cambodia is not mentioned there, will be found in Hanbury's and Flückiger's *Pharmacographia*, Art. 'Rhubarb': Watt, *Commercial Products*, 912 f.; Yule, *Marco Polo*, ii. 144; Bernier, 425; Barbosa, ed. Dames, i. 93 f.

[3] These rubies, so called, were doubtless only garnets.

As for Hungary, it has a mine whence opals [1] are obtained; they are not found in any other place in the world.

Turquoise occurs only in Persia, and it is obtained in two mines. One of them which is called 'the old rock' is three days' journey from Meshed towards the north-west and close to a large town called Nichabourg; [2] the other, which is called 'the new', is five days' journey from it. These stones from the new are of an inferior blue, tending to white, and are little esteemed, and one may purchase as many of them as he likes at small cost. But for many years the King of Persia has prohibited mining in 'the old rock' for anyone but himself, because there are no gold workers in the country except those who work in thread, who are ignorant of the art of enamelling on gold, and without knowledge of design and engraving, and he uses for the decoration of swords, daggers, and other work, instead of enamel, these turquoises of 'the old rock' which are cut and arranged in patterns like flowers and other figures which the jewellers make. This catches the eye and passes as a laborious work, but it is wanting in design.

As for the emerald, it is an ancient error of many people to suppose that it was originally found in the East [3] [because

[1] There are early references to the occurrence of opal in India, at Poona, Bījāpur, and Sītābaldī (Watt, *Economic Dict.*, ii. 175), but Ball had never been able to identify any local source there. Hungary still retains pre-eminence in this respect, but very beautiful opals are now found in Australia.

[2] Nishapur in Meshed is the classic locality for the true turquoise. Its mode of occurrence there will be found described in a paper by Mr. A. H. Schindler published in the *Records of the Geol. Survey of India*, vol. xvii, 1884, p. 132. Vambéry, *Life*, 290, also describes these mines. Turquoise has been found in some other places in Asia, as for instance in the province of Ferghana at Mount Karumagar, 24 miles NE. of Khojend. It occurs there in veins in a decomposed felspar porphyry. It is also found in South America. The best account of the Nishapur mines is that of Lord Curzon (*Persia*, i. 264 ff.). He could find only inferior stones at Meshed, near Nishapur, all the best being exported; the poor stones are kept in damp earthenware pots, until they are sold, when they turn to a sickly green colour (*ibid.*, i. 167, 267; *Russian Central-Asia*, H. Lansdell, 515).

[3] Tavernier appears to have been wholly unaware of the true source of the emerald in early times. Although common beryl is abundant in

before the discovery of America they could not believe otherwise][1], and the majority of jewellers and artisans, when they see an emerald of high colour inclining to black, are still accustomed to call it an oriental emerald, in which they are mistaken [since the East has never produced them]. I confess I have not been able to find the places in our Continent from whence these kinds of stones are obtained. But I am assured that the East has never produced them, either on the mainland or on the islands; and having made a strict inquiry during all my journeys, no one has been able to indicate any place in Asia where they are found. It is true that since the discovery of America some few rough stones have often been carried by the Southern Sea from Peru to the Philippine Islands, whence they have been exported in due course to Europe; but that does not justify these being called 'oriental', nor support the view that their source is in the East, since both before this discovery and this passage there was no want of emeralds for disposal throughout the whole of Europe, and because at present, having left this route, they are all conveyed by the North Sea (Atlantic) to Spain.[2] In the year 1660 I saw 20 per cent. less price

India the emerald, though highly esteemed, and well known at a very remote epoch, does not appear to have been found there. All records, and indeed many might be quoted since the times of the Ptolemies, point to certain mines in Egypt, especially at Mount Zabara on the Red Sea, as having afforded the supply. Prof. Maskelyn, *Edin. Rev.* 1866, p. 244, records that when this locality was visited by Sir G. Wilkinson he found several emeralds of pale and poor quality (Wilkinson, *Ancient Egyptians*, ed. 1878, i. 33). The matrix was mica schist. Among other authors who have mentioned Egypt as supplying emeralds to India, the following are the principal: Pliny, the Monk Cosmas, *circa* A. D. 545, Masūdī, and the Muhammadan travellers of the ninth century. The emeralds of Siberia do not appear to have been discovered before the present century. F. Leguat (*Voyage*, ii. 269) denies that they are found in Java.

[1] The passages in square brackets do not occur in the 1678 edition of Tavernier, but are in that of 1713.

[2] The foregoing passage is thus recast in the edition of 1713: 'I believe that long before that part of the world which is called the West Indies had been discovered, emeralds were carried from Asia into Europe; but they came from mines in the Kingdom of Peru. For the Americans, before we had knowledge of them, trafficked in the Philippine

given in India for emeralds than they would be sold for in France.

But concerning this commerce by sea between America and the Philippine Islands, it should be remarked that when the Americans arrive at these islands,[1] the people of Bengal, Arakan, Pegu, Goa, and other places, carry thither all sorts of cloths, and a quantity of worked stones, such as diamonds and rubies, with many manufactured articles of gold and silver, silken stuffs, and Persian carpets. But it should be added that they are unable to sell anything directly to these Americans, but only to those who reside in the Manillas, and that they resell them again when the former have left. Similarly, if any one obtained permission to return from Goa to Spain by the Southern Sea he would be obliged to pay 80 or 100 per cent. for transmitting money as far as the Philippines, without being allowed to buy anything, and to do the same from the Philippines as far as New Spain.

[This then was the course of trade in emeralds before the West Indies were discovered, for they came to Europe only by this long way and tedious journey. All that were not fine remained in this country, and all those that were passed on into Europe.] [2]

Islands, where they carried gold and silver; but more silver than gold, as there was more profit on the one than the other, on account of the abundance of gold mines in the East. To-day this trade still continues, and the people of Peru go annually to the Philippines with two or three vessels, whither they only carry silver and a small quantity of rough emeralds, and indeed for some years they have ceased to carry the emeralds, sending them all to Europe by the Northern Sea.'

[1] This early traffic between Peru and the Philippine Islands, by which our author strives to explain the source of the emeralds, is corroborated by recent researches by Prof. Elliot Smith and others. It is curious to note that the agreement between the Spaniards and the Portuguese, that the former should extend their conquests only to the west and the latter to the east of Europe, was disturbed when vessels first crossed the Pacific from South America to Manilla. The Spaniards, so far as is known with certainty, probably first carried Peruvian emeralds to the Eastern nations.

[2] Interpolated in the edition of 1713.

CHAPTER XX

Concerning Pearls and the places where they are fished for.

PEARLS are found in the eastern and western seas, and although I have not been in America, both for the satisfaction of the reader and so as to avoid omitting anything important, I shall mention all the places where there are pearl-fisheries, commencing with those in the East.

In the first place, there is a pearl-fishery round the island of Bahrein,[1] in the Persian Gulf. It belongs to the King of Persia, and there is a good fortress there, where a garrison of 300 men is kept. The water drunk in this island and that used on the coast of Persia is salt, and has an unpleasant taste, and it is only the people of the country who can drink it. As for strangers, it costs them not a little to obtain good[2] water, for they have to get it out at sea from half a league distance from the island up to nearly two leagues. Those who go in boats for it should number five or six, one or two of whom dive to the bottom of the sea, and hang from their waistbands a bottle or two, which they fill with water and then cork them well. For at the bottom of the sea, for about two or three feet in depth, the water is fresh, and the best that can be drunk. When those who dive to the bottom of the sea to get this water, pull a small cord which is attached

[1] Bahrein Island, the well-known centre of the pearl-fishery in the Persian Gulf.

[2] See vol. i, p. 214. 'Bahrein . . . is still noted for the fresh springs which rise from the earth under the sea, and from which the Arabs contrive to water their ships by placing over the spot a vessel with a syphon attached to it' (J. Morier, *A Journey through Persia, Armenia, and Asia Minor*, 52). At Bahrein freshwater springs bubble up from the bottom of the sea, even at a depth of 18 feet, and some miles from the shore (Curzon, *Persia*, ii. 457). Cases of water-springs flowing from under the sea are reported in many places. At Anavolo in Greece a body of fresh water rises from the sea, 50 feet in diameter, about a quarter of a mile from the narrow beach under the cliffs (Sir J. Frazer, *Pausanias*, iii. 306, and for a similar case, *ibid.*, iv. 198 f.). For the pearl-fishery see *Journal, Royal Asiatic Society*, xii. 189 ff.; Varthema, 94 ff.

to one of those who remain in the boat, it is the signal to their comrades to haul them up.

While the Portuguese held Hormuz and Muscat, each terate [1] or boat which went to fish was obliged to take out a licence from them, which cost 15 ʽabbāsīs,[2] and many brigantines were maintained there, to sink those who were unwilling to take out licences. But since the Arabs have retaken Muscat, and the Portuguese are no longer supreme in the Gulf, every man who fishes pays to the King of Persia only 5 ʽabbāsīs,[3] whether his fishing is successful or not. The merchant also pays the King something small for every 1,000 oysters.

The second pearl-fishery is opposite Bahrein, on the coast of Arabia Felix, close to the town of Al Katīf,[4] which, with all the neighbouring country, belongs to an Arab Prince.

The pearls fished in these places are for the most part sold in India, because the Indians are not so particular as we are. All pass easily, the baroques [5] as well as the round ; each has its price, all being saleable. Some of them are taken also to Bassora. Those which go to Persia and Russia are sold at Bandar-Congo,[6] two days distance from Hormuz. In all the places which I have named, and in other parts of Asia, the water tending slightly to yellow is preferred to the white,[7] because it is said that pearls the water of which

[1] Spelt terrade in *Persian Travels*, p. 232, Paris edition, 1676. Various forms of the word, which means a galley or a small ship of war, occur in Portuguese, Spanish, and Arabic, but its etymology is uncertain. Dalboquerque (*Commentaries*, Hakluyt Society, i. 105) speaks of Terradas, explained as ' Shore boats '.

[2] Or, allowing 1*s*. 6*d*. for the ʽabbāsī, £1 2*s*. 6*d*.

[3] 7*s*. 6*d*. [not 3*s*. 9*d*. as in 1st ed.]

[4] This is Catifa in the original. Al Katīf, on the Persian Gulf, is a considerable Arabian town, with a district of some extent (Curzon, *Persia*, ii. 454).

[5] The term baroques, which is sometimes written barocche, is from the French baroque, Span. barruco, Port. barroco signifying irregular or uncouth : it is applied to irregularly-shaped pearls. They are much used for grotesque figures. Castellani says they are specially esteemed in Spain and Poland. (*History of Gems*, p. 172.)

[6] Kongūn, on the Persian Gulf, 100 miles west of Gombroon. Bandar-Congo is mentioned as a port for Lār in the *Persian Travels*, pp. 232–4 (Curzon, *Persia*, ii. 408 ; Yule, *Hobson-Jobson*, 246).

[7] The statement at the end of this chap. (xx) contradicts this.

is slightly golden retain their brightness and never change, but that when they are white they do not last for thirty years without losing their brightness, and, on account both of the heat of the country and the perspiration of the body, they assume a vile yellow colour.

Before leaving the Gulf of Hormuz I shall speak a little more fully than I have done in my account of Persia [1] of that splendid pearl which is possessed by the Arab Prince who took Muscat from the Portuguese. He then assumed the name of Imenhect, Prince of Muscat, having been previously called Asaf bin Ali,[2] Prince of Norenuaé. This is but a petty Province, but the best in Arabia Felix. All

'Generally speaking, the Bahrein pearls are not so white as Ceylon pearls, but are larger and more regular in shape, while they are said to retain a lustre for a longer period' (Curzon, *Persia*, ii. 457).

[1] The account in the *Persian Travels* is that the pearl belonged to the Amīr of Vodana, who showed it to M. Constant and our author at Hormuz; it was perfectly round and transparent, and weighed 17 'abbās, or 14⅞ carats, the 'abbās being equal to ⅞ of a carat. On behalf of the Governor of Surat, the latter, on a subsequent occasion, offered 60,000 rupees, say £6,750, to the owner for it, but he refused to sell it (*Persian Travels*, bk. ii, ch. ix.).

[2] Aceph Ben-Ali in the original. Mr. E. Heawood has kindly investigated the question of Vodana and Norenuaé. Ptolemy is evidently the source of the Vodana of Ortelius and others, but as in bk. vi, ch. 7 the position assigned to it is in the very centre of Southern Arabia, it can hardly be connected with the actual Wadām. Yet even in D'Amville's Atlas Vodana still appears in 'Omān, but there it is placed as a Wadī debouching not, as in Ortelius, on the Persian Gulf, but on the outer coast. Regarding Norenuaé nothing has been discovered, save the suggestion that it may represent some honorific title. The first syllable may be Persian *nūr*, 'bright', as Nūr-chashmī, 'light of the eyes', a beloved daughter. Imenhect may represent some title like Shaikh Imām. As regards the capture of Maskat, Nāsir-bin-Murshid was succeeded by his cousin, Sultān-bin-Saif, who determined to drive the Portuguese from Maskat. He was repulsed several times, but finally the place was captured by the treachery of a Banian, Narūtam, who induced the commandant, Pareira, to empty the water-tanks, clear out the provisions, and remove the gunpowder. This seems to have occurred in 1651–2 (G. P. Badger, *History of the Imāms and Seyyids of 'Omān*, Introd., xxvi f., 79 ff., 89 note). For another account see A. Hamilton, *A New Account of the East Indies*, in Pinkerton's *Collection of Voyages and Travels*, viii. 284 f. Maskat was captured by the Imām of 'Omān in 1650 (Sir P. Sykes, *Hist. of Persia*, 2nd ed., ii. 194).

that is necessary for the life of man grows there, and more especially splendid fruits, and in particular excellent grapes, from which very good wine can be made. This Prince possesses the most beautiful pearl in the world, not by reason of its size, for it only weighs $12\frac{1}{16}$ carats, nor on account of its perfect roundness; but because it is so clear and so transparent that you can almost see the light through it. As the Gulf opposite Hormuz is scarcely 12 leagues wide from Arabia Felix to the coast of Persia,[1] and the Arabs were at peace with the Persians, the Prince of Muscat came to visit the Khān of Hormuz, who entertained him with magnificence, and invited the English, Dutch, and some other Franks, in which number I was included, to the festival. At the close of the feast the Prince took this pearl out of a small purse which he carried suspended from his neck and showed it to the Khān and the rest of the company. The Khān wished to buy it, to present to the King of Persia, and offered up to 2,000 tomāns,[2] but the Prince was unwilling to part with it. Since then I crossed the sea with a Banian merchant whom the Great Mogul was sending to this Prince to offer him 40,000 écus[3] for this pearl; but he refused to accept that sum.

This account proves that fine jewels ought not always to be taken to Europe,[4] but rather from Europe to Asia, as I have done, because both precious stones and pearls are esteemed there very highly when they have unusual beauty;

[1] According to Yule's map (*Marco Polo*, i. 108) the distance from Jerum, or New Hormuz, to Old Hormuz on the Persian coast, is about 40 miles. Badger, in his note on Varthema (p. 95), says that the channel between Hormuz and the mainland, directly opposite, is only 4 miles broad; between the island and Bandar 'Abbās it averages between 11 and 12.

[2] About £6,900.

[3] i. e. £9,000. Its value is stated to have been £32,000. (See Streeter, *Precious Stones and Gems*, 3rd. edition, part iii, p. 14.)

[4] Ball recalled a case in India a few years since illustrative of this, which gave rise to a trial. One or two persons residing at Simla bought some stones as a speculation and sent them to England, where they were valued at a lower price than had been given for them. The purchasers thereupon sought by an action to recover their money from the native jewel merchant, but lost their suit

but an exception must be made in the case of China and Japan, where they are not valued.[1]

The other locality in the East where there is a pearl-fishery is in the sea near a large town called Manār, in the island of Ceylon.[2] The pearls found there are the most beautiful, both as regards water and roundness, of all the fisheries; but one is rarely found which exceeds 3 or 4 carats in weight.

Moreover, on the coast of Japan, there are pearls of very beautiful water and good size, but they are very imperfect; nevertheless they are not fished for, because, as I have said, the Japanese do not esteem jewels.

Although the pearls which are found at Bahrein and at Al Katīf tend somewhat to yellow, they are esteemed as highly as those of Manār, as I have remarked, and throughout the East it is said that they are mature or ripe, and that they never change colour.

I come now to the fisheries of the West, which are all situated on the great Gulf of Mexico, along the coast of New Spain, and there are five of them which succeed one another from east to west.

The first is near the island of Cubagua,[3] which is only 3 leagues in circuit, and is distant about 5 from the mainland. It is in 10° 30 of N. Lat., and 160 leagues from S. Dominique[4] in the Isle of Spain. It is a very barren land, wanting in

[1] The Chinese prefer to invest their money in porcelain, lacquer, and other works of art, and ridicule the craze for precious stones: but both Chinese and Japanese women wear jade, gold, and pearl necklaces (Pyrard de Laval, ii. 173; *Ency. Brit.*, vi. 173; Chamberlain, *Things Japanese*, 3rd ed. 116). Ornaments are less worn by the Chinese than by other Asiatics (S. W. Williams, *The Middle Kingdom*, 4th ed. ii. 37).

[2] The best account of the pearl-fisheries in the Gulf of Manaar will be found in the Report by Prof. Herdman (Royal Society, London, 1903–6). In 1905 the fisheries realized 25 lakhs of rupees, and have since that time been leased for £20,000 per annum (Watt, *Economic Products*, 557 f.; *Ency. Brit.*, xxi. 24 ff.). For early accounts of the fisheries see Dames, *Book of Duarte Barbosa*, ed. 1921, vol. ii. 115, 123. Small pearls are found in the Thāna creek, Bombay, and being ground and mixed with lime juice, are used as a nerve tonic (*Bombay Gazetteer*, xiii, part i, 55).

[3] Cubagua is one of the Antilles group. It lies between the isle of Margarita and the coast of Cumana, and belongs to Venezuela. It was formerly a centre of the pearl-fisheries (*Ency. Brit.*, xxvii. 989).

[4] San Dominique, also one of the Antilles.

all things, and especially water, which the inhabitants are obliged to obtain from the mainland. This island is renowned throughout the west, because here the most considerable pearl-fishery is situated, although the largest pearls do not exceed 5 carats. The second fishery is in the island of Marguerite, that is to say, the island of pearls, at 1 league from Cubagua, which it surpasses much in size. It produces all that is necessary to life except that, like Cubagua, it lacks water, which has to be sent for to the river Cumana, near New Cadiz.[1] This fishery is not the most abundant of all the five in America ; but it is considered the principal, because the pearls which are found there surpass the others in perfection, both as regards water and size. One of the latter which I possessed, of well-formed pear shape, and of fine water, weighed 55 carats, and I sold it to Shāista Khān, uncle of the Great Mogul.[2]

Many are astonished to learn that pearls are taken from Europe to the East, whence they come in abundance, but it should be remarked that in the Oriental fisheries they are not found of as great weight as in those of the West, added to which all the kings and great nobles of Asia pay much better than do people in Europe, not only for pearls, but for all kinds of jewels—when they are out of the common run—excepting only the diamond.

The third fishery is at Comogote,[3] near the mainland. The fourth is at Rio de la Hacha,[4] along the same coast. The fifth, and last, is at Sainte Marthe, 60 leagues from Rio de la Hacha. All these three fisheries produce pearls of good weight ; but generally they are ill-formed and are of a leaden-coloured water.

Finally, as for the pearls of Scotland, and those which are found in the rivers of Bavaria,[5] although necklaces are

[1] The positions of Marguerite and Cumana are indicated in the previous note.

[2] See vol. i. (112 f.) for details of the sale, and the quarrel it gave rise to.

[3] Comogote is not marked in ordinary maps, but it is near Cubagua.

[4] Rio de la Hacha, a province and its chief town, is in Columbia.

[5] Obtained from the Unio and Anodonta, freshwater mussels (*Ency. Brit.*, xxi. 26 ; *Notes and Queries*, 2nd Ser. v. 400 f.). Pearl-fishing has

made of them which are worth up to 1,000 ecus [1] and beyond, they cannot enter into comparison with those of the East and West Indies.

It is possible that none of those who have written before me concerning pearls have recorded that some years back a fishery was discovered in a certain part of the coasts of Japan, and I have seen some of the pearls which the Dutch brought from there. They were of very beautiful water, and some of them of large size, but all baroques. The Japanese, as I have said above, do not esteem pearls. If they cared about them it is possible that by their means some banks might be discovered where finer ones would be obtained.[2]

Before concluding this chapter I shall make a very important remark in reference to pearls and the differences in their waters, some being very white, others tending to yellow, and others to black, and some which are, so to speak, lead-coloured. As for the last, they are found only in America, and this colour is caused by the nature of the bottom, which is muddier than in the East. In a return cargo which the late M. du Jardin,[3] the well-known jeweller, had in the Spanish galleons, there were included six perfectly round pearls, but black as jet, which weighed altogether 12 carats. He gave them to me with some other things to take to the East, to see if they could be disposed of, but I brought them back again, as I found no one who would look at them.[4] As for the pearls tending to yellow, the colour is due to the fact that the fishermen sell the oysters in heaps, and as the merchants wait sometimes as long as fourteen or fifteen days till the shells open of themselves, in order to extract the pearls, some of these oysters lose their water during this time, decay, and become putrid, and the pearls become yellow by contact. This is so true that in all oysters which have

been resumed on the river Ugie in north-east Aberdeenshire; in former times this was a lucrative industry (*The Sunday Times*, 26th March 1922).

[1] £225.

[2] The Japanese have recently started the industry of producing pearls in oysters by artificial means.

[3] See p. 125, below.

[4] Black pearls do not suit dark complexions so well as the lighter kinds.

retained their water the pearls are always white. They are allowed to open of themselves, because if they are opened by force, as we open our oysters in the shell, the pearl may be damaged and broken. The oysters of the Manār Strait open of themselves, spontaneously, five or six days sooner than those of the Gulf of Persia, because the heat is much greater at Manār, which is at the 10th degree of North Latitude,[1] while the island of Bahrein is at about the 27th. And consequently among the pearls which come from Manār there are few yellow ones found. Finally, all the Orientals are very much of our taste in matters of whiteness, and I have always remarked that they prefer the whitest pearls,[2] the whitest diamonds, the whitest bread, and the whitest women.

CHAPTER XXI

Concerning the manner in which Pearls originate in Oysters how they are fished for and at what Seasons.

I AM aware that according to the testimony of some ancient authors, who were not well instructed in these matters, it was commonly believed that the pearl originates from the dew of heaven, and that but one is found in each oyster ;[3] but experience proves the contrary. For, as regards the first, the oyster does not stir from the bottom of the sea, where the dew cannot penetrate, and sometimes it is necessary to dive for them to a depth of 12 cubits, as we shall see presently ; and as for the other, it is common to find as many as six or seven pearls in a single oyster, and I have seen one in which there were ten or so in process of formation. It is true that they are not all of the same size, because they are produced in the oyster in the same manner as eggs are in a fowl : as the largest egg advances towards the orifice and goes out

[1] The true Latitude of Manār, a gulf or arm of the sea between Ceylon and Southern India, is about 8° to 9° N. Lat., and of Bahrein about 27° as stated.

[2] On p. 85 it was stated that slightly yellow pearls have the preference.

[3] Pliny, *Nat. Hist.*, ix. 54 ; Fryer, ii. 362 f.

first, while the small eggs remain inside to complete their formation ; so the largest pearl advances first, and the other smaller ones, not having arrived at their full perfection, remain under the oyster at the bottom of the shell until they have attained the size which nature gives them.[1] But it cannot be said that there are pearls in all oysters, and many may be opened in which none are found.

Moreover, it should not be supposed that a great profit is earned by those who fish for pearls ; for if the poor people who engage in it had anything else to do they would leave the fishing, which merely saves them from dying of hunger.[2] I have remarked in my account of Persia, that from Bassora up to Cape Jasque,[3] on both coasts of the Gulf of Persia, the land produces nothing. The people there are so poor, and live in so miserable a way, that they never have any bread or rice, and only dates and salt fish for their food, and you must travel nearly 20 leagues inland before finding grass.

This fishing in the Eastern seas takes place twice in the year, the first being in March and April, and the second in August and September, and the sale lasts from the month of June till November, but this fishing does not take place every year. For those who fish like to know beforehand whether it will pay. In order not to be deceived they send to the fisheries seven or eight boats, each of which brings back about 1,000 oysters, which are opened, and if there is not found in every thousand oysters the value of 5 fanos of pearls—that is to say a half écu of our money [4]—it is accepted as a proof that the fishing will not be good, and that these poor people will not recover the outlay which they have had

[1] This physiological explanation will hardly receive acceptance at the present time. (Cf. Pliny, *Nat. Hist.*, ix. 55, 57.)

[2] Diamond and gold washing have always, likewise, been the most miserably requited trades in India.

[3] Cape Jask, or the Rās Jāshak of the Arabs, is 'a point on the eastern side of the Gulf of 'Omān near the entrance to the Persian Gulf, and 6 miles south of a port of the same name. The latter was frequented by the vessels of the English Company whilst the Portuguese held Hormuz. After the Portuguese were driven out of Hormuz (1622) the English trade was moved to Gombroon' (Yule, *Hobson-Jobson*, 453).

[4] Or 2*s.* 3*d.* The écu being worth 2 rupees, or 4*s.* 6*d.*, therefore these fanos were worth 5·4*d.* each.

to incur. For both on account of their outfit and for their food during the time of the fishing they borrow money at the rate of from 3 to 4 per cent. per month. Accordingly, if, at the worst, 1,000 oysters do not yield 5 fanos worth of pearls, they do not fish during that year. The merchants buy the oysters on chance, and content themselves with what they find inside. It is a great piece of good fortune when large pearls are found, but it rarely occurs, especially at the Manār fishery which produces no large ones, as I have said, the majority being only pearls to be sold by the ounce and ground into powder.[1] Only a few among them weigh half a grain or a grain, and it is a great event when any of 2 or 3 carats are found. In some years the 1,000 oysters contain as much as 7 fanos worth, and the whole fishing yields 100,000 piastres and over.[2] While the Portuguese were masters of Manār they levied toll from every boat, and the Dutch, who have taken possession of it from them, now levy 8 piastres from each diver, and sometimes up to 9; this yields them a revenue in the best years amounting to 17,200 reals. The reason why the Portuguese took this revenue from these poor people, and why the Dutch take it still, is that they are obliged to protect them against their enemies, the Malabaris, who come with armed boats to capture and enslave the fishers.

Whilst the fishing lasts the Dutch always keep two or three armed boats at sea on the quarter whence the Malabaris come, these precautions being taken so that the work may proceed in safety. The fishermen are for the most part idolaters, but there are also Musalmāns who have boats of their own. They never mingle with one another, and the Dutch levy more from the latter than from the others. For the Musalmāns, besides having to pay as much as the idolaters, have also to give one day's take, the particular day being left to the choice of the Dutch.

The heavier the rainfall in the year, the better is the pearl-fishery. But since many think that at the greatest depths

[1] The term aljofar was applied by the Portuguese to seed pearls said to be from *al-jauhar*, Arab., (the) jewel. (Yule, *Hobson-Jobson*, 12.)

[2] With the piastre at 4*s*. 6*d*. this would be equal to £22,500.

at which the oyster is found, the pearl is whitest, because the water is not so hot there, and the sun has more difficulty in penetrating to the bottom, it is necessary to correct this error. The fishing is carried on in from 4 to 12 cubits depth on the banks, where there are sometimes up to 250 boats. In the majority of the boats there is but one diver, and in the largest only two. These boats sail from the coast every day before sunrise, with a land wind which never fails and lasts till 10 a.m. In the afternoon they return with a wind from the sea, which succeeds the land-wind, and does not fail to blow at 11 or 12 o'clock, as soon as the other has ceased. The banks are 5 or 6 leagues out to sea, and when the boats have arrived there the oysters are fished for in the following manner :—

A cord is tied under the arms of those who dive, which those who remain in the boats hold by the end. A stone of 18 to 20 pounds weight is attached to the diver's great toe which those who remain in the boat also hold by a rope. They have a net made like a sack, the mouth of which is surrounded by a hoop to keep it open, and this net is attached like the rest. Then the diver plunges into the sea, and as soon as he reaches the bottom, which he does quickly, on account of the weight of the stone attached to his great toe, he removes the stone, and those who are in the barque draw it up. For as long as the diver is able to hold his breath he puts oysters into the net, and as soon as he feels that he is unable to hold out longer, he pulls the cord which is tied under his arms ; this is the signal for him to be drawn up, which those who are in the boat do as quickly as they can. The people of Manār are better fishers, and remain for a longer time under the water than those of Bahrein and Al Katīf, for they do not place any clips on their noses nor cotton in their ears to keep the water from entering, as is done in the Persian Gulf.

After the diver has been drawn into the boat the nets containing the oysters are hauled up, and it requires about seven or eight minutes to lift the oysters and to give the diver time to regain breath, after which he returns to the bottom as before ; this he does many times during ten or twelve hours, and then returns to land. Those who are in want of money sell what they have taken, at once, but those who have what they require to live on, keep the oysters until the whole fishing is finished. The oysters are left unopened, and as they decay open of themselves. There are some of these shells which are four times as large as those of our Rouen oysters, but as the flesh of this kind of oyster, of which we speak, is poor and of bad flavour, it is not eaten but thrown away.

To conclude the discourse on pearls, it should be remarked that throughout Europe they are sold by carat weight, which is equal to 4 grains, the same as the diamond weight, but in Asia the weight is different. In Persia the pearls are weighed by the 'abbās, and an 'abbās is an eighth less than our carat. In India, and in all the territories of the Great Mogul and the Kings of Golkonda and Bījāpur, they are weighed by ratis, and the rati is also an eighth less than the carat.[1]

Goa was formerly the place where there was the largest trade in all Asia in diamonds, rubies, sapphires, topazes, and other stones.[2] All the miners and merchants went there to sell the best which they had obtained at the mines, because they had there full liberty to sell, whereas, in their own country, if they showed anything to the Kings or Princes, they were compelled to sell at whatever price was fixed. There was also at Goa a large trade in pearls, both of those which came from the island of Bahrein in the Persian Gulf, and those fished for in the straits of Manar on the coast of the island of Ceylon, as also of those which were brought from America. It should be known then, that in Goa and in all the other places which the Portuguese hold in India, they have a particular weight for pearls which is not used in the other places where there is a trade in pearls, neither in Europe, Asia, nor America. I do not include Africa, because this trade is unknown there, and because in that part of the

[1] Kelly in the *Universal Cambist*, i, p. 278, gives the value of the Persian 'abbās as 3·66 diamond grains = 2·25 (2·9 ?) troy grains. But it has been shown that the pearl rati of our author was equal to 2·77 troy grains. (See vol. i, Appendix, p. 333.)

[2] Cf. Linschoten, i. 225, and on the great trade of Goa, Pyrard de Laval, ii. 212 f.

world the women content themselves, in lieu of jewels, with pieces of crystal, beads of false coral, or yellow amber, of which they make necklaces and bracelets to wear on their arms and legs.

The Portuguese, then, in all the places in India where they are in authority, sell pearls by a weight which they call chegos, but buy them of the merchants, according to the places from whence they bring them, by carats, ʿabbās, or ratis. The table which follows shows the ratio between these chegos and carats.

Carats.	Chegos.	Carats.	Chegos.	Carats.	Chegos.	Carats.	Chegos.
1	5	11	84	21	306	31	667¼
2	8	12	100	22	336	32	711
3	11½	13	117	23	367¼	33	756¼
4	16	14	136	24	400	34	802¾
5	21	15	156	25	430	35	850½
6	27	16	177¾	26	469¼	36	900
7	34	17	200½	27	506¼	37	950½
8	44	18	225	28	544½	38	1002¾
9	56	19	250½	29	584	39	1056
10	69	20	277¾	30	625	40	1111¼ [1]

[1] With such an extraordinary table of equivalents one may easily understand the difficulty that is experienced in reconciling statements about weights and measures. If 1 carat equals 5 chegos, it might be supposed that 20 carats would equal 100 chegos, and 40 carats 200; but it will be seen that the equivalents above given are 277¾ and 1111¼ respectively.

This table has been explained by Mr. A. Rambaut, Assistant Astronomer Royal for Ireland. For the first six equivalents the equation $y = 3 + 1\frac{3}{4}x + \frac{3}{8}x^2$, represents the relation when y = the number of chegos and x the number of carats, subject, however, to the condition that wherever an uneven number of eighths of a carat occurs, one is rejected. If this table is followed the precise figures of Tavernier's table are obtained. From 7 carats onwards a very simple rule is followed to obtain the number of chegos. It is to multiply the number of carats by 10, divide by 12, and square the result—thus $36 \times 10 \div 12 = 30$, which squared $= 900$. There is one exception to this rule in the case of 25 carats, which in the table is given equal to 430 chegos, whereas it ought to be, when calculated as above, 434·05 chegos. This discrepancy is probably due to a misprint, so that the table should be corrected accordingly.

On the difficult word Chego Mr. M. Longworth Dames writes: "I find that the word Chego is in Dalgado's *Glossario Luso-Asiatico*. It appears to be an ingenious method of combining weight with size, according to Ficalho in his note on a passage in his edition of Garcia da Orta's *Collo-*

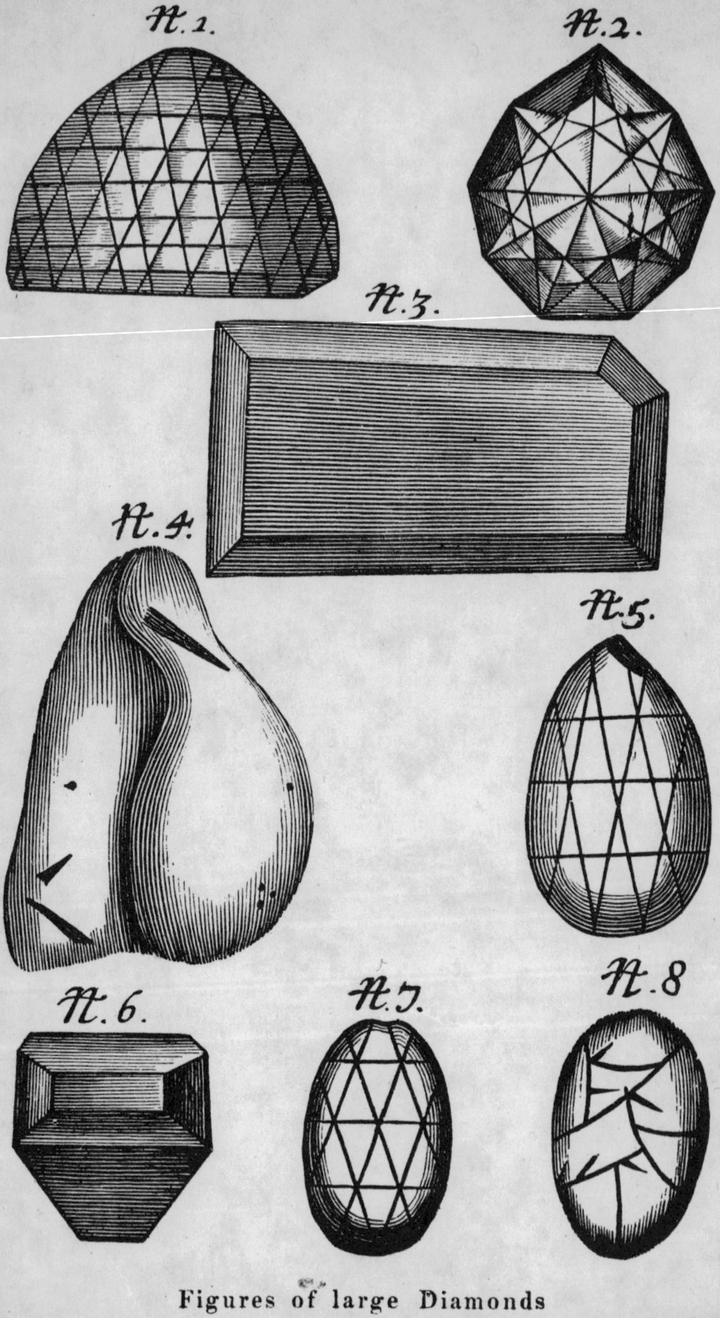

Figures of large Diamonds

CHAPTER XXII

Remarks upon the largest and most beautiful Diamonds and Rubies which the Author has seen in Europe and Asia, the figures of which are here given, together with those of large Stones which he sold to the Emperor on his return from his last Journey to India, with a representation of a magnificent Topaz, and the largest Pearls in the World.

I SHALL follow the order of the figures as they are arranged [in Pl. II] by their numbers, and I shall commence with the heaviest diamond of which I have any knowledge :

No. 1. This diamond [1] belongs to the Great Mogul, who did me the honour to have it shown to me with all his other jewels. You see represented here its form after having been cut, and, as I was allowed to weigh it, I ascertained that it weighed $319\frac{1}{2}$ ratis, which are equal to $279\frac{9}{16}$ of our carats. When in the rough it weighed, as I have elsewhere said, 907 ratis, or $793\frac{5}{8}$ carats. This stone is of the same form as if one cut an egg through the middle.[2]

quios, quoted by Dalgado. Orta does not use the word Chego, although he describes the process of passing the pearls through a sieve. The earliest mention appears to be that in Teixeira (see Ferguson's note on p. 179 of the Hakluyt Society ed., 'The Kings of Ormus'). He says 'the reckoning and weighing is by Chegos, by a method not easy, but very subtle and ingenious'. The system appears to have been used for seed-pearls mainly or only in the Ceylon fishery. Dalgado says the word is not now in use, and he has not been able to trace its origin."

The relationship between the real weight called the mangelin in Madras, and the nominal weight called chow, though it does not elucidate this table, throws some light on the subject. *Rule*—Square the number of mangelins, and divide three-fourths of this product by the number of pearls. The quotient is the number of chows. *Example*—To find value of 21 pearls weighing 16 mangelins at 12 pagodas per chow, $16 \times 16 \times \frac{3}{4} = 192$, $192 \div 21 = 9$ chows $9\frac{1}{7}$ = parts, which at 96*s.* per chow = £43 17*s.* $8\frac{1}{4}$*d.* (See Kelly, *Universal Cambist*, p. 92.)

[1] For full discussion of all the facts connected with the Great Mogul's diamond, see Appendix I.

[2] This operation may be performed in either of two ways ; from the figure given by Tavernier he evidently means transversely. The Koh-i-Nūr as it was when brought to England might be described as of the shape of half an egg, cut longitudinally, but this difference of form,

No. 2 represents the form of the Grand Duke of Tuscany's diamond, which he has had the goodness to show me upon more than one occasion. It weighs $139\frac{1}{2}$ carats, but it is unfortunate that its water tends towards the colour of citron.[1]

No. 3 is of a stone [2] weighing $176\frac{1}{8}$ mangelins, which amount to $242\frac{5}{16}$ of our carats. The mangelin, as I have said, is the weight used in the Kingdoms of Golkonda and Bījāpur and it amounts to $1\frac{3}{8}$ of our carats. When at Golkonda in the year 1642, I was shown this stone, and it is the largest diamond I have seen in India in the possession of merchants. The owner allowed me to make a model of it in lead, which I sent to Surat to two of my friends, telling them of its beauty and the price, namely 500,000 rupees, which amount to 750,000 livres of our money.[3] I received an order from them, if it was clean and of fine water, to offer 400,000 rupees, but it was impossible to purchase it at that price. Nevertheless, I believe that it could have been obtained if they would have advanced their offer to 450,000 rupees.

No. 4 represents a diamond which I bought at Ahmadābād for one of my friends. It weighed 178 ratis, or $157\frac{1}{4}$ of our carats.[4]

No. 5 represents the shape of the above mentioned diamond after it had been cut on both sides. Its weight was then $94\frac{1}{2}$

as will be explained, was the result of the mutilation to which it was subjected. (See Appendix I.)

[1] For identification of this stone with the Austrian yellow, once the property of the Emperor of Austria, and known as the Florentine, see Index. Its weight, as recently determined by Schrauf, is $133\frac{1}{5}$ Vienna carats, or 27·454 gramms. His figure of it corresponds with that given by our Author. The figures of the Austrian yellow given by Murray, and following him by Emanuel, erroneously represent a distinct stone.

[2] It is not known whether this stone still exists in the form it had when seen by Tavernier. Mr. Streeter (*Great Diamonds*, 88 ff.) devotes a chapter to it under the title 'The Great Table'. Ball could not ascertain the source whence the story which he gives as to its discovery by a Bhīl Chief is derived. What has become of it is not known; it has most probably been broken up. Prof. Maskelyne has suggested that it is the Daryā-i-Nūr, or Ocean of Light, but it is difficult to compare them, as we are ignorant of the thickness of the stone described by Tavernier. The Daryā-i-Nūr is said to be $\frac{3}{8}$ inch in thickness.

[3] £56,250.

[4] The equivalent should be $155\frac{3}{4}$ carats.

carats, the water being perfect. The flat side, where there were two flaws at the base, was as thin as a sheet of thick paper. When I had the stone cut I had all this thin portion removed, together with a part of the point above, where a small speck of flaw still remains.[1]

No. 6 represents another diamond which I bought in the year 1653 at the Kollūr mine. It is beautiful and pure, cut at the mine. It is a thick stone, and weighs 36 mangelins, which are equal to $63\frac{3}{8}$ of our carats.[2]

Nos. 7 and 8. The two pieces represented are from a cleaved stone, which, when whole, weighed $75\frac{5}{8}$ mangelins, or 104 carats.[3] Although of good water, there appeared so much impurity inside it, that, as it was large and high-priced there was no one among the Banians who dared to purchase it. At length a Dutchman named Bazu ventured to do so, and, having had it cleaved, he found inside it about 8 carats weight of impurity like decomposed vegetable matter.[4] The small piece was clean, save for a nearly imperceptible flaw; but as for the other, where the flaws traversed right through, it had to be divided into seven or eight pieces. The Dutchman risked much in cleaving this stone, and it was a great piece of good luck for him that it did not break into a hundred fragments. Still, for all that, it did not repay him; this makes it sufficiently plain that where the Banians refuse to bite there is nothing to be hoped for by the Franks.

[1] Mr. Streeter (*Great Diamonds*, 140 ff.) heads a chapter with this, the 'Ahmadābād Diamond', but, so far as the stone is concerned, all that can be said is that nothing is certainly known of its subsequent history. It may have been disposed of in Persia.

[2] The equivalent of 36 Kollūr or Golkonda mangelins, in carats at $1\frac{3}{8}$, is $49\frac{1}{2}$ carats, and in Rammalakota mangelins at $1\frac{3}{4}$ (see p. 69) = 63 carats. Nothing further is known of this stone.

[3] Strictly $103\frac{63}{64}$ carats, in round numbers therefore 104, the mangelins being those of Golkonda at $1\frac{3}{8}$ carats in this case.

[4] This case has been quoted in connexion with investigations into the nature and origin of the diamond. Mr. Streeter devotes a chapter to this diamond. (See *Great Diamonds*, ch. xxx, p. 218.) Bazu, on his return to Europe, sold a number of diamonds and pearls to Louis XIV.

Figures of twenty Diamonds which the Author sold to the King on his return from his last Voyage to India. The figures before the Reader show the weight, the extent, and thickness of each Stone.[1] [Pl. III.]

Here [in Pl. IV] are the figures of the most beautiful rubies in the world, and of the topaz of the Great Mogul, in the order in which they are arranged here by numbers.

No. 1. Figure of a ruby which belongs to the King of Persia. It is of the thickness and shape of an egg, is bored through and of very high colour, beautiful and clean, with the exception of a small flaw at the side. The custodians refuse to say what it cost, as is also the case with the pearl belonging to the same King, which is represented further on; they are likewise unwilling that any one should know the weight of either. Those who keep the registers of the King of Persia's jewels merely say that this ruby has been in the possession of the King for many years.

No. 2 represents a large stone believed to be a ruby, and sold as such to Ja'far Khān, the Great Mogul's uncle, who bought it for the sum of 95,000 rupees, which amount to 1,425,000 livres.[2] He presented it to the Great Mogul, with

[1] The violet-blue diamond A, and the two rose-coloured diamonds B and C, which are here figured, are referred to in 'A Note about some unusual Diamonds', published in the *Phil. Trans.* for 27th April 1674, No. 102, p. 26, as being in a representation of a considerable number of diamonds, which were sold by Tavernier to the King of France. Louis XIV paid 220,000 livres for it. Hence it would seem that this plate reached the Royal Society in London before the publication of the travels in 1676. The adamantine hardness of the stones, in spite of their unusual colours, caused them to be admitted to be diamonds. The history of the blue diamond is well told in Mr. Streeter's work on *The Great Diamonds*. The blue diamond which belonged to Mr. Hope, weighing 44¼ carats, is believed to be a fragment of this stone, which was stolen from the Garde Meuble in 1792.

[2] There is here a mistake on one side or the other; a cipher should either be added to the rupees or subtracted from the livres. See vol. i, p. 310, where the total value of a present made by Ja'far Khān is put at 1,050,000 livres, hence perhaps it may be concluded that the figure here should be 142,500 livres, but it is not certain that the occasions referred to were identical. Bernier (p. 271) says that it was valued at 40,000 crowns, but 'Chah-Jehan, who understood better than any man the

many other precious things, on the King's festival, that is to say, the day whereon he is weighed, as I have elsewhere said. This stone having been priced at a little less than it cost, there happened to be present at that time an old Indian who had previously been chief jeweller to the King, but had been dismissed from his charge through jealousy. Having taken this stone in his hands, he maintained that it was not a balass [1] ruby, that Ja'far Khān had been cheated, and that the stone was not worth more than 500 rupees. The King having been informed of the discussion, summoned the old Indian, with all the other jewellers, who maintained on their side that the stone was a balass ruby. As in the whole Empire of the Great Mogul there was no one more proficient in the knowledge of stones than Shāhjahān, who was kept as a prisoner at Agra by Aurangzeb, his son, the latter sent the stone to the Emperor, his father, asking for his opinion. After full consideration he confirmed the verdict of the old jeweller, and said that it was not a balass ruby, and that its value did not exceed 500 rupees. The stone having been returned to Aurangzeb, he compelled the merchant who had sold it to take it back and return the money he had received.

Nos. 3 and 4 are figures of a ruby which belongs to the King of Bījāpur. No. 4 shows the height of the stone above the ring, and No. 3 the circuit of the chaton.[2] It weighs 14 mangelins, which equal $17\frac{1}{2}$ of our carats, the mangelin at Bījāpur being 5 grains.[3] It is hollowed from beneath, [i. e. cut *en cabuchon*] clean, and of the first quality. The King of Bījāpur bought it in the year 1653 for the sum of 14,200 new pagodas, the pagoda being then worth $3\frac{1}{2}$ rupees, this, in our money, would be equal to 74,550 livres.[4]

value of every kind of precious stone, discovered it to be worth less than five hundred, to the great confusion of the principal Jewellers, who in this instance had been completely deceived.'

[1] Ballet in the original, for balass. (See vol. i. 303 *n.*)

[2] The chaton is the bezel of a ring which holds a jewel in position.

[3] On p. 98 the Bījāpur mangelin is said to be equal to $1\frac{3}{8}$ carats (i. e. $5\frac{1}{2}$ diamond grains). and 14 mangelins should therefore be equal to $19\frac{1}{4}$ carats.

[4] £5,591 5*s.*

No. 5 is the figure of a ruby which a Banian merchant showed me at Benares during my last visit to India. It weighs 58 ratis, or $50\frac{3}{4}$ [1] carats, and is of the second quality. Its form is of an almond cabuchon somewhat hollowed beneath, and bored near the point. I was willing to give 40,000 rupees for it, which make 60,000 livres,[2] but the merchant to whom it belonged asked 55,000 rupees. I believe I could have got it for 50,000 rupees.[3]

No. 6 is the figure of the large topaz of the Great Mogul. I did not see him wear any other jewel during the time I remained at his Court on my last visit to India. This topaz weighs $181\frac{1}{8}$ ratis, or $157\frac{1}{4}$ carats.[4] It was bought at Goa for the Great Mogul, for the sum of 181,000 rupees, or 271,500 livres of our money.[5]

No. 7. These grand monarchs of Asia are not the only ones in the world who are in possession of beautiful stones. I have not seen as large rubies in any of the thrones of the Great Mogul as are those represented in the plate Nos. 7, 8, and 9, which belong to our great King, the most powerful and magnificent, in all respects, among the Monarchs of the earth !

[1] At the rate of one *rati* = $\frac{7}{8}$th of a carat.

[2] £4,500.

[3] £5,750. The following reference to two great rubies may be quoted : 'In the aforesaid island of Sylen [Ceylon] is a very potent King, who hath precious stones of every kind under heaven, in such quantity as to be almost incredible. Among these he hath two rubies, of which he weareth one hung round his neck, and the other on the hand wherewith he wipeth his lips and his beard ; and each is of greater length than his breadth of four fingers, and when held in the hand it standeth out visibly on either side to the breadth of a finger. I do not believe that the universal world hath two stones like them, or of so great a price, of the same species' (Friar Jordanus, *Wonders of the East*, ed. Yule, p. 30 ; cf. Yule, *Marco Polo*, ii. 254, 256).

[4] $181\frac{1}{8}$ ratis = $158\frac{1}{2}$ carats nearly. In vol. i, p. 319, it was said to weigh 6 melscals = 1 Fr. once. It was probably the stone referred to in vol. i, p. 296. Bernier, already quoted, alludes to it as a 'beautiful oriental topaz of matchless size and splendour, shining like a little sun' (*Travels in the Mogul Empire*, 268).

[5] £20,412 10*s*.

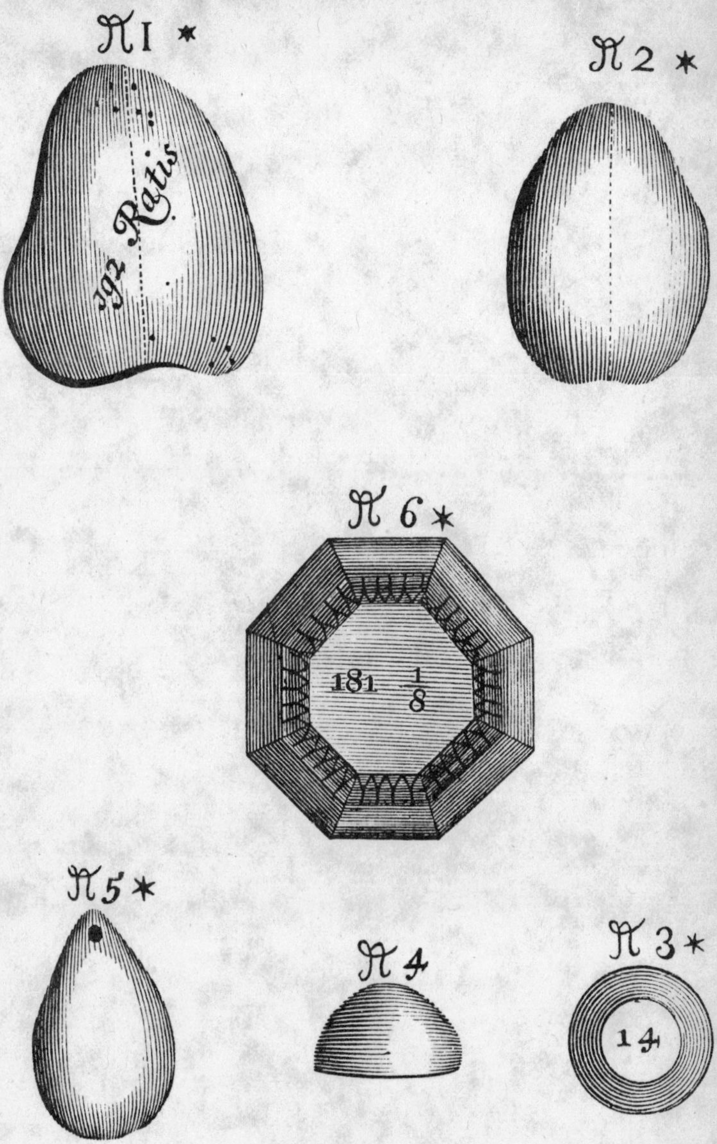

Figures of Rubies and Topaz

Here again [in Pl. V] *are figures of the largest pearls of which we have knowledge, in the order of their numbers.*

No. 1 is the figure of a pearl which the King of Persia bought in the year 1633 from an Arab who had just received it from the fisheries at Al Katīf. It cost him 32,000 tomāns, or 1,400,000 livres of our money at the rate of 46 livres and 6 deniers per tomān.[1] It is the largest and most perfect pearl ever discovered, and it has not the least defect.

No. 2 is the figure of the largest pearl which I saw at the Court of the Great Mogul. It is suspended from the neck of a peacock made of precious stones, and rests on the breast, and this peacock surmounts the throne.

No. 3 is the figure of a pearl which I sold, on my last journey, to Shāista Khān,[2] uncle of the Great Mogul and Governor of Bengal. It weighs 55 carats, but the water is somewhat dead ; it is the largest pearl which has ever been taken from Europe to Asia.

No. 4 is the figure of a large pearl perfect both as regards its water and its form which is like that of an olive. It is in the middle of a chain of emeralds and rubies that the Great Mogul sometimes wears round his neck, and it hangs down to his waist.

No. 5. As a round pearl of perfect form, this is the largest I know of, and it belongs to the Great Mogul. Its equal has never been found, for which reason the Great Mogul has not worn it, but has left it with other jewels which are unmounted. For if a match for it had been found, the pair might have been used as ear pendants, and each of the two pearls would have been placed between two rubies or two emeralds, in

[1] 32,000 × 46*l.* 6*d.* = 1,472,800 livres = £110,460, and 32,000 tomāns at £3 9*s.* = £110,400. Ainslie, referring to this in his chapter on pearls as a drug, erroneously states that Tavernier himself paid the enormous sum of £110,000 for this pearl. (*Materia Medica*, vol. i, p. 294.) A value of £64,000 for this pearl is mentioned by Streeter (*Precious Stones and Gems*, 3rd edition, part iii, p. 14), but that sum appears to have been derived from an underestimate of the equivalent values of the livre and tomān, as known to Tavernier.

[2] See for the incidents connected with the sale of this pearl, vol. i, p. 113. It was the cause of serious disagreement between Tavernier and Shāista Khān. Tavernier states that it came from the American pearl fishery.

conformity with the custom of the country, every one, rich or poor, in proportion to his means, wearing in each ear a pearl set between two coloured stones.

CHAPTER XXIII

Concerning Coral and Yellow Amber and the places where they are found.

ALTHOUGH coral does not rank among precious stones in Europe, it is nevertheless held in high esteem in the other quarters of the globe, and it is one of the most beautiful of nature's productions, so that there are some nations who prefer it to precious stones. I shall set down here, in a few words what I have been able to ascertain about the places where it is fished for, and of the manner in which it is obtained.

I shall say in the first place that there are three fisheries on the coast of Sardinia. That obtained at Arguerrel [1] is the best and the most beautiful of all, the second locality is called Boza,[2] and the third is close to the island of St. Pierre.[3] There is another fishery on the coasts of the island of Corse,[4] and the coral found there is slender but beautiful in colour. It is found at two other places on the coast of Africa—one near the Bastion de France,[5] and the other at Tabarque ;[6] the coral from this locality is fairly thick and long, but the colours are pale. There is a seventh fishery on the coast of Sicily, near Trapano ;[7] the coral there is slender, but of good colour. There is still another locality on the

[1] Alghero, near Cape Caccia, on west coast of Sardinia.

[2] Boza, on the west coast of Sardinia, about 5 miles from Cagliari. The coral fishery, mainly on the west coast, has now lost its importance (*Ency. Brit.*, xxiv. 212).

[3] St. Pierre is probably some small islet not on ordinary maps.

[4] Corsica.

[5] The Bastion de France was one of the forts belonging to France on the coast of Algiers before the nineteenth century. It was near La Callé, which in 1594 belonged to France, and was the centre of a coral fishery. It is now destroyed.

[6] Tabarka, a rocky islet on north coast of Tunis, near La Callé.

[7] Trepani, the Drepanum of the ancients, 18 miles north of Marsala.

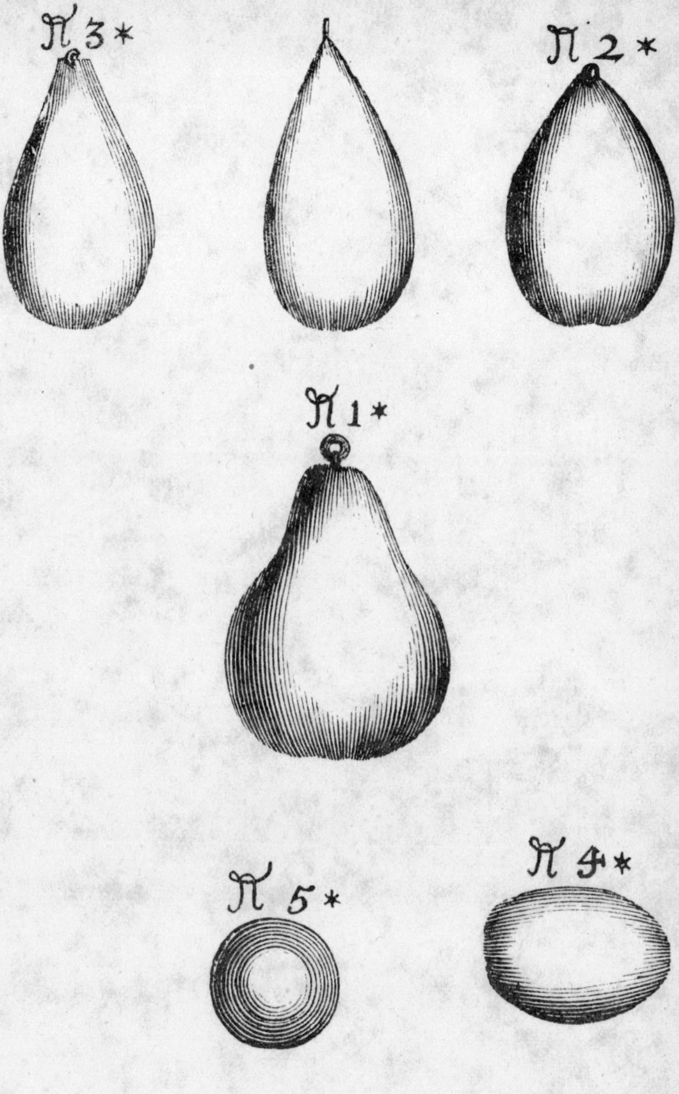

Figures of Pearls

coast of Catalogne, towards Cape de Quiers;[1] the coral there is of excellent colour and thick, but the branches are very short. There is, moreover, a ninth fishery in the island of Majorque,[2] of the same nature as that of the island of Corse; and these are all the places in the Mediterranean where there are coral fisheries,[3] for there are none in the Ocean.[4] The following is the method of fishing for it.

As coral grows under hollowed rocks where the sea is deep, the following device is used in order to obtain it. The fishers bind two rafters together in the form of a cross, and place a large lump of lead in the centre to make them sink to the bottom. They then bind tufts of hemp about the rafters, and twist them irregularly to the size of the thumb, and attach the wood by two ropes, one of which hangs from the bow and the other from the stern of the boat. They then allow the wood to drift with the current across the rocks, and the hemp becoming entangled about the coral, it sometimes requires five or six boats to hoist the rafters; and when exerting the great strain necessary, if one of the cables breaks all the rowers are in danger of perishing; it is a very risky trade. When dragging up the coral thus, by force—for as much as is drawn out an equal quantity falls back into the sea, and the bottom being generally very muddy—the coral is injured from day to day, as our fruits on the earth are, by worms, so that the sooner it is extracted from the mud the less is it deteriorated. In reference to this I may say that

[1] Catalonia, in Spain; Cape de Quiers, possibly C. Servère,

[2] Majorca. The fact of there being so much variation in the characters of the coral from these different localities should be of some interest to naturalists.

[3] 'The most important fisheries extend along the coasts of Tunis, Algeria, and Morocco, but red coral is also obtained in the vicinity of Naples, near Leghorn and Genoa, and on the coasts of Sardinia, Corsica, Catalonia, and Provence. [It is said that it attains greater perfection in the East than in the South, and that it is rarely found in a western, and never in a northern aspect.]' (*Encyclopædia Britannica*, vii. 131.) In 11th ed. the passage in brackets is omitted.

[4] This is now known to be not correct, since 'red or precious coral occurs at San Jago and also at St. Vincent . . . It occurs in about 100 or 120 fathoms, and is dragged for with swabs as in the Mediterranean.' (H. N. Moseley, *Notes of a Naturalist on the Challenger*, 65.)

I have seen, at Marseilles, something wonderful in a shop where coral was worked. There was a piece as big as the thumb, and as it was somewhat glassy it was cut in two, and a worm was found inside, which I saw wriggle ; it had been kept alive for some months by shutting it up in its hole. For it should be remarked that among some branches of coral there grows a sort of sponge similar to our honeycombs, where small worms ensconce themselves like bees—in such ways does nature delight to diversify her works. Some persons believe that coral is soft in the sea, but, as a matter of fact, it is hard. It i .owever, true that in certain months of the year one can express from the ends of the branches a kind of milk as from the breast of a woman.[1] This may be the seed which, falling upon whatsoever it meets with in the sea, produces another branch of coral—thus, for instance, it has been found on a human skull, upon the blade of a sword, and upon a grenade which had fallen into the sea, where it was interlaced in the branches of coral to the height of six inches ; and I have had the grenade in my hands.

The coral fishery lasts from the beginning of April to the end of July, and generally 200 boats are engaged in it, some years more and some less. They are built on the Genoa river,[2] and are very light. They carry much sail in order to sail fast, there is no other part of the Mediterranean where boats carry so much, and there are no galleys able to outstrip them. There are seven men to each boat, with a boy to attend on them. The fishing is carried on from 25 to 40 miles from the land, where it is believed there are rocks, the boats not advancing farther to sea for fear of pirates, from whom they escape, when they meet them, by swift sailing.

I have to make a remark here about coral in reference to certain nations of the East. The Japanese, as I have said, esteem neither pearls nor precious stones,[3] but they value

[1] This refers to the ova of the coral polypes.

[2] [Surely 'Genoese Riviera'.]

[3] See vol. ii, p. 88 above. It is also remarkable that red coral seems to have been little used as an ornament in Egypt and Phoenicia, but the material may have crumbled away, or been dissolved (Hastings, *Dict. Bible*, i. 478 and cf. *Ency. Biblica*, i. 895 f.).

beautiful beads of coral, which serve to close their bags; these bags are made, as they were formerly, in France. It is for this purpose that they use the largest beads of coral, to run on a silken cord which closes the bag; so that if you are able to offer them one of the size of an egg, beautiful and clean, without any spot upon it, they will pay whatever you ask. The Portuguese, who formerly did a large trade in Japan, have often assured me that they could obtain for one as much as 20,000 écus.[1] It is much to be wondered that the Japanese give so much money for a fine piece of coral, since they have a contempt for jewels, caring only for things which are little thought of elsewhere. They attach great value to the skin of a particular fish, which is rougher than shagreen; this fish has on the back, as it were, six small bones, and sometimes eight, which are elevated and form a circle, with another in the middle, resembling a rose of diamonds.[2] They make sword scabbards of these fish-skins and the more symmetrically these small bones form the rose and are arranged, the more money is given for them—sometimes up to 10,000 écus,[3] as the Dutch have assured me. To return to coral and to finish the discourse about it, it should be added that the common people wear it and use it as an ornament for the neck and arms throughout Asia, but principally towards the north in the territories of the Great Mogul, and beyond them, in the mountains, of the Kingdoms of Assam and Bhutān.[4]

[1] £4,500.

[2] This appears to have been the skin of some kind of shark or ray. Ball had seen, but could not refer to, figures of it in some of the old Dutch and Portuguese travels. A common kind of it is still to be seen on the handles of the Japanese swords, of which such large numbers have been recently imported. In his chapter on the *Conduite des Hollandois en Asie*, published in the *Recüeil*, ed. 1679, p. 17, Tavernier gives a further account of it. He says a perfect skin was worth up to 10,000 écus, an ordinary one being obtainable for 1 écu. The fish, he adds, occurred in the Persian Gulf (*Ency. Brit.*, xxiv. 769).

[3] The French editions of 1679 and 1713 have 1,000 écus.

[4] The reason for the preference shown for coral is probably to be attributed to the way its tints adapt themselves to set off a dark skin, and also look well with a white garment. It is much worn in the Himalayas (Yule, *Marco Polo*, i. 162; Baden Powell, *Economic Products of the Punjab*, 48).

Yellow amber is not found except on a particular coast of Ducal Prussia, in the Baltic Sea,[1] where the sea during certain winds throws it from time to time on the sand. The Elector of Brandenburg, who is the proprietor of it, farms out all this coast for from 18,000 to 20,000 écus a year, and sometimes up to 22,000 écus ; and the farmers employ watchmen, who traverse the length of the shore, the sea throwing the amber sometimes on one side and sometimes on the other, so that no one can steal it ; and whoever ventures to do so receives corporal chastisement.

Amber is nothing more than a congelation of a species of gum which forms in the sea. This experience sufficiently proves, because numerous pieces are to be seen which contain flies and other insects congealed in them.[2] I have had many such pieces, and one, among others, which had four or five small flies inside it.

As I have made a remark about coral in reference to Japan, I shall make another about amber in reference to China. It is a custom among the Chinese that when any great noble gives a feast, his reputation for grandeur and magnificence depends upon his having brought in, at the close of the repast, three or four perfume-pans and his having thrown into each of them a large quantity of amber, sometimes to the value of 1,000 écus and upwards, in consideration of the fact that the more he burns, and the larger the pieces, the more magnificent is the entertainment regarded, for a piece weighing one livre is worth 200 to 300 écus.[3] They use amber for this purpose because they adore fire, and because amber, thrown in the fire, yields a certain odour which is not unpleasing to the Chinese ; as it contains a kind of oil it gives out a flame

[1] The source of amber in Upper Burma in the Hukung valley was not known to Tavernier. (See *Economic Geology of India*, p. 57 ; Watt, *Economic Products*, 64 ; Scott & Hardiman, *Gazetteer*, Part i, vol. ii. 289 ff. for a description of the mines there.)

[2] Tavernier had therefore an approximately correct idea as to the true nature and origin of amber as a fossilized vegetable production.

[3] i. e. £45 to £67 10*s*. per livre. This use of amber has not been traced in modern authorities, but that of incense sticks is common (J. D. Ball, *Things Chinese*, 4th ed., pp. 64, 74, 551, 553, 643; Hastings, *Ency. Religion and Ethics*, vii. 204 f.).

exceeding most other flames. This profusion and waste explain the reason why amber is one of the best articles of merchandise that one could carry to China if trade had been open to foreigners, but the Dutch Company strictly reserve to themselves the trade in it—the Chinese coming to buy it from them at Batavia.

I am unwilling to finish this chapter without making some remarks on ambergris also. We do not very well know either how it is formed or where it is found; but it would appear as though it can only be in the seas of the East, although it has sometimes been found on the English and other European coasts.[1] The largest quantity of it is found on the coast of Melinda, principally towards the mouths of the rivers, and especially at the mouth of that which is called Rio di Sena.[2] When the Governor of Mozambique returns to Goa at the close of three years, the term of his government, he generally brings with him about 300,000 pardos' worth of ambergris, and the pardo, as I have elsewhere said, amounts to 27 sols

[1] Ambergris, as is now well known, consists of the fæces of the Cachelot or Sperm whale, Physeter macrocephalus, which inhabits the Indian Ocean. Multitudes of small cuttlefish are swallowed whole, and their horny beaks are not digested. This causes irritation, which produces ambergris (Dr. C. F. Sonntag, London Zoological Society; cf. *Daily Mail*, 10th May 1922). Garcia da Orta (*Drugs and Simples of India*, 24) in his chapter on ambergris speaks of ambergris containing beaks of birds. These were no doubt the beaks of the cuttlefish upon which these whales feed. A form of this story is told by Barbosa (ed. Dames, ii. 107), who says ambergris is the guano of birds which has been swallowed and voided by whales. Chardin (iv. 47) doubts the connexion with birds, but mentions a number of alternative myths as to its origin. Ainslie and Watt (*Materia Medica*, i. 15–17; *Commercial Products*, 64) give an interesting account of it, and refer to a vegetable ambergris yielded by a tree in Guiana. Ainslie says, like many other authors, that the best ambergris was obtained on the coast of Madagascar. (See *Voyage of F. Leguat*, Hakluyt Society, ii. 152 ff.) In the *Daily Press* there once appeared a paragraph headed 'An Ambergris King', in which one William A. Atkins, the owner of a fleet of Cape Cod whalers, is described as having the monopoly of the ambergris trade of America—the ambergris being for equal weight worth more than gold. Owing to ambergris being called *ambra* by some nations, very erroneous statements occur in many authorities as to the distribution in the East of true amber, for which it has been mistaken. (See *Economic Geology of India*.)

[2] The Zambezi, see p. 126 below.

of our money.[1] Sometimes pieces of ambergris of considerable size and weight are found. In the year 1627 a Portuguese vessel sailing from Goa to the Manillas, after it had passed the Straits of Malacca was overtaken by a tempest which lasted many days and nights; the sky was always concealed, and it was impossible for the pilot to take observations. Meanwhile the rice and other articles of food began to be exhausted, and the crew discussed whether they should not throw the blacks who were in the vessel into the sea in order to preserve the food for the white men. They were about to carry this plan into execution, when one morning the sun showed itself, and disclosed an island tolerably near, but they were unable to anchor till the following day, the sea being high and the wind unfavourable. There were in the vessel a Frenchman, named Marin Renaud, of Orleans, and his brother, who on going on shore found a river and, together with two Portuguese corporals and a sergeant, went to bathe at its mouth. One of the corporals when bathing perceived in the water a large mass which floated near the shore, and which he concluded, on going near it, was a sort of spongy stone. So he left it without another thought, as did the four others, who also went to look at it and handled it without being able to make out what it was. When he returned to the vessel the corporal reflected during the night what this object, of which he had been unable to ascertain the nature, could be, and having heard ambergris spoken of, began to think that it might be it, in which he was not mistaken. The following day, without saying anything to his comrades, he took a sack and got himself put on shore, and going to the river as though he wished to bathe again, found the piece of ambergris and carried it secretly to the vessel, where he placed it in his box. He could not help communicating the fact the same evening to Marin Renaud, who was unwilling to believe at first that it was really ambergris, but having well considered it thought at length that the corporal was right. Taking all chances, he offered the piece to Marin for two pains of Chinese gold, and the golden

[1] 27 sols = 2*s*. ·03*d*., or say 2*s*. 300,000 pardos therefore = £30,000. On the finding of ambergris in the Indian Ocean see Linschoten, ii. 92 f.

pain is equal to 600 livres[1] of our money; but Marin was only willing to give one; the other held out on his side and kept the piece in his box. A few days afterwards, either spite at not being able to get the piece of ambergris for what he had offered caused Marin to speak, or the matter was discovered in some other way; the report, however, was spread throughout the vessel that the corporal had a big piece of ambergris in his box, which he had found by chance on the shore of the island near which the Portuguese were at anchor, and the sailors and soldiers then insisted on having their share. Marin Renaud out of petty revenge set the ball a-rolling and taught them their lesson. They told the corporal that, being all comrades and all running the same risks, it was just that they should all share in common the benefits which fortune offered them; and, moreover, that he was not the only one to whom she had disclosed this piece of ambergris, which should consequently be divided between all the crew. The corporal defended himself as well as he could, and as there were some who took his part, in the hope of having a better share of the piece if there were few pretenders to it, the dispute became so hot that at length it gave rise to a disturbance, which the captain of the vessel at once prudently sought to allay. He pointed out to the sailors and soldiers that this large piece of ambergris, which, when it was weighed in their presence, proved to be 33 livres in weight, being a rare piece and worthy of being presented to the King, it was a pity to break it into so many small pieces; that they would find it pay them better to keep it till their return to Goa, where if it was presented to the Viceroy, he would not fail to pay handsomely for it, and by this means they would each receive much more. This suggestion of the captain was generally approved. They pursued their voyage to the Manillas, and on their return the piece of ambergris was taken to the Viceroy. The captain told him beforehand how the matter stood, and they concerted together how they could secure the ambergris without it

[1] Literally 'loaves'. The English name for the ingots of gold used in currency by the Chinese was 'shoes'; the equivalent value here would be £45. See vol. i, p. 331; Yule, *Hobson-Jobson*, 830.

costing the Viceroy anything. Those who presented it to him on the part of the sailors and soldiers were thanked for it, and the Viceroy told them that he recognized their goodwill by so splendid a present which he would send to the King, who at that time was Philippe the Fourth,[1] to whom Portugal was still subject. Thus all the pretenders to the piece of ambergris were defrauded of their expectations, and neither from the Viceroy nor the King himself, to whom the ambergris was sent, did they receive any gift.

I shall say one other word concerning a piece of ambergris weighing 42 livres. In the year 1646 or 1647 a Zealander, of one of the best families of Middlebourg, who commanded for the Dutch Company in the Island of Maurice, which is to the east of that of St. Laurens,[2] found this piece on the shore and sent it to the Company. As these people always have enemies, and there being a mark on the piece as if some one had broken a portion off, the Commander was accused of having stolen half, but he cleared himself of this charge at Batavia. But the suspicion, however, dwelt in the minds of many persons, and the Commander seeing that they would not give him another appointment, returned to Zealand on the same vessel on which I was a passenger.

CHAPTER XXIV

Concerning Musk and Bezoar and some other medicinal stones.

Musk and bezoar being included among the rarest articles of trade, and the most precious which Asia furnishes us with, I have considered it appropriate to devote a chapter to them, and present the reader with some remarks about these two articles.

The best kind and the greatest quantity of musk come

[1] Philip IV, King of Spain, 1605–65.

[2] Mauritius and Madagascar, the latter having been known to the Portuguese as St. Lorenzo. Some say the Portuguese landed there first on the festival of the Saint, others that it was discovered by Lorenzo de Almeyda in 1506. (Varthema in Hakluyt Soc. ed., 296; Pyrard de Laval, i. 29; Fryer, i. 54.)

from the Kingdom of Bhutān, whence it is conveyed to Patna, the principal town of Bengal, to be sold to the people of that country. All the musk sold in Persia comes from there, and the merchants who sell musk prefer to receive in exchange yellow amber and coral, rather than gold and silver, because they make great profits out of these two commodities. I had the curiosity to take to Paris[1] a skin of this animal, which is here represented.

After this animal has been killed, the bladder, which is situated under the belly, is cut off—it is of the size of an egg, and is closer to the genital parts than to the navel. The musk is then extracted from the bladder which contains it—it is then like coagulated blood. When the peasants wish to adulterate it, they insert some of the liver and the blood of the slaughtered animal mixed together, instead of the musk which they have withdrawn. This mixture generates in the bladders certain small worms which eat the good musk, so that when one opens them he finds that much has gone bad. Other peasants, when they have cut the bladder and have drawn as much musk as they can without its appearing to be excessive, put in its place small pieces of lead to make up the weight. The merchants who buy it and transport it into foreign countries prefer this fraud to the other, because it does not generate these little worms. But it is still more difficult to discover the fraud when they make small purses of the skin of the animal's stomach, which they sew up with threads of the same skin, so as to resemble the true bladders; these purses are filled with what has been removed from the good bladders, together with the fraudulent mixture which is added to it, so that it is difficult for the merchants to discover anything.[2] It is true that if they bind the bladder directly

[1] The figure in the original, which it is needless to reproduce here, is a tolerable representation of the musk deer, *Moschus moschiferus* (Linn.). The trade now recognizes three grades of musk; Cabardien or Russian; Tonquin or Chinese; and Assam, including all the Indian varieties, reaching Europe via Calcutta (Watt, *Economic Products*, 786, and see Linschoten, ii. 94 f.; Fitch, ed. Ryley, 189).

[2] A still more remarkable method of adulteration is that mentioned by Barbosa, which consists, in short, in putting leeches on the living animal, after the musk has been removed, and then allowing them to

they cut it, without letting the air get to it, and without giving time to the odour to lose some of its strength by evaporation while they take out what they want to remove, if this bladder should be held to any one's nose, blood would immediately issue from it in consequence of the pungency of the odour, which for this reason must be tempered to render it agreeable and prevent it from injuring the brain. The odour from the skin of this animal, which I took to Paris, was so strong that it was impossible to keep the skin in my rooms, as it caused headache to all the people in the house, and it was necessary to put it in a garret, where at length my servants cut off the bladder, but this did not prevent its always retaining some of the odour. You do not begin to meet with this animal till about the 56° of latitude; but at 60° it is in great abundance, the country there being well wooded. It is true that in the months of February and March, after these animals have suffered from famine in their own country on account of the snow, which falls in abundance to depths of 10 or 12 feet, they come south to 44° and 45°, to eat the corn and new rice, and it is at this time that the peasants entrap them, in snares which they set, and kill them with arrows and blows of sticks. Some persons have told me that the deer are so thin and feeble in consequence of the hunger from which they have suffered, that many allow themselves to be captured by coursing. There must be an enormous number of these animals, as each has but one bladder, the largest of which is ordinarily of the size of a hen's egg, and only yields half an ounce of musk. It sometimes requires even three or four of these bladders to make an ounce.[1]

gorge themselves with the blood, after which they are dried in the sun and pounded, and the substance so prepared is placed in counterfeit pods made of the skin of the animal. (*The Book of Duarte Barbosa*, ed. Dames, ii. 1921, 161.) Linschoten says that the Chinese adulterated it with the livers of cattle, dried and beaten to powder (ii. 95). According to Varthema (p. 102), the test of true musk is to take a bladder of it in the morning fasting, let three or four men smell it, and if it is genuine it will make their noses bleed.

[1] 'The musk deer is found throughout the Himalayas, always at great elevations, and in summer rarely below 8,000 feet, and as high as the limits of forest. It extends through the Himalayas to Central and

The King of Bhutān, of whom I shall speak in the following Book, in the description which I shall give of his Kingdom, fearing that the fraud done in musk might stop the trade, especially as musk is also obtained in Tonquin or Cochin-China, but is much dearer because it is not so abundant there—this King, I say, fearing lest this falsification of goods might divert the trade from his territories, some time ago ordered that the bladders should not be stitched, but should be brought open to Bhutān, which is his place of residence, to be examined and sealed with his seal. Those which I bought were of this kind; but notwithstanding all the King's precautions, the peasants open them secretly, and place small pieces of lead in them, as I have said; this the merchants tolerate, because the lead does not spoil the musk, and causes no injury, save in the weight. On one of my journeys to Patna I bought 7,673 bladders, which weighed 2,557½ ounces, and 452 ounces without the bladders.[1]

Bezoar [2] comes from a district of the Kingdom of Golkonda,

Northern Asia as far as Siberia. A good musk pod is valued at from 10 to 15 rupees. One ounce is about the average produce of the pod.' (Jerdon, *Mammals of India*, 268; Blanford, *Mammalia*, 552 f.; Yule, *Marco Polo*, i. 242, 245.) Adulteration, as it is described by Tavernier, appears to be still practised.

[1] Barbosa (ed. Dames, 1921, vol. ii, p. 159) says that musk was abundant in Ava. From this, with similar statements about other commodities, we see that Tavernier did not limit his mercantile transactions to precious stones and he shows the abundance of the animal in his time. On p. 201 below, he again refers to this purchase (?), and says he bought 26,000 rupees' worth—a Fr. ounce in the capsule costing 4 livres and 4 sols, i. e. about 6*s*. 3*d*., and out of the capsule 8 francs, or say 6*s*. 8*d*., or if livres are intended, 12*s*. But at these prices the quantity here mentioned falls far short of making the total sum of 26,000 rupees. This, supposing the occasions to be identical, as appears to be the case, is a characteristic Tavernier discrepancy.

[2] Bezoar is from Persian *pādzahr*, Arabic *bāzahr*, *bādizahr*, 'counter-poison, antidote' the name given to intestinal calculi. It was formerly so highly esteemed in the East as a drug that the early European travellers all seemed to believe in its efficacy, and accounts of it are to be found in the writings by many of them. (See note 1, on p. 119; Yule, *Hobson-Jobson*, 90.) It has at present no medicinal value (See *Ency. Brit.*, i. 668, xi. 418; Blanford, *Mammalia*, 503); Garcia da Orta (*Colloquies on the Simples and Drugs of India*, ed. Sir C. Markham, p. 362 ff.) has much to say on the subject.

towards the north-east. It is found in the fodder in the paunches of goats which browse on a tree, the name of which I have forgotten. This plant bears little buds, about which, and also on the tips of the branches, which the goats eat, the bezoar concretes in the bellies of these animals. It assumes a form according to the shape of the buds and the ends of the branches, and this is why one finds it in so many different shapes. The peasants, by feeling the belly of the goat, know how many bezoars it contains, and they sell the goat for a price in proportion to the number which are therein. In order to ascertain this, they run both hands under the belly of the goat and beat the paunch along both sides, so that all the stones fall to the middle, and they then estimate exactly, by touch, how many bezoars are in it. The value of bezoar depends on the size, although the small possess no less virtue than the large. But in this respect one is often deceived by the fact that there are people who enlarge the bezoar with a kind of paste made of gum and other materials of the same colour as the bezoar. They understand, even, how to give as many coats as the natural bezoar ought to have. One can detect this fraud easily by two methods. The first by weighing the bezoar and placing it to steep for some time in lukewarm water; if the water does not change its colour, and if the bezoar does not lose weight, it has not been adulterated. The other means is to touch the bezoar with a pointed hot iron; if the iron enters it and makes it fry, it is a sign that it is a mixture, and that it is not genuine.[1] For the rest, the larger the bezoar the higher the price, which rises in proportion like that of the diamond. For if 5 or 6 bezoars weigh an ounce, the ounce will be worth from 15 to 18 francs, but if it is a bezoar of one ounce, the ounce will be worth fully 100 francs. I have sold one of 4¼ ounces for as much as 2,000 livres.[2]

I had the curiosity to investigate all that can be ascertained regarding bezoar,[3] having already made several visits

[1] Fryer recommends touching it with a hot iron, or rubbing the stone on paper smeared by the application of chalk, when, if it leaves an olive colour, it is good (ii. 141).

[2] £150.

[3] Bezoar is the Jadah stone of Central Asia, often alluded to by Bābur, and said to be able to produce rain and snow; the word has no

to Golkonda, which is the place where there is the most considerable sale, without being able to ascertain in what part of the body of the goat it is found. On my fifth journey some persons who were in the services of the English and Dutch Companies, and who dared not trade on their own account, were indebted to me because I purchased about 60,000 rupees' worth of bezoar for them. The merchants who sold it, wishing to show their gratitude, and make me some present, I refused, and told them I had never taken anything from anyone for a service which I was able to render. But I let them know that I would be able to serve them again in the approaching monsoon, and that they would oblige me, on their part, if they would get three or four of these goats which produce the bezoar for me, promising to pay them for them whatsoever they were worth. The merchants appeared much surprised at this demand, and replied that the prohibition was so strict that if any one dared to remove the goats out of the Province he would be executed without fail. I saw plainly that this request troubled them, for on the one side they feared punishment and on the other they were afraid lest I might prevent them from making another sale; this would have been a great loss to these poor people, who, whether they do or do not sell, are obliged to pay the King, for the farm, 6,000 old pagodas, which amount to 45,000 livres of our money.[1] Fifteen days or so afterwards, when I had thought nothing further about them, three of them knocked at my door before daylight. As soon as they entered my chamber, where I was still in bed, they asked me if all my servants were foreigners. As I had none from the town, and they were all either Persians or from Surat, I told them they were all foreigners, upon which they withdrew without replying. Half an hour afterwards they returned with six of these goats, which I examined at my leisure. It should be said that they are beautiful animals,

connexion with Jade (N. Elias & E. D. Ross, *Hist. of the Moghuls of Central Asia*, 1898, p. 32, note 4).

[1] There may be some mistake here, as 6,000 old pagodas are only equal to 45,000 livres when the pagoda is taken at 5 rupees, whereas Tavernier in general gives the old pagoda the value of only 4½ rupees, 45,000 livres = £3,375.

very tall, and having fine hair, like silk. As soon as the goats were safely in my hall, the eldest of the three merchants who had brought them, began by paying me a compliment, and told me that since I had not been willing to take the present which they wished to make me, for having procured the sale of so large a parcel of bezoar, at the least I would not refuse these six goats which they gave me with their whole hearts; but as I did not wish to take them entirely as a gift, as they desired, I asked what the value of them was; and, after having made great difficulty about telling me, I was at length much surprised and thought they were joking when they said that one of the goats which they pointed out was worth three rupees, that each of the two next were worth four rupees, and each of the three which remained four and a quarter rupees. Upon which I asked them why some of the goats were dearer than others, and I learnt that it was because one had only one bezoar in the stomach, and the others had two or three or four of them; this they made me see for myself, forthwith, by tapping the belly, as I have above described. These six goats had 17 bezoars, and a half one, like the half of a nut. The inside was like the soft dropping of a goat, as these bezoars grow amongst the food in the belly of the goat. Some have told me that bezoars originate close to the liver, others maintain that it is close to the heart, but I was never able to ascertain the truth.[1]

Both in the East and West there are an abundance of bezoars obtained from cows, and there are some which weigh up to 17 or 18 ounces, such an one having been given to the Grand Duke of Tuscany. But nothing is thought of this kind of bezoar, six grains of the other having a greater effect than thirty of it.

As for the bezoar obtained from monkeys, as some believe, it is so strong that two grains of it do as much as six from that of the goat; but it is very rare, and it is found particu-

[1] That Tavernier was not well versed in anatomy is sufficiently apparent from this passage, but at the period at which he wrote it, more than two centuries ago, such references to the heart and liver, and their communication with the stomach, would probably have passed without criticism.

larly in the species of monkeys which live in the Island of Macassar. This kind of bezoar is round, while the other is of diverse forms, according to the shapes of the buds and ends of branches which the goats have eaten. As these stones, which it is believed come from monkeys, are much rarer than the others, they are also much dearer and much more sought after; and when one is found of the size of a nut it is valued at more than 100 écus. The Portuguese, more than other nations, attach great value to bezoar, because they are always on their guard, one against the other, fearing that an enemy may wish to poison them.[1]

There is still another much esteemed stone which is called the porcupine stone, which this animal has in its head, and is more efficacious against poison than bezoar. When it is placed to steep in water for a quarter of an hour, the water becomes so bitter that there is nothing in the world to equal it in bitterness.[2] This animal has also sometimes, in its belly, a stone which is of the same nature and equally good as that which comes from the head, except with this difference, that it loses nothing of its weight or size by steeping in water, while there is diminution of the other. During my life I have bought three of these stones. One cost me 500 écus, and I disposed of it subsequently with advantage to the Ambassador Dominico de Santis,[3] of whom I have spoken in my accounts of Persia. I paid 400 écus for another, which I still

[1] Garcia da Orta (*Drugs and Simples*, 362 ff.), who devotes a chapter to bezoar, highly extols its merits as a medicine in cases of ague, measles, as an antidote to poison, and in the treatment of abscesses; he mentions that it was supposed, moreover, to possess aphrodisiac properties. It is not now believed to have any therapeutic value—to be, in fact, neutral.

[2] It seems probable that the substance supposed to be obtained in the head of the porcupine was a vegetable drug, to which that mythical origin was ascribed (Garcia da Orta, 470 f.). Castanheda mentions a stone obtained in the head of an animal called bulgoldorf, which was exceedingly rare, and was said to be an antidote against all kinds of poison (Kerr, *Voyages and Travels*, ii. 439). A. Hamilton (in Pinkerton, viii. 450) says that at Lingen, near Johore, he has seen pieces of porcupine bezoar as big as, and shaped like, a walnut, valued at 600 pieces of eight.

[3] See *Persian Travels*, Paris, 1576, bk. ii, ch. v, p. 181. He was an ambassador from the Venetian Republic.

keep; and the third was sold to me for 300 écus, and I made a present of it to a friend.

I shall finally make mention of the snake-stone, which is nearly of the size of a double,[1] some of them tending to an oval shape, being thick in the middle and becoming thin towards the edges. The Indians say that it grows on the heads of certain snakes, but I should rather believe that it is the priests of the idolaters who make them think so, and that this stone is a composition which is made of certain drugs.[2] Whatever it may be, it has an excellent virtue in extracting all the poison when one has been bitten by a poisonous reptile. If the part bitten is not punctured it is necessary to make an incision so that the blood may flow; and when the stone has been applied to it, it does not fall off till it has extracted all the venom which is drawn to it. In order to clean it it is steeped in woman's milk, or, in default of it, in that of a cow; and after having been steeped for ten or twelve hours, the milk, which has absorbed all the venom, assumes the colour of matter. One day, when I dined with the Archbishop of Goa, he took me into his museum, where he had many curiosities. Among other things he showed me one of these stones, and in telling me of its properties assured me that but three days since he had made trial of it, and then he presented it to me. As he traversed a marsh on the island of Salsette, upon which Goa is situated, on his way to a house in the country, one of his pallankeen bearers, who was almost naked, was bitten by a serpent and was at once cured by this stone. I have bought many of them; it is only the Brahmans who sell them, and it is that which makes me think that they make them. You employ

[1] Doubloon? A Spanish gold coin, formerly worth 33*s.* or 36*s.*, now £1.

[2] Thévenot says that they were made of the ashes of the root of a certain plant, mixed with a particular kind of clay (*Voyages*, p. 94). Some snake-stones appear to have been made of charred bone. (See for an exhaustive account of this subject Yule, *Hobson-Jobson*, 847; Tennent, *Ceylon*, i. 197; Fryer, 138 f.; *Voyage of F. Leguat*, ii. 234.) The belief in their efficacy is still very general in India; by some they are supposed to be found in the head of the adjutant bird (see Ball, *Jungle Life in India*, 82; Prof. W. R. Halliday, *Folk-lore*, xxxii. 262 ff., xxxiii, 118 f.).

two methods to ascertain if the snake-stone is good, and that there is no fraud. The first is by placing the stone in the mouth, for then, if good, it leaps and attaches itself immediately to the palate. The other is to place it in a glass full of water, and immediately, if it is genuine, the water begins to boil, and small bubbles ascend from the stone which is at the bottom, to the top of the water.

There is still another stone which is called 'stone of the hooded snake.'[1] It is a kind of snake which has, as it were, a hood which hangs behind the head, and it is behind this hood that the stone is found, the smallest being of the size of a hen's egg. There are snakes in Africa and in Asia of an enormous size,[2] and up to 25 feet in length, as was that one whose skin is preserved at Batavia. This snake had swallowed a girl of eighteen years, of which fact I have elsewhere given an account.[3] You find these stones only in snakes which are, at the least, two feet in length. The stone, which is not hard, when rubbed against another stone yields a kind of slime which, when dissolved in water and drunk by a person who has some poison in his body, has the property of driving it out at once. These snakes are only to be found on the coasts of Melinda, and you can obtain the stones from Portuguese sailors and soldiers on their return from Mozambique.

CHAPTER XXV

Concerning the places from whence gold is obtained in Asia and Africa.

JAPAN consists of many islands to the east of China trending northwards; some even believe that Niphon, which is the largest of them, is, as it were, in contact with the mainland; it is the region of all Asia which furnishes the greatest quantity

[1] Cobra di capello—*Naja tripudians.* The figure referred to is a spirited one of a cobra, but is not reproduced here.

[2] Pythons. Marco Polo's great snakes were probably alligators (ii. 45, 49). For pythons nearly 30 feet long see *Ency. Brit.*, xxii. 704.

[3] Ball could not find the account to which Tavernier refers.

of gold, but it is thought that the principal part of it comes from the island of Formosa, from whence it is carried to Japan. Since the Dutch have held Formosa they have been unable to develop the trade of the particular locality where they believe the gold to occur.[1] Gold also comes from China, and the Chinese exchange it for the silver taken to them, for, price for price, they prefer silver to gold, because they have no mines of silver. This gold is of one of the lowest standards of any found in Asia.

The island of Celebes or Macassar[2] also produces gold, which is obtained from the rivers, where it occurs mingled with the sand. In the island of Achīn or Sumatra,[3] after the rainy season, and when the waters in the streams have subsided, veins of gold are found in the pebbles of different sizes which the rains have carried down from the mountains facing the north-east. On the west coast of the same island, where the Dutch go to ship pepper, the peasants bring an abundance of gold, but it is of very low standard, even inferior to the gold of China. Towards Tibet, which is identical with the Caucasus of the Ancients, in the territories of a Rājā beyond the Kingdom of Kashmīr, there are three mountains, close to one another, one of which produces gold of excellent quality, another grenat, and another lapis.[4] Finally, gold

[1] The occurrence of gold in China, Japan, and Formosa is not a subject that can be treated of exhaustively in these notes. That mines occur in China and Japan is well known, but Ball was not able to find conclusive evidence with reference to Formosa. See *Ency. Brit.*, x. 670. There is little in Japan (*ibid.*, xv. 197). Ainslie (*Materia Medica* i. 516) quotes the *Asiatic Journal* for December 1824 in support of the statement that the island abounds in gold. From a cursory examination of Mr. Locke's great work on gold, it seems to contain no reference to Formosa. For gold in China see *Ency. Brit.*, vi. 178.

[2] Gold occurs in the rivers of the northern and south-western peninsulas of Celebes. (Crawfurd, *Dictionary*, 144; *Ency. Brit.*, v. 578.)

[3] According to Crawfurd a small gold coin called mas (worth 1*s.* 2*d.*) from the Malay name of the metal, has been coined at Achīn. Gold dust, however, was the common medium of exchange. The Achinese have learnt the use of the touchstone from Telugu settlers. The gold filigree work of the Malays of Sumatra is very beautiful. A total of £1,000,000 worth of gold was considered by Crawfurd to cover the annual yield of all the Malayan islands in 1856.

[4] This indication as to the three mountains is somewhat vague. In all probability the grenat mine may be identified with the ruby, or

comes from the kingdom of Tippera,[1] of which I shall give a description in the following Book, but this gold is of bad quality, being of about the same standard as the gold of China.

These are all the places in Asia [2] whence gold comes, and I shall now say something of the gold of Africa, and of the region where it is obtained in greatest abundance.[3]

It should be remarked, under this head, that the governor

rather spinel mine, which is situated on the banks of the Shignān, a tributary of the Oxus in Badakhshān. As pointed out in vol. i, p. 303 *n.*, the name balass was derived from this locality. The lapis mine is near Firgāmu, also in Badakhshān, Lat. 36° 10′ Long. 71°. (Yule, *Marco Polo*, i. 150, 153.) The Tibet gold mines, famous since the days of Herodotus, are somewhat numerous. Each of these localities will be found described in the *Economic Geology of India*, pp. 213, 430, 529, where, also, an explanation of the myth of the gold-digging ants is suggested. See Watt, *Dict. Economic Products*, iii. 529. Khoten is famous for its gold, of which there are several mines under the mountains near Kiria to the east of Khoten (R. Shaw, *Visits to High Tartary, Yārkand, and Kāshghar*, 476). For Mīrzā Haidar's account of Tibetan gold mines see N. Elias & E. D. Ross, *Hist. of the Moghuls of Central Asia*, 409, 411 f. On various explanations of gold guarded by griffins or dug by ants in Sir J. Frazer, *Pausanias*, ii. 328 f. Sir T. Holdich (*Tibet the Mysterious*, 2 f.) points out that the myth is based on the practice of Tibetan miners, covered with blankets, who excavate gold by means of deer horns. The subject is fully discussed in *Indian Antiquary*, iv. 225 ff. The stone most frequently associated with Media was the highly-prized lapis lazuli, said to be found in Mount Demavand. But nothing is known of the locality of this mine, which must have been one of the most ancient in the world (Sir P. Sykes, *Hist. of Persia*, 2nd ed. i. 33).

[1] Tipra in the original. Ball did not know of any evidence for the occurrence of gold in Tippera; possibly what was brought thence in Tavernier's time was received from Assam, China, or Burma, in exchange for other commodities. Our Author devotes ch. xvi of bk. iii to a description of this Kingdom, which see.

[2] It is strange that Tavernier should have been unaware of the occurrence of gold in any part of the Indian Peninsula, there being so many localities where it is obtained, some of which were most probably worked in his time. (*Vide* for distribution of gold *Economic Geology of India*, ch. 'Gold'.) For gold-mining in neolithic times at Maski in the Nizam's Dominions see *The Foote Collection of Indian Prehistoric and Protohistoric Antiquities*, Madras, 1916, ii. 29, 125.

[3] Of the existence of gold in Eastern Africa there is abundant evidence. Of that which reaches the coast, however, a large proportion probably comes from afar off in the interior. Alluvial gold has long been collected in the Zambezi watershed (Sir H. H. Johnston, *British Central Africa*, 463).

of Mozambique has subject to him the commanders of Sofāla [1] and of Shupanga.[2] The first of these two small governments is on the river Sena 60 leagues from its mouth, and the other is 10 leagues higher up. From the mouth of the river up to these places on both sides there are many settlements of negroes, each of which is commanded by a Portuguese. These Portuguese have for a long time been masters of the country, and act like petty princes, making war against one another on the smallest pretext, there being some among them who have as many as 5,000 Cafres, who are their slaves. The Governor of Mozambique, to whom these petty princes are subject, furnishes them with cloth and other necessary goods, each of which he sells according to its market value. When the Governor of Mozambique [3] leaves Goa to assume charge of his government, which is the best of those subject to the Viceroy, he takes with him a great quantity of goods, and especially calicoes dyed black. His correspondents at Goa also send him every year two vessels laden with the same goods, which he forwards to Sofāla and Shupanga, and up to the town of Monomotapa,[4] capital of a Kingdom of the same name, otherwise called Voubebaran—the town being about 150 leagues distant from Shupanga. The ruler of all

[1] The position ascribed to Sofāla is incorrect, as it was not on the river named, but some two degrees, or say 70 leagues, to the south of the Delta of the Zambezi, on which the town of Sena is situated. A very interesting collection of notices referring to Sofāla and its gold is given in Yule, *Hobson-Jobson*, 849 f. Tavernier calls the river '*Sene*'.

[2] Chepon-Goura in the original. The modern Shupanga on the Zambezi is probably Tavernier's Chepon-Goura; it is between Sena and the coast.

[3] Castanheda says that the Moors took from India to Mozambique 'silver, linen cloth, pepper, ginger, silver rings, many pearls and rubies, and from a country inland they procured gold'. He also states that much gold was brought from the interior to Sofāla. (See Kerr, *Voyages and Travels*, ii. 317, 427.)

[4] The name is spelt Monomopata and Monomotapa in the original. Monomotapa is the old name of an extensive region on the Zambezi, and to the south of it. The meaning is uncertain, one explanation being that it means 'lord of the hippopotamus'. Its capital was Zumubany, a corruption of Zimbabwe, the Voubebaran of the text. See a full account in *Ency. Brit.*, xviii. 731 f.; Sir H. H. Johnston, *British Central Africa*, 56; Barbosa, ed. Dames, i. 9 ff.; Sir R. Burton, *Lands of Cazembe*, 22; Linschoten, i. 26.

this country takes the name of Emperor of Monomotapa, and his authority extends up to the confines of Preste Jan.[1] It is from these territories of Monomotapa whence the purest and finest African gold comes, and it is extracted without great difficulty by excavating in the ground to a depth of only 2 or 3 feet. In certain places in this country which are not inhabited, because there is no water there, gold is found on the surface of the ground in nuggets of all kinds of shapes and weights, and there are some of these nuggets which weigh an ounce. I have had, as curiosities, some pieces which I have presented to my friends, and some of them weighed as much as 2 ounces. I still have one of them weighing an ounce and a half or thereabouts.[2] When at Surat with M. d'Ardilière,[3] son of M. du Jardin, of whom I have made mention in my account of Persia, an Ambassador from the King of Abyssinia arrived, whom we went to salute. I presented him with a pair of pocket pistols decorated with silver, and when he invited us to dine with him he showed us the presents which he was carrying to the Great Mogul on behalf of the King, his master. They consisted of fourteen

[1] i.e. Abyssinia. The name Prester John was given to the ruling monarch by the Portuguese. (Varthema, Hakluyt Society, 63; Barbosa, ed. Dames, i. 39; Yule, *Marco Polo*, i. 205 ff.)

[2] For the Portuguese gold trade from Monomotapa, see Linschoten, i. 30 ff.

[3] The references to M. du Jardin and his son are very perplexing. In the *Persian Travels*, bk. ii, ch. vi, Tavernier says he started on his fourth journey from Paris with M. d'Ardilière, son of M. du Jardin. When landing at Masulipatam he refers to his companion as M. Louis du Jardin (vol. i, p. 206). He again mentions him as being with him at Madras (vol. i, p. 215), and on p. 245 he records his death in the year 1652. In vol. ii, p. 191, he speaks of being in M. d'Ardilière's company on the road from Golkonda to Surat in 1653. From all of which it would seem to be the legitimate conclusion that both father and son travelled with him in India, as is suggested on pp. 336 and 690. However, it is due to M. Joret to say that he may be right in treating these notices as all referring to the same person, and consequently the date 1653 must be wrong, if du Jardin died in 1652: *J.-B. Tavernier*, pp. 131, 114. But it should be added that this present notice seems to contradict that view, as M. du Jardin died within a few days of their arrival at Surat. Fryer in 1671 mentions M. Jordan (? Jardin) as having, with M. Rezin, succeeded Tavernier in the trade of carrying diamonds to and from Europe (i. 226, with the editor's note).

beautiful horses, which were all that remained out of thirty he had taken from his country, the others having died in the vessel when crossing the sea from Mocha to Surat. Also a number of young slaves of both sexes; and finally, this being the most important and worthy to be admired, there was a tree of gold 2 feet 4 inches high, and about 5 or 6 inches round the stem.[1] It had ten or twelve branches, some of which were nearly half a foot long and an inch broad, others being smaller. In some parts of the large branches there was to be seen some roughness, which in a manner resembled buds. The roots of this tree which had been thus naturally formed, were small and short, the longest not being more than 4 or 5 inches.

The people of this Kingdom of Monomotapa, knowing the time that the calicoes and other goods arrive at Sofāla [2] and Shupanga, come punctually to provide themselves with what they require. Many Cafres from other Kingdoms and Provinces also come, and the Governors of these two towns sell them calicoes and other things of which they have need, trusting for the payment which they undertake to make the following year by bringing gold, to the amount agreed upon; for if the Governor did not trust them thus there would be no trade between the Portuguese and the Cafres. It is almost the same with the Ethiopians who every year carry gold to Cairo, of which I have spoken in my account of the Seraglio of the Grand Seigneur. These people of Monomotapa do not live a long time on account of the bad water in their country. At the age of twenty-five years they begin to be dropsical, so that it is considered a marvel when they exceed forty years in age. The Province where the river Sena rises is called Moukaran,[3] and belongs to another King, commencing at 100 leagues or thereabouts above

[1] This description suggests a manufactured article, but it is possible that it was really, as Tavernier supposed, a natural arborescent nugget.

[2] Sofāla, a district and town on the East African coast, the most remote settlement towards the south made on that coast by the Arabs (Yule, *Hobson-Jobson*, 849; Barbosa, ed. Dames, Hakluyt Society, i. 6 ff. Shupanga is situated on the lower Zambezi (*Ency. Brit.*, xxviii. 952).

[3] Sir H. H. Johnston kindly writes: 'Sena is the lower Zambezi: Moukaran is probably the country of Karana or Karanga'.

Shupanga. The people of this Province find much gold dust in several rivers which join the Sena; but this gold is inferior to the other kind, and it is also taken to Shupanga and Sofāla. The country is very healthy, and the inhabitants live as long as those of Europe. In certain years Cafres arrive there from much farther than the Province of Moukaran, and even from the neighbourhood of the Cape of Good Hope. The Portuguese know of the country and its name, but have not induced the Cafres to reveal more than that their country, called Sabia,[1] is governed by a King, and that they generally spend four months on the road to Sofāla. The gold which they bring is excellent, and is in nuggets, like that of Monomotapa; they say that they find it on high mountains, where they only have to excavate the ground for it to the depth of 10 or 12 feet. They also bring an abundance of elephants' tusks, and say that there are so many elephants in the country that they are to be seen in troops in the fields, and that all the palisades of the fortresses and parks are made of elephants' tusks; this I have also observed elsewhere.[2] The ordinary food of these Cafres is the flesh of this animal, and four of them, with their assegais,[3] which are a kind of short pike are able to bring an elephant to the ground and kill it. All the water in their country is very bad, which is the reason why they have swollen legs, and it is a marvel when any one escapes this disease.

Above Sofāla there is a country commanded by a King called the King of Baroé. In some part of his country there grows a root which is an inch thick, and of a yellow colour. It cures all kinds of fever by causing vomiting; but as very little of it is found the King forbids, under severe penalty, any of it to be carried out of his Kingdom. While Dom Philippe de Mascarenhas was Viceroy of Goa the King of

[1] Sabia, Sir H. H. Johnston writes: 'is almost certainly the basin of the upper Sabi'.

[2] See vol. i, p. 221.

[3] Ageagayes in the original, for assegais, the well-known hurling spears used in Africa. The word is from the Berber zaghāya, with the Arabic article prefixed. It occurs commonly in travellers' accounts of other countries besides those included in Africa. (See Yule, *Hobson-Jobson*, p. 38.)

Baroé sent him a piece of this root [1] about 3 feet long, garnished with gold at both ends, and with rings of gold in the middle. The Viceroy having received it made great account of it, and causing it to be cut up into several pieces presented them to certain of his friends. He sent two to Surat to Mr. Fremlin, the English President, who showed them to me, and when I placed a piece of the root on my tongue I found the taste very bitter.

As for silver mines, there are none in the whole of Asia,[2] save only in the Kingdom of Japan. Some years ago very rich mines of tin were discovered at Delegore, Sangore, Bordelon, and Bata ; [3] this has done some injury to the English, because there is no longer need of their tin as formerly, sufficient being now produced in Asia. Tin is only used in this country to tin cooking-pots, kettles, and other copper utensils.[4]

CHAPTER XXVI

Account of a notable act of perfidy done to the author when he was about to embark at Gombroon for Surat.

In the month of April 1665, I was about to leave Gombroon, and on the point of embarkation for Surat in a vessel belonging

[1] De Lacerda speaks of the Baroé, probably the Barue of Livingstone, to the west of Sena and north of Māniça, the Bambire, or people of Baroé (Sir R. Burton, *Lands of Cazembe*, 44).

[2] Tavernier is here in error, as there are undoubted sources of silver in India and on the confines of Assam and Burma, which have been largely worked. (See *Economic Geology of India*, ch. iv, 'Silver'; Watt, *Dict. Economic Products*, vi. part iii, 239 f.) Silver certainly occurs also in other parts of Asia. (See pp. 212, 220, below.) For its occurrence in Burma see Scott & Hardiman, *Gazetteer, Upper Burma*, part i, vol. ii, p. 303 f.

[3] Ball identified these places with Delhi, Salangor, Billiton, and Banka. But Col. G. E. Gerini (*Journal Royal Asiatic Society*, 1904, p. 720 f.) points out that Delegore is Ligor ; Sangore, Senggora or Singora ; Bordelon, P'hattalang ; Bata, Pate, on the east coast of the Malay Peninsula, between Siam and Patāni.

[4] The artificer is known as the Qala'igar. Copper vessels, to be safely used, must be tinned at least once a month, the vessel to be heated and the tin (qala'ī) applied by means of sal-ammoniac (W. Hoey, *Monograph on Trades and Manufactures of Northern India*, 162 f.).

to the broker of the Dutch Company, and commanded by Captain Hans, when the Agent of the English gave me a packet of letters, which had arrived by express from England, to deliver to the President of Surat. This packet was very large, because, besides the Company's letters, he had included in it those which were addressed to private persons in Surat and other parts of India. I received the packet from him, on the evening of my embarkation, in presence of M. Casembrot, a Dutchman, who had come to Persia by land, and was related to M. Henry Van-Wück, Commander at Gombroon.[1] Casembrot managed to accompany me on all occasions when I went to see the English Agent, and Van-Wück asked me at each visit which I paid him, whether the Agent had not entrusted me with letters for Surat. I replied ingenuously that he had told me that he would give me some, without suspecting anything of the evil intention of both these men. Their object, as appeared subsequently, was to obtain possession of this packet in consequence of the rumour which was in circulation of a rupture between England and Holland,[2] and because they thought that the English had received definite news of it, as some days previously an Arab had arrived by the desert route and had brought a packet to the English Agent; this caused the Commander Van-Wück much anxiety.

As soon as I had received the packet from the Agent, Casembrot, who was always on the watch, and was looking on, as it was put into my hands, reported it to Van-Wück, and told him of its form and size. I pledged the Agent in a glass of wine which he offered me when wishing me a good passage, and went to take leave of Van-Wück, who would not allow me to go till after I had supped with him. He kept me, as it were by force, in order to have more time to accomplish his coup. He excused himself for being unable

[1] Henrik van Wijk, at this time Chief in Persia (1663–5). He is mentioned in W. Foster's *English Factories in India, 1651–1654*, p. 181, who refers, for this incident of the packet entrusted to Tavernier, to Report (1913) of the Hist. MSS. Commission on the Finch MSS., vol. i, p. 439. Tavernier spells his name Van-Wück in the ed. of 1678.

[2] War between England and Holland was declared on 14th March 1665,
10 and ended with the Peace of Breda, signed on 31st July 1667 N. S.

to accompany me on account of the arrival of three vessels which cast anchor while we were at table, and lent me his own boat to go on board, together with four or five of the principal officers of his staff, whom he sent with me, under pretext of escorting me, and with them the captain of the vessel also, to whom he gave the word. As soon as we were on board the captain offered me his own cabin, where he had already directed my bed to be placed by my servants, who had been on board for two days before, and on my making a difficulty about accepting it, he told me that the Commander had ordered him to do so; to which I replied that I would not accept his cabin, except on the condition that I should only occupy half of it, while he took the other. This having been arranged, I drew the packet of English letters from the pocket of my greatcoat, and giving it to one of my servants to place in my boucccha,[1] which is the valise of these countries, he put the boucccha between the side of the vessel and the head of my bed. There had come with us to the ship two small boats, bringing more than sixty bags of silver, some of 50 and others of 100 tomāns,[2] all the bags being made in Persia in that manner. Immediately the boats were alongside, the crew commenced to hoist the bags, one after the other, into the vessel, but did so very slowly, with the object of delaying us the whole night, and compelling me to go to bed. But as they observed that I was unwilling to retire, the captain, the pilot, and the Company's Broker, to whom, as I have said, the vessel belonged, consulted with the Dutch, and all together conspired to let a bag of 100 tomāns fall into the sea when hoisting it into the vessel; this was done in order to have time to accomplish their design. As soon as the bag fell into the sea they sent a boat to Gombroon to fetch a diver, who reached the vessel by daybreak, to dive for the sack. Seeing then that the vessel could not leave before the following day at two or three o'clock, I went to lie down, my boucccha being all the time in the same place, half under the head of my bed and half outside. My servants went to rest in the gunner's cabin, and while I slept alone

[1] Pers. *buqcha, bughcha,* 'a knapsack, wallet, bundle'.
[2] Tomān (see i. p. 331).

in that of the captain my bouccha was quietly drawn out, and from it the packet of letters was taken, and another well sealed and of similar form and size, which contained only white paper was put in its place. The bag which they had purposely allowed to fall into the sea in order to accomplish this wicked coup having been pulled up, we made sail, and arrived at the port of Surat on the 5th of May of the same year. The Dutch Commander did me the honour to send a barque 2 or 3 leagues out to sea to fetch me, and immediately on landing, which was about midnight, as I specially desired to pay my respects to him, I asked two Capuchin Fathers, who were at the port on our arrival, to deliver to the English President the packet which I had taken out of my bouccha, a service they willingly undertook. But they told me that, as it was an unseasonable hour, and that the President, who was gouty, might be then asleep, they did not consider it proper to awake him, and would wait till the morrow to accompany me, when I should be able to deliver the packet to the President myself. But the gout from which he suffered not permitting him to sleep much, it was delivered to him the same hour. The President opened the packet in presence of the chief officers of his staff, but they found only white paper folded like letters inside it. When this was reported to me, I realized at once the bad turn which Van-Wück and his accomplices had played me. What confirmed me further as to this perfidy was, that on going to examine my bouccha I found that a jewel which I had tried to sell to the Governor of Gombroon had also disappeared. As I was unable to agree with him as to the price, he returned it to me some hours before I embarked for Surat, and I had placed it in haste with the packet of letters in my bouccha, where I did not find it on my arrival at Surat.

The theft of this packet of letters, thus accomplished, incensed the President against me so much that he refused to allow me to justify myself, and I was moreover subjected to the displeasure of many private Englishmen affected by the loss of the letters in the packet, which were addressed to them. They went so far on different occasions as to attempt my life, as I am able to prove by the evidence and affidavits of many men of honour, and particularly of M. Hartman, who was then the second officer in the factory at Surat. So, to protect myself from snares which were set for me, I was obliged to be constantly accompanied by many people, and I was even unable to go to Golkonda, where there is a great trade in diamonds, as I was warned by my friends that ten or twelve English awaited me in that part of the world to do me some injury. The treachery which was thus done to me disturbed all my plans and caused me considerable loss; besides which I was obliged to carry back to Persia a large sum of money, in consequence of my not being able to invest it in India.

This is a copy of the letter which I sent on this subject to Batavia, to the General of the Dutch Company and the members of his Council, dated Surat, the 16th May 1665.

'GENTLEMEN—I take the liberty to write to you these lines in order to testify the displeasure I have experienced at the affront done me by Commander Henri Van-Wück at Gombroon, who has ignored the letters of recommendation which I received from the Ambassador to the States, an Officer of my King, addressed, one to the Chief Officer of the Company at Ispahān, another to the Commander at Gombroon, and a third to the Commander in this town of Surat, asking all three to assist me as much as possible, except in so far as the Company was interested. But M. Henri Van-Wück has disregarded that addressed to him, and has done me the most signal affront that a man of honour, as I, an Officer of his Royal Highness, the brother of my King, could ever receive, which was to have my baggage opened, in which there were many jewels, some of which have been lost, and to have ordered a large packet of letters to be taken which the Agent of the English at Gombroon entrusted to me to deliver to the President of the English in this town of Surat, having had another packet containing blank paper placed in its stead. I leave you to reflect what kind of esteem the President and all the English hold me in at present, and whether I have not good cause for making my complaints and asking justice from you. And, if it should please you gentlemen to send me permission to wait upon you at Batavia, in order to testify, by word of mouth, the displeasure which I feel on account of what M. Van-Wück has done to me in order to accomplish a crime of this nature, and to inform you in detail of the manner in which all this affair has happened, you would oblige me much. At the least, I ask you to give me some satisfaction in respect to the author of the theft, in default of which I shall not fail, as soon as I have, by the grace of God, returned to France, to make my complaints through the King my master, who has honoured me with his protection, and through his Royal Highness, his only brother, to MM. the States, and to their Ambassador, to obtain satisfaction, at whatever cost, from the said Van-Wück, and by this means re-establish my honour. Moreover, if I return by Ispahān, I shall not neglect to bring it to the notice of the King of Persia, and shall tell him that, after all the honour His Majesty has done me, and notwithstanding all the passports which I have had from him, the said M. Van-Wück has treated me in this fashion. I believe also that His Majesty will not be pleased to hear that all the patterns of jewels, which I was to buy and have made for him both in India and Europe, were lost when the packet of letters was stolen. I can also advise him of the plots and conspiracies which M. Van-Wück has carried on at Gombroon with a Prince, an enemy of Persia, who came to that place in disguise. Finally, I know enough to make him receive an equal or greater affront than he has done me; and by his receiving it the Company will receive it also. This, Gentlemen, is what I am resolved to do if you do not decide to give me complete satisfaction, though I believe I shall not have that trouble. Hoping that you will not omit to do me justice before I leave this country to return to Europe, where as in all other places I shall always be, Gentlemen, your very humble, &c.'

It is rare to see treason unpunished, and the principal actors in this plot all had miserable ends.

In the following monsoon the vessels which arrived from Surat at Gombroon spread in that region the tidings of the black villany which had been done to me; and a short time after, when M. Van-Wück was attacked by a kind of fever, the Rev. Father Balthasar, Carmelite Monk, went to see him, and sought to get him to speak of this affair in which he was so prominently involved. He strongly defended himself against the charge, and making use of an equivocation, said, that if it was true that he had taken the letters, he wished to die without speaking, and not to live three days. He had not in truth committed the theft, but he had arranged for its being done ; and he died at the end of three days, and without speaking. His Lieutenant, named Bozan, one of those whom he had sent to escort me to the vessel, and who apparently had opened the bouccha and committed the theft, after a great debauch, lay down on the terrace of the house to sleep in the fresh air, and as these terraces have neither parapet nor anything to prevent a fall, on moving and rolling in his sleep, he fell over, and on the following day was found dead on the seashore. As for the Captain of the vessel, who was also in the plot, four or five days after his arrival at Surat, as he pursued his way, a Musalmān, jealous of his wife, whom he had beaten, and excited to rage against some Franks who separated them, believing this Captain, whom he found alone, to be a member of the band, stabbed him five or six times with a dagger, upon which he fell dead on the ground. Such were the miserable ends of all these people.

BOOK III

Concerning the religion of the Musalmāns and that of the Idolaters of India: the voyage of the Author by sea from Surat to Batavia, and from Batavia to Holland; and of many peculiarities in different Kingdoms of the East.

CHAPTER I

Concerning the religion of the Musalmāns in the East Indies.

THE diversity which exists among the Musalmāns consists not only in the different explanations which they give of their Korān,[1] but also in the different opinions which they entertain regarding the first successors of Muhammad. From this cause two sects, entirely opposed to one another, have sprung; the one calling itself the Sunnīs is followed by the Turks, the other the Shī'as,[2] which is the sect of the Persians. I shall not delay here to say more as to the difference between these two sects, which divide the Musalmān world, having spoken sufficiently of them in my accounts of Persia, and I shall only describe the present condition of this false religion, both in the Empire of the Great Mogul and in the Kingdoms of Golkonda and Bījāpur.

At the first establishment of Islām in India the Christians[3] of the East were very ostentatious [estoient fort superbes] but not very devout, and the Idolaters were effeminate people unable to make much resistance. Thus it was easy for the Musalmāns to subject both by force of arms. This they did with so much success that many Christians and Idolaters embraced the Law of Muhammad.

The Great Mogul with all his Court followed the sect of

[1] Alcoran in the original.

[2] Sounnis and Chias in the original, and Sunnis and Schiais in the *Persian Travels*, bk. iv, ch. vii. The former revere the direct successors of Muhammad, and the latter maintain that 'Alī and his sons Hasan and Husain are the true successors to the caliphate. Sunnīs predominate in the Musalmān population of India, but there are also many Shī'as there, some of them being descendants of Persian immigrants. (See *Islām in India*, Oxford, 1921, ch. i.)

[3] M. Thévenot states that about the year 1665 some believed that there were 25,000 families of Christians in Agra, but all were not agreed as to this estimate (*Voyage des Indes*, 102). Colonel Sleeman, who refers to this, adds that he himself came upon a colony of 2,000 in the year 1814 in Bettiah in Tirhūt (*Rambles and Recollections*, ed. 1915, pp. 11 ff.; Smith, *Akbar, The Great Mogul*, 136 ff.).

the Sunnīs, the King of Golkonda that of the Shī'as, and the King of Bījāpur had in his territories both Sunnīs and Shī'as.[1] The same might also be said of the Court of the Great Mogul, on account of the number of Persians who came to serve in his armies. It is true that although they regard the Sunnīs with horror they nevertheless follow, in outward show, the religion of the Monarch, believing that to make or secure their fortune they may conceal their true belief, and that it suffices for them to cherish it in their hearts.[2]

As for the Kingdom of Golkonda, Qutb Shāh, who reigns at present [1625–72], maintains with great zeal the law of the Shī'as, and as the nobles of his Court are nearly all Persians, they observe the customs of the sect of the Shī'as with the same strictness and the same freedom from restraint as in Persia.

I have elsewhere remarked that among the native Musalmān subjects of the Great Mogul there are but few in positions of command ; this is the cause why many Persians, oppressed by want, or ambitious of better fortune than they can hope for in their own country, go to seek for it in India. Being clever they are successful in finding means to advance themselves in the profession of arms, so that in the Empire of the Great Mogul, as well as in the Kingdoms of Golkonda and Bījāpur, the Persians are in possession of the highest posts.[3]

[1] It is curious that half of the Bījāpur Kings were Sunnī and half Shī'a—the Sunnī being Ibrāhīm I, Ibrāhīm II, and his son Mahmūd, and probably Sikandar, the last of the dynasty ; while 'Alī 'Ādil Shāh, Yūsuf, and Ismāil were Shī'as (*Bombay Gazetteer*, xxiii. 413 note 4).

[2] This is the Shī'a doctrine of Taqīa, whereby he believes that he is justified in smoothing down or in denying the peculiarities of his religious belief, in order to save himself from religious persecution (Hughes, *Dict. of Islām*, 628).

[3] On the Persian adventurers who crowded out the Courts of the Mughal Emperors and the Musalmān Kingdoms of Southern India see Erskine, *Hist. of India*, ii. 24 f. ; Smith, *Akbar, The Great Mogul*, 357, 362. Persian influence is strong at Haidarābād even at the present day. Also see Bernier, 209 : 'The court itself does not now consist, as originally, of real Mogols ; but is a medley of Usbecs, Persians, Arabs, and Turks, or descendants from all these peoples, known, as I said before, by the general appellation of Mogols.'

Aurangzeb, especially, shows great zeal for the Sunnī sect, of which he is so faithful a follower that he surpasses all his predecessors in external observance of the Law, which has been the veil by means of which he has concealed his usurpation of the kingdom. When he took possession of the throne he proclaimed that it was with the design of insisting upon the Law of Muhammad being observed in all its strictness, as it had been relaxed during the reigns of Shāhjahān his father and Jahāngīr his grandfather. To show himself still more zealous for the Law he became a Dervish or Fakīr, i. e. a professional beggar, and under this false mantle of piety cleverly made his way to the Empire. Although he had, as I have said, numerous Persians in his service, he did not allow them to celebrate the festival of Hasan and Husain,[1] sons of 'Alī, who were killed by the Sunnīs, as I have mentioned in my account of Persia; and they themselves, to please the Emperor and advance their own fortunes, made no scruple about conforming themselves outwardly to the cult and customs of the Sunnīs.

CHAPTER II

Concerning Fakīrs or Musalmān beggars in the East Indies.[2]

It is estimated that there are in India 800,000 Musalmān Fakīrs, and 1,200,000 among the idolaters, which is an enormous number.[3] They are all vagabonds and idlers, who blind the eyes of the people by a false zeal, and lead them to believe that all that falls from their own mouths is oracular.

There are different kinds of Musalmān Fakīrs; some are almost naked, like the Fakīrs of the idolaters, who have no

[1] Hosen and Heussin in the original. The observance of the Shī'a Muharram festival was prohibited in 1669 (Jadunath Sarkar, *Hist. of Aurangzib*, iii. 104). On Aurangzeb becoming a Fakīr see i. 264.

[2] See *Islām in India*, the *Qānūn-i-Islām* of Ja'far Sharīf, Oxford, 1921, pp. 283 ff.

[3] The numbers of Fakīrs, Hindu and Musalmān, are great, but no exact figures are available, because at recent enumerations it has been found impossible to distinguish them from ordinary beggars.

regular dwellings, and abandon themselves to all kinds of impurity without any shame. They persuade simple souls that they are privileged to do all kinds of evil without sin.

There are other Fakīrs who are clad in garments of so many pieces of different colours that one is unable to say what they are. These robes extend half-way down their legs and conceal the miserable rags beneath. These Fakīrs generally travel in companies, having a chief or superior over them who is distinguished by his garment, which is poorer and made up of more pieces than those of the others. He, moreover, drags a heavy iron chain attached to one leg; it is 2 cubits long and thick in proportion. When he prays it is with a great noise, which he makes with this chain and a loud voice; this is accompanied by an affected gravity, which attracts the veneration of the people.[1] The people, however, bring him and his followers food to eat, which is served to him in the place where he halts, generally a street or public place. His carpets are spread by his disciples, and he seats himself on them while he gives audience to those who wish to consult him. Moreover, his disciples proclaim throughout the country the great virtues of their master and the favours he receives from God, Who reveals to him the most important secrets, and confers upon him the power to aid afflicted persons with good advice. The people give him easy credence, regard him as a holy man, approach him with great devotion, and when one of them comes close to him, he removes the shoes off his feet, prostrates himself before the Fakīr and kisses his feet. Then the Fakīr, in order to show his humility, extends his arm and gives his hand to be kissed, after which he makes those who come to consult him sit near him, and listens to each in turn. He boasts of possessing a prophetic spirit, especially for indicating to women who are sterile the way in which they may obtain children, and how to constrain anyone they wish to manifest love for them.

Some Fakīrs have more than 200 disciples, whom they assemble by the sound of the drum and with a horn similar

[1] Bernier (p. 317) notes the habit of Fakīrs dragging chains, of which there are many modern instances; cf. *Islām in India*, 289 f.

to those of our huntsmen. When marching, the disciples carry their standard, lances, and other arms, which they plant in the ground near their master when he halts to rest anywhere.[1]

The third class of Fakīrs of the East Indies consists of those who, being born of poor parents, and wishing to know the Law thoroughly, in order to become Mullās or doctors, take up their abode in mosques, where they live on charity bestowed upon them. They occupy their time in reading the Korān, which they learn by heart, and when they are able to add to this study some little knowledge of natural things, with the example of a good life, according to their ideas, they become heads of mosques, and reach the dignity of Mullās and judges of the Law.[2] Fakīrs of this class marry wives, and some of them through piety and their great desire to imitate Muhammad, take three or four of them, believing that they render to God signal service, by becoming fathers of many children who will follow the Law of their Prophet.

CHAPTER III

Of the Religion of the Gentiles or Idolaters of India.

THE idolaters of India are so numerous that for one Musalmān there are five or six Gentiles.[3] It is astonishing to see how this enormous multitude of men has allowed itself to be subjected by so small a number, and has readily submitted to the yoke of the Musalmān Princes. But astonishment ceases when one remembers that the idolaters have no union among themselves, and that superstition has introduced

[1] Ja'far Sharīf gives a full account of the organization of these bands (*ibid.*, 169 ff.). P. della Valle describes them as begging and sounding a trumpet (i. 94).

[2] For a good account of the qualifications and duties of the Mullā and other Muslim officials see *Bombay Gazetteer*, ix, part. 2, 132 ff. A man who knows the Korān by heart is called Hāfiz. Mosque schools, as described in the text, still exist.

[3] At the Census of 1911 Hindus numbered 217 millions and Musalmāns 66 millions, the proportions to the total population being respectively 69 and 21 per cent.

so strange a diversity of opinions and customs that they never agree with one another.[1] An idolater will not eat bread nor drink water in a house belonging to anyone of a different caste from his own, unless it be more noble and more exalted than his; thus they can all eat and drink in the houses of the Brāhmans,[2] which are open to all the world. Among these idolaters a caste is, so to speak, what a tribe was among the Jews, and although it is commonly believed that there are seventy-two of these castes, I have ascertained from the most accomplished of their priests that they can be reduced to four principal castes from which all others derive their origin.[3]

The first caste is that of the Brāhmans, the successors of the ancient Brachmanes or philosophers of India, who specially studied astrology. Their ancient books, in the reading of which the Brāhmans generally occupy themselves, still exist and they are so skilled in their observations that they do not make a mistake of a minute in foretelling eclipses of the sun and moon. In order to preserve this science among themselves, they have a kind of university in a town called

[1] This has ever been the strength of those who have conquered India.

[2] Bramines in the original. Brāhmans' houses are certainly not now open to all the world; the very reverse is the case. The accuracy of this statement, even in Tavernier's time, may be doubted. True as it is that a man of lower caste may eat from the hand of a Brāhman, a Brāhman has, himself, to guard against defilement by contact with men of lower caste. Dubois, who allows that Brāhmans permit no stranger to enter their kitchens, was admitted into their houses by Brāhmans (*Hindu Manners, Customs, and Ceremonies*, ed. 1906. Introd. x. 181, 201 f.) and Mrs. Stevenson was admitted to eat in Brāhman houses in Kāthiāwār (*Rites of the Twice-born*, 240). But these cases are exceptional.

[3] The number of castes at the present day is enormous; see the list in the *Census Report, India*, 1911, vol. i, Part 2, pp. 177 ff., and Sir E. A. Gait's analysis of the Statistics in Part 1, ch. xi. He remarks that earlier writers 'accepted his view that the classes [Tavernier's four castes] had gradually developed into castes. It has, however, been shown by Senart and others that the division into castes has no direct relation with the division into classes. The castes came into existence independently, without regard to the classes.' The best short summary of the question will be found in Sir E. A. Gait's article 'Caste' in Hastings, *Encyclopædia of Religion and Ethics*, vol. iii, p. 230 ff.

Benares,[1] where they study astrology principally, but they also have doctors who teach the Law, which is observed with very great strictness. This caste is the most noble of all, because it is from among the Brāhmans that the priests and ministers of the law are selected. But as they are very numerous and cannot all study in their university, the majority of them are ignorant and consequently very superstitious, those who pass as the most intellectual being the most arrant sorcerers.

The second caste is that of the Rājputs or Ketrīs,[2] i. e. warriors and soldiers. These are the only idolaters who are brave, and distinguish themselves in the profession of arms. All the Rājās, of whom I have often spoken, are of this caste. They are like so many petty kings, whose disunion has made them tributaries to the Great Mogul; but as the majority are in his service, they are highly recompensed for the small tribute which they pay him by the large and honourable salaries which they receive from him. These Rājās, and the Rājputs their subjects, are the most firm supports of the Great Mogul's kingdom; and it was the Rājās Jaisingh and Jaswantsingh who placed Aurangzeb on the throne. But it should be remarked that this second caste does not exclusively consist of people who follow arms as a profession. It is only the Rājputs who go to war, and who are all cavaliers; but as for the Ketris they have degenerated from the bravery of their ancestors, having quitted arms for merchandise.[3]

The third caste is that of the Banians,[4] who attach them-

1 Benarez in the original, elsewhere written Benarow or Banarous.

2 Kshatriya, Chhatrī.

3 He refers to the Khatrī caste of Northern India, who claim Kshatriya descent, but are merchants (Rose, *Glossary of Tribes and Castes, Panjab*, ii. 501 ff.).

4 Tavernier spells this word Baniane, which has been altered in the text to Banian. It is otherwise, and perhaps more properly, spelt Banyan, or Vānya in Western India. It signifies a trader or merchant, especially in Gujarāt. In Calcutta it is a title still used for the Indian brokers attached to houses of business. It is derived from Vānya (Gujarāti Vāniyo), and that from the Sanskrit Vanij, a trader. Our author's testimony as to the astuteness of the men of this caste is borne out by many authors, notably P. F. Vincenzo de Maria, who says to make one it takes three Chinese, and three Hebrews to make a Chinese,

selves to trade, some being Shroffs, i. e. money-changers or bankers, and the others brokers, by whose agency the merchants buy and sell. The members of this caste are so subtle and skilful in trade that, as I have elsewhere said,[1] they could give lessons to the most cunning Jews. They accustom their children at an early age to shun slothfulness, and instead of letting them go into the streets to lose their time at play, as we generally allow ours, teach them arithmetic, which they learn perfectly, using for it neither pen nor counters, but the memory alone, so that in a moment they will do a sum, however difficult it may be. They are always with their fathers, who instruct them in trade, and do nothing without at the same time explaining it to them. These are the figures which they use in their books, both in the Empire of the Great Mogul, as well as in other parts of India,[2] although the languages may vary. If anyone gets in a rage with them they listen with patience, without replying, and withdraw coldly, not returning to see him for four or five days, when they anticipate his rage will be over. They never eat anything which has enjoyed sentient life, and they would rather die than slay the least animal, not even excepting an insect or vermin, being in this respect very zealous observers of their Law. It is sufficient to add that they never strike one another, and that they never go to war, and can neither eat nor drink in the houses of the Rājputs, because they slay animals and eat meat, with the exception of that of the cow, which is never eaten.

The fourth caste is called Charados or Soudra.[3] Like that of the Rājputs, it occupies itself with war; but with this difference, that the Rājputs serve on horse, and the Sūdras on foot. Both glory in dying in battle, and a soldier, whether of the cavalry or foot, is esteemed for ever infamous

therefore a Banian ought to possess the subtlety of nine Jews. (Yule, *Hobson-Jobson*, 63.)

[1] Vol. i. 24. 'The chief Pleasure of the Gentiles, or Banyans, is to Cheat one another, conceiving therein the highest Felicity' (Fryer, i. 281).

[2] These figures are not reproduced here.

[3] Sanskrit Sūdra. Tavernier confines the name to infantry in the Indian armies, perhaps with reference to the Nāyars of Malabar, who, by an extension of the term, rank as Sūdras.

if, in the moment of combat, he runs away. It is regarded as an eternal disgrace in his family, and in this connexion I shall relate a story which was told me in the country. A soldier who loved his wife passionately, and by whom he was equally beloved in return, fled from the field of battle, not out of fear of death, but simply on account of his wife's sorrow in case she might find herself a widow. When she heard the cause of his flight, as she saw him approach the house she closed the door, and told him she was unable to recognize as a husband a man who had preferred the love of a woman to honour; that she did not wish to see him any more, to avoid leaving a blot on the reputation of her family, and to teach her children to have more courage than their father. This woman remained firm in her resolution. The husband, to regain his reputation and his love, returned to the army, where he performed noble actions which redounded to his credit, and having splendidly repaired his fault, the door of his house was opened to him, and his wife received him with pleasure.[1]

The remainder of the people, who do not belong to either of these four castes, are called Pauzecour.[2] They all occupy themselves with mechanical arts, and do not differ from one another except in the trades which they follow from father to son; so that a tailor, although he may be rich, is unable to advance his children, except in his own calling, nor to marry them, be it a son or a daughter, to others than those of his trade. So also when a tailor dies all those of his calling go to the place where his body is burnt, and the same custom is observed among all the other artisans.

Among the special castes there is one that is called Halāl-

[1] Tod and Bernier tell a similar story about Jaswant Singh, who was so treated by his wife on his return from the battle of the 17th April 1658. (Tod, *Annals of Rajasthān*, ed. 1920, ii. 724; Bernier, 40 f.; A. Hamilton, in Pinkerton, *Voyages*, viii. 311.)

[2] The origin of the name is uncertain. Tavernier may have heard of the Panchama, a general name for a class of artisans or menials in Madras, and may have confounded them with the Pānchgaur, or Pancha-gauda, a term applied to the five classes of the northern Brāhmans (Thurston, *Castes and Tribes of Southern India*, vi. 43 f.; J. Wilson,
11 *Indian Caste*, ii. 124 ff.).

khor,[1] who engage only in cleaning houses, each house paying them something monthly, according to its size. If a man of quality in India, whether a Musalmān or an idolater, has fifty servants, not one of them will use a broom to clean the house, for he would consider himself contaminated by it, and one of the greatest insults that one can do to a man in India is to call him Halālkhor. It is proper to remark here that each of these servants has his own special duty, the one to carry the vessel of water for drinking by the way, another to have the pipe of tobacco ready, and if the master asks one to perform the service for which the other is employed, that service will not be performed, and the servant remains as though he were immovable. As for slaves, they have to do whatever their master orders. As the caste of Halālkhors is only occupied in removing the refuse from houses, it gets the remains of what the others eat, of whatever caste they may be, and it does not make any scruple about eating indifferently of all things. It is the people belonging to this caste alone, who make use of asses, to carry the sweepings from the houses to the fields; while all other Indians will not touch this animal. It is otherwise in Persia, where asses are used both for baggage and for riding. It is also the Halālkhors in India who alone feed pigs and use them for food.[2]

[1] Alacors in the original. The name Halālkhor signifies an eater of lawful food, or rather, one to whom all kinds of food are lawful, euphemistically applied to the Sweepers, to whom all things are lawful. (Yule, *Hobson-Jobson*, 409; Ovington, 382.)

[2] Dhobīs, or washermen, use asses to convey clothes backwards or forwards from a river or tank, and Kumhārs, or potters, employ the asses for carrying clay, but both these castes are held in low esteem. Many menial castes, besides Halālkhors, or sweepers, keep swine, such as the Chamārs, or leather-dressers; Kumhārs and Dhīmars, or fishermen and palanquin-bearers of the Central Provinces, breed pigs, which they sell to people of low caste to be used in sacrifice (Russell, *Tribes and Castes, Central Provinces*, iv. 8).

CHAPTER IV

Concerning the idolatrous Kings and Princes of Asia.

It is necessary to place in the front rank of the idolatrous Kings of Asia, the King of Arakan, the King of Pegu, the King of Siam, the King of Cochinchina, the King of Tonquin, and, as for the King of China, we know that he was an idolater before the irruption of the Tartars into his territories; but since that time one can say nothing certain about him, because these Tartars, who are now the masters of the country, are neither idolaters nor Musalmāns, being, rather, both combined.[1] In the principal islands, firstly, the King of Japan, next the King of Ceylon, and some small Kings of the islands of the Moluccas, and, finally, the Rājās, both of the Empire of the Great Mogul and of the neighbourhoods of the Kingdoms of Bījāpur and Golkonda, are all idolaters. In general, all the common people, whether in the territories subject to the Great Mogul, or the Kings of Golkonda and Bījāpur, and the islands of Achīn, Java, and Macassar, the Kings of which, as I have elsewhere said, are Musalmāns,—all the common people, I say, of these countries are idolaters.

I have stated that the King of Ceylon[2] is an idolater, and it is true. But it is true also that about fifty years ago a King of Ceylon became a Christian, and received at his baptism the name of Jean, having been previously called the Emperor Priapender.[3] As soon as he embraced Christianity, the

[1] Tavernier knew little about the Chinese.

[2] The ruler of Ceylon at this period was the merciless tyrant, Rājāsingha II, who being unable to resist the Dutch in the low country, practised ruthless cruelty against his subjects in the hills (Tennent, *Ceylon*, ii. 49).

[3] Although the period of his reign was somewhat more remote than Tavernier states, it seems probable that this Emperor Priapender was Don Juan Dharmapāla, who was raised to the throne in 1542 by the Portuguese, and reigned thirty-nine years. He was baptized by Wilponte Alphonso Perera, who went to Ceylon from Goa for the purpose. A number of his chiefs and people also became Christians at the same time. He was opposed throughout his reign by Rājā Singha, who ultimately superseded him (Forbes, *Eleven Years in Ceylon*, ii. 315). Ribeiro calls him Paria Pandar, which is like Tavernier's form of the name (Dames'

Princes and priests of the country established another King in his stead. He did what he could to induce all his people to imitate him, and for this purpose assigned to the Jesuit Father twelve of the largest villages which were around Columbo, so that from the revenue of these places they might support the children of the country in colleges, where, being well instructed, they would afterwards be able to teach others. For the King represented to these Fathers that it was impossible for them to learn the language of the country well enough to preach to the people, and in effect they found that the youth of Ceylon were so quick and intelligent that they learnt, in six months, more Latin, philosophy and other sciences, than Europeans acquire in a year, and they questioned the Fathers with such subtlety, and so deeply, that they were amazed.

Some years after the King had become a Christian, a very accomplished man and good native philosopher, named Alegamma Motiar,[1] as one might say master of the philosophers, after having conversed some time with the Jesuit Fathers and other priests at Columbo, was inspired to become a Christian. With this object he went to see the Jesuit Fathers, and told them that he desired to be instructed in the Christian faith, but he inquired what Jesus Christ had done and left in writing. He set himself then to read the New Testament with so much attention and ardour that in less than six months there was not a passage which he could not recite, for he had acquired Latin very thoroughly. After having been well instructed, he told the Fathers that he wished to receive holy baptism, that he saw that their religion was the only good and true one, and such as Jesus Christ had taught, but what astonished him was, that they did not follow Christ's example, because, according to the Gospel, he never took money from anyone, while they on the contrary took it from everyone, and neither baptized nor buried anyone without it. This did not prevent him

Book of Duarte Barbosa, ed. 1921, vol. ii, p. 114 ; see Tennent, *Ceylon*, ii. 14 f.).

[1] Mudaliyar, a Cingalese title, meaning a headman. Alegamma has not been identified (Yule, *Hobson-Jobson*, 569 f.).

from being baptized, and from working for the conversion of the idolaters afterwards.

Such is the present condition of the idolaters throughout Asia. I come now to those of India in detail and to their gross errors, after which I shall speak of their customs and of the penances of their Fakīrs.

CHAPTER V

Concerning the belief of the Idolaters with respect to the Deity.

THE idolaters of India yield to creatures like the cow, the ape, and different monsters, honours which are only due to the true Deity, although it is certain that they acknowledge one infinite God, all-powerful and all-wise, Creator of the heavens and the earth, who is omnipresent. They call him in some places Permesser, in others Peremael,[1] as, for example, towards the coast of Malabar; and Vvistnou [2] in the language of the Brahmans who inhabit the coast of Coromandel. As the idolaters have perhaps heard that the circle is the most perfect of all figures, they have thought to improve upon it by saying God is of an oval figure, and it is for this reason that they generally keep in their pagodas an oval pebble, which they obtain from the Ganges,[3] and adore as God. They

[1] Perumāl, 'great man', is the most common title of Vishnu in the Tamil country (B. Ziegenbalg, *Genealogy of the South-Indian Gods*, Madras, 1869, p. 83); Permesser in the text represents Paramesvara, 'Supreme Lord'.

[2] Vishnu, the preserver, one of the Hindu triad. He is represented as a dark man with four arms—one hand holds a club, another a shell, the third a chakra, or metal quoit, and the fourth the lotus.

[3] This is the so-called Sālagrām stone. The Son river supplies some which are, it is believed, silicious pebbles derived from the basalt; others are obtained from the Himalayas, and these are said to include fossils, ammonites. The Sālagrām is connected with the worship of Vishnu, but it may be worshipped as representing for the time being any god. According to Ward (*History of the Hindus*, ed. 1815, ii. 221 ff.; Sleeman, *Rambles*, ed. 1915, p. 121; Dubois, *Hindu Manners*, ed. 1906, p. 648 f.) the Sālagrām is black, hollow, and nearly round, and is obtained from the Gandak river. As much as 2,000 rupees was given for one of the

are so strongly fixed in this foolish idea that the wisest among the Brahmans will not listen to any argument against it, and thus it is not to be wondered at if a people who have such evil guides fall into this gross and monstrous idolatry. There is a caste so superstitious about this, that those who belong to it keep these oval stones suspended from their necks, and press them against their bodies while they pray.

In this gross and pitiable ignorance the idolaters, like the ancient pagans, regard their gods as men, and even bestow wives upon them, thinking that they love the same things as those in which men take pleasure. Thus they regard their Rāma as a great deity on account of the wonders which they believe he performed during his life. The following are the fables which they relate regarding him, as I have learnt from the most accomplished among their Brahmans :—

Rāma was the son of a powerful Rājā, who called himself Deseret,[1] and the most virtuous of many children which he had by two legitimate wives. He was particularly beloved by his father, who had destined him to be his successor. The mother of Rāma having died, the other wife of the Rājā, who possessed entire control over her husband, induced him to drive Rāma and his brother Lakshman [2] from his house and territories ; this was done, and by the exclusion of these two brothers, the son of this other wife was declared to be heir to the Rājā. Rāma and his brother having then received an order to depart, obeyed the command of their father, and as they were about to leave, Rāma went to bid farewell to his wife Sītā, whom these idolaters regard as a goddess. She was unwilling to part from him, and protested that she would follow him everywhere, and so they all three left the house of the Rājā, to seek their fortunes. They were unlucky

first class. Vast sums of money are sometimes expended on the festivities connected with the marriage of the Sālagrām to the Tulsī plant (*Ocymum sanctum*). But Tavernier may confuse it with the Lingam worn by the Lingāyat sect.

[1] Rāma, son of Dasaratha, King of Ayodhya. What follows is a tolerably correct version of the Rāmāyana epic, for a popular abstract of which see J. C. Oman, *The Great Indian Epics*, 1899, and for criticism, Hastings, *Ency. Religion and Ethics*, x. 574 ff.

[2] Lochman in the original.

at first, for while passing through a forest, Rāma went in pursuit of a bird, and remained a long time absent, when Sītā, fearing that some disaster had happened to her husband, by force of her entreaties obliged Lakshman to go in search of him. He strongly objected, because Rāma told him not to leave Sītā, having foreseen by a spirit of prophecy what would happen if she remained alone. Nevertheless Lakshman, moved by the earnest prayers of his sister-in-law, went to seek his brother Rāma. In the meantime Rāvana,[1] another god of the idolaters, appeared to Sītā in the garb of a Fakīr and asked alms of her. Rāma had told Sītā not to go beyond the spot where he had left her; this being well known to Rāvana he refused to receive the alms which Sītā offered him unless she left the place. Sītā either by mistake or forgetting the command of Rāma, passed beyond the limits which he had prescribed, and then Rāvana seized her and took her into the depths of the forest where his followers awaited him, with whom he departed to his territories. When Rāma returned from the chase, and missed Sītā, he fell senseless from grief, but Lakshman his brother brought him to his senses, and they went together to search for Sītā, who was tenderly beloved by her husband.

When the Brāhmans recount this ravishment of their goddess Sītā they do so with tears and demonstrations of excessive grief,[2] and they add to the story a multitude of ridiculous fables, extolling the great bravery of Rāma in the pursuit of the ravisher of Sītā. All the animals were employed in order to discover her, among which the monkey Hanumān[3] alone had the good fortune to be successful. He crossed the sea with a bound, and arrived in the gardens of Rāvana, where he found Sītā in the deepest affliction, and she was much surprised on beholding a monkey, who spoke on behalf of her husband. At first she was not willing to give credence to such an ambassador, but the monkey, to authenticate

[1] Rhevan in the original. Rāvana was the demon king of Lankā or Ceylon.

[2] This is done at the Rāmlīlā or mystery play, describing the adventures of Rāma and Sītā, who are impersonated by boys, performed in Northern India in September–October. See Oman, *The Great Indian Epics*, 75 ff.

[3] Harman in the original.

his mission, handed her a ring which her husband had given her, but which she had left in her baggage. She had much difficulty in believing such a miracle, and that Rāma her husband had been able to make a beast give her news of him, and such certain indications of his love. The monkey Hanumān did wonders at this interview, and being recognized as a spy by the servants of Rāvana, who wished to burn him, he made use of the fire which they had prepared for him to set alight the palace of Rāvana, which was consumed almost entirely, by means of the rags which they tied to his tail and body and set on fire. He threw himself immediately among the straw and other combustible matter, which caused a great conflagration in the palace. The monkey realizing that he would not escape from Rāvana if he again fell into his power, promptly retraced the road by which he had come, and having bathed himself in the sea, which he recrossed at a single bound, he gave Rāma an account of his adventures, and told him of the affliction in which he had found Sītā, who was in despair at finding herself so far removed from her husband. Rāma, touched by the affection of his wife, resolved at any cost to deliver her from the hands of Rāvana. This was accomplished, the monkey serving him as guide, and with the aid of forces which Rāma had collected from different places. With much difficulty he approached the palace of Rāvana, which was still smoking, so great had been the fire; and the subjects of this Prince having been dispersed, it was easy for Rāma again to see his beloved Sītā, whom Rāvana abandoned and fled in fear to the mountains. Rāma and Sītā experienced infinite joy at seeing one another again, and did much honour to the monkey Hanumān, who had rendered them so great a service.

As for Rāvana, he passed the remainder of his days as a poor Fakīr, his country being altogether ruined by the troops of Rāma, who avenged the injury he had received, and it is from this Rāvana that this incredible number of Fakīrs, whom one sees in peregrination throughout India, have taken their origin.[1] These Fakīrs lead a life of such

[1] Tavernier was possibly misinformed. Sir G. Grierson, who has kindly made inquiries, has failed to trace any legend connecting Rāvana

austerity that their penances amount to prodigies, and I have had the curiosity to collect several pictures of them, some of which I shall show to the reader in the following chapter.

CHAPTER VI

Concerning Fakīrs, or the professional Mendicants of India, and their penances.[1]

THE Fakīrs, as I have just said, take their origin from Rāvana, whom Rāma despoiled of his kingdom; on that account he felt so much remorse that he resolved to wander like a vagabond throughout the world, poor and bereft of all property, and completely nude. He soon found many people to follow him in this kind of life, which afforded them all kinds of license. For being reverenced as saints, they had abundant opportunities of doing whatever evil they wished.

Fakīrs ordinarily travel in troops, each of which has its Chief or Superior. As they go perfectly nude, winter and summer, always lying on the ground, and since it is sometimes cold, the young Fakīrs and other idolaters who are the most devoted, go in the afternoon to search for the droppings of

with any of the mendicant or ascetic Orders. Many legends about him are told at Gokaru in Kānara (*Bombay Gazetteer*, xv, part 2. 290). The story in the Rāmāyana tells that Rāma, mounted on Indra's chariot, slew Rāvana with an arrow forged by Brahmā. Ovington (p. 360) tells the same story: 'The Original of these Holy Mendicants is ascrib'd, according to their Account, to a certain Prince named *Revan*, who quarell'd with *Ram*, a Knowing and Victorious Prince'. Russell, however (*Tribes and Castes, Central Provinces*, iii. 155 f.) describes an Order of Gosāīns, called Rāvanvansī, or 'of the race of Rāvana'. When Rāma left his wife, Sītā, in the forest, Rāvana disguised himself as a beggar and begged alms from her. She told him to come within the magic circle which Rāma had cast round her, but he refused, and induced her to leave the circle, whereupon he seized her and carried her to Lankā or Ceylon. This Order claims descent from him.

[1] The subject of Fakīrs and their austerities attracted much attention from the earlier writers; for example, Ovington, 363 ff.; Mundy, ii. 176 ff; Bernier, 316 ff.; Fryer, i. 257 ff. Though at the present day the clothing of a Fakīr is scanty, absolute nudity is prohibited by the police and municipal regulations.

cows and other animals, which are dried by the sun, and with them they kindle fires. They seldom use wood through fear lest it may contain some living animal which would be killed—that which is used to burn the dead is a kind of drift-wood which does not engender worms. These young Fakīrs, having collected a quantity of these droppings mingled with dry earth, make many large fires according to the size of the troop, and ten or twelve Fakīrs seat themselves around each fire. When sleep overtakes them, they let themselves fall on the ground, upon which they spread ashes to serve as a mattress, and they have only the heavens for a covering. As for those who perform the penances, of which I shall presently speak, when they lie during the night in the same position as one sees them during the day, fires are kindled for them on either side, without which they would be unable to withstand the cold; this will be seen at the end of this chapter in the illustrations which I give of the penances. Wealthy idolaters consider themselves happy, and believe that their houses receive the blessings of heaven, when they have as guests some of these Fakīrs, whom they honour in proportion to their austerity; and the glory of a troop is to have someone in it who performs a notable penance, like those of which I shall hereafter speak.

These troops of Fakīrs assemble in numbers to go on pilgrimage to the principal pagodas, and to the public bathing-fairs which are held on certain days of the year, both in the river Ganges, which they specially esteem, as also in that which separates the territories of the Portuguese at Goa from those of the King of Bījāpur.[1] Some of the most austere Fakīrs dwell in miserable huts near their pagodas, where they are given food, for the love of God, once in every twenty-four hours.

The tree, of which a picture will be seen at the end of this chapter, is of the same kind as that near Gombroon, of which I have given a description in the accounts of Persia.[2] The

[1] The Kistnā, though it may be doubted if the authority of Portugal extended so far to the east and north-east.

[2] Namely the Banyan, *Ficus Indica*, Linn. The reference is to Book V, ch. xxiii, of the *Persian Travels*. See Curzon, *Persia*, ii. 421.

Franks call it the tree of the Banians, because, in places where there are any of these trees, the idolaters sit under them and cook their food there. They reverence them specially, and generally build their pagodas either under or close to one of these great trees. The one which the reader will see depicted further on is at Surat,[1] and in its trunk, which is hollow, a monster is represented like the head of a deformed woman, which is said to be the representation of the first woman, whom they call Mamaniva.[2] Every day a large number of idolaters assemble there to adore this monster, near whose shrine there is constantly some Brāhman detailed for its service, and to receive the offerings of rice, millet, and other grains made to it. On all those who have prayed in the pagoda, both men and women, the Brahman makes a mark on the middle of the forehead with a kind of vermilion, with which the idol is also painted. With this mark on them they do not fear that the devil will injure them, because they are, as they say, under the protection of their God.

I give here the explanation of the figures represented under the tree of the Banians, marked by the numbers 1, 2, 3, etc.[3]

Another example with its numerous stems is the famous Kabīr bar on an island in the Narbadā 12 miles above Broach. At one time it covered an area of 2,000 feet in circumference, and had upwards of 3,250 separate stems. It has afforded shelter to 7,000 men at a time, but is now much reduced in size (Yule, *Hobson-Jobson*, 277). The particular tree at Gombroon referred to by our author is also mentioned by Mandelslo, Valentijn, and della Valle. The Persian name for the tree is lūl. This is a species distinct from the famous Bo tree (*F. religiosa*) of Ceylon, one of which, having a known history, recorded in full detail by Sir Emerson Tennent (*Ceylon*, ii. 613), was planted 288 B.C.

[1] The tree at Surat has frequently been described; Fryer, i. 265; Mundy, ii. 34; and see Yule, *Hobson-Jobson*, 65 ff.

[2] It has been suggested that this word is a corruption of Māriamma, the 'death mother', who, in Southern India, controls epidemic disease (B. Ziegenbalg, *Genealogy of the South Indian Gods*, 138 ff.; G. Oppert, *Original Inhabitants of Bharatavarsa or India*, 471 ff.; B. L. Rice, *Mysore*, 2nd ed. i. 456). But, as the reference is to a goddess at Surat, the term probably represents Mahāmāi, or Māmā Devī, the mother of the gods. But Tavernier, working through an interpreter, confuses names of this kind, not connected with his business. For Māmā Devī see Tod, *Annals of Rajasthan*, ii. 781.

[3] This plate is not reproduced here or in Ball's edition, being rudely drawn and of no great interest or importance.

1. Is the place where the Brāhmans dress up a representation of some one of their idols, as Mamaniva, Sītā, Madedina,[1] and similar images which are very numerous. 2. Is the figure of Mamaniva which is in the pagoda. 3. Is another pagoda close to the preceding. It has a cow at the door, and inside a representation of the god Rāma. 4. Is another pagoda, where Fakīrs betake themselves for penance. 5. Is a fourth pagoda dedicated to Rāma. 6. Is the form of a grave into which several times during the year a Fakīr retires, where he gets no light except through a very small hole. He sometimes remains there nine or ten days without drinking or eating, according to his powers of devotion—a thing which I could not easily have believed if I had not seen it. Curiosity led me to go to see this penitent in company with the Dutch Commander of Surat, who ordered a watch to be set in order to see whether he did not receive something to eat by day or night. The watch were unable to discover that he received any nourishment, and he remained seated like our tailors without changing his position either by day or night. He whom I saw was not able to remain more than seven days out of the ten which he had vowed to spend, because the heat stifled him on account of the lamp in the grave.[2] The other kinds of penance, of which I am about to speak, would still further exceed human belief if thousands of men were not witnesses of them. 7. Is the position of a penitent who has passed many years without ever lying down either by day or night. When he wishes to sleep he leans on a suspended cord, and in that position, which is very strange and inconvenient, the humours descend to the legs, which become thereby

[1] Mahādeva ?—another name for *Shiva*.

[2] Ibn Batuta (ed. Lee, p. 159) speaks of Jogīs who used to allow themselves to be buried for months, or even for a whole year on end, and were afterwards revived, upon which Col. Yule remarks, 'This art, or the profession of it, is not yet extinct in India'. A very curious account of one of its professors will be found in Major-General A. H. E. Boileau's *Personal Narrative of a Tour through the States of Rajwara*: Calcutta, 1837, 41–4. (See *Cathay and the Way Thither*, 413; *post*, p. 173; N. Chevers, *Manual of Medical Jurisprudence in India*, 656; Carpenter, *Human Physiology*, 4th ed. 1103; J. Braid, *Observations on Trance or Human Hybernation*, 1850.)

swollen.[1] 8. These are the positions of two penitents who, till death, keep their arms elevated in the air, so that the joints become so stiff that they are never able to lower them again. Their hair grows below the waist, and their nails equal their fingers in length. Night and day, winter and summer, they remain stark naked in this position, exposed to the rain and heat, and to the stings of mosquitoes, without being able to use their hands to drive them away. With regard to the other necessities of life, as drinking and eating, they have Fakīrs in their company who wait on them as required. 9. Is the position of another penitent, who stands for several hours daily on one foot, holding in his hands a chafing-dish full of fire, upon which he throws the incense which he offers to his god, at the same time fixing his eyes on the sun. 10 and 11. These are the postures of two other penitents, seated, who have their hands elevated in the air. 12. Is the position in which the penitents sleep without ever lowering their arms ; this without doubt is one of the greatest torments which the human body can suffer. 13. Is the position of another penitent, whose weakness has caused his hands to fall behind his back, not being able to lower his arms, which are dried up from lack of nutrition.

There are an infinity of other penitents, some of whom assume positions altogether contrary to the natural attitude of the human body, turning their eyes always towards the sun ; others who have their eyes directed to the ground, without ever looking anyone in the face, or saying a single word ; and the diversity is so great that it would be sufficient to form the subject of a long discourse.

In order to give more satisfaction to the curious, and to enable them to understand matters more distinctly, I shall add here other pictures of these same penitents, which I have drawn, on the spot, after nature. Modesty has compelled me to conceal the parts which they have no shame about exposing to view, for at all times, both in the country and in the towns, they go about altogether as naked as they came from their mothers' wombs ; and although the women

[1] Cf. Bernier, 317 ; M. Monier-Williams, *Brahmanism and Hinduism*, 4th ed. 88.

approach them out of devotion in order to do what cannot be named for shame, you do not see in them any sign of sensuality; but on the contrary, as they pay no attention to anyone, and roll their eyes terribly, you would say they are absorbed in abstraction.

CHAPTER VII

Concerning the belief of the Idolaters touching the condition of the soul of man after death.

It is one of the articles of belief of the idolaters that the souls of men on leaving their bodies after death are presented to God, who, according to the life the owners have led, allots them other bodies to inhabit, so that the same person is several times reborn into the world. And God sends the souls of men of evil life, degraded in their habits and plunged in all kinds of vices, after being separated from the bodies, into the bodies of inferior animals, such as asses, dogs, cats, and others, in order that they may perform penance for their crimes in these infamous prisons. But it is believed that the souls which enter the bodies of cows are supremely happy, because these animals are regarded as divinities. If a man dies with a cow's tail in his hand, that will suffice, it is said, to render him altogether happy in a future life.[1]

As the idolaters believe in this passage of human souls into the bodies of animals, they abhor the slaughter of any kind of animal, through fear of being guilty of the death of some one of their relations or friends who may be doing penance in one of these bodies.[2]

If these men, during their lives, perform virtuous actions, such as pilgrimages and the giving of alms, it is believed that after death their souls pass into the bodies of some powerful

[1] For the doctrine of Metempsychosis or transmigration of souls see Manu, *Laws*, xii. 1 ff.; Dubois, *Hindu Manners*, 556 ff; Mrs. S. Stevenson, *Rites of the Twice-born*, 195 f., 198 f., 225, 436 ff. For notices by early travellers, P. della Valle, i. 79; Ovington, 283 f.; Fryer, i. 95.

[2] The doctrine of Ahimsa, or veneration for animal life, exemplified in Buddhism (V. A. Smith, *Asoka*, 27 ff. E. W. Hopkins, *Religions of India*, 199 f.).

Rājās or other rich persons, who enjoy the pleasures of life as a reward for the good deeds they had done in other bodies.

This is the reason why the Fakīrs, of whom I have spoken in the preceding chapter, perform such horrible penances; and as all men are not able to bring themselves to suffer so much in this world, they seek during their lives to make up by good works for the want of penances, and by their wills direct their heirs to give alms to Brāhmans, to the end that, by the power of the prayers which they order them to say, God may assign them the body of some grand personage. In the month of January of the year 1661 the Shroff or money-changer of the Dutch Company, named Mondās Parek,[1] died at Surat. He was a rich man and very charitable, and bestowed much alms during his life on the Christians as well as on the idolaters; for the Rev. Capuchin Fathers[2] of Surat used to live for a part of the year on the rice, butter, and vegetables which he sent to them. This Banian was ill only for four or five days, and during that time, as well as for eight or ten days after his death, his brothers distributed 9,000 or 10,000 rupees, and burnt his body, adding to the ordinary wood much sandal and aloes, believing that by this means the soul of their brother, on passing into another body, would become a great noble in some other country. There are some among them who are foolish enough to bury their treasures during their lifetime, as, for instance, nearly all the rich men of the Kingdom of Assam, so that if they enter, after death, the body of any poor and miserable mendicant, they can have recourse to the money which they have buried in order to draw from it at necessity.[3] This is the reason why so much gold and silver and so many precious stones are buried in India,[4] and an idolater must be poor indeed

[1] His name was perhaps Mohandās, 'slave of the captivating one', Krishna: pārakh, 'a money-tester'.

[2] Manucci (i. 62) speaks of 'a little church', at Surat, 'belonging to the French Capuchin Fathers, whose superior was the famous priest Brother Ambrozio'. Cf. Fryer, i. 225.

[3] See p. 219 below.

[4] The enormous absorption of gold by India and its disappearance, is explained by many writers in the same way. Bernier, (p. 223) among others may be mentioned, but the subject is too extensive to be entered

if he has no money buried in the earth. I remember one day buying in India, for 600 rupees, an agate cup 6 inches high and of the size of one of our silver plates.[1] The seller assured me that more than forty years had elapsed since it was buried in the earth, and that he preserved it to serve his need after death, as it was a matter of indifference to him whether he buried the cup or the money. On my last voyage I bought from one of these idolaters sixty-two diamonds weighing about 6 grains apiece, and on expressing my astonishment at seeing so fine a parcel, he replied that I need not be surprised seeing that it took nearly fifty years to accumulate them for his wants after death; but his affairs having changed, and having need of money, he had been obliged to dispose of them. These buried treasures were once of great service to the Rājā Sivajī, who took up arms against the Great Mogul and the King of Bījāpur. This Rājā having taken Callian Bondi,[2] a small town of the Kingdom of Bījāpur, by the advice of the Brāhmans, who assured him that he would find a considerable amount of buried treasure, he ordered

on here. See *Imperial Gazetteer*, iii. 269. Not many years ago about £5,000,000 of hoarded treasure, including precious stones, was taken from pits and wells sunk in the palace zenāna at Gwalior.

[1] This was probably of the kind known to the Romans as the Murrhine cups. The custom of roasting the agates to develop the colours doubtless gave rise to the idea that the material was some form of porcelain; while the suggestion that they were made of fluor-spar may be rejected, as that mineral is not known in India, and there is no trace of its ever having been imported or worked by the lapidaries of Western India. But the true Murrhine cups were probably made of fluor-spar (*Ency. Brit.*, x. 578). The writer of the article Murrhina, Murrea Vasa (Smith, *Dict. Greek and Roman Antiquities*, 3rd ed. ii. 181 f.) discusses the various substances from which they have been supposed to have been made, and regards the problem as unsolved. Also see Sir J. Frazer, *Pausanias*, iv. 255. On the modes of working the so-called Cambay stones, agate and carnelian, see Watt, *Commercial Products*, 561 f.

[2] Kalyān in Thānā District, 33 miles north-east of Bombay. Grant Duff (*Hist. of the Mahrattas*, Oxford, 1921, i. 110) states that it formerly belonged to Ahmadnagar and was ceded to Bījāpur under the treaty of 1636. The northern part extended from Bhiundī, the 'Bondī' of Tavernier, to Nagothana in Kolāba District. The other Kalyānā or Kalyāni is situated in the Kulbarga District, Nizām's Dominions. See Bilgrami & Willmott, *Hist. Sketch of the Nizām's Dominions*, ii. 616 ff.; Manucci, iv. 425; Bernier, 24, 28.

it to be partly demolished, and found in fact great riches, with which he supported his army, consisting of more than 30,000 men. It is impossible to disabuse these idolaters of their errors, because they will not listen to reason, and they entirely subordinate their own judgement to their ancient customs, the principal of which is to burn the bodies of the deceased.

CHAPTER VIII

Concerning the Idolaters' custom of burning the bodies of the deceased.

THE custom among the Gentiles of burning bodies after death is very ancient; they generally burn them on the banks of rivers, where they wash the bodies of the deceased to complete the cleansing of those sins from which they have not been purified during life. This superstition goes to such extremes that very often sick persons, when on the point of death, are carried to the margin of a river or tank, and their feet are placed in the water. According as nature fails the body is pushed forwards, and at last it is held by the chin only, so that at the moment when the spirit departs and leaves the body, both the one and the other can be purged of all defilement by plunging the body wholly into the water, after which it is burned in the same place, which is always close to some pagoda.[1] There are people who make it their business to collect wood, and there is a fixed rate of payment for their trouble.[2] When an idolater is dead, all those of his caste or tribe who are in the place assemble at the house of the deceased, and the body having been placed on a litter covered by some fine cloth, according to the station of the deceased and the property which he has left, they accompany it to the place where it is to be burnt, following the litter, which is carried on the shoulders of those appointed for that

[1] For the custom in Bengal see Ward, *The Hindoos*, 2nd ed., i. 192, and Bernier, 315.

[2] For the extortions of the Doms at Benares, who provide fuel for the funeral pyre, see Crooke, *Tribes and Castes, North-West Provinces and Oudh*, ii. 329.

duty. They always proceed chanting some prayers to their god, and calling out Rām! Rām! and, while carrying the body, there is someone who sounds a small bell to give notice to the living to pray for the deceased. The body having arrived at the margin of the river or tank, it is plunged into the water, and afterwards burnt.[1] This is done in three different ways, as I shall describe in the following chapter. According to the wealth of the deceased, more or less sandal-wood or other scented wood is mingled with the ordinary wood which is collected for burning the corpse.

But the idolaters burn not only dead bodies; their cruel superstition goes further, for they also burn the bodies of the living. They make scruple about killing a serpent, and even a bug, yet they regard it as a highly meritorious action to cause a living woman to be burnt in the fire together with the body of her deceased husband.[2]

CHAPTER IX

How the women burn themselves with the bodies of their deceased husbands in India.

It is also an ancient custom among the idolaters of India that on a man dying his widow can never remarry; as soon, therefore, as he is dead she retires to weep for her husband, and some days afterwards her hair is shaved off, and she despoils herself of all the ornaments with which her person was adorned; she removes from her arms and legs the bracelets which her husband had given her, when espousing her, as a sign that she was to be submissive and bound to him, and she remains for the rest of her life without any consideration, and worse than a slave, in the place where previously she was mistress.[3] This miserable condition causes her to detest

[1] For the custom in Kāthiāwār see Mrs. S. Stevenson, *Rites of the Twice-born*, 149.

[2] See a curious case of self-inhumation of a water-carrier woman attendant with her mistress, mother of the Rāo (Mrs. M. Postans, *Cutch*, 72 ff.).

[3] In Gujarāt the widow on the day of her husband's death breaks her bracelets, and has her head shaved on the tenth day; but a young

life, and prefer to ascend a funeral pile to be consumed alive with the body of her deceased husband, rather than be regarded by all the world for the remainder of her days with opprobrium and infamy. Besides this the Brāhmans induce women to hope that by dying in this way, with their husbands, they will live again with them in some other world with more glory and more comfort than they have previously enjoyed. These are the two reasons which make these unhappy women resolve to burn themselves with the bodies of their husbands; to which it should be added that the priests encourage them with the hope that at the moment they are in the fire, before they yield up their souls, Rām will reveal wonderful things to them, and that after the soul has passed through several bodies it will attain to an exalted degree of glory for all eternity.

But it should be remarked that a woman cannot burn herself with the body of her husband without having received permission from the Governor of the place where she dwells, and those Governors who are Musalmāns, hold this dreadful custom of self-destruction in horror, and do not readily give permission.[1] On the other hand, it is only childless widows who can be reproached for not having loved their husbands if they have not had courage to burn themselves after their death, and to whom this want of courage will be for the remainder of their lives a cause of reproach. For widows who have children are not permitted under any circumstances to burn themselves with the bodies of their husbands; and so far from custom obliging them, it is ordained that they

Brāhman widow is allowed to wear her bracelets till she is about thirty years old, and then, when another death occurs in the family, her bracelets are broken, her head is shaved, and she wears the dark dress of a widow (*Bombay Gazetteer*, ix, part i, 50. Mrs. S. Stevenson, *Rites of the Twice-born*, 203).

[1] On Mughal efforts to repress Satī see Ovington, 344; Bernier, 306; Smith, *Akbar, the Great Mogul*, 226. At a later time Sleeman (*Rambles*, 18 ff.) was asked to allow a Satī, and failed to save the woman's life. Akbar prohibited the burning of a widow against her inclination (Smith, *Akbar, the Great Mogul*, 382). The custom was prohibited by the Sikh Gurus, and does not prevail among the Nāmbutirī Brāhmans of Malabar. (M. A. Macauliffe, *The Sikh Religion*, i. Introd. xxii; E. Thurston, *Castes and Tribes of S. India*, v. 189.)

shall live to watch over the education of their children. Those to whom the Governors peremptorily refuse to grant permission to burn themselves pass the remainder of their lives in severe penances and in doing charitable deeds. There are some who frequent the great highways either to boil water with vegetables, and give it as a drink to passers by, or to keep fire always ready to light the pipes of those who desire to smoke tobacco. There are others among them who make a vow to eat nothing but what they find undigested in the droppings of oxen, cows, and buffaloes,[1] and do still more absurd things.

The Governor, seeing that all the remonstrances with women, who are urged to burn themselves even by their relatives and by the Brāhmans, fail to turn them from the damnable resolution which they have taken to die in so cruel a fashion, when his secretary indicates by a sign that he has received a bribe, at length allows them to do what they wish, and in a rage tells all the idolaters who accompany them that they may 'go to the devil'.

Immediately on permission being obtained, all kinds of music are heard, and with the sound of drums, flutes, and other instruments, all go to the house of the deceased, and thence, as I have said, accompany the body to the margin of a river or tank, where it is to be burned.

All the relatives and friends of the widow who desires to die after her husband congratulate her beforehand on the good fortune which she is about to acquire in the other world, and on the glory which all the members of the caste derive from her noble resolution. She dresses herself as for her wedding-day, and is conducted in triumph to the place where she is to be burnt. A great noise is made with instruments of music and the voices of the women who follow, singing hymns to the glory of the unhappy one who is about to die. The Brāhmans accompanying her exhort her to show resolution and courage, and many Europeans believe that in order to remove the fear of that death which man naturally abhors, she is given some kind of drink that takes away her senses and removes all apprehension which the preparations for her

[1] See i. 226 above.

death might occasion.[1] It is for the interest of the Brāhmans that these unhappy women maintain the resolution they have taken to burn themselves, for all the bracelets which they wear, both on arms and legs, with their earrings and rings, belong of right to the Brāhmans, who search for them in the ashes after the women are burnt. According to the station and wealth of the women, the bracelets, earrings, and rings are either of gold or silver ; the poorest wear them of copper and tin ; but as for precious stones, they do not wear them at all when going to be burnt.[2]

I have seen women burnt in three different ways, according to the customs of different countries. In the Kingdom of Gujarāt, and as far as Agra and Delhi, this is how it takes place : On the margin of a river or tank, a kind of small hut, about 12 feet square, is built of reeds and all kinds of faggots, with which some pots of oil and other drugs are placed in order to make it burn quickly. The woman is seated in a half-reclining position in the middle of the hut, her head reposes on a kind of pillow of wood, and she rests her back against a post, to which she is tied by her waist by one of the Brāhmans, for fear lest she should escape on feeling the flame. In this position she holds the dead body of her husband on her knees, chewing betel all the time ; and after having been about half an hour in this condition, the Brāhman who has been by her side in the hut goes outside, and she calls out to the priests to apply the fire ; this the Brāhmans, and the relatives and friends of the woman who are present immediately do, throwing into the fire some pots of oil, so that the woman may suffer less by being quickly consumed. After the bodies have been reduced to ashes, the Brāhmans take what ever is found in the way of melted gold, silver, tin, or copper, derived from the bracelets, earrings, and rings which

[1] Preparations of bhang, or Indian hemp, used to be given for this purpose, but in many cases the excitement alone, in all probability, produced an insensibility to pain. In a case which occurred in Cutch, it was suspected that the woman had been dosed with opium, but when she was examined by two doctors, this was found not to be the case (Mrs. M. Postans, *Cutch*, 65).

[2] For some contemporary accounts see Bowrey, 36 ff., 86, 203 f ; Fryer, i. 95 f., ii. 18, 117.

the woman had on; this belongs to them by right, as I have said.

In the Kingdom of Bengal women are burnt in another manner. A woman in that country must be very poor if she does not come with the body of her husband to the bank of the Ganges to wash it after he is dead, and to bathe herself before being burnt. I have seen them come to the Ganges more than twenty days' journey, the bodies being by that time altogether putrid, and emitting an unbearable odour. There was one of them who came from the north, near the frontiers of the Kingdom of Bhutān, with the body of her husband which she had conveyed in a carriage, and travelled all the way on foot herself, without eating for fifteen or sixteen days, till she arrived at the Ganges, where after washing the body of her husband, which stank horribly, and bathing herself also, she had herself burnt with him with a determination which surprised those who saw it. I was there at the time. As throughout the course of the Ganges, and also in all Bengal, there is but little fuel,[1] these poor women send to beg for wood out of charity to burn themselves with the dead bodies of their husbands. A funeral pile is prepared for them, which is like a bed, with its pillow of small wood and reeds, in which pots of oil and other drugs are placed in order to consume the body quickly. The woman who intends to burn herself, preceded by drums, flutes, and hautboys, and adorned with her most beautiful jewels, comes dancing to the funeral pile, and ascending it she places herself, half-lying, half-seated. Then the body of her husband is laid across her, and all the relatives and friends bring her, one a letter, another a piece of cloth, this one flowers, that one pieces of silver or copper, asking her to give this from me to my mother, or to my brother, or to some relative or friend, whoever the dead person may be whom they have most loved while alive. When the woman sees that they bring her nothing more, she asks those present three times whether they have any more commissions for her, and if they do not reply she wraps all they have brought in a

[1] This remark is of interest as showing that the scarcity of fuel, which is now so much felt, had already been experienced in these regions.

taffeta,[1] which she places between her lap and the back of the body of her dead husband, calling upon the priests to apply fire to the funeral pile. This the Brāhmans and the relatives do simultaneously. There is, as I have remarked, but little wood in the Kingdom of Bengal ; so as soon as these miserable women are dead and half burnt, their bodies are thrown into the Ganges with those of their husbands, where they are eaten by the crocodiles.

I should not forget here an evil custom which is practised among the idolaters of the same Kingdom of Bengal. When a woman is delivered, and the infant, as often happens, is unwilling to take its mother's breast it is carried outside the village and placed in a cloth, which is tied by the four corners to the branches of a tree, and is thus left from morning to evening. In this way the poor infant is exposed to the crows, which torment it, and some have been found whose eyes have been torn out of their heads, which is the reason why many idolaters are seen in Bengal who have but one eye, and others who have both injured or altogether gone. In the evening the infant is taken to try whether it is willing to suckle during the following night, and should it happen that it still refuses the breast, it is taken back on the following day to the same place ; this is done for three days in succession, after which, if the infant is unwilling to take the breast, in the belief that it is a demon, they cast it into the Ganges, or some other river or tank which is nearer at hand. In places where there are many monkeys these poor children are not so exposed to the attacks of crows, for this reason, that as soon as a monkey discovers a nest of these birds he climbs the tree, and throws the nest on one side and the eggs on the other. On the other hand, there are among the English, Dutch, and Portuguese charitable persons who, moved to compassion for the misfortune of these infants, remove them when they are thus exposed and hung in a tree and take care to have them brought up as I have once seen

[1] Pers. *tāfta,* silken or linen cloth ; *tāftan,* 'to shine, twist, spin' ; originally applied to various kinds of silk cloth ; at present various mixtures of silk, wool, cotton. or jute. (*New English Dict.* s.v. ; Yule, *Hobson-Jobson,* 708.)

an example of at Hugly; this is done in the places near their factories.[1]

Let us see now what is the practice along the coast of Coromandel when women are going to be burnt with the bodies of their deceased husbands. A large hole of 9 or 10 feet deep, and 25 or 30 feet square, is dug, into which plenty of wood is thrown, with many drugs to make it burn quickly. When the hole is well heated, the body of the husband is placed on the edge, and then his wife comes dancing, and chewing betel, accompanied by all her relatives and friends, and with the sound of drums and cymbals. The woman then makes three turns round the hole, and at each time she embraces all her relatives and friends. When she completes the third turn the Brāhmans throw the body of the deceased into the fire, and the woman, with her back turned towards the hole, is pushed by the Brāhmans, and falls in backwards. Then all the relatives throw pots of oil and other drugs of that kind, as I have said is elsewhere done, so that the bodies may be the sooner consumed. In the greater part of the same Coromandel coast the woman does not burn herself with the body of her deceased husband, but allows herself to be interred, while alive, with him in a hole which the Brāhmans dig in the ground, about 1 foot deeper than the height of the man or woman. They generally select a sandy spot, and when they have placed the man and woman in the hole, each of their friends fills a basket of sand, and throws it on the bodies until the hole is full and heaped over, half a foot higher than the ground, after which they jump and dance upon it till they are certain that the woman is smothered.[2]

[1] The exposure of children is said to have been a Vedic practice, but it merely meant that the child, if a girl, was laid aside, while a boy was lifted up and acknowledged (Macdonell & Keith, *Vedic Index*, i. 395; ii. 114 f.). Various modes of infanticide are described by Chevers (*Manual of Medical Jurisprudence in India*, 750 ff.). In stating that in Bengal the excess of children blind of one eye is due to exposure, Tavernier exaggerated the case. Blindness in Bengal is largely due to climatic causes—glare and dust (*Census Report, Bengal*, 1901, i. 288; 1911, i. 419).

[2] Thévenot alludes to the custom of burying widows alive, but says that when they were covered with clay up to the neck, they were strangled by the Brāhmans (*Voyages*, 253). This probably gave rise to the tale of Sindbad the Seaman being buried with his dead wife (Burton,

When any of the idolaters of the Coromandel country are on the point of death, their friends do not act like those elsewhere, who carry them to die at the margin of a river or tank, so that their souls when leaving the body may be cleansed of their impurity. They simply carry them into the vicinity of the fattest cow which they are able to find.[1]

. . . . . .

If a cow happens to be sick the owner must lead it to the margin of a tank or river, for should it die in his house the Brāhmans inflict a fine upon him.[2]

CHAPTER X

Remarkable histories of several women who have been burnt after the death of their husbands.

AMONG several examples of this more than barbarous custom of the women of the idolaters of India of burning themselves with the corpses of their husbands, I will relate three remarkable cases, of two of which I was a witness.

A Thousand Nights and a Night, ed. 1893, iv. 381 ff.). Numerous other writers also refer to the custom. As is the case with Satī, this practice is now extinct, but were the restraint removed it is most probable that there would be reversion to both in some parts of India. For this form of Satī by burning in a pit see Fra Paolino da San Bartolomeo, *A Voyage to the East Indies,* trans. W. Johnston, 1800, p. 91 f.; Sleeman, *Rambles,* 19; Caesar Fredericke, in Hakluyt, *Principal Navigations,* Everyman's Library, iii. 214.

[1] The remainder of this passage has been omitted, as the ceremony described is too disgusting for reproduction. This refers to the common use of the Panchagavya, the five sacred products of the cow—milk, curds, butter, urine, dung (Dubois, *Hindu Manners,* 42 f., 152 ff.).

[2] These fines, as described by Ward, were very heavy, sufficient in some cases to cripple a man's resources for the remainder of his life. If one of the Tiyar caste in the Central Provinces kills a cow, he must live in the cowshed for 21 days, lying down when the cows lie down, standing up when they stand up; then he must make a pilgrimage, partake of the five products of a cow, and give a feast to the caste (Russell, *Tribes and Castes,* i. 415). Among the Tellis of Madras, if a cow dies with a rope round its neck, or on the spot where it is tethered, the family must get rid of the pollution by a pilgrimage, or by bathing in a sacred river (Thurston, *Castes and Tribes of Southern India,* vii. 16). See also Fra Paolino da San Bartolomeo, *A Voyage to the East Indies,* 299; F. Buchanan, in Martin, *Eastern India,* ii. 140.

The Rājā of Vellore,[1] of whom I have spoken in the first book of this account of India, having at the same time lost both this town and his life by the victory which the General of the King of Bījāpur gained over him, there was great mourning in all his Court. Eleven of the women of his household were keenly affected by his death, and all resolved to burn themselves when his body was burnt. The General of the Bījāpur army having heard of this resolve, thought that he would be able to dissuade these desperate women by flattering them, and promising them all kinds of good treatment. But seeing that this was of no effect, and that they were absolutely determined to be burnt with the body of the deceased, he directed that they should be kept shut up in a room. He who received this order, on going to execute it, was told by the infuriated women that it was in vain, that he might do his best, but that it was useless to keep them prisoners, and that if they were not allowed to do what they wished, they had resolved that in three hours there would not be one of them left alive. He jeered at this threat, and would not believe that it could be carried into effect. But the officer in charge of the women, on opening the door at the end of three hours, found the eleven all dead and stretched on the ground, without any apparent indications that they had hastened their deaths, either by steel, rope, or poison, nor could anyone see how they had been able to make away with themselves. On this occasion it was assuredly the case that the evil spirit had played his game. Let us pass to another history.

Two of the most powerful Rājās of India, who were brothers came to Agra in the year 1642 to pay their respects to Shāhjahān, who then reigned. As they had not behaved themselves properly on this occasion, in the opinion of the Grand Master of the Emperor's palace, he one day said to one of the two

[1] Velou in the original (see vol. i. 130). This refers to Rāma Rājā, of Vijayanagar, who was defeated at the battle of Talikota, 23rd January 1565, by a confederacy of the Kings of Bījāpur, Bīdar, Ahmadnagar, and Golkonda, and being captured, was beheaded by Husain Nizām Shāh of Ahmadnagar, with his own hands (Smith, *Oxford Hist. of India*, 296 f.). No contemporary account of the Satī, which certainly occurred, has been traced.

Rājās, who were together under the gallery of the palace, in the presence of the Emperor, that this was not the sort of demeanour that should be observed towards so great a monarch as the Emperor his master. As this Rājā regarded himself as a King and a great Prince, and had brought 15,000 or 16,000 horse in his suite with the other Rājā, his brother, he was offended by the boldness the Grand Master showed in reprimanding him in that fashion, and drawing his dagger slew him on the spot, in the presence of the Emperor, who witnessed the deed from an elevated position, where, as I have elsewhere said, he generally administers justice. The Grand Master fell at the feet of his brother, who was close to him, and the latter immediately set himself to avenge his death, but was anticipated by the brother of the Rājā, who stabbed him in the breast with his dagger and flung his dead body on that of the Grand Master. The Emperor, who beheld these two murders, one after the other, was frightened and withdrew into his harem; but forthwith all the Omrahs and other people who were present under the gallery, threw themselves on the two Rājās and cut them to pieces. The Emperor, indignant at such an action being committed in his palace and in his presence, ordered the bodies of the Rājās to be thrown into the river; but as soon as the troops they had left near Agra heard of the affront which was intended to the memory of their Princes, they threatened to enter the city and pillage it; this caused the Emperor, rather than expose the city to this danger, to order that the bodies should be handed over to them. This was done, and the Rājputs were appeased by this means. As they went to burn them they beheld thirteen women of the households of these two Rājās approaching, dancing and leaping, who forthwith encircled the funeral pile, holding one another by the hand, mounted it, and being immediately enveloped in the smoke, which suffocated them, they all fell together into the fire. The Brāhmans then threw upon them a quantity of wood, pots of oil, and other drugs, according to custom, in order that the bodies should be quickly consumed.[1]

[1] This refers to the famous tragedy of the assassination of Salābat Khān in the Palace at Agra, on 5th August 1644. See the narrative, with references, in Tod, *Annals of Rajasthan*, ed. 1920, ii. 976 ff.

I remember another strange occurrence which happened one day in my presence at Patna, a town of Bengal. I was with the Dutch at the house of the Governor of the town, a venerable noble, nearly eighty years old, who commanded 5,000 or 6,000 horse, when a young and very beautiful woman, scarcely more than twenty-two years of age, entered the reception room where we were seated. She, with a firm and resolute voice, required the Governor's permission to burn herself with the body of her deceased husband. The Governor, touched by the youth and beauty of the woman, sought to turn her from her resolution, but seeing that all that he could say was useless, and that she only became more obstinate, and asked him with a bold and courageous voice if he believed that she feared fire; he enquired if she knew any torment equal to fire, and if she had never happened to burn her hand. 'No, no,' this woman then replied to him with more courage than before; 'I do not fear fire in any way, and to make you see that it is so, you have only to order a well-lighted torch to be brought here.' The Governor, horrified at the language of the woman, did not wish to hear more, and dismissing her told her in a rage that she might go to the devil. Some young nobles who were by him asked him to allow them to test the woman and to order a torch to be brought, persuading him that she would not have the courage to burn herself with it. At first he was unwilling to consent, but they continued to urge him the more; so that at length, by his order, a torch was brought, which, in India, is nothing more than a cloth twisted and steeped in oil, and fixed on the end of a stick like a chafing dish; this, which we call a lamp (*fallot*), serves us at need in the crossways of towns. As soon as the woman saw the torch, which was well lighted, she ran in front of it, held her hand firmly in the flame without the least grimace, and pushed in her arm up to the elbow, till it was immediately scorched; this caused horror to all who witnessed the deed, and the Governor commanded the woman to be removed from his presence.

Since we are at Patna I shall relate yet another strange thing which happened there one day in my presence. A Brāhman from outside entered the town, summoned all his tribesmen and told them that they must give him 2,000 rupees and 27 cubits of cloth, which are, as I have said, the ells of this country. The principal among them told him that it was impossible, and that they were poor, but he persisted in his demand to have what he asked, and declared that he would remain there without drinking or eating till they had brought the cloth and the 2,000 rupees. With this resolution he climbed up a tree in the square, seated himself on a forked branch, and remained in this position without eating or drinking for several days. The report of this extravagance reached the ears of the Dutch, with whom I then was, and we gave money to keep men on the watch all night close to the tree, to see if it was true that this man was able to remain for so long a time without eating or drinking, which he did indeed for thirty days. Besides the people whom we had engaged for the purpose, there were more than 100 other witnesses whom his tribesmen had sent, who never moved day or night from the vicinity of the tree. At length, on the thirty-first day of such a surprising and extraordinary fast, the idolaters, fearing that the Brāhman would not be able to hold out longer against hunger, and having a scruple about allowing one of their priests to die for want of that which he asked, taxed themselves all round and took him the 27 ells of cloth and the 2,000 rupees.[1] As soon as the Brahman saw the money and cloth he descended from the tree, reproached all those of the tribe who were present at this spectacle with their want of charity to the poor, and distributed to the poorest the whole sum, reserving only 5 or 6 rupees for himself. He did the same with the cloth, which he cut up into many pieces, keeping for himself only what was sufficient to cover his waist, and when all this was done he disappeared, and in spite of inquiries no one knows what became of him. This

[1] This is what is known in India as sitting Dharnā—to enforce payment of a demand; it is now an offence under the Indian Penal Code. As to the possibility of a man remaining for so long a period without food, India furnishes numerous apparently well authenticated instances. Besides which we have Dr. Tanner's case in America, many in different countries of Europe, and that of McSwiney, Lord Mayor of Cork, who died in Brixton Prison, on 25th October 1920, after 73 days' hunger strike. (See p. 156 above.) On 'sitting Dharnā' see Yule, *Hobson-Jobson*, 315.

ought to show sufficiently that in these matters the work of the devil is manifested.

As there are many Chinese at Batavia, I shall give here an account of a custom which I have observed among these idolaters. When a Chinaman is at the point of death, all the relatives and friends crowd about him, and ask him, with tears, where he wishes to go, that if he wants anything he has only to say so and they will give it to him, be it gold, silver, or women.[1] When death occurs many ceremonies are performed at their funerals; these consist principally in displays of fireworks, in which the Chinese excel all the other nations of the world, for a man must be very poor if something is not expended on them at his death. Moreover, some silver is placed in a small box, which is buried near the deceased, and a quantity of food is placed near the grave in the belief that he will come to eat it. As some soldiers of the garrison are sent out of Batavia every evening to make the circuit of the town during the night, on one occasion they took it into their heads to go to the graves, and ate up that which had been left; this they continued to do for some nights in succession. When the Chinese were aware of this, in order to deter them from returning, on three or four occasions they poisoned the food which they placed on the graves of their dead; this caused a great disturbance in Batavia. The Chinese occupy a leading position in commerce, and are more cunning than the Dutch, but as they are not liked by the people of the town, the latter took the part of the soldiers, and accused the Chinese of having poisoned

[1] This is apparently a version of the custom of placing with the dead articles for their use in the next world. The exact custom in the text has not been traced. See J. J. M. de Groot, *Religious Systems of China*, i. 3 ff.; J. M. Gray, *China*, i. 278 ff. 'The Burials of the Chineses are perform'd with great Ceremony. When a sick Person is at the point of Death, all his Friends and Relations gather about him, and ask him frankly whither he is going, and why he will leave them? Questions very edifying and much to the purpose! They tell him he need only acquaint them what he wants, and assure him very obligingly he shall immediately have all he can ask' (*The Voyage of François Leguat*, Hakluyt Society, ii. 254 f.). Leguat, who speaks contemptuously of Tavernier, may have borrowed this passage from him.

some of them. But they defended themselves from this charge very cleverly, saying, that if greed had caused these soldiers to die from eating the food which had been left on the graves of their dead, they were not responsible, as it was not for the soldiers they had left it, and that till then among the great number whom they had interred not one of the dead persons had ever complained of such a thing; thus nothing more was said about it, and the soldiers dared not meddle with them any further.

CHAPTER XI

Concerning the most celebrated Pagodas of the Idolaters of India.

THE idolaters of India have, both in the towns and country parts, a great number of temples, large and small, called pagodas, where they go to pray to their gods and make offerings; but many of the poor people who dwell in the forests and mountains, far removed from villages, take a stone, and rudely trace a nose and eyes with yellow or red colour upon it, and all the family then worship it.[1]

The four most celebrated pagodas are, Jagannāth, Benares, Muttra, and Tirupati,[2] of each of which I shall give a separate description.

Jagannāth is the name of one of the mouths of the Ganges,[3] upon which the great pagoda is built, where the Great Brāhman, that is to say the High Priest of the idolaters, resides. The form of the choir or interior of this pagoda is as follows: it is similar, in proportion, to all the others, which are built upon the same model, in the form of a cross. The great idol on the altar of the choir[4] has two diamonds for his eyes and

[1] For stone worship in India see Hastings, *Ency. Religion and Ethics*, xi. 871 ff.

[2] Jagrenate, Banarous, Matura, and Tripeti in the original.

[3] The position of Jagannāth is on the sea coast of Orissa, at Purī, which is many miles from the nearest mouth of the Ganges. Bernier, Tavernier's contemporary, was better informed, as in a letter to M. Chapelain he states it was situated on the Gulf of Bengal (p. 304). For an account and plan of the temple see Hunter, *Orissa*, i. 128 and Bowrey, 12 f., who calls it Jno. Gernaet.

[4] Of late years no European has been allowed to enter Jagannāth.

a pendant from his neck which reaches to the waist, and the smallest of these diamonds weighs about 40 carats; he has bracelets on his arms, some being of pearls and some of rubies, and this magnificent idol is called Kesora.[1] The revenues of this great pagoda are sufficient to feed 15,000 or 20,000 pilgrims daily, and these numbers are often to be found there, the pagoda being the object of the highest devotion by the Indians, who visit it from all quarters. It should be remarked that jewellers, who come like others, are not now permitted to enter the pagoda, since one of them intending to steal it, who allowed himself to be shut up during the night, extracted a diamond from one of the eyes of the idol. As he was about to leave in the morning, when the pagoda was opened, this thief, they say, died at the door, and the idol performed this miracle as a punishment for sacrilege. What makes this grand building the principal pagoda in India, is, that it is situated on the Ganges, the idolaters believing that the waters of that river have a special virtue, which cleanses them from defilement when they bathe in it. The great wealth of this pagoda (for it supports upwards of 20,000 cows) depends upon the amount of the offerings made every day by the incredible multitude of people who arrive from all parts. But these alms are not altogether at the discretion of those who give them, as they are fixed by the High Priest, who before granting permission to the pilgrims to shave themselves, to bathe in the Ganges, and do the other things necessary

On the occasion of the late Lord Mayo's last journey, which was cut short by his murder in the Andaman Islands, he had it in contemplation to visit Purī on his return to Calcutta, and a rumour was then abroad that a special concession about entering the temple was to be made in his favour. The temple has been described by Hindus, and in especial detail by Dr. Rajendra Lāla Mitra, in his *Orissa*.

[1] Kesava Rāī, 'he with the flowing locks', or Krishna. The bones of Krishna, who had been killed by a hunter, were placed inside an image, which was never completed owing to the impatience of King Indra, who, however, obtained from Brahma a concession that the idol should become famous as Jagannāth. (Ward, *The Hindoos*, 2nd ed., ii. 163.) The story of the bones of Krishna is based on the veneration of relics in Buddhism, of which many survivals are found in the Vaishnava customs of Jagannāth (Hastings, *Ency. Religion and Ethics*, vii. 464).

in fulfilment of their vows, taxes each one according to his means, of which he is very exactly informed. Thus he receives enormous sums, from which he himself derives no profit, all being expended on the feeding of the poor and the support of the pagoda. The Grand Brāhman distributes each day to the pilgrims whatever food is required, consisting of butter, milk, rice, and flour; but to the poor, who are in want of utensils to cook their food with, it is given read cooked.[1] It is a surprising thing, and well worthy of notice, to observe how the food is distributed to the poor people who have no pots. In the morning the rice is cooked in earthen pots of different sizes, and when the hour has come when the poor pilgrims come for food, if, for example, there are five, the chief Brāhman orders another Brāhman to take a pot full of cooked rice, which he lets fall, and the pot is broken into five equal parts, of which each pilgrim takes one, and likewise in proportion, more or less, according to the number of people who present themselves to receive their shares. The Brāhmans never cook twice in the same earthen pot, but frequently use copper pots, and they have for plates certain leaves larger than our walnut leaves,[2] which are stitched together. They use, however, a kind of dish about a foot in diameter to melt butter, in which they dip the rice with their fingers when eating, and a small ladle for the melted butter, which is drunk as we drink a glass of Spanish wine after a repast.

I come now to a more detailed description of the idol on the altar of the pagoda of Jagannāth. It is covered from the neck to the base with a grand mantle which hangs on the altar, and this mantle is of gold or silver brocade according to the nature of the ceremonies. At first this idol had neither feet nor hands, and this is how this fact is explained. After one of their prophets was taken up into heaven, when they were all plunged in tears and lamentation at losing him, God sent to them from heaven an angel like the prophet, whom they treated with great honour and respect. But while

[1] This is a distorted version of the distribution of the consecrated food to the pilgrims. See Hastings, *op. cit.*, vii. 464 f.; Hunter, i. 146. The same custom prevails at other Vaishnava shrines (Mrs. S. Stevenson, *Rites of the Twice-born*, 317).

[2] See ii. 60 above.

the angel was engaged in making the idol, impatience seized upon them, and they removed it to the pagoda, although, as yet, it was unprovided with feet and hands. But as it was deformed, they made hands for it out of the small pearls which we call 'pearls by the ounce'.[1] As for the feet, they cannot be seen, being concealed under the mantle. There is nothing left uncovered save the hands and face; the head and body are made of sandal wood.[2] Round the elevated dome in which the idol is seated, from the base up to the top, there are many niches containing other images, the majority of which represent hideous monsters made of stone of various colours. On each side of this great pagoda there are others, much smaller, where the pilgrims make their petty offerings, and those who, on account of sickness or in their business, have made a vow to some god, take there an image or semblance of the object in memory of the benefit which they believe they have received.[3] This idol is anointed every day with scented oils which make him quite black. He has on his right hand his sister who is called Sotora, who is also represented standing and clothed; and on his left his brother, also clothed, who is called Balbader.[4] In front of the great idol, somewhat to the left, his wife is to be seen, who is called Kemui,[5] she is of massive gold, and represented standing, the three others are made of sandal wood.

The other two pagodas are intended for the residence of the chief Brāhman, or High Priest, and the other priests who serve in the great pagoda. All these Brāhmans go about with bare heads, and the majority are shaved, having for sole garment a piece of cloth, a part of which is wrapped

[1] Seed pearls, aljofar of the Portuguese. (See p. 93.)

[2] The legend was invented to explain how a rude fetish block, an object of worship by some non-Aryan tribe, became adopted as a form of Vishnu (Hastings, *op. cit.*, vii. 464).

[3] A similar custom is followed in some Catholic countries of Europe; see vol. i, p. 210 above.

[4] The names are Subhadra and Balbhadra or Balarāma. The triple image is said to represent Buddha, his Law and Congregation (see Hastings, *op. cit.*, vii. 464).

[5] The word may represent Kāminī 'an amorous woman', applied to Rādhā, mistress of Krishna.

round the body, and the remainder worn like a scarf. Near the pagoda the tomb of one of their prophets, named Cabir,[1] to whom they do great honour, is to be seen. It should be remarked that all these idols are on a kind of altar surrounded by gratings, for no one is allowed to touch them, with the exception of certain Brāhmans appointed by the High Priest for that purpose.

I come to the pagoda of Benares, which, after that of Jagannāth, is the most famous in all India, and of equal sanctity, being built on the margin of the Ganges,[2] and in the town of which it bears the name. The most remarkable thing about it is that from the door of the pagoda to the river there is a descent by stone steps, where there are at intervals platforms and small, rather dark, chambers, some of which serve as dwellings for the Brāhmans, and others as kitchens where they prepare their food. For after the idolaters have bathed, and have gone to pray and make their offerings in the pagoda, they prepare their food without anyone but themselves touching it, through the fear they have lest anyone who approached it might be unclean. But above all things, they ardently desire to drink the water of the Ganges, because, as soon as they have drunk it, they believe, as I have said, that they are cleansed from all their sins. Every day large numbers of these Brāhmans are to be seen going to the clearest part of the river to fill round, small-mouthed, earthen pots, which hold about a bucketful, with this water. When they are full they are taken to the chief priest, who directs the mouth to be covered with a very fine cloth of fire-colour, in three or four folds, upon which he applies his seal. The Brāhmans carry this water at the end of a stick, flat like a lath, from which hang six small cords, and to each of them one of these pots is attached. They rest themselves by changing the shoulder frequently,

[1] Kabīr, a Saint and writer, flourished about the close of the fifteenth century. (Hastings, *op. cit.*, vii. 632 ff.) It is a corroboration of Tavernier's knowledge that a monastery, called after Kabīr, still exists at Purī (Hunter, *op. cit.*, i. 103).

[2] Here the mistake about Jagannāth, being on the Ganges (see p. 175, *n.*) is repeated, as it is also elsewhere in the following pages.

and they sometimes travel three or four hundred leagues of country with this load,[1] and then sell it, or make a present of it, but only to the richest persons, from whom they expect a liberal reward. Some of these idolaters, when they celebrate any festival—especially when their children are married—drink this water at a cost of 400 or 500 écus. It is drunk only at the end of the repast, as we drink hypocras or muscat in Europe, each guest receiving a cup, or two, according to the liberality of the host. The principal reason why this water of the Ganges is so highly esteemed, is, that it never becomes bad, and engenders no vermin ; but I do not know whether we should believe what is said about this, taking into consideration the number of bodies which are constantly being thrown into the Ganges.[2]

Returning to the pagoda at Benares.[3] The building, like all the other pagodas, is in the figure of a cross, having its four arms equal. In the middle a lofty dome rises like a kind of tower with many sides terminating in a point, and at the end of each arm of the cross another tower rises, which can be ascended from outside. Before reaching the top there are many niches and several balconies, which project to intercept the fresh air ; and all over the tower there are rudely executed figures in relief of various kinds of animals. Under this great dome, and exactly in the middle of the pagoda, there is an altar like a table, of 7 to 8 feet in length, and 5 to 6 wide,

[1] This is what is known as a banghy in India. Men who are accustomed to carrying weights in this way, when on occasion they have only a load for one end, make up an equipoise of a stone or clod of earth for the other. A similar carrying-stick is used in China. Formerly, if not still, troops of these water-carriers were to be seen on the Grand Trunk road, which affords a scene of much animation and interest. Photographs of men carrying water from the Ganges and Nerbudda will be found in Russell, *Tribes and Castes, Central Provinces*, i. 184, ii. 100.

[2] The reader will do well not to believe this story, but rather to conclude that much of the water when drunk is in a very unwholesome condition, and is the cause of disease. At the same time, it is believed that it becomes rapidly purified by oxidation.

[3] The mosque at the Panchgangā Ghāt, the minarets of which overlook the city, occupies the site, and is constructed out of materials of the great temple dedicated to Siva, known as Bisheshar (Visvesvara) and destroyed by orders of Aurangzeb in 1669 (Jadunath Sarkar, *Hist. of Aurangzīb*, iii. 321). Tavernier's account of the original temple is valuable.

with two steps in front, which serve as a footstool, and this footstool is covered with a beautiful tapestry, sometimes of silk and sometimes of gold and silk, according to the solemnity of the rite which is being celebrated. The altar is covered with gold or silver brocade, or some beautiful painted cloth. From outside the pagoda this altar faces you with the idols upon it; for the women and girls must salute it from the outside, as, save only those of a certain tribe, they are not allowed to enter the pagoda. Among the idols on the great altar one stands 5 or 6 feet in height; neither the arms, legs, nor trunk are seen, only the head and neck being visible; all the remainder of the body, down to the altar, is covered by a robe which increases in width below. Sometimes on its neck there is a rich chain of gold, rubies, pearls, or emeralds. This idol has been made in honour and after the likeness of Bainmadou,[1] formerly a great and holy personage among them, whose name they often have on their lips. On the right side of the altar there is also the figure of an animal, or rather of a chimera, seeing that it represents in part an elephant, in part a horse, and in part a mule. It is of massive gold, and is called Garou,[2] no person being allowed to approach it but the Brāhmans. It is said to be the resemblance of the animal which this holy personage rode upon when he was in the world, and that he made long journeys on it, going about to see if the people were doing their duty and not injuring anyone. At the entrance of the pagoda, between the principal door and the great altar, there is to the left a small altar, upon which an idol made of black marble is seated, with the legs crossed, and about two feet high. When I was there, near it, on the left, sat a small boy, son of the chief priest, and all the people who came there threw him pieces of taffeta, or brocade like handkerchiefs, with which he wiped the idol and then returned them to the owners.

1 Benīmādho, Sanskrit *veni*, 'a triple braid', the impersonation of the junction of the three sacred rivers, Ganges, Jamnā and Sarasvatī, at Prayāg, or Allāhābād. Mādhava, 'honey-sweet', is a title of Vishnu or Krishna.

2 Garuda, the mythical bird, vulture, half-man, half-bird, on which Vishnu rides, represented with the head, wings, talons, and beak of an eagle, and the body and limbs of a man.

Others threw him chains made of beads like small nuts, with a naturally sweet scent, which these idolaters wear on their necks and use to repeat their prayers over each bead. Others threw chains of coral or yellow amber, others fruits and flowers. Finally, with everything which is thrown to the chief Brāhmaṇ's child he wipes the idol and makes him kiss it, and afterwards, as I have just said, returns it to the people. This idol is called Morli Ram,[1] that is to say, the God Morli, brother of the idol on the great altar.

Under the principal entrance of the pagoda one of the chief Brāhmans is seated, and close to him is a large dish full of yellow pigment mixed with water. All the poor idolaters one after the other present themselves to him, and he anoints their foreheads with some of this colour, which is continued down between the eyes and on to the end of the nose, then on the arms and in front of the chest; and it is by these marks that those who have bathed in the Ganges are distinguished.[2] Those who bathe only in their houses—for they are all obliged to bathe before eating, and even before cooking—those, I say, who have bathed only in well-water, or in that brought from the river, are not properly purified, and so they cannot be anointed with this colour. It may be remarked that the idolaters, according to their castes, are anointed with different colours; and in the Empire of the Great Mogul, those who are anointed with yellow belong to the most important tribe, and are the least impure. For, when attending to the ordinary necessities of nature, the others content themselves with carrying a pot of water to wash themselves, while these always use a handful of sand, with which they first rub themselves, and then bathe. So they can say their bodies are clean, that no impurity remains, and that they may then take their food without fear.

Adjoining this great pagoda, on the side which faces the setting sun at midsummer, there is a house which serves as

[1] Muralīdhara, Krishna in the form of a flute-player, muralī, 'a flute or pipe'. See an engraving in W. J. Wilkins, *Hindu Mythology*, 186.

[2] The Tilak, or mark characteristic of the Vaishnava sect, is perpendicular; that of the Saivas horizontal. See drawings in Russell, *op. cit.*, ii. 102; *Census Report, Bengal*, 1911, i. 254.

a college, which the Rājā Jai Singh,[1] the most powerful of the idolatrous princes in the Empire of the Great Mogul, has founded for the education of the youth of good families. I saw the children of the Prince, who were being educated there by several Brāhmans, who taught them to read and write in a language which is reserved to the priests of the idols,[2] and is very different from that spoken by the people. Entering the court of this college, being curious to see it, and throwing my eyes upwards, I perceived a double gallery which ran all round it, and in the lower the two Princes were seated, accompanied by many young nobles and numerous Brāhmans, who were making different figures, like those of mathematics, on the ground with chalk. As soon as I entered, the Princes sent to inquire who I was, and having learnt that I was a Frenchman they invited me to ascend, when they asked me many things about Europe, and especially about France. One of the Brāhmans had two globes, which the Dutch had given him, and I pointed out the position of France upon them. After some conversation of this kind they presented me with betel; and before I took leave I asked the Brāhmans at what hour I should be able to see the pagoda open. They told me to come on the following morning a little before sunrise, and I did not fail to be at the house by that time, where the Rājā had built a pagoda on the left of the entrance. In front of the door there is, as it were, a gallery sustained by pillars, where many people were already assembled—men, women, and children—awaiting the opening of the door. When the gallery and a part of the court are full of people, eight Brāhmans approach, four on each side of the door of the pagoda, each carrying a censer; and there are many other Brāhmans who make a great noise with drums and other instruments. The two oldest of the Brāhmans chant a canticle, and all the people, after they have intoned it, repeat it while singing and playing instruments, each one waving a peacock's tail, or other kind of fan, to drive away the flies; so that when the door of the pagoda is opened the

[1] At a later period than this, namely 1693, Jai Singh erected the famous observatory at Benares (Sherring, *Sacred City of the Hindus*, 131 ff.).

[2] Sanskrit.

idol may not be inconvenienced by them. All this fanning and music lasted a good half-hour, when the two principal Brāhmans began to sound two large bells three times, and, with a kind of small mallet, they then knocked at the door. At the same moment it was opened by six Brāhmans, who were inside the pagoda, and 7 or 8 paces from the door there was an altar with an idol upon it, which is called Ram-Kam, who is the sister of Morli Ram.[1] She has on her right a child in the form of Cupid, who is known as the god Lakshmī, and on her left arm she carries a small girl called the goddess Sītā. As soon as the door of the pagoda was opened, and after a large curtain had been drawn, and the people present had seen the idol, all threw themselves on the ground, placing their hands upon their heads and prostrating themselves three times; then rising they threw a quantity of bouquets and chains in form of chaplets, which the Brāhmans placed on the idol, and then returned to the people. An old Brāhman in front of the altar held in his hand a lamp with nine lighted wicks, upon which, from time to time, he threw a kind of incense when moving the lamp towards the idol. All these ceremonies lasted about an hour, after which the people retired, and the pagoda was closed. The people presented the idol with a quantity of rice, flour, butter, oil, and milk, of which the Brāhmans let nothing be lost. As this idol has the form of a woman, all the women invoke her, and regard her as their patron; this is the reason why the temple is always crowded with women and children.

The Rājā desiring to have this idol in the pagoda of his house and to remove it from the great pagoda, has expended in gifts to the Brāhmans and in alms to the poor more than 500,000 rupees, which make 750,000 livres[2] of our money.

On the other side of the street in which this college is

[1] The image of 'Ram-Kam' is that of Annapūrnā, 'she who fills with food', a beneficent goddess, represented as a fair woman, standing on a lotus, holding in one hand a rice bowl, and in the other the spoon with which the rice is stirred when it is being boiled (W. J. Wilkins, *Hindu Mythology*, 265 f.). Tavernier supposed that she was the sister of Muralidhara, Krishna represented as a flute-player. Lakshmī or Srī is the goddess of fortune, consort of Vishnu, and mother of Kāma, god of love, the Cupid of the text.

[2] £56,250.

situated, there is another pagoda called Richourdas,[1] from the name of the idol on the altar inside, and lower down on another small altar is the idol whom they call Goupaldas,[2] brother of this Richourdas. Only the faces of these idols, which are made of stone or wood, are exposed to view. They are black as jet, with the exception of the image of Morli Ram, which is in the great pagoda and is uncovered. As for the idol Ram-Kam, which is in the pagoda of the Rājā, it has two diamonds in the eyes which the Prince has placed there, together with a large necklace of pearls, and a canopy sustained by four silver pillars over its head.

At eight days' journey from Benares, due northwards, is a mountainous country [3] which at intervals has beautiful plains sometimes 2 to 3 leagues wide. They are very fertile, producing corn, rice, and vegetables, but what injures and ruins the people of this country is the abundance of elephants [4] which eat a considerable proportion of the vegetables and grain. If a caravan of travellers passes through this country where there are no caravansarāīs, as they are compelled to camp in the open fields, they have much trouble in defending themselves during the night from the elephants which often come to carry away the food. In order to prevent this the travellers light fires, fire musket-shots, and from time to time some of them cry with all their might, and make a great noise to frighten these animals.

In this country there is another pagoda, well-built and very ancient, and ornamented within and without with many figures, which are representations of girls and women only. Men never go there to worship, and on that account it is called the girls' pagoda. It has an altar in the middle like the other pagodas, and upon this altar there is an idol of massive gold about 4 feet high, which represents a girl, standing, whom they call Ram-Marion.[5] She has on her right an

[1] Ranchhordās, 'he who fled from the battle field', a form of Krishna.

[2] Gopāla, Krishna as a keeper of cows.

[3] Ajodhya, not in the hills, but in the plain of Oudh, on the river Gogra, about 105 miles north of Benares. It is the birthplace of the deified hero, Rāma, and the centre of his cultus (*Imperial Gazetteer*, v. 175 f.).

[4] See p. 205.

[5] Rāmnārāyan, the deified Rāma of Ajodhya. Nārāyana, usually

image of a child, standing, made of massive silver, and nearly 2 feet in height, and it is said that this girl living a holy life, the infant was taken to her by the Brāhmans to learn her creed and how to live well; but at the end of three or four years, during which the child had dwelt with the girl, it became so clever and accomplished that all the Rājās and Princes of the country wished for it, and, at last, one of them carried it off one night and it has not since been seen. This idol has on her left, at the base of the altar, another idol representing an old man, whom they say had been the servant of Rām-Marion and the child, and the Brāhmans pay great reverence to this idol. They come to it only once a year for worship, and it is necessary for them to arrive on a prescribed day, which is the first day of the moon in November, because the pagoda is only opened at full moon.[1] During the fifteen days which intervene all the pilgrims, both men and women, must fast at times, and bathe three times every day, without leaving a single hair on their bodies, all being easily removed by the use of a certain earth with which they rub themselves.[2]

CHAPTER XII

Continuation of the description of the principal Pagodas of the Idolaters of India.

AFTER the pagodas of Jagannāth and Benares, the most considerable used to be that of Muttra,[3] about 18 coss from

interpreted to mean 'he that moves on the waters', really means 'Son of Nara, the Primal Male', in Hindu belief. Tavernier, writing from hearsay, represents the image as that of a goddess.

[1] The reference is perhaps to the Rāmlīlā, or miracle play describing the exploits of Rāma, held from the 8th day of the waning moon of the month Kuār, September–October, until the 15th of the waxing moon. But there is an important local bathing fair in honour of Rāma in October–November (*Imperial Gazetteer*, v., 176).

[2] The reference is to the use of lime and arsenic as depilatories.

[3] Matura in the original. The antiquities of Muttra, or, as it is properly called, Mathurā, have been very fully described by F. S. Growse, *Mathurā*, 3rd ed. Allāhābād, 1883. The temple on the platform described by Tavernier was that of Kesavadeva, Krishna with the long locks, which

Agra, on the road to Delhi. It is one of the most sumptuous buildings in all India, and was visited by the greatest concourse of pilgrims; but at present scarcely any are to be seen there, the idolaters having gradually lost the devotion which they had for this pagoda, since the river Jumnā, which used to pass close to it, has changed its course, and now flows half a league away.[1] For when pilgrims have bathed in the river it takes them too much time to return to the pagoda, and during that period they may encounter something which renders them impure and unclean. Although this pagoda, which is very large, is in a hollow, it is visible from more than 5 or 6 coss distance, the building being very elevated and magnificent. The stones which were used in its construction are of a red colour, and are obtained from a large quarry near Agra. They split like our slates, and some of them, which are 15 feet long and 9 or 10 feet wide, are not 6 fingers in thickness, that is to say, they are split by the quarrymen to the required size; beautiful columns are made of them also. The fortress of Agra, the walls of Jahānābād, the palace of the Emperor, the two mosques, and some houses of the great nobles are built of the same stone.[2]

Returning to the pagoda, it is seated on a great platform of octagonal shape faced with cut stone, around which there are two courses of animals, chiefly monkeys, carved in relief. One of the courses is only 2 feet from the ground floor, and the other 2 feet from the level of the platform. It is reached

was destroyed by Aurangzeb in 1669–70, and a mosque built on the site (Growse, 126 ff.; Jadunath Sarkar, *History of Aurangzib*, iii. 321).

[1] The main channel of the Jumnā can never in historic times have flowed near the temple. The traces of fluvial action are unmistakable, but they date from remote antiquity (Growse, 129).

[2] For an account of these sandstones, which are derived from the Vindhyan formation, reference may be made to the chapter on Building Stones in the *Economic Geology of India*. Tavernier's statements as to the fissile character and the large size of the pieces which can be obtained are quite accurate. One of the most remarkable, though not the most successful uses to which they have been put in modern times is in the manufacture of telegraph-wire posts. Latterly these have been replaced by metal posts. The best quarries are at Fatehpur Sīkrī, in Agra District, and Bansi Pahārpur in Bharatpur State (Watt, *Dict. Economic Products*, vi, part 3, 369 f.; *Imperial Gazetteer*, v. 78, viii. 82; *Āīn-i-Akbarī*, ii. 180 f.).

by two staircases of fifteen or sixteen steps each, the steps being only 2 feet long, so that two persons are unable to ascend side by side. One of these staircases leads to the great gate of the pagoda, and the other behind the choir. But the pagoda occupies scarcely half the platform, the other half serving as a grand area in front. Its form, like those of the other pagodas, is that of a cross, and in the middle there rises a lofty dome, with two others a little smaller at the sides. On the exterior of the building, from base to summit, there are numerous figures of animals such as rams, monkeys, and elephants, carved in stone, and all round are niches containing different monsters. From the foot of each of the three domes up to their summit, at intervals, there are windows from 5 to 6 feet high, and at each a kind of balcony where four persons can sit. Each balcony is covered by a small canopy, and some are sustained by four columns, others by eight, but then they are in pairs and in contact with one another. Around these domes there are also niches full of figures which represent demons, one with four arms, another four legs ; some of them have the heads of men on the bodies of beasts, with horns and long tails which twine round their legs. There are, finally, numerous images of monkeys, and it is a terrible thing to have before the eyes so many ugly representations. The pagoda has but one door, which is very high, and on both sides there are many columns and images of men and monsters. The choir is enclosed by a screen of stone columns 5 to 6 inches in diameter, and no one may enter these except the principal Brāhmans, who have access by a small secret door which I could not see. When I visited this pagoda I asked some Brāhmans who were there if I might see the great Rām Rām, that is to say the great idol. They replied that if I gave them something they would go to ask leave of their Superior ; this they did as soon as I had placed two rupees in their hands. I waited less than half an hour when the Brāhmans opened a door inside the middle of the screen, for on the outside there is none, the screen itself being closed. I saw across it, at about 15 or 16 feet from the door, as it were a square altar covered with a piece of old brocade of gold and silver, and on it the great idol which they call Rām Rām.[1] Only the head, which is of black marble, can be seen, and he has for eyes what appear to be two rubies. All the body from the neck to the feet is covered by a robe of red velvet with some embroidery, and the arms cannot be seen. There are two other idols beside him 2 feet in height or thereabouts ; they are arranged in the same manner, save that they have the faces white, and they are called Becchor.[2] I also saw in this pagoda a machine 15 to 16 feet square and about 12 to 15 feet high, covered with painted calico on which all kinds of demons are represented. This machine was supported on four small wheels, and I was told that it was the car on which their great god is placed at the solemn days when he goes to visit the other gods, and is taken to the river by the people on the occasion of their principal festival.[3]

The fourth pagoda is that of Tirupati,[4] in the province of Carnatic, towards the Coromandel coast and Cape Comorin. I went to see it when I was going from Masulipatam to Gandikota [5] to join the Nawāb Mīr Jumla. It is a large pagoda, surrounded by numerous small ones, and by many dwellings for the Brāhmans ; this makes it appear like a town. It has around it many tanks, and the superstition is so great that a passer-by dare not take water from them unless a Brāhman give it to him.

[1] Kesavadeva, Krishna.

[2] This word represents none of the many names of Krishna and his consorts unless the word is a corruption of Ranchhor (see p. 185 above).

[3] Growse (*op. cit.*, 261) gives a photograph of the great car used at the Seths' temple.

[4] Tripeti in the original ; more correctly it is Tirupati, commonly called Tripatty, in the District of North Arcot. In some respects it is regarded as the most sacred temple in Madras. The principal temple is at Tirumala, 6 miles distant. From all parts of India pilgrims flock there, bearing large offerings with them (*Imperial Gazetteer*, xxiii. 393 f.).

[5] Indecote in the original. In vol. i, p. 217, Tavernier gives his route between Madras and Gandikota when he saw this temple. There he speaks, however, of Courua or Kuruva-bandalu, which is a different place.

CHAPTER XIII

Concerning the pilgrimages of the Idolaters to their Pagodas.

ALL the idolaters who are subjects of the Great Mogul and other Princes on either side of the Ganges at least once in their lives make a pilgrimage to perform their devotions at one of the four pagodas which I have named, and most commonly to that of Jagannāth, it being the principal and most considerable of all. The Brāhmans and rich people make this pilgrimage more than once, some every four years, others every six or every eight years, when they place the idols of their pagodas in litters and accompany their Brāhmans in procession to the pagoda for which they have most reverence ; but it is most frequently, as I have said, to that of Jagannāth, and also to that of Benares, because both are on the Ganges, the water of which is held in special veneration by them.

These pilgrimages[1] are not made as in Europe, by one or two individual pilgrims, but the people of a town or several villages assemble and travel together in company. The poor who come from afar, sometimes 300 or 400 leagues, with all the savings which they have accumulated for that purpose during their lives, are unable to bear the expenses of the journey, and they are assisted by the rich, who expend very great sums in such alms. Each one travels according to his station and means, some in pallankeens or litters, others in carriages ; and the poor, some on foot and others on oxen, the mother carrying her child and the father the cooking utensils.

The god whom they carry in procession[2] from the place they are leaving, to visit and pay his respects to the great Rām Rām, reposes at full length in a rich pallankeen covered with gold brocade with silver fringes, with a mattress and cushion of the same material under his head, feet, and elbows, as we see in the effigies on our tombs. The Brāhmans distri-

[1] On pilgrimages in India see Sleeman, *Rambles*, 588 ff. ; Hastings, *Ency. Religion and Ethics*, x. 24 ff. Pilgrimages are not confined to the four temples described by Tavernier.

[2] See vol. i. 236.

bute among the most important persons in the troop fans with handles 7 or 8 feet long, and covered with plates of gold and silver, the fan being at the end in the form of a kiln-shovel of 2 to 3 feet in diameter, and covered with the same brocade as the pallankeens. It is surrounded with peacock feathers, and makes a great current of air ; to it bells are sometimes attached to give a kind of music,[1] and there are generally five or six of these fans to drive away the flies from the face of the idol ; those who carry them take turns from time to time, like those who carry the pallankeens, so that many may share in this honourable task. This custom should not appear more strange to us than that which I have seen practised in Saxony, and in many other parts of Germany, where, while a funeral oration for a man or a woman is delivered in the church, the body reposes at full length on a bier which is uncovered, and the people on both sides fan it constantly, when it is summer time, to drive away the flies attracted to the face of the deceased, who has then no more power of feeling than an idol.

In the year 1653, on the road from Golkonda to Surat in company with M. d'Ardilière, of whom I have elsewhere spoken, we met near Daulatābād more than 2,000 persons, including men, women, and children, who came from the direction of Tatta [2] with their idol, which they carried in a rich pallankeen, on their way to visit the great idol of the pagoda at Tirupati. The idol was laid on a mattress of red crimson velvet, and the covering and cushions were of the same stuff. The bamboo or stick which served to carry the pallankeen was covered with gold and silver brocade, and no one except the Brāhmans had permission to approach it. We saw this long procession pass, and we could not help

[1] And to scare evil spirits.

[2] M. Joret (*l.c.* p. 131) is probably mistaken in assuming that this occasion of meeting pilgrims is identical with one described in vol. i. 236, which took place in the year 1652 at Emelipata, i. e. Vemulakota, a stage between Gandikota and Golkonda. He adds as a further mistake of Tavernier's that M. d'Ardilière had died before 1653. (See Preface.) As we know that Tavernier went back to Golkonda in 1653, and was in Surat in 1654, he may very possibly have met the pilgrims exactly as he says, when on his return towards the end of 1653.

feeling much compassion for the blindness of these poor people.

[Here are the figures of the most famous idols, which I had the curiosity to have drawn on the spot.[1]]

CHAPTER XIV

Concerning various customs of the Idolaters of India.

THE Brāhmans possess much knowledge of astrology, and know how to predict eclipses of the sun and moon for the people.[2] On the 2nd of July 1666 at one o'clock p.m. an eclipse of the sun was visible at Patna, a town of the Kingdom of Bengal.[3] It was a wonderful sight to watch the multitude of people, men, women, and children, who came from all quarters to bathe in the Ganges. But they must begin this bathing three days before they see the eclipse, during which time they remain day and night on the banks of the river preparing all kinds of rice, milk, and sweetmeats to throw to the fishes and crocodiles. Immediately when the Brāhmans give the word, and they know it is the fortunate hour, whichever kind of eclipse it may be, of the sun or moon, the idolaters break all the earthen vessels used in their households, and

[1] These figures are not given in any of the editions which are accessible. Probably they were never reproduced.

[2] 'The Brachmanes of this Kingdome [Bengal] are great Students of the Magick art, and make their Sorceries more apparent than they of any Other Kingdome in Asia' (Bowrey, 205). Similar accounts will be found in Roe, i. 192; Terry, 236 f.; Fryer, ii. 102; Bernier, 161, 244 f. For modern accounts see A. K. L. Anantha Krishna Iyer, *Cochin Tribes and Castes*, ii. 217 ff.; Russell, *Tribes and Castes, Central Provinces*, iii. 255 ff.; Thurston, *Castes and Tribes, Southern India*, i. 10; Dubois, *Hindu Manners*, 379 ff.

[3] Bernier (p. 300) gives a lively account of eclipse observances at Delhi in 1666. On modern ceremonies see Crooke, *Popular Religion and Folklore of N. India*, i. 21; *Bombay Gazetteer*, ix, part i, 395; Mrs. S. Stevenson, *Rites of the Twice-born*, 351 f. Compare Fryer, i. 275, ii. 306 f. The 'fortunate hour', mentioned by Tavernier, is the Sā'at or Mahūrat. The earthen vessels are broken because they are believed to be defiled by the presence of the demon Rāhu, who causes the eclipse by swallowing the sun or moon.

leave not one piece whole—this causes a terrible noise in a town.

Every Brāhman has his book of magic, in which there are a number of circles and semicircles, of squares and triangles, and many other kinds of figures.[1] They draw divers figures on the ground, and when they perceive that the fortunate hour has arrived they all cry aloud to the people to throw food into the Ganges. Then a terrible noise is made with drums, bells, and large disks made of a metal similar to that of our cymbals, which they strike one against the other; and as soon as the food is thrown into the river all the people should enter and continue rubbing themselves, and bathing until the eclipse is over. As this eclipse appeared at a time when the Ganges is usually very low, after the end of the rains, which last from the month of July to the end of October, for more than 3 leagues above and below the town, and as many as the river extends in width, nothing was to be seen but heads in the water. As for the Brāhmans, they remain on land to receive the richest pilgrims and those who give them most, dry their bodies, and give them fresh clothes to cover their waists. Then they make them sit in chairs, at a place where the richest of the idolaters have brought abundance of Indian corn, rice, and all kinds of vegetables, with milk, butter, sugar, flour, and wood. Before each chair the Brāhman makes a very clean place about 5 or 6 feet square, after which he takes cattle droppings steeped in a great dish of yellow pigment, to rub over all the place, through fear lest some ant might come there and be burnt.[2] If possible their ceremonies are conducted without burning any wood, and for cooking their food they generally use cattle droppings. When they are obliged to use wood they take care that it has no maggots or other insects inside it, as I have elsewhere remarked, because of their belief in the transmigration of souls into different bodies, lest the soul of a relative or friend may be burnt with this small animal. In the place which they have carefully cleaned,
14 they trace many kinds of figures, such as triangles and half

[1] Bernier (p. 244) explains how this book is used.

[2] The true object is to preserve the purity of the enclosures.

triangles, ovals and half ovals, made with powdered chalk. On each figure they place a little cow-dung, with two or three small branches of wood, which they rub well for fear any insect should be present ; and they place on one of the branches wheat, on another rice, on the others vegetables, and all the kinds of food they have. Then they throw on each heap a quantity of butter, and set fire to them, when according to the appearance of the flames they predict whether there will be in that year an abundant harvest of corn, rice, and other products.[1]

At the March full moon there is a solemn festival for the idol in the form of a serpent, of which I have spoken in the first Book of this account of India.[2] This festival lasts nine days, and while it lasts both men and beasts remain idle ; the majority of the latter are ornamented with circles of vermilion around the eyes, with which the horns are also painted, and when any animal is specially loved leaves of tinsel are added. Every morning the idol is worshipped, and the girls dance round it for an hour to the sound of flutes and drums, after which all eat together and enjoy themselves till the evening, when they worship the idol again and dance round it a second time.

Contrary to the usual custom of the idolaters who consume no kind of drink, during this festival they drink palm wine, and, in villages far removed from the great routes, a spirit is made from this wine, because Musalmān governors do not

[1] For the Homa or fire-sacrifice see Monier-Williams, *Brahmanism and Hinduism*, 4th ed. 366 ff. ; Mrs. S. Stevenson, *Rites of the Twice-born*, 225 ff. Omens are taken from the direction in which the smoke rises. This is also done in Northern India in the case of the Holi, or spring fire-festival. See for the rules Crooke, *Rural and Agricultural Glossary, North-West Provinces and Oudh*, 125.

[2] Snake worship. See vol. i. 35. The chief snake festival is the Nāgpanchamī, held on 5th Srāvan (July–August), in the rainy season, when snakes are most dangerous (B. A. Gupte, *Hindu Holidays and Ceremonials*, 2nd ed. 176 ff.). The feast mentioned in the text has not been exactly identified : but in Madras the Nagarapanchamī is held in the beginning of February, to propitiate the cobra (Dubois, 571). Mr. A. L. K. Anantha Krishna Iyer writes that snakes are venerated in Madura and other places in South India in connexion with the worship of Subrahmanya or Kārttikeya, god of war, in the month of Phālgun, February–March.

allow them to distil it, or to sell wine brought from Persia or elsewhere. The spirit is made in this way—In large earthen vessels, glazed inside, which are called martabans,[1] and of different sizes, holding as much as 300 Paris pints of palm wine, they place 50 or 60 pounds of black sugar—unrefined, and looking like yellow wax—with about 20 pounds of a thick black bark of a kind of thorn,[2] very like that which our tanners use in Europe to tan their leather. This bark serves to make the palm wine ferment in four or five days like our new wine, so that the sweetness changes into sourness like that of our wild pears. The whole is then distilled, and, according to the flavour which is desired, they throw into a kettleful either a small bag of cloves, or three or four handfuls of aniseed or mace, large cauldrons serving for the distillation. This spirit can be made of whatever strength is desired. One day, as I had a fancy to distil some for myself, I filled ten of those bottles which come from England, the glass of which is of the thickness of a white crown (écu blanc); they hold each about 4 pints, Paris measure, and are used for wines which it is desired to keep. But during the night the spirit effervesced in the bottles and I found them all cracked in the morning by the strength of the liquor.

When I was at Agra in the year 1642 a somewhat strange thing happened. An idolater called Voldas,[3] who was the Dutch broker, and about seventy years old, received news that the Chief Priest of the pagoda of Mathura was dead. Immediately he went to see the Chief of the Dutch factory to ask him to examine his accounts and close them, because, as he said, their Chief Priest being dead he also wished to die, to serve that holy man in the other world. As soon as

[1] Martavane in the original. This name was given to large vessels of glazed pottery, which were made in Martaban, and thence largely exported. A number of examples of its use will be found in Yule, *Hobson-Jobson*; Dames, *Book of Duarte Barbosa* ed. 1921, vol. ii. 158.

[2] This does not appear to be the common Cutch or Catechu (Acacia catechu); but the gum of *acacia leucophloea*, which is used in distillation (Watt, *Commercial Products*, 15, 759). For methods of distillation see *ibid.*, 1043 ff.

[3] His name may have been Vitthaldās, called after Vitthal or Vithobā, the form of Vishnu worshipped at Pandharpur in Sholāpur District (*Bombay Gazetteer*, xx. 420).

his accounts had been examined he entered his carriage accompanied by some relatives who followed him, and as he had neither eaten nor drunk since he had received the news, he died on the road, refusing to take any food.

The idolaters of India observe this custom, that when any one yawns they crack their fingers, while crying out many times Ginarami,[1] that is to say, remember Narami, who passes among the idolaters as a great saint. This cracking of the fingers is done, it is said, to prevent any evil spirit entering into the body of the yawner.

When I was at Surat in the year 1653 one of the soldiers called Rājputs, who had upon his horse two or three pieces of cloth, was brought before the Governor to be made pay duty on them. The Rājput in a firm tone of voice asked the Governor boldly, if a soldier who had served the Emperor all his life ought to pay duty on two or three miserable pieces of calico which were not worth more than 4 or 5 rupees, and were intended to clothe his wife and children. The Governor, stung by this protest, called him Bethico, that is to say, son of a strumpet,[2] adding that even if he were a Prince he would make him pay the Emperor's due. The soldier, exasperated by this abuse, made as though to take out the money to pay what was demanded, and advancing towards the Governor gave him seven or eight stabs with his dagger in the stomach, from which he died, and the soldier was at once hacked to pieces by the attendants.

Although these idolaters are in the depths of blindness as to a knowledge of the true God, that does not prevent them from leading in many respects, according to nature, moral lives.[3] When married they are rarely unfaithful to

[1] Jai Nārāyan! a name of Vishnu, with the exclamatory prefix Jai! signifying 'victory to'. The custom referred to is well known, its object being to prevent evil spirits taking advantage of the involuntarily open mouth in order to obtain an entrance into the body of the yawner, or that his soul may not escape. See Crooke, *Popular Religion and Folk-lore of N. India*, i. 240; P. Saintyves [M. Nourry], *l'Éternuement et le Baillement dans la Magie, l'Ethnographie, et le Folk-lore Médical*, Paris, 1921.

[2] This is not an exact translation of the term, but may be allowed to pass as such here (Yule, *Hobson-Jobson*, 56). [See Introd.]

[3] Many early travellers give a favourable account of Hindu morals,

their wives, adultery is very rare among them, and one never hears unnatural crime spoken of.[1] They marry their children at the age of seven or eight years, through fear lest they should abandon themselves to this crime. And, in a few words, these are the ceremonies which are observed at their marriages. On the eve of the nuptials the bridegroom, accompanied by all his relatives, goes to the house of the bride with a pair of large bracelets two fingers in thickness, but hollow inside, and in two pieces, with a hinge in the middle to open them by. According to the wealth of the bridegroom these bracelets are more or less costly, being of gold, silver, brass, or tin,[2] those of the poorest being of lead only. When the bridegroom arrives, he places one of these bracelets on each leg of his bride, to indicate that he holds her thenceforward enchained, and that she can never leave him. On the morrow the feast is prepared in the house of the bridegroom, where all the relatives on either side are present, and at 3 p.m. the bride is brought.[3] Several Brāhmans are present, and their Chief makes the head of the bridegroom touch that of the bride, and pronounces several words while he sprinkles water on their heads and bodies. Then on plates or on large leaves of the fig tree [4] many kinds of food and pieces of stuff and calico are brought. The Brāhman asks the bridegroom if what God gives to him he will share with his wife, and if he will strive to support her by his labour. When he has said 'yes,' all the guests seat themselves at the feast which has been prepared for them, and each one eats apart. According to the wealth of the bridegroom and the credit he enjoys with great persons, the nuptials

as Friar Jordanus, *Wonders of the East*, 22; Marco Polo, ii. 303. Max Müller has made a large collection of similar evidence (*India, What can it teach us?* ed. 1905, p. 34 ff.). Both sides of the question are discussed in *Bombay Gazetteer*, ix, part i, 78.

[1] This testimony as regards homosexual practices is very different from that given by some other writers of the same period as Tavernier, who himself describes cases (vol. i, pp. 44, 100). See Fryer, i. 245; Linschoten, i. 100; Dubois, 311; Grose, 219; Chevers, *Handbook of Medical Jurisprudence*, 705 ff.; Russell, *Tribes and Castes, Central Provinces*, iii. 209 ff.

[2] Leton and estain in the original.

[3] For the rites among Brāhmans see Mrs. S. Stevenson, *Rites of the Twice-born*, 46 ff.

[4] The plantain (vol. i. 197, and vol. ii. 3).

are celebrated with pomp and great expenditure. He is seated on an elephant and his bride in a carriage, all who accompany them bearing torches in their hands. He borrows, moreover, for this ceremony from the Governor of the place and from other great nobles among his friends as many elephants as he can, together with show horses, and they march about thus for a part of the night with fireworks, which are exploded in the streets and open spaces. But the chief outlay is on Ganges water,[1] for those who are sometimes 300 or 400 leagues distant from the river; as this water is considered sacred, and drunk from religious motives, it has to be brought from a great distance by the Brāhmans in earthen vessels glazed inside, which the Grand Brāhman of Jagannāth has himself filled with the cleanest water in the river,[2] and has marked with his own seal. This water is not given except at the end of the repast, as I have said before; for each of the guests three or four cupfuls are poured out, and the more of it the bridegroom gives them to drink the more generous and magnificent he is esteemed. As this water comes from so far, and the Chief Brāhman charges a tax on each pot, which is round and holds about as much as one of our buckets, there is sometimes 2,000 or 3,000 rupees worth of it consumed at a wedding.[3]

On the 8th of April, when I was in Bengal at a town called Mālda,[4] the idolaters made a great feast which is peculiar to the inhabitants of that place. They all leave the town and attach hooks of iron to the branches of trees, to which many of these poor people hook themselves, some by the sides and others by the middle of the back. These hooks enter their bodies, and they remain suspended, some for an hour and others for two, till the weight of the body drags the flesh, when they are compelled to retire.[5] It is a surprising

[1] See vol. ii. 180. [2] See vol. ii. 179.

[3] Ganges water is used as a means of purification, more usually at funeral than at marriage rites.

[4] Malde in the original. See vol. i. 110. Mālda is a well-known town at the junction of the Kālindrī and Mahānadī rivers in the district of the same name in Bengal. Formerly it was a port and centre of manufactures, but is not now important. (*Imperial Gazetteer*, xvii. 82.)

[5] This is the so-called Charakh pūjā or swinging festival, now forbidden

thing not to see a drop of blood come from this cut flesh, and not to see a sign of it even on the hook, and in two days they are entirely cured by the drugs which the Brāhmans give them. There are others at this festival who make beds for themselves with points of iron and lie upon them; these points enter deep into the flesh, and while both are doing these penances their relatives and friends bring them presents, such as betel, money, or pieces of calico. When the penance is finished the penitent takes all these presents and distributes them to the poor, not wishing to profit by them himself.[1] I asked some of these people why they gave this feast and underwent this penance, and they said it was in memory of the first man, whom they called Adam like us.[2]

I shall relate also an example of a strange kind of penance which I saw when sailing up the Ganges on the 12th of May 1666. A clean place on the margin of the river had been prepared, in which one of these poor idolaters was condemned to place himself on the ground many times during the day, supported only on his hands and feet, and to kiss the ground three times before rising, without daring to touch it with the rest of his body. When he rose it was necessary for him to do so on the left foot, with the right foot in the air, and every morning during a whole month, before drinking or eating, he was obliged to place himself in this position fifty times in succession, and kiss the ground one hundred and fifty times. I was told that the Brāhmans had inflicted this penance on him for having allowed a cow to die in his house, not having taken it to the margin of the water according to custom, in order that it might be bathed while dying.[3]

in British India. On one occasion, in the Rājmahāl hills, a deputation of Santāls waited on Ball to ask for his intercession with the Government to permit its revival, on the ground that their neglected deities, out of revenge, caused injury to their families and flocks. See a full account of the rite by J. H. Powell, *Folk-Lore*, xxv. 147 ff., with photographs. It is not peculiar to the Mālda District. On swinging as a magical rite see Frazer, *The Golden Bough*, The Dying God, 277 ff.

[1] For the penance of lying on a spiked bed see Crooke, *Popular Religion and Folk-lore*, i. 92; *Id.*, *The People of Northern India*, 128; Greaves, *Kashi*, 54, with photographs.

[2] Tod (*Annals of Rajasthan*, iii. 1754) heard a Rājput call Siva-Mahādeva Bābā, or Father, Adam.

[3] See vol. ii. 169.

Here is yet another rather curious custom. When an idolater loses a coin or a sum of gold, be it by mistake or that he has been robbed, he is bound to take as much as he has lost to the Chief Brāhman, and if he does not do so and it gets known he is driven with ignominy out of his caste, through policy, to make people careful.[1]

Beyond the Ganges, northwards, towards the mountains of Nagarkot,[2] there are two or three Rājās who, like their people, believe neither in God nor devil. Their Brāhmans have a certain book which contains their creed, and which is only filled with rubbish for which the author, who is called Baudou, gives no reason.[3] These Princes are vassals of the Great Mogul and pay tribute to him.

Finally, as a last remark and to finish this chapter, I may say that the Malabaris in general carefully preserve the nails of their left hands, and allow their hair to grow like that of a woman. Their nails, which are sometimes half a finger long, serve them as combs, indeed they have no others, and it is with this left hand also that they perform all impure duties, never touching their faces nor that which they eat save only with the right hand.[4] I now come to some remarks

[1] Dr. L. D. Barnett and Mr. S. K. Chatterjī have kindly inquired into this custom, of which they have found no corroboration. It seems to be based on a misunderstanding.

[2] Naugrocot in the original. Nagarkot is to a certain extent synonymous with Kāngrā, the capital of which is situated on the Rāvi Bāngangā Torrent. The name in many early travels indicates the mountainous region of the N.W. Himalayas. See *Āīn-i-Akbarī*, ii. 312 f.

[3] This is rather an unceremonious way of discussing the tenets of Buddhism. The Buddhists form a comparatively small part of the population of Kāngrā at present. For Buddhism in the Panjāb hills see Rose, *Glossary, Tribes and Castes Panjāb and N. W. Frontier Province*, 166 ff.; *Census Report, Panjāb*, 1911, i. 192.

[4] The Nāyars of Malabar let their nails grow, according to Linschoten, (i. 282) to show that they are 'gentlemen' and do not engage in manual labour. As is well known, the Chinese do so likewise, for the same reason. Alberuni (*India*, i. 180) erroneously notes it as a general custom. The Nambūtiri Brāhmans of Malabar grow their nails more than a foot long, 'which serve several useful purposes' (Thurston, *Castes and Tribes of Southern India*, v. 169). Compare the Chinese customs (J. F. Davis, *The Chinese*, i. 267 f.; S. W. Williams, *The Middle Kingdom*, 4th ed., ii. 38).

which I have made in my journeys regarding kingdoms which lie to the north-east of the territories of the Great Mogul, as those of Bhutān, Tippera, Assam, and Siam, of which I believe that we Europeans have not much knowledge; and I would also speak of the Kingdom of Tonquin,[1] if I did not know that two different authors have filled two volumes with it.

CHAPTER XV

Concerning the Kingdom of Bhutān, whence comes musk, good rhubarb, and some furs.

THE Kingdom of Bhutān is of very wide extent, but we have not been able to acquire an exact knowledge of it as yet.[2] This is what I have ascertained during several journeys in India, from people of the country who come from there to trade; but I was better informed regarding it on the last occasion than I had been previously, as I was at Patna, the largest town in Bengal and the most famous for trade—at the time that the merchants of Bhutān arrive to sell their musk. During the two months I spent there I bought to the extent of 26,000 rupees worth of musk, an once (Fr.) in the capsule costing me 4 livres and 4 sols of our money, and out of the capsule at the rate of 8 francs,[3] and were it not for the custom duties which have to be paid in India, as well as in Europe, there would be a great profit to be made on it. The best kind of rhubarb[4] also comes from the Kingdom of Bhutān; the same country produces also the seed which yields worm powder,[5] and other kinds of drugs, and from

[1] In his third volume Tavernier gives an account of Tonquin, or Tunquin as he calls it. In the opinion of some critics it is very inaccurate. See S. Baron, *A Description of the Kingdom of Tonqueen*, in J. Pinkerton, *A General Collection of Voyages and Travels*, ix. 656 ff., who criticizes some of Tavernier's statements.

[2] For a full account of Bhutān see *Imperial Gazetteer*, viii. 154. The name is derived from Sanskrit Bhotānta, 'the end of Bhot or Bod', Tibet (L. A. Waddell, *Buddhism of Tibet*, 44).

[3] See vol. ii. 115 for another account of this purchase, and a comparison showing the discrepancy. Here for francs we should probably read livres.

[4] See p. 203 *post*.

[5] This is probably a species of *Artemisia*—*A. maritima* (Watt,

thence also beautiful furs are brought. But as for rhubarb, you risk much in its carriage, by whatever road you take it; for if you go by the north towards Kābul the damp spoils it, and if you take the southern direction, as the way is long, the rains which may supervene are still more to be feared, so that there is no kind of merchandise which is more likely to be spoilt, and requires more care than it does.

As for musk, during the hot season the merchant does not make any profit by it, because it becomes dry and loses weight. Upon this article 25 per cent. duty has generally to be paid at Gorakhpur,[1] the frontier town of the territories of the Great Mogul in the direction of the Kingdom of Bhutān,[2] although they extend 5 or 6 leagues farther. When Indian merchants arrive in that town they call on the customs officer, and tell him that they are going to the Kingdom of Bhutān, one to buy musk, another rhubarb, and they make declarations of the sums which they intend to expend, these the customs officer enters in his register with the names of the merchants. Then the merchants, instead of 25 per cent., which they ought to pay, agree for 7 or 8 per cent., and take a certificate from the customs officer or the Kāzī,[3] so that on their return they may not be asked for any more. If it should happen that they are unable to obtain a fair composition from the customs officer, they take a different road, which is both very long and very difficult, as the mountains are nearly always covered with snow, and in the level country

Commercial Products, 93. It is the *Flores cinæ*, or *Semen cinæ*, or *Santonica* of the pharmacopœias. Most of it which reaches Europe comes through Russia, but the drug now to be found in Indian bazars is similar, consisting of the small unopened flower heads. It is found in great abundance on the steppes of the Kirghiz, in the northern part of Turkestan. (See *Pharmacographia*, by Hanbury and Flückiger. London, 1874.)

[1] Gorrochepour in the original. Gorakhpur is the chief town of the District of the same name in the United Provinces of Agra and Oudh. It adjoins Nepāl on the north, through which territory the merchants travelled to Bhutān.

[2] This geographical indication is not correct, as Northern Bengal lies nearer to Bhutān; but it is evident from other references that Tavernier's knowledge of the extent and position of Bhutān was vague.

[3] For the Kāzī, a State minister in the Himalayan Kingdoms, see Yule, *Hobson-Jobson*, 475.

there are vast deserts to be crossed. They have to go up to the 60th degree of latitude, and then they turn towards the west to Kābul,[1] which is at the 40th, and it is in that town that the caravan divides, one portion going to Balkh,[2] and the other to Great Tartary. It is where those who come from Bhutān barter their goods for horses, mules, and camels, for there is little money in these countries. Then these Tartars carry their goods into Persia, to Ardabīl,[3] and Tabrīz; this it is which makes Europeans believe that rhubarb and the seeds (*semencine*)[4] come from Tartary. It is quite true that rhubarb comes from thence, but it is not nearly so good as that which comes from the Kingdom of Bhutān, as it is much more tainted, rhubarb being subject to decay at the heart. The Tartars carry away from Persia silken stuffs of small value which are made at Tabrīz and Ardabīl, and some English and Dutch cloths which the Armenians bring from Constantinople and Smyrna, whither they are brought from Europe. Those merchants who come from Bhutān and Kābul go to Kandahār and on to Ispahān, and they generally take back coral beads, yellow amber, and lapis wrought into beads when they can obtain them. The other merchants, returning from the regions about Multān, Lahore, and Agra, take calicoes, indigo, and an abundance of carnelian and

[1] That they travelled so far north as the 60th degree is most improbable. That there was a northern route is well known, however. The true latitude of Kābul (Caboul) is only 34° 21′.

[2] Balch in the original. Balkh is an ancient city of Turkestan, south of the Oxus. (See vol. i. 75 *n.*)

[3] Ardeüil in the original. Ardabīl is near the Caspian, in the rugged northern province of Persia called Azarbaijān, wherein Tabrīz is also included.

[4] See *ante*, p. 201. Commercial rhubarb, known as Chinese and East Indian, is said to be obtained from Rheum officinale and R. palmatum, which grow in South-east Tibet and North-West China (Watt, *Commercial Products*, 912 f.) Nishapur, in North Persia, is also famous for its rhubarb. Sir P. Sykes (*Hist. of Persia*, ii. 20) quotes a verse by Ya'qūb:

'Its stones are turquoises, its bushes rhubarb,
And its dust edible clay. How could I leave such a land?'

Barbosa names rhubarb as one of the products of Malabar, but his editor, Dames, suggests that it came from China via Malacca (i. 93, f., ii. 230).

crystal beads. Finally, those who return by Gorakhpur, and have an understanding with the customs officer, take from Patna and Dacca coral, yellow amber, tortoise-shell bracelets, and others of sea shells,[1] with numerous round and square pieces of the size of our 15-sol coins, which are also of the same tortoise-shell and sea shells. When I was at Patna four Armenians, who had previously made a journey to the Kingdom of Bhutān, came from Dantzic, where they had had made numerous images of yellow amber, which represented all kinds of animals and monsters; these they were taking to the King of Bhutān to place in his pagodas, he being, like his people, exceedingly idolatrous. Wherever the Armenians see that money is to be made they have no scruple about supplying materials for the purposes of idolatry,[2] and they told me that if they had been able to get an idol made which the King had ordered from them they would have been enriched. It was a head in the form of a monster, which had six horns, four ears, and four arms, with six fingers on each hand, the whole to be of yellow amber,[3] but the Armenians could not find sufficiently large pieces for the purpose. I was inclined to believe that they lacked money, for it did not appear that they had much of it; it is, however, an infamous trade to furnish the instruments of idolatry to these poor people.[4]

Coming now to the road which must be followed from

[1] For the Chank or Conch fishery and industry see J. Hornell, *The Sacred Chank of India*, Madras, 1914: Watt, *op. cit.*, 989.

[2] Ball notes that 'Bohemia, it is said, at present sends idols made of cast glass to India, which undersell the marble images of Agra.'

[3] Huge pieces of amber were employed in the manufacture of the boxes made in the shape of geese included in the King of Burma's treasure, which is in the South Kensington Museum. It has been stated that the largest piece of amber ever known was recently discovered near the Nobis Gate at Altona. It weighed 850 grammes. Dr. Meyer of Dresden (*Nature*, 29th November 1888), commenting on this, says that besides smaller pieces, elsewhere, there are specimens in the Berlin Mineralogical Museum weighing 6·5 and 9·5 kilogrammes; they were obtained on the sea-coast of North Germany.

[4] For an example of a form of trade equally disgraceful see A. Hamilton, *New Account of the East Indies*, in Pinkertom, *Voyages and Travels*, viii. 439.

Patna to the Kingdom of Bhutān, upon which the caravan spends three months.[1] It leaves Patna generally at the end of December and arrives on the eighth day at Gorakhpur, which, as I have said, is the last town in this direction in the territories of the Great Mogul, where the merchants obtain their supplies for a portion of the journey. From Gorakhpur to the foot of the high mountains there are still eight or nine days' marching, during which the caravan suffers much, because the whole country is full of forests, where there are numerous wild elephants,[2] and the merchants instead of sleeping at night must remain on the watch, making large fires and firing their muskets to frighten these animals. As the elephant moves without noise, he takes the people by surprise, and is close to the caravan before they are aware of it. He does not intend to do injury to man, for he contents himself with carrying off whatever food he can seize, a sack of rice or flour, or a pot of butter, of which there is always a large supply. One can go from Patna to the foot of these mountains in Indian carriages or pallankeens, but oxen, camels, or the horses of the country are generally used. These horses are by nature so small that when a man is upon them his feet nearly touch the ground, but they are otherwise strong, and go at an amble, doing up to 20 leagues at a stretch, and eating and drinking but little. There are some of them which cost as much as 200 écus,[3] and when you enter the mountains you can only use that means of carriage, it being necessary to leave all the others behind, which become useless on account of the numerous and very narrow passes. The horses even, though strong and small, often have difficulty in getting through, and it is for this reason, as I shall presently

[1] Three months is a long time for the journey to have lasted between Patna and any portion of Bhutān territory, as now known. The Bhutān of Tavernier seems to have included Lhassa.

[2] The Tarāī. It was in a part of this region that the Prince of Wales, afterwards King Edward VII, took part in the elephant captures arranged for him by Sir Jang Bahādur.

[3] £45, a very high price indeed for a country pony in Ball's day. These hill ponies, known as Gūnth, or Tāngan, stand usually about 13 hands high, are short-bodied, clean-limbed, deep in the chest, and extremely active and sure-footed (Yule, *Hobson-Jobson*, 387, 898).

say, that one has recourse to other expedients for traversing these lofty mountains.

At 5 or 6 leagues beyond Gorakhpur you enter the territories of the Rājā of Nepāl,[1] which extend to the frontiers of the Kingdom of Bhutān. This Prince is a vassal of the Great Mogul, and sends him an elephant every year as tribute.[2] He resides in the town of Nepāl, of which he bears the name, and there is very little trade or money in his country, as it consists of forests and mountains.

The caravan having arrived at the foot of the high mountains, known to-day by the name of Nagarkot,[3] which cannot be crossed in less than nine or ten days, as they are very high and narrow, with great precipices,—many people come from different places, the majority being women and girls, who strike a bargain with the people of the caravan, to carry the men, goods, and provisions to the other side of the mountains. This is the method by which they carry them. The women have a strap on the shoulders to which a large cushion hanging on the back is attached; upon it the man seats himself.[4] It takes three women, who change in turns, to carry a man; and as for the baggage and provisions, they are loaded on goats which carry up to 150 livres weight each. Those who desire to take horses into these mountains are often obliged, in the narrow and difficult passes, to haul them up with ropes; and it is, as I have said, on account of this difficulty that but little use is made of horses in this

[1] See p. 202 *n*. It is Nupal in the original.

[2] The finest elephant Ball ever saw he met on its way down the Grand Trunk Road to Calcutta from Nepāl. It was a gift from Sir Jang Bahādur to Lord Mayo. If the Mughals claimed suzerainty over Nepāl, it was of a very shadowy kind. The capital of Nepāl is Kathmāndū. The finest elephant Sir S. W. Baker ever saw belonged to the Rājā of Nandgaon in the Central Provinces. A perfect elephant should be 9 feet 6 inches high at the shoulder: Baker gives the other points. (*Wild Beasts and their Ways*, 44.)

[3] See p. 200, *n*. This takes us to the Panjāb hills, a long way from the Gorakhpur route.

[4] In some parts of the Himalayas women still offer themselves for carrying travellers on their backs. But in Kāngrā the practice seems to have ceased, though the women are so strong that one of them is said to have carried a grand piano up the hill.

country. They are fed only in the morning and evening. In the morning a pound of flour, half a pound of black sugar and half a pound of butter, are mixed together with water for the horse. In the evening it must be contented with a few horn peas,[1] crushed and steeped in water for half an hour; this is all their food during the space of twenty-four hours. The women who carry the men receive only 2 rupees each, for the ten days of the journey, and as much is paid for every quintal[2] that the goats or sheep carry, and for every led horse.

After passing these mountains, for carriage to Bhutān, oxen, camels, and horses, and even pallankeens[3] are procurable for those who wish to travel more at their ease. The country is good, and produces corn, rice, vegetables, and wine in abundance. All the people, both men and women, are clad during the summer in coarse cotton or hempen cloth, and during the winter in a thick cloth like felt. The headdress for both sexes is a cap made very like those English caps which they call bouquin-kans,[4] and it has pigs' teeth around it for ornament, with round and square pieces of tortoise-shell of the size of one of our 15-sol coins; the richest add to them beads of coral or yellow amber, of which the women also make necklaces. The men, like the women, wear bracelets only on the left arms, and from the wrist to the elbow. Those worn by the women are very narrow, but those of the men are two fingers wide. They wear a silken cord on the neck, to which a bead of coral[5] or yellow amber is suspended, or a pig's tooth, which hangs down to the waist; and on their

[1] 'd'un peu de poids cornus,' i. e. gram, cicer arietinum.

[2] Quintal, Arabic qintār, 100 lb.

[3] Probably a modified form of pallankeen, or dooly, suitable for hill travelling.

[4] We have not found a full explanation of the term. Bouquin means an old book-cover. The caps of felt worn in these regions are somewhat similar to what used to be called 'pork pie' hats a few years ago in England. C. A. Sherring (*Western Tibet and the British Borderland*, 1906) does not mention the use of pigs' teeth as ornaments, but they are worn in Assam (p. 223 below).

[5] Tibetan women wear silver disks on the sides and back of their heads, 'and all were loaded with coral and sham or real turquoise' (W. Gill, *The River of Golden Sand*, 201).

left side they have bands from which more of these same beads of coral, amber, or pigs' teeth hang in strings. Although they are great idolaters they eat all kinds of meat, except that of the cow, which they worship as the mother and nurse of all men, and they are very fond of spirits. They also observe some of the Chinese ceremonies; for, after having fed their friends, when the repast is finished they burn yellow amber, although they do not worship fire like the Chinese. I have elsewhere given the reason why the Chinese burn amber at the conclusion of their feasts;[1] this causes this article to have a good sale in China. In Patna, even, pieces of yellow amber which are not worked, of the size of a good nut, clear and of good colour, are bought by these Bhutān merchants at 35 and 40 rupees the ser, and the ser, both for amber, as also for ambergris, musk, coral, rhubarb, and other drugs, is equal to 9 onces (Fr.) of our weight. Saltpetre, corn, rice, sugar, and other articles of food, are also sold by sers in Bengal; but this ser is 72 of our livres at 16 onces to the livre, and 40 sers make a maund, which would amount to 2,880 livres weight of Paris.[2] When I left that country the maund of rice was selling for 2 rupees.

To return to the yellow amber, for a piece of a ser or 9 onces (Fr.) weight, according to its colour and beauty, from 250 to 300 rupees is paid, and the other pieces cost the same in proportion to their size and beauty.[3] Coral in the rough or worked into beads is saleable with sufficient profit, but the rough is much preferred, for this reason, that it can be cut according to their own fashion; and most frequently women and girls are employed at this work. They also make beads of crystal and agate, and the men bracelets of tortoise-shell and sea shells, as also those small pieces of the same shell, both round and square, of which I have spoken above.[4] All

[1] See vol. ii. 108.

[2] This is an extraordinary jumble of figures. A ser of 72 livres, 40 of which went to the maund, making a maund of 2,880 livres, is surely due to a copyist's mistake. It is possible that a Bengal maund of 40 sers may have been equal to 72 livres, or more than double the Surat maund of 40 smaller sers = 34 livres (see vol. i. 334), but the statement as it stands is clearly wrong.

[3] See vol. ii. 108.

[4] See vol. ii. 204.

the people of the north, men, women, girls, and boys, suspend them from their hair and ears. There are in Patna and Dacca more than 2,000 persons who occupy themselves with these trades, all that is produced by them being exported to the Kingdoms of Bhutān, Assam, Siam, and other countries to the north and east of the territories of the Great Mogul.[1]

As for the semencine,[2] or worm powder, it cannot be harvested like other grains. It is a herb which grows in the fields, and must be allowed to die, and the evil is that when it approaches maturity the wind causes a great part to fall among the herbage, where it is lost, and it is this which makes it so dear. As it cannot be touched by the hand, because it would thereby be quickly spoilt, and even when taking a sample, it is collected in a porringer; when they want to gather what remains in the ear, the following is the method adopted. The people who collect it have two baskets with handles, and when walking in the fields they wave one of these baskets from right to left, and the other from left to right, as though they cut the herb, of which nevertheless they only touch the upper part—that is to say, the ear, and all the grain thus falls into the baskets. Semencine also grows in the Province of Kermān,[3] but it is not so good as that of Bhutān, and there is not more of it than is required in the country itself. This grain not only serves to relieve children from worms, but the Persians and all the people who live towards the north, and even the English and Dutch, use it like aniseed to flavour comfits.

As for rhubarb, it is known to be a root which is cut in pieces, ten or twelve of them being strung together and then dried.

If the people of Bhutān had as much skill as the Muscovites in slaying the marten, an abundance of rich furs might be obtained, since there are numbers of these animals. As soon as it shows its head outside its hole the Muscovites, who are

[1] For the Sānkhāris, or shell-workers of Dacca and other parts of Eastern Bengal see J. Wise, *Notes on the Races, Castes, and Trades of Eastern Bengal*, 364 ff.; T. N. Mukharji, *Art-Manufactures of India*, 135, 281.

15 [2] See p. 201, *n.* 5. [3] In South-East Persia.

on the watch, shoot it without fail, generally in the nose or the eyes, for if it is shot in the body the skin will be worth nothing on account of the blood which flows from the wound, and causes the hair moistened by it to fall out.

The King of Bhutān always employs 7,000 or 8,000 men as his guard. These people are armed with bows and arrows, and the majority also carry axes and shields, the former having a point on one side like a war mace. It is long since the Bhutānese first acquired the use of the musket, iron cannon, and gunpowder,[1] which is of long grain, and is very strong. I have been assured that on their guns figures and letters are visible which are more than 500 years old.[2] They cannot be taken out of the kingdom without the express permission of the Governor, and no one dare carry away a musket unless his nearest relatives go bail that it will be faithfully returned. Except for this difficulty I would have brought one away with me. By the characters on the gun, as those who were able to read assured me, it had been made 180 years. It was very thick, the mouth shaped like a tulip, and the interior polished like a mirror. On two-thirds of the gun there were bands in relief, and some gilt and silvered flowers between two of them, and the ball which it carried was an once (Fr.) in weight. The merchant of Bhutān being so particular about the return of the musket, no matter what offer I made, I could never persuade him to sell it to me, and

[1] In his paper on *Early Asiatic Fire Weapons* General Maclagan says, 'While there appears to be no good evidence in support of the idea that Asia had a knowledge of gunpowder and used firearms before Europe, there are plain indications that the knowledge of the most improved weapons of war, both before and since the introduction of gunpowder, and the skill to make and use them, came from Europe to India and other Asiatic countries': *Journ. Asiatic Society of Bengal*, vol. xlv, p. 64. He concludes, too, that there is no good evidence to support the belief that the Arabs were the first to use powder. He considers the European nations were the first to discover its most important form and application: p. 70 (*Ency. Brit.*, xii. 723 f.; *Cambridge Hist. of India*, i. 271). Were space available, much interesting information might be given here of the huge size of the guns which were used in India. One at Bījāpur was 4 feet 8 inches diameter at the muzzle, and had a calibre of 2 feet 4 inches. It was cast at Ahmadnagar in 1549. (*Asiatic Journ.*, 1827, p. 65; *Bombay Gazetteer*, xxiii. 638 ff.)

[2] This carries back to the year A. D. 1150 or thereabouts. See p. 217.

he even refused to give me a sample of his powder. But I have brought to France two guns of nearly the same kind, one of which was made in the island of Ceylon, and the other in Bengal.[1]

There are always fifty elephants about the house of the King of Bhutān for his guard, and twenty or twenty-five camels, which carry on the saddle a small piece of artillery, with a ball of about half a pound in weight. A man is seated on the crupper of the camel, as I have elsewhere described, and he manipulates this piece as he pleases, high or low, to the right or to the left, it being fixed on a fork attached to the saddle.[2]

There is no king in the world who is more feared and more respected by his subjects than the King of Bhutān, and he is even worshipped by them. When on the seat of justice or when he gives an audience, all those who present themselves before him raise their joined hands to their foreheads, and at some distance from the throne, prostrate themselves to the ground without daring to raise the head. In this humble posture they make their supplications to the King, and when they withdraw they walk backwards till they are out of his presence. The Brāhmans make these poor people believe that the King is a god upon earth, and principally those who come from the north.[3] . . . [Passage not translated.]

The people of Bhutān are robust men and of fine stature, but have somewhat flat faces and noses. I am informed that the women are taller and more vigorous than the men, but that they are more subject than them to goitre, from

[1] This is the bell-mouthed blunderbuss, not uncommon, sometimes called Sherbachha, 'tiger-cub' (Hon. W. Egerton, *Illustrated Handbook of Indian Arms*, 142.)

[2] Known as Zambūrak, 'little wasp', Shuturnāl, 'camel-gun', Shāhīn, 'falcon' (Irvine, *Army of the Indian Moghuls*, 135 f.; Bernier, 217).

[3] It seems probable that this so-called King of Bhutān, who was described to Tavernier, was really the Grand Lama of Tibet, and this is the more likely from the statement as to his sanctity in the passage which is not reproduced, being unsuitable for publication. The armaments and elephants mentioned above seem, however, to be scarcely compatible with the surroundings of the Grand Lama. On this use of stercus humanum see Manucci, ii. 440, iv. 438; Dubois, 594.

which few of them escape. They know nothing of war, and have no one to fear but the Great Mogul. But his territory, which lies to the south of them, is, as I have said, a country of high mountains and narrow passes; on the north there is nothing but forests and almost perpetual snow, and both on the east and west there are vast deserts where one finds nothing but bitter water; and whatever inhabited country there is belongs to Rājās who have not much power.

There is apparently a silver mine in the Kingdom of Bhutān,[1] for the King coins pieces of the value of rupees. These pieces are not round but octagonal, and there are characters on them which are neither Indian nor Chinese. Nevertheless, the merchants of Bhutān, who told me at Patna of all these things, could not inform me where the mine was, and as for gold the little they have of it is brought to them by the merchants who come from the east.

This is all that I have been able to learn concerning the Kingdom of Bhutān, beyond which the ambassadors passed whom the Duke of Moscovie sent to China in the year 1659. They passed through the length of Great Tartary to the north of Bhutān, and arrived at the court of the King of China with considerable presents. They were some of the most distinguished nobles of Moscovie, and were at first very well received. But when it became necessary for them to salute the King—the custom being to prostrate oneself three times on the ground—they would not consent to do so, saying that they would salute according to their own method, and in the manner that they saluted their own Emperor, who was as great and as powerful as he of China. As they remained firm in this resolution they had no audience,

[1] This is extremely probable; but it is inconsistent with our author's own statement on p. 128 that there are no silver mines in Asia except in Japan. Ainslie (*Materia Medica*, vol. i. 563) gives a number of references to authorities on the subject. Silver mines in the Patkāi country, between Assam and Upper Burma, have been recently described by Colonel Woodthorpe. (See *Pro. Geogl. Soc.*, January 1887.) A number of mines where argentiferous ores occur in India will be found enumerated in the chapter on silver in the *Economic Geology of India*. On Tibetan gold mines see N. Elias & E. D. Ross, *Hist. of the Moghuls of Central Asia*, 409, 411 f.

and returned with their presents without having seen the King.[1] It would have answered better if the Grand Duke had chosen for this embassy some persons of lower rank than these three nobles, who would have shown themselves less scrupulous about formalities, which are often the cause of envoys being unable to accomplish great designs. If these Moscovite ambassadors had consented to conform to the customs of China—which they might have done without compromising the honour of their master—we should have, without doubt, at this time, a road opened by land from Moscovie to China, through the north of Great Tartary, and a greater knowledge of the Kingdom of Bhutān, which is in its vicinity, and of some others of which we scarce know the names; this would have been a great advantage for all Europe.[2]

As I have just spoken of the Moscovites, I remember that in my journeys, and particularly on the road from Tabrīz to Ispahān, where you generally meet Moscovite merchants, several of them have assured me that in the year 1654, in one of the towns of Moscovie, a woman aged eighty-two gave birth to a male child, which was taken to the Grand Duke, who wished to see it, and had it brought up at his own court.[3]

[1] Envoys to the Emperor of China about the year 713, who refused to kotow, were tried and pronounced worthy of death, but were subsequently pardoned. See Yule, *Marco Polo*, i. 349; *Cathay and the Way Thither*, i. lxxxi. The Russian embassy to China arrived in 1656 (*Ency. Brit.*, vi. 198).

[2] This passage is of considerable interest when regarded in connexion with the subsequent extension of Russia's influence in this direction, and our own hitherto futile attempts to establish a regular trade route through Tibet, which however, have been advanced by the war in 1903–4.

[3] Mr. A. Keith, F.R.C.S. LL.D. Conservator of the Museum of the Royal College of Surgeons, in a letter dated 12th January 1921, writes: 'Two years ago a correspondence was carried on in the *British Medical Journal* to ascertain the latest age at which a woman was known to have borne a child. It was found that there was no authenticated case of any one over 50 bearing a child, and that such cases were very rare.'

CHAPTER XVI

Concerning the Kingdom of Tippera.

SOME persons up to this hour believe that the Kingdom of Pegu bounds China, and I myself shared this error until three merchants of the Kingdom of Tippera corrected me. They passed as Brāhmans in the hope that they might be treated with special respect, but they were in truth only merchants who came to Patna and Dacca, where I saw them, to buy coral, yellow amber, tortoise-shell, and sea-shell bracelets, and other toys which, as I have said in the preceding chapter, are made in these two towns of Bengal. I saw one of them at Dacca, and met the two others at Patna, and invited them to dine with me. They were people who spoke but little, either because it was their nature, or the usual custom of their country; one of them knew the Indian language. When they bought anything they made their calculations with small stones resembling agates, and of the size of the finger nail, upon which there were figures. They each had scales made like steelyards.[1] The arms were not of iron, but of a kind of wood as hard as bresil,[2] and the ring which held the weights, when put in the arm to mark the livres, was a strong loop of silk. By this means they weighed from a dram up to ten of our livres. If all the inhabitants of the Kingdom of Tippera resemble these two merchants whom I met at Patna, one might conclude that this nation loves drinking very much; and I experienced a pleasure in giving them sometimes spirits, sometimes Spanish wine, and other kinds, such as those of Shīrāz, Rheims, and Mantua, never having been without a supply in all my journeys, except during the last, in the deserts of Arabia, which I was unable to traverse in less than sixty-five days, for the reasons I have elsewhere stated. I should have been able to learn

[1] See H. Ling Roth, 'Oriental Steelyards and Bismars', *Journal, Royal Anthropological Institute*, xlii, 1912, p. 200 ff.

[2] The Brazil wood of commerce is at present derived from Cæsalpinia Brasiliensis, a native of Pernambuco. (*Ency. Brit.*, iv. 463.) The Indian Sappan wood is Cæsalpinia Sappan: Watt, *Economic Products*, 194 ff. (See Yule, *Hobson-Jobson*, 113.)

many things from these Tippera merchants in reference to the nature and extent of their country if they had known how to give me as good as account of it as they did of my good wine when I proposed a health. For my interpreter had scarce finished paying them a compliment, on my behalf, before the wine was drunk, when they gazed at one another, smacked their lips, and strook their hands two or three times on their stomachs with a sigh.[1] These three merchants had come by way of the Kingdom of Arakan, which lies to the south and west [2] of that of Tippera, partly bounded by Pegu in the direction of the winter sunset, and they told me that they spent about fifteen days in traversing their country, from which one cannot very well estimate its extent, because the stages are unequal, being sometimes longer and sometimes shorter, according as water is to be found.

For the conveyance of goods they use, as in India, oxen and horses, which are similar to those I have described above, small in size, but otherwise excellent. As for the King and the great nobles, they travel in pallankeens,[3] and have elephants trained for war. The inhabitants of Tippera are not less troubled by goître than those of Bhutān. I was told that it attacked some of the women on the breasts. Of the three men from Tippera whom I saw in Bengal, the one who was at Dacca had two goîtres, each of the size of the fist; they are caused by the bad water, as in many other countries of Asia and Europe.[4]

Nothing is produced in Tippera which is of use to foreigners. There is, however, a gold mine, which yields gold of very low standard; and silk, which is very coarse.[5] It is from

[1] 'Drunkenness among them [the Tipperas] does not take an amorous or a pugnacious direction; it generally expends itself in vehement dancing, until such time as the head becomes giddy, and the dancer lies down to sleep off what he has drunk' (T. H. Lewin, *Wild Races of South-Eastern India*, 201).

[2] East.

[3] The King, without reason, claims descent from the Rājput Lunar Race (*Imperial Gazetteer*, xiii. 118).

[4] For early explanations of the origin of goître see Mundy, i. 117. It seems to be due to telluric or malarial causes, combined with drinking water impregnated with salts of lime and magnesia (*Ency. Brit.*, xii. 192). It is prevalent in the Sub-Himalayas and the adjoining districts.

[5] Tippera, as now understood, does not produce gold—the gold brought from thence may have been originally obtained elsewhere

these two articles that the King's revenue is derived. He levies no taxes from his subjects, save that those below the rank, corresponding to that of the nobility of Europe, have to work for him for six days every year either in the gold mine or at the silk. He sends both the gold and silk to be sold in China, and receives silver in return, with which he coins money of the value of 10 sols.[1] He also coins small gold money like the aspres [2] of Turkey, and has two kinds of them, of one of which it takes four to make an écu, and of the other a dozen. This is all I have been able to ascertain concerning a country which has been unknown to us up to the present, but about which we shall hereafter have more information, as also of others which the accounts of travellers have made known to us, all not having been discovered in a day.[3]

CHAPTER XVII

Concerning the Kingdom of Assam.

It was never properly known what the Kingdom of Assam was till after that great Captain Mīr Jumla, to whom I have often referred in the history of the Moguls, had secured the Empire for Aurangzeb by the death of all his brothers and the imprisonment of his son. He concluded, that when the war was finished, he would be no longer esteemed at Court

(see vol. ii, p. 157 *n.*). In Assam, it is said that it was once the custom for the Rājās to require their subjects to wash for gold for a certain number of days every year. Regular gold washers were taxed. For gold in Upper Burma see Scott & Hardiman, *Gazetteer*, Part i, vol. ii. 304 f.

[1] These coins were therefore worth 9*d.*

[2] The Turkish asper (ἄσπρος, 'white': see *New English Dict.* s.v. asper) was both a small coin, and a money of account. Its value varied with that of the piastre. It therefore represented about a halfpenny in value, if there were 80 to 100 in a piastre. The coins here mentioned by Tavernier were worth 1*s.* 1½*d.* and 4½*d.* respectively.

[3] For the people of Tippera see 'On the Manners, Religion, and Laws of the Cucis, or Mountaineers of Tipra' by J. Rawlins (*Asiatic Researches*, ii, 1799, pp. 187 ff.); and more recent accounts by Sir E. Gait (*Bengal Census Report*, 1901, vol. i. 186 f., 438), Sir H. Risley (*Tribes and Castes of Bengal*, ii. 323 ff.); T. H. Lewin (*Wild Races of South-Eastern India*, 190 ff.).

as highly as he had been when Commander-in-Chief of the armies of Aurangzeb, and all powerful in the Kingdom where he had a great number of supporters. In order, therefore, to retain for himself the command of the troops, he resolved to undertake the conquest of the Kingdom of Assam, where he knew he would not meet with much resistance, the country having had no war for 500 or 600 years, and the people being without experience in arms.[1] It is believed that this people in ancient times, first discovered gunpowder and guns, which passed from Assam to Pegu, and from Pegu to China; this is the reason why the discovery is generally ascribed to the Chinese. Mīr Jumla brought back from this war numerous iron guns, and the gunpowder made in that country is excellent. Its grain is not long as in the Kingdom of Bhutān, but is round and small like ours, and is much more effective than the other powder.

Accordingly Mīr Jumla left Dacca with a powerful army for the conquest of the Kingdom of Assam.[2] At 5 leagues from Dacca one of the rivers which comes from the Lake of Chiamay,[3] which like other rivers of India takes different names according to the places it passes, joins an arm of the Ganges, and at the place where these two rivers meet there are forts on each side, both armed with good pieces of bronze cannon, which shoot at a level with the water. This is where Mīr Jumla embarked,[4] his army ascending the river to the

[1] Bernier (p. 171) says that Mīr Jumla was sent to Assam because 'Aurangzeb justly apprehended that an ambitious soldier could not long remain in a state of repose, and that, if disengaged from foreign war, he would seek occasion to excite internal commotions.' Ostensibly he was appointed Viceroy of Bengal to punish the lawless Zamīndārs of Assam and Arakan (Jadunath Sarkar, *History of Aurangzīb*, iii. 178).

[2] On 1st November 1661. An account of Assam at the time of its conquest by Mīr Jumla in 1663, based on the *'Ālamgīr-nāma* of Muhammad Kāzim-ibn-Muhammad Amīn Munshī, by Kavirāj Syāmal Dās, translated by Bābū Rāma Prasāda, has been published in the *Indian Antiquary* for July 1887, pp. 222-6. The authorities for the campaign are Elliot & Dowson, *Hist. of India*, vii. 144; *Asiatic Researches*, ii. 172 ff.; Jadunath Sarkar, iii. 166 ff.

[3] Lake Chiamay was a myth believed in by early travellers. (Yule, *Hobson-Jobson* 190; Scott & Hardiman, *Gazetteer of Upper Burma*, Part ii, vol. ii, 659 f.)

[4] Gorāghāt on the west bank of the Karatoyā river in the district

29th or 30th degree, where the frontier of Assam is situated, and thence he led it by land through a country abounding with all the necessaries of life, and with but little means of defence, especially as the people were taken by surprise. As they are all idolaters, the army, which consisted wholly of Musalmāns, did not spare their pagodas, but destroyed them wherever they met with them, burning and sacking all, up to the 35th degree.[1] Mīr Jumla then heard that the King of Assam was in the field with a larger force than had been expected; that he had many guns, and an abundance of fireworks, somewhat like our grenades, which are fixed at the end of a stick as long as a short pike, as I have elsewhere described, and carry more than 500 paces.[2] When Mīr Jumla received this intelligence he did not consider it prudent to advance farther, but the principal cause of his return was that the cold season had commenced, and to effect the conquest of that country it would have been necessary to go as far as the 45th degree of latitude; this would have involved the loss of his army. For the Indians are so susceptible to cold, and fear it so much, that it is impossible to make them pass the 30th, or at the most the 35th degree, except at the risk of their lives, and of all the servants whom I took from India to Persia, it was a great feat for them to come as far as Kasvīn,[3] and I never succeeded in taking any of them to Tabrīz. As soon as they saw the mountains of Medea covered with snow I had to allow them to return home.

As Mīr Jumla was unable to go farther north, he resolved to turn to the south-west, and laid siege to a town called Azoo,[4] which he took in a short time, and found great riches

of Dinājpur, an ancient city now marked by ruins, according to Muhammad Ḳāzim, was the starting point of Mīr Jumla on the 21st November 1662. This was after he had conquered Kuch Bihār. The route is fully given by Jadunath Sarkar, and cannot be reconciled with the text (Jadunath Sarkar, iii. 181 ff.).

[1] The Mughal forces can scarcely have gone beyond Garhgāon, which they reached on 17th March 1662 or about the 28th degree of latitude, at the farthest.

[2] Rockets (see vol. i, p. 311).

[3] Casbin in the original.

[4] Azoo or Ḳoch Hājo, a kingdom on the left bank of the Brahmaputra river, extending up to Kāmrūp. The town of Hājo was on the frontier of Assam. A full account of it will be found in the *Pādishāh-*

there. Many are of opinion that his original design was merely to take this town and pillage it, and afterwards return, as he in fact did.[1] It is in this town of Azoo that the tombs of the Kings of Assam and of all the members of the royal family are situated. Although the Assamese are idolaters, they do not burn the bodies of the dead, but bury them. They believe that after death they go to another world, where those who have lived well in this world lack nothing, and enjoy all kinds of pleasure ; but, on the contrary, those who have lived badly, and have taken the property of others, suffer much, principally hunger and thirst, and accordingly it is prudent to bury something with them to serve them at need. Thus it was that Mīr Jumla found such a quantity of riches at Azoo,[2] since for many centuries every King has built for himself in the great pagoda a sort of chapel where he was to be buried, and during their lifetime, each of them sent, to be placed in the grave where he was to be buried, a quantity of gold and silver, carpets and other articles. When the body of a dead king is buried, all his most precious possessions are also placed in the grave, such as the household

nāma. (See Blochmann in *Journ. Asiat. Soc. Bengal*, vol. xli. p. 53.) Here Tavernier copies Bernier (p. 172), but it is difficult to follow his story. The Mughals seem to have been in possession of Hājo since 1612 (Jadunath Sarkar, iii. 169).

[1] Muhammad Kāzim says that Mīr Jumla, finding his army tired of the difficulties with which they were surrounded, 'came to terms with the Assamis (on the 17th January 1663), who, besides surrendering two districts, which were added to the crown lands, gave 20,000 tolās of gold, 128,000 rupees in hard cash, 120 elephants, and the King's daughter to the conqueror. He then returned to Bengal via Lakhughar and Kajli, and reached Khizarpur on the 8th April A. D. 1663, where he paid the debt of nature after suffering for a time from consumption' (*l.c.*, p. 223). For the terms of peace and a review of the results of the campaign, which, except for the blockade of the Mughals, was successful, see Jadunath Sarkar, iii. 201 ff. ; Bernier, 172 f. It was at Garhgāon, not Hājo, that the booty was taken.

[2] Muhammad Kāzim says 90,000 rupees worth of gold and silver was obtained by Mīr Jumla's soldiers from these graves (*l. c.* 225). 'The tumuli constructed over the graves of the Asam (Ahom) sovereigns are very extensive, and when opened the remains of the dead have been found in coffins of massive timber, with gold and silver ornaments, and outside the coffin various utensils, arms, and implements of agriculture.' (E. T. Dalton, *Descriptive Ethnology of Bengal*, 9.)

idol of gold or silver which he worshipped during life, and all things which it is believed will be required by him in the other world. But it is most strange, and savours much of barbarism, that as soon as the King is dead, some of his most beloved wives and the principal officers of his house kill themselves by means of a poisoned decoction, in order to be interred with him, so that they may serve him in the other world. Besides which an elephant, twelve camels,[1] six horses, and numerous sporting dogs are buried with him, it being believed that all these animals will come to life again, after they are dead, and serve the King.

This Kingdom of Assam is one of the best countries in Asia, for it produces all that is necessary to the life of man, and there is no need to go for anything to the neighbouring States. There are mines of gold, silver, steel, lead, and iron,[2] and much silk, but it is coarse. There is a kind of silk which is produced on trees, and is made by an animal like our silkworm, but it is rounder and remains for a whole year on the trees.[3] The stuffs which are made of this silk are very brilliant, but soon fray and do not last long. These silks

[1] Muhammad Kāzim gives a similar account, but does not mention camels. Elsewhere he states camels were unknown in Assam (*l. c.*, p. 224). The climate of Assam does not suit camels. (*Imperial Gazetteer*, vi. 36.) The practice, if it once prevailed, of burying animals with the dead, has now practically disappeared from India, though among some of the tribes in the Vindhyan hills the habit of placing in the grave tools or implements used by men or women still survives as in the case of the Majhwārs of the United Provinces (Crooke, *Tribes and Castes of the North-Western Provinces*, iii. 433). And in Bengal, when a Khambu dies, a pig is brained with the pestle used for husking corn, its tail and ears being cut off and placed under the dead man's armpits before he is buried (*Census Report, Bengal*, 1911, i. 512).

[2] Muhammad Kāzim says, 'Gold and silver are got from the sand of the rivers draining the Gol (i. e. northern circle). About 12,000 Assamis according to some people, 20,000 as others state, are generally engaged in washing these noble metals, and have to pay one tola of gold per head per annum to the Chief' (*l. c.*, 224). See *Economic Geology of India*, p. 231, for details as to the gold of Assam. See also *ante*, p. 128, where it is stated incorrectly that there are no silver mines in India. Iron is still worked to a small extent; alluvial gold is no longer washed; there is some silver and platinum (*Imperial Gazetteer*, vi. 71 f.).

[3] The production of silk is now important (*ibid.*, vi. 73). For Upper Burma see Scott & Hardiman, *Gazetteer*, Part i, vol. ii, 372 f.

are produced, and the gold and silver mines are situated in the southern part of the country. The country also produces an abundance of shellac, of which there are two kinds.[1] That formed on trees is of a red colour, with it they dye their calicoes and other stuffs, and when they have extracted the red colour they use the lac to lacquer cabinets and other objects of that kind, and to make Spanish wax.[2] A large quantity of it is exported to China and Japan, to be used in the manufacture of cabinets ; it is the best lac in the whole of Asia for these purposes. As for the gold, no one is permitted to remove it out of the Kingdom, and it is not coined into money but is kept in large and small ingots, which the people make use of in local trade, and do not export it ; but as for silver, the King coins it into money of the size and weight of rupees, and of an octagonal shape, and they may be taken outside the Kingdom. Although the country abounds, as I have said, with all things necessary to life, among all articles of food the flesh of the dog[3] is especially esteemed ; it is the favourite dish at feasts, and every month, in each town in the Kingdom, the people hold markets where they sell only dogs, which are brought thither from all directions. There are also quantities of vines and good grapes, but no wine, the grapes being merely dried for distilling spirits. Finally, as regards salt, there is none in the Kingdom but what is manufactured, which is done in two ways.[4] The first is to collect vegetable matter which

[1] The manufacture of shellac is declining (Watt, *Economic Products*, 1059).

[2] See p. 18 for an account of shellac and lac dye. For shellac in Upper Burma see Scott & Hardiman, *Gazetteer*, Part i, vol. ii. 393 ff. 'In his [King of Pegu] country there is found much lacca' (Varthema, 222).

[3] Muhammad Kāzim says the Nanaks (Nāgas) eat the flesh of dogs, cats, serpents, &c. (*l.c.*, p. 224). The Nāgas still eat dog's flesh (Dalton, *Descriptive Ethnology of Bengal*, 43 ; T. C. Hodson, *Naga Tribes of Manipur*, 59 f. ; J. H. Hutton, *The Angami Nāgas*, 81) ; and so do the Akhas in Upper Burma (Scott & Hardiman, *Gazetteer*, Part i, vol. i. 589).

[4] The chief sources of supply of salt in Assam were formerly the brine springs at Borhāt and Sadiyā in Lakhimpur. The vessels used in the manufacture for boiling the brine were simply sections of bamboos, which were pared so thin that the percolating moisture prevented their

is found in stagnant water, such as ducks and frogs eat. This is dried and burnt, and the ashes derived from it being boiled and strained as is described below, serve as salt. The other method, which is that most commonly followed, is to take some of those large leaves of the kind of fig tree which we call Adam's fig,[1] they are dried in the same manner and burnt, and the ashes from them consist of a kind of salt which is so pungent that it is impossible to eat it unless it is softened, this being done in the following way. The ashes are put into water, where they are stirred about for ten or twelve hours, then this water is strained three times through a cloth and boiled. As it boils the sediment thickens, and when the water is all evaporated, the salt, which is white and fairly good, is found at the bottom of the pot.

From the ashes of fig leaves in this country the lye is made to boil silk, which becomes as white as snow, and if the people of Assam had more figs than they have, they would make all their silks white, because white silk is much more valuable than the other, but they have not sufficient to bleach half the silks which are produced in the country.

Kemmerouf[2] is the name of the town where the King of Assam resides, twenty-five or thirty days' journey from the former capital of the Kingdom and it bore the same name. The King takes no tribute from his people, but all the mines of gold, silver, lead, steel, and iron belong to him, and to avoid oppressing his subjects, he employs only the slaves

burning. Imported salt is now largely used in Assam. (See *Economic Geology of India*, p. 491.) The manufacture of salt is now confined to some hill tribes (Watt, *Dict. Economic Products*, vi, part 2, 400).

[1] This manufacture of salt from the leaves of the plantain is mentioned by Muhammad Kāzim, *l. c.*, p. 224. (See *ante*, p. 3.) The pungency is probably due to the presence of potash salts. The ashes of the leaves are, as Tavernier says, still used for dyeing in Bengal (Watt, *op. cit.*, v. 296).

[2] Kāmrūp, now known as the name of a District in Assam of which Gauhātī is the chief town. It is certain that Mīr Jumla was defeated by the Ahāms here, and this was the seat of the Ahām Viceroy, but the King of Assam's capital was at Nāzira or Garhgāon (Kargānv) in the Sibsāgar District. (See Jadunath Sarkar, iii. 183 ff.; *Imperial Gazetteer*, xix. i f.) The palace is described in Robinson's *Descriptive Account of Assam*. According to Muhammad Kāzim, who also describes it, its circuit was 1 kos and 14 chains (= 840 yards).

whom he buys from his neighbours for working the mines.[1] Thus all the peasants of Assam are at their ease, and there is scarcely anyone who has not a separate house in his land, a well surrounded by trees, and the majority even keep elephants for their wives. These idolaters, unlike those of India, who have but one wife, have four, and when a man marries one, in order that there may be no dispute among them, he says to her, 'I take you to serve me in my household for this purpose', and to another, 'I destine you for another', and thus each of the women knows what she has to do in the house. The men and women are of fine build, and of very good blood; but the people dwelling on the southern frontier are somewhat olive coloured, and are not subject to goître like those of the north. The latter are not of so fine stature, and the majority of their women have somewhat flat noses. The people of the southern part go about naked, having only a piece of calico with which they cover that which modesty requires them to conceal, with a cap like English caps, around which they hang an abundance of pigs' teeth.[2] They have their ears pierced so that one might easily pass the thumb through the holes, some carry ornaments of gold in them and others of silver.[3] The men wear their hair down to their shoulders, and the women let it grow as long as it can. In the Kingdom of Assam, as well as that of Bhutān, there is a large trade in tortoise-shell bracelets, and sea shells as large as an egg, which are sawn into small circles, but the rich wear bracelets of coral and yellow amber.

[1] This may have been true of the silver mines, but as above stated, subjects had to wash for gold.

[2] Muhammad Kāzim says, 'A head-piece of gunny (*gonī*), a cloth round the loins, and a sheet over the shoulders, form all the articles of their dress' (*l.c.*, p. 225). Dalton, *op. cit.*, plate xiii, gives a photograph of an Abor chief whose head is decorated with tusks of the wild boar.

[3] On the practice, common among Hindu women, of distending the ears with heavy rings see P. della Valle, i. 195; Pyrard de Laval, i. 343, 419; Barbosa, ed. Dames, i. 114; Linschoten, i. 77. In the Central Provinces 'to have the hole torn open is one of the worst social mishaps which can happen to a woman. She is immediately put out of caste for a long period, and only readmitted after severe penalties, equivalent to those inflicted for getting vermin in a wound' (Russell, *Tribes and Castes*, iv. 529).

When a man dies all his relatives and friends should come to the burial, and when they place the body in the ground they take off all the bracelets on their arms and legs and bury them with the deceased.

CHAPTER XVIII

Concerning the Kingdom of Siam.[1]

THE greater part of the Kingdom of Siam is situated between the Gulf of the same name and the Gulf of Bengal, adjoining Pegu on the north and the peninsula of Malacca on the south. The shortest road and the best which Europeans can take to reach this Kingdom is to go from Ispahān to Hormuz, from Hormuz to Surat, from Surat to Golkonda, and from Golkonda to Masulipatam, where they should embark for Denouserin,[2] which is one of the ports of the Kingdom of Siam. From Denouserin to the capital town, which bears the name of the Kingdom, there are about thirty-five days' journey; one part is traversed by ascending a river, and the remainder in a cart or upon elephants. The road both by land and water is uncomfortable, because on the land portion one must always be on guard against lions[3] and tigers; and by water, as the river makes rapids in many places, it is difficult to make the boats ascend, but this is accomplished by the aid of machinery. It is the route which I recommended, on the return from one of my voyages to India, to three bishops whom I met on the road. The first was the Bishop of Beryte,[4] whom I met at Ispahān; the second the Bishop of Megalopolis,[5] when crossing the Euphrates;

[1] One of the most important early accounts of Siam is that of Simon de la Loubère, *Du Royaume de Siam*, Amsterdam, 1691, of which an English translation, by A. P. Gem, R. S. S., was published in London, 1693, under the title of *A New Historical Relation of the Kingdom of Siam*. The references in the notes are to the latter work.

[2] Tenasserim, which, however, was included in the Kingdom of Pegu, though at times conquered and held by Siam (Yule, *Hobson-Jobson*, 914).

[3] There are no lions in Siam.

[4] Beyrout, in Syria.

[5] Metellopolis of Finlayson, *Mission to Siam*, 257: perhaps Megalopolis in Arcadia.

the third the Bishop of Heliopolis,[1] who arrived at Alexandretta as I was leaving it for Europe. The whole of Siam abounds with rice and fruits, the principal of which are called mangues, durions, and mangoustans.[2] The forests are full of deer, elephants, tigers, rhinoceros, and monkeys, and everywhere is to be seen an abundance of bamboos, which are large and very tall canes, hollow throughout, and as hard as iron.

At the ends of these canes nests, of the size of a man's head, are suspended; they are made by ants from a fat earth which they carry up. There is but a small hole at the base of these nests, by which the ants enter, and in these nests each ant, like honey bees, has his separate chamber. They build their nests on the canes, because if they made them on the ground, during the rainy season, which lasts four or five months, they would be exterminated, all the country being then inundated. One must take precautions after night-fall against snakes. There are some snakes which are 22 feet long and have two heads,[3] but the head at the extremity which answers to the tail, and where the snake ends, does not open the mouth and has no movement. There is also in Siam a very venomous animal which is not more than a foot long. Its tail is forked and has two points, and its form is somewhat like what we picture the salamander.[4]

The rivers of this Kingdom are very beautiful, and the

[1] Heliopolis or Bambyke, near Carchemish on the Euphrates. Le Blanc identified Hieropolis with Aleppo (*Voyages*, Paris Edition, 1648, p. 8).

[2] Mangoes, durians, and mangosteens.

[3] This fable of two-headed snakes is common in India; sometimes it is said of the Dhamin snake—Ptyas mucosus. The statement that the head, at the tail end, has no movement, and that the mouth does not open, is a charmingly ingenuous admission. See Mundy, 308 f., with an illustration; *Bombay Gazetteer*, x. 48. Like the case of the Birds of Paradise, referred to on p. 13, the description illustrates the persistence of myths.

[4] This poisonous, forked-tailed reptile was certainly mythical. A species of Eublepharis? is called bishkhaprā by the natives of India, and though unprovided with fangs is believed to be very poisonous. (Yule, *Hobson-Jobson*, 95 f.) A. Hamilton describes a dangerous animal, shaped like a lizard, and called Jackoa (Pinkerton, *Voyages*, viii. 453).

one at Siam is of nearly uniform size throughout.[1] The water in it is very wholesome, but it is full of crocodiles of enormous size, which often devour men who are not on their guard.[2] The rivers aré in flood during the time that the sun traverses the northern signs ; this contributes much to the fertility of the land where the waters spread themselves, and where, by a wonderful provision of nature, the ear of rice ascends to the surface as the waters rise.[3]

Siam,[4] the capital town of the Kingdom, and the ordinary residence of the King, is surrounded by walls, and is more than 3 of our leagues in circuit. It is on an island, the river surrounding it on all sides ; canals might easily be made through all the streets if the King were willing to expend on that work a part of the vast amount of gold which he lavishes on the idol temples.

The Siamese have thirty-three letters in their alphabet ;[5] they write as we do, from left to right, or contrary to the people of Japan, China, Cochin-China, and Tonquin, who write from the right hand to the left, and from the top of the page to the bottom.

All the common people of this Kingdom are in slavery either to the King or to the nobles.[6] The women cut their hair like the men, and their garments are not very copious. Among the civilities which the Siamese observe towards

[1] The principal rivers of Siam are the Menam, Mekong, Meklong, Petriü, Tachin, and the Chantibun (Crawfurd, *Dictionary*, 380).

[2] The Siamese take their revenge by eating crocodiles' eggs.

[3] The period of floods is during the south-west monsoon, from June to November, and the plain fertilized by them has an area of 6,750 geographical square miles.

[4] Bangkok, on both banks of the Menam river, 24 miles from the sea, is the present capital of Siam. The old capital, called Siam or Yuthia, or Ayuthia, from Sanskrit Ayodhya, is 54 miles farther to the north ; it was destroyed by the Burmese in 1768, and Bangkok was founded in 1769 (Crawfurd, *Dictionary*, 384 f. ; Yule, *op. cit.*, 56 f., 465 f.).

[5] The Siamese alphabet contains 32 vowels and 44 consonants—in all, 76 distinct characters (*Ency. Brit.*, xxv. 9). The language consists of two dialects—the court and the vulgar. The sacred language is distinct, being Pali or Prakrit (Crawfurd, *Dictionary*, 387).

[6] For an interesting account of slavery or serfdom in Siam at the present day, see E. Young, *The Kingdom of the Yellow Robe*, 125 ff. ; de la Loubère, 77 f.

one another, one of the principal is never to pass anyone to whom respect is due, without previously asking permission; this is done by elevating both hands. The richest have many wives, as is the case in the Kingdom of Assam.[1]

The money of the country is of silver and nearly of the shape of a musket bullet.[2] The lowest denomination consists of small shells, which are brought from the Manillas. There are good tin mines in Siam.[3]

The King of Siam is one of the wealthiest monarchs in the East, and he calls himself in his edicts King of heaven and earth, although he is a tributary to the Kings of China. He shows himself but rarely to his subjects, and gives audience only to the principal persons of his court, strangers having no admission to his palace. He confides the government to his ministers, who very often make ill use of the authority with which they are invested. He shows himself in public only twice in the year; this he does with much splendour. The first time is when he goes in state to a pagoda in the town,[4] the tower of which is gilt throughout, both inside and outside. It contains three idols, from 6 to 7 feet high, and made of massive gold; by means of liberal alms to the poor, and presents to the priests of these false gods, he believes that he makes himself pleasing to them. He goes there accompanied by all his court, and displays all his richest possessions. Among other indications of magnificence there

[1] Young, 99 ff.

[2] The coins here referred to are probably those which our author figures in his chapter on coins (p. 22 of the original Paris ed. of 1676). Ball suggests that this peculiar form imitates the curious-shaped coco-de-mer, or double coco-nut of the Seychelles islands, for which fabulous prices were given in the Malayan countries and India. (See Yule, *Hobson-Jobson*, 229 for an account of this coco-nut.) Gold and silver bullet coins are still current (Young, 140). See an illustration of these coins in de la Loubère, 72. Porcelain coins are still current (Carl Bock, *Temples and Elephants*, 142).

[3] Tin is obtained in four of the provinces, which extend from Lat. 8° to Lat. 13°; and also in the tributary Malay States (*Ency. Brit.*, xxv. 5).

[4] This pagoda, or the one next referred to, is probably the one still standing, though much ruined, near Yuthia; it is 400 feet high, and has a gigantic gilt bronze statue of Buddha. It is said to have been built in the year 1387 A. D. (Crawfurd, *Dictionary*, 387).

are 200 elephants in Siam, one of them being white; and it is so highly esteemed by the King that he glories in calling himself 'the King of the white elephant'.[1] These elephants live for several centuries, as I have elsewhere remarked.[2]

The second time that the King goes forth in public is for the purpose of visiting another pagoda, 5 or 6 leagues from the town up the river. No one can enter this pagoda save the King and his priests. As for the people, as soon as they see the door of it each one must fall with his face to the ground. On this occasion the King appears on the river with 200 richly gilt and decorated galleys of an enormous length, each having 400 rowers.[3] As this second sortie of the King happens in the month of November, when the river begins to fall, the priests make the people believe that it is the King alone who is able to arrest the course of the waters by the prayers and offerings which he makes in this pagoda; and these poor people persuade themselves that the King goes to cut the waters with his sword, to dismiss them and order them to retire into the sea.[4]

The King goes, moreover, but on this occasion without any state, to a pagoda which is in the island where the Dutch have their factory. There is, at the entrance, an idol seated after the manner of our tailors, having one hand on one of

[1] In the year 1821–2 the envoys from the Governor-General of India found five white elephants in the possession of the King. Finlayson gives an interesting account of them (*Mission to Siam*, p. 154). See Sir J. Bowring, *Siam*, i. 220 f. 'In Siam the representation of the white elephant is everywhere conspicuous. The national flag is a white elephant on a scarlet ground. The mercantile flag is a white elephant on a blue ground. On every temple and official building in the land there is a representation in stone, plaster, or colour, of this wonderful creature' (E. Young, *The Kingdom of the Yellow Robe*, 389); Hastings, *Ency. Religion and Ethics*, xi. 483. Dames, *Book of Duarte Barbosa*, ed. 1921, ii. 154 f.

[2] See vol. i, p. 223.

[3] Drawings and descriptions of these fine royal barges, called Balon (see Yule-Burnell, *Hobson-Jobson*, 53), are given by de la Loubère, p. 40, and see Turpin, *Hist. of Siam*, in Pinkerton, *Collection of Voyages*, ix. 581; Young, 349; and compare the royal boats in the Burmese Court (Scott & Hardiman, *Gazetteer Upper Burma*, part i, vol. ii. 157 ff.).

[4] A good instance of mimetic magic.

his knees and the other at his side. It is more than 60 feet high, and around this large idol there are more than 300 others of different sizes, which represent all kinds of attitudes of men and women.[1] All these idols are gilt, and there is a prodigious quantity of these pagodas in all the country. This results from the fact that every rich Siamese builds one to perpetuate his memory. These pagodas have towers and bells, and the walls inside are painted and gilt, but the windows are so narrow that they give but little light. The altars are laden with costly idols, among which there are generally three of different sizes close to one another.[2] The two pagodas to which, as I have said, the King goes in state, are surrounded by many beautiful pyramids, all well gilt; and that in the island where the Dutch have their house has a cloister connected with it, the facade of which is very fine. In the middle there is, as it were, a great chapel all gilded within, where a lamp and three wax candles are kept alight in front of the altar, which is covered with idols, some being of fine gold and the others of gilt copper. The pagoda in the middle of the town, and one of the two which the King visits once in the year, as I have related, contains nearly 4,000 idols, and it has around it, like that 6 leagues from Siam, a number of pyramids, the beauty of which causes one to wonder at the industry of this nation.

When the King appears all the doors and windows of the houses have to be closed, and all the people prostrate themselves on the ground without daring to raise their eyes towards him. As no one should be in a place more elevated than the King when he is passing through the streets, all those who are in their houses must descend. When his hair is cut one of his wives is employed on that duty, as he does not allow

[1] It is possible that this is a mistake, as some images of Buddha have an effeminate appearance. For images in pagodas at Bangkok, see Young, *op. cit.*, 272 ff.; Hastings, *Ency. Religion and Ethics*, xi. 482.

[2] Vast accumulations of figures of Buddha characterize these temples, even those which are deserted. The well-known seated and recumbent figures of Buddha, made of marble or lacquered wood, which are brought to Europe, have generally been obtained from deserted pagodas in Burma or Siam.

a barber to place a hand upon him.[1] This prince is passionately attached to certain elephants, which he supports as the favourites and ornaments of his kingdom. When they are sick the greatest nobles of the court show the utmost care for them in order to please their sovereign; and when they die, as much magnificence is displayed for them as at the funerals of the nobles of the Kingdom.[2] These funerals of the nobles are conducted in the following manner:—A kind of mausoleum is adorned with reeds covered on both sides with paper of many colours. As all kinds of scented wood are sold by weight, as much as the body weighs is placed in the middle of the mausoleum, and after the priests have finished pronouncing some benedictions they burn the whole to ashes. Those of the rich are preserved in urns of gold or silver, but as for those of the poor they are cast to the winds.[3] As for criminals who have finished their lives with a disgraceful death, the Siamese do not burn their bodies, but bury them.[4]

The King authorizes public women, but they have to live in their own separate quarter, under a chief who protects them from insult. When one of them dies her body is not burnt as is that of a respectable woman, but is thrown into a place where it becomes the food of dogs and crows.

It is estimated that there are in this Kingdom more than 200,000 priests called Bonzes,[5] who are held in great veneration

[1] On respect paid to the heads of royal personages, see Young, *op. cit.*, 131. It is a well-known characteristic of these sacred kings that their heads are regarded as sacrosanct. Hence no one is allowed to appear above the level of the King's head, and this must not be touched except under careful precaution (Sir J. G. Frazer, *The Golden Bough*, 3rd ed.; *Taboo and the Perils of the Soul*, 252 ff.).

[2] Turpin (Pinkerton, ix. 590) describes the cremation of a favourite parrot of the King.

[3] See the account by de la Loubère, 123 f.; Young, *Kingdom of the Yellow Robe*, 239 ff.

[4] According to Turpin (Pinkerton, ix. 590) the honour of cremation is denied to executed criminals, women dying in childbed, and all who have perished by a violent death. Young (*op. cit.*, 245) describes a poor man's funeral, while the corpses of paupers and criminals are exposed to be devoured by vultures at one of the Bangkok temples, see Hastings, *Ency. Religion and Ethics*, xi. 487.

[5] This is the ordinary term to denote the priests of Buddha in Siam. Its origin is obscure (Yule, *Hobson-Jobson*, 105).

both by the court and by the people. The King himself regards some of them with such awe as to humiliate himself in their presence. The extraordinary respect which everyone shows them has sometimes inspired in them so much pride, that they have ventured to attempt to occupy the throne, But when the King discovers anything of the kind he takes their lives, as was the case some time ago in a rebellion, the author of which was a Bonze, whom the King executed.

These Bonzes are clad in yellow, and wear on their loins a small red cloth as a waistband. They make an outward show of great modesty, and they never appear to manifest the smallest degree of passion. At four o'clock in the morning they rise at the sound of bells to say their prayers, and they do the same towards evening. There are certain days of the year when they withdraw from the conversation of men to live in retreat.[1] Some live on charity, and others have well-endowed dwellings. As long as they wear the garb of Bonzes they cannot possess wives, and they must relinquish it if they desire to marry. They are for the most part very ignorant, and know not what they believe. It appears, however, that like the idolaters of India they believe in the transmigration of the soul into many bodies. They are forbidden to take the lives of animals; nevertheless, they make no scruple about eating animals which others have slain, or which have died naturally.[2] The god whom they worship

[1] This is the retreat practised by monks in the rainy season (vassavāsa, vassa, Sanskrit vārsika) when the country is swamped, and the roads are impassable (H. Kern, *Manual of Indian Buddhism*, 80).

[2] Ball quotes a story, which may be a libel, of Burmese chasing fowls till they died of exhaustion, by which kind of 'killing no murder' they believed they had not done wrong, though they ate the fowls. The Burmese are always glad to dispose of any animal a sportsman may shoot, and will even eat snakes if he kills them. The King of Burma (Ava), it is said, used to keep sheep, one of which would conveniently die whenever meat was required at the palace. (See H. Gouger, *The Prisoner in Burmah*, 1860, p. 52.) Buddha did not forbid the use of meat, and he is said to have died after a meal on wild boar's flesh which, as a Rājput, he was permitted to eat; but Rhys Davids (*Buddhism*, 80) thinks that it means mushrooms. A saying of his is quoted: 'Those who take life are in fault, but not the persons who eat the flesh: my priests have permission to eat whatever food it is customary to eat in any place or country' (Hardy, *Manual of Buddhism*, 327). Modern

is a phantom, of whom they speak blindly, and they are so obstinate in maintaining their gross errors that it is difficult to confute them. They say that the God of the Christians and theirs are brothers, but that theirs is the elder. If anyone asks them where their god is they reply that he has disappeared, and that they know not where he is.

The standing army of the kingdom consists mainly of infantry, which is fairly good. The soldiers are inured to fatigue, and have for their sole garment a piece of calico to cover their waists. All the remainder of the body—the chest, back, arms, and thighs—is uncovered, and the skin, which is all tattooed,[1] as when one applies cupping-glasses, represents many kinds of flowers and animals. After the skin is cut and the blood has flowed from it, these figures of flowers and animals are rubbed in with whatever colours they wish ; and seeing these soldiers from a distance you would say that they were clad with some flowered silken stuff or painted calico, for the colours once applied never fade. They have for arms bow and arrow, musket and pike, and an azagaye,[2] which is a stick of 5 or 6 feet long, tipped with iron at the end, which can be hurled with skill against an enemy.

In the year 1665 there was in the town of Siam a Neapolitan Jesuit called Father Thomas.[3] He fortified the town and the King's palace, which is on the margin of the river, and he had previously erected good bastions on both sides. On account of this the King allowed him to dwell in the town, where he had a small church with a house where M. Lambert, Bishop of Beyrout, went to lodge on arriving in Siam. But these two did not long remain on good terms, and the Bishop found it advisable to have a separate chapel.

The port where vessels arrive from Cochin-China and other

Burmese occasionally, but not often, eat meat (Sir J. G. Scott, *Burma*, 1906, p. 90).

[1] As is well known, tattooing is a fine art in Siam (de la Loubère, 276) : and in Burma, Sir J. G. Scott, *op. cit.*, 77 f.

[2] Assegai (vol. ii, 127).

[3] De la Loubère (p. 91) tells how a few years before his time the King employed a priest of the Mission of St. Lazarus at Paris, named Brother René Charbonneau, to make a wooden fort on the Pegu frontier.

places is only half a league from the town, and as there are always some Christian sailors there, the Bishop built a small house and a chapel there in order to perform mass.[1]

CHAPTER XIX

Concerning the Kingdom of Macassar and the Dutch Embassy to China

THE Kingdom of Macassar, otherwise called the Island of Celebes,[2] commences at the 5th degree of south latitude. The heat is excessive during the day, but the nights are fairly temperate, and the land is beautiful and very fertile; but the people of this island do not know how to build well. The capital town bears the same name as the kingdom, and is situated close to the sea. The port is free; and the vessels which carry thither a quantity of merchandise from the neighbouring islands do not pay any custom dues. The inhabitants poison their weapons, and the most dangerous poison which they use is made of the juice of certain trees which grow in the island of Borneo; they temper it according to the effect, whether slow or quick, which they wish the poison to produce.[3] It is said that the King alone knows the secret of weakening its effect, and he boasts of having some of it so quick that there is no remedy in the world capable

[1] On the whole, this must be allowed to be an excellent account of Siam. Very probably Tavernier obtained his information from the bishops and Jesuit priests. The reader is referred to Crawfurd's *Dictionary of the Indian Islands* for a valuable epitome of information on this subject, and to other authorities referred to on p. 224 above. Full bibliographies will be found in *Ency. Brit.*, 11th ed., xxv. 8 f.; Hastings, *Ency. Religion and Ethics*, xi. 488. Finlayson's *Account of the Mission to Siam*, p. 379, London, 1826, contains an interesting account referring to a period when Siam had scarcely been affected by European nations. On Siam as it now is, there are numerous authorities.

[2] The Island of Celebes extends from Lat. 1° 45′ north to 5° 45′ south (*Ency. Brit.*, v. 596 ff.). For Macassar, *ibid.*, xvii. 193.

[3] The reference is perhaps to the upas poison, for which see Yule, *Hobson-Jobson*, 952 ff.; *Journal Royal Anthropological Institute*, xxxii. 239 ff.; Skeat & Blagden, *Pagan Races of the Malay Peninsula*, i. 263, ii. 315.

of neutralizing it. One of my brothers,[1] whom I had taken to India, and who died there, one day witnessed a remarkable proof of the quickness with which this poison takes effect. An Englishman in a rage killed one of the subjects of the King of Macassar, and the Prince forgave him, but all the Franks, English as well as Dutch and Portuguese, who were in Macassar, feared that if this murder was left unpunished the islanders would take their revenge by attacking some of them, and besought the King to execute the Englishman, and they urged him so strongly that at length he consented. My brother was much beloved by the King, who invited him to take part in all his amusements, and especially at drinking parties. When the Englishman was condemned to death, the King told my brother that he would not allow the victim to languish long, and at the same time to prove the extraordinary power of his poison, he would wound the criminal himself with one of his arrows. These are small poisoned arrows which are fired with a sumpitan,[2] and the King, in order to show his skill, asked my brother in what part of the body he wished him to strike the criminal. My brother, who was anxious to see if what the King had told him of the rapid effect of his poison were true, asked him to strike him on the great toe of the right foot; this the King did exactly and with wonderful skill. Two surgeons, one English and the other Dutch, were ready to cut the toe well below the wound, but they were unable to accomplish it before the poison, more rapid, had reached the heart, and the Englishman died at the same moment. All the kings and princes of the East similarly cherish with care the strongest poisons, and the King of Achīn one day made a present of fifteen or twenty of these poisoned arrows to M. Croke,[3]

[1] This was his brother Daniel. (See Introduction, vol. i, p. x.)

[2] The word is sarbatane in the original; it means a blow-tube, or rather the object blown through. Owing to the virulence of the poison on the darts it is a terrible instrument of offence. Though frequently mentioned by writers, there is no stronger testimony of its power than that given by our author. As an alleged antidote stercus humanum, diluted with water, is mentioned by Friar Odoric (see Yule, *Cathay*, 91; *Hobson-Jobson*, 795, 868).

[3] Later on Tavernier calls him M. Croc (vol. ii, 249).

Envoy-General of Batavia, who was subsequently Chief of the factory at Surat. He had not thought of trying them for some years after they came into his possession, and one day when I was with him we shot many squirrels which fell dead immediately on being struck.

The King of Macassar is a Musalmān, and he allows none of his subjects to become Christians. The Jesuit fathers in the year 1656 found means to build a fairly good church at Macassar, but in the following year the King ordered it to be thrown down, as also that of the Dominican fathers, who said mass for the Portuguese traders in the kingdom. The parochial church, which was conducted by some secular priests, remained standing until the Dutch attacked Macassar with a powerful fleet, and by force of arms they compelled the King to drive all the Portuguese out of his territories.[1] The bad conduct of the Prince was partly the cause of this war, to which the Dutch were also driven by the resentment they felt in consequence of the Portuguese Jesuits having opposed their embassy to China. Besides which they had committed serious outrages against the Dutch at Macassar, having even flung on the ground the hat of one of the envoys who had come to conclude a treaty with the King. Thus the Dutch, unable to avoid resenting this affront, resolved to unite their forces with the Bugis,[2] who were in rebellion against their King, and to avenge, at whatever cost, so gross an insult. On the other hand, as I have said, the Dutch had been much ill-used by the Portuguese Jesuits, who by their intrigues prevented the Deputy whom the former sent to the Emperor of China from accomplishing what he desired, and it happened in this way:

Towards the end of the year 1658 the General of Batavia and his Council sent one of the chiefs of the Dutch Company to the Emperor of China. On his arrival at the Court with splendid presents, he sought to obtain access to the Mandarins, who are the great nobles of the kingdom, so that by their

[1] In 1660 (Crawfurd, *Dict.*, 91).

[2] Bouquins in the original. The Bugis are so called by the Malays, their proper name is Wugi. They are the dominant race in Celebes (Crawfurd, *Dict.*, 74; *Ency. Brit.*, iv. 759 f.).

credit he might obtain permission to trade in China. But the Jesuits, who knew the language and were acquainted with the nobles of the Court, in consequence of the long sojourn they had made in the country, in order to prevent the Dutch Company from gaining a footing, to the prejudice of the Portuguese nation, represented many things to the Emperor's Council to the disadvantage of the Dutch. They told them that in Ceylon they had broken the promise they had given to the King of that island to make over to him the places which they jointly captured from the Portuguese; that they were not people of good faith; and that they had likewise fooled the King of Achīn after the capture of Malacca, and many other Princes in the Molucca islands; that after having taken, by terms of capitulation, the country of some of them together with their persons, promising to maintain them all their lives according to their dignity, they had not treated them with any further consideration once they got them into their power, but had transported them as slaves to the Island of Maurice[1] to cut ebony wood. All these things and many others of the same kind having been represented to the Emperor's Council, the Dutch deputy was immediately dismissed, and left China without having accomplished anything. He learnt from a letter which a spy wrote to him after his departure, the bad turn which the Portuguese Jesuits had played him, and on his return to Batavia he reported it to the General and his Council, who were much annoyed, and resolved to take ample vengeance. According to the accounts which the Deputy handed in, the cost of the voyage amounted to 50,000 écus;[2] and the Council reflected how they could recover double that amount from the Portuguese. They were aware of the trade which the Jesuit fathers conducted annually in the island of Macao and the Kingdom of Macassar, and that they fitted out on their own account as many as six or seven vessels laden with all kinds of Indian as well as Chinese goods. The Dutch calculated the time when these vessels should arrive at Macassar, and on the 7th of June 1660 there appeared at that port two of the Company's vessels, which came in advance to facilitate the withdrawal

[1] Mauritius.

[2] £11,250.

of the Dutch who were on land. The Dutch fleet was composed of more than thirty sail, and anchored at the island of Tanakeke,[1] at 7 leagues from Butagne.[2]

The King felt compelled to defend himself against these enemies whose power he feared, and with the vessels of Macao, which were in the roads, attempted for some time to resist the Dutch attack. The combat was obstinate on both sides, the Dutch divided their fleet, and while thirteen vessels devoted themselves to the Portuguese, the remainder incessantly battered the fortress, which was carried without much resistance. It is said that on this day the Dutch fired more than 7,000 cannon shots, and that the King was so much terrified that he ordered the Portuguese not to fire any more, so as not to irritate the enemy further. The Prince Patinsaloa died during this engagement, and this was a great loss to the King of Macassar, who had become formidable to his neighbours by the diplomacy of this minister, upon whom he entirely relied. As the vessels of Macao found themselves surprised and unprepared for defence, it was not difficult for the Dutch fleet to destroy the Portuguese; they burnt three of their vessels, sent two to the bottom, and took from them a quantity of costly goods; thus it was that the Dutch reimbursed themselves profitably for the cost of the deputation to China.

On the 13th of June the King of Macassar, named Sumbaco, through fear of seeing himself reduced to the last extremity, ordered a white flag to be hoisted on another fortress, whence, surrounded by his wives, he watched the fight. During the truce which they granted him, he sent one of the highest of the nobles of his court to the General of the Dutch fleet to ask for peace, which was granted to him only on condition that he would send an ambassador to Batavia, that he would expel the Portuguese from the island, and that his subjects should no longer trade with them.

As the articles of the treaty were to be ratified at Batavia

[1] Tanahkeke, or the 'Island of Sorcerers', in S. Lat. 5° 30′ towards the extreme end of the south-western peninsula of Celebes (Crawfurd, *Dict.*, 426).

[2] Bontaing, Bonthein, Bonti (*ibid.*, 57) on S. coast of Celebes.

by the General and his Council, the King of Macassar equipped his galleys and sent there eleven of the grandest nobles of his court with a following of 700 men, and the chief of this embassy was the brother of the late Prince Patinsaloa. They were instructed to present to the General of Batavia 200 loaves (*pains*) [1] of gold to redeem the royal fortress, and had orders to submit to all the conditions which the Dutch proposed to them, provided that they did not affect the law of Muhammad. The General received this embassy, which was a great honour for him, and profiting by the opportunity, and the good fortune of his arms, he himself prepared the terms of the capitulation, which were signed by the ambassadors of Macassar and were strictly observed. For immediately all the Portuguese left the country, some passing to the Kingdoms of Siam and Cambodia,[2] and the remainder withdrawing to Macao and Goa. Macao, which was some years ago regarded as one of the most famous and richest towns of the East, was the principal object of the Dutch embassy to China, and as it was the best port which the Portuguese then had in these regions, the design of the Dutch was to ruin it completely. To-day this town, which is at the 22° of north latitude, in a small peninsula of the Province of Canton,[3] which is a part of China, has lost much of its former renown.

The Jesuit fathers and the Portuguese merchants were not recompensed by it for the disgrace which they had experienced at Macassar, and they sustained still another blow close to Goa. The Chief of the Dutch factory at Vengurla, which is only 8 leagues from that town, heard of the ill-success of Dutch affairs in China, and thought of a means to avenge it. On his part he was not ignorant of the fact that the Jesuit fathers of Goa and other places in India did a large trade in rough diamonds which they sent to Europe, whither they carried them when returning to Portugal. And in order to conceal this trade they used to send one or two of their number

[1] 'Loaves' of gold. (See Appendix, vol. i. 331. 200 = £9,000.)

[2] Camboye in the original.

[3] Xanton in the original. Macao is near the mouth of the Canton river and belongs to the Portuguese. The local, not the foreign, trade of Macao is still very considerable, but largely in the nature of smuggling (*Ency. Brit.*, xvii. 191).

in the garb of Fakīrs or Indian pilgrims; this was easy for them to do, because there are among them fathers born in the country, who know the Indian language perfectly. The garb of Fakīrs consists of the skin of a tiger, worn on the back, and one of a goat which covers the waist and hangs down to the knees. For cap they have the skin of a lamb or a kid, the four feet of which hang on the forehead, and neck, while their ears are pierced, and in them are inserted large rings of crystal. Their legs are naked, and they have large wooden sandals on the feet, and carry a bundle of peacocks' feathers to fan themselves with, and drive away the flies. One day as I was dining in company with MM. L'Escot and Raisin,[1] at the house of the Augustin fathers who reside at the Court of the King of Golkonda, one of these Jesuit fathers who had come from Goa entered the chamber clothed in the manner I have described. He told us that he was going to St. Thomé on the business of the Viceroy of Goa; upon which I remarked that to travel through India it was not necessary to disguise himself, and that other religious persons, to whatever order they belonged, did not disguise themselves in that manner.

The chief of the Vengurla factory then seized his opportunity to revenge himself on the Jesuit fathers, and having learnt that two of them were going to the mines to buy 400,000 pardos[2] worth of diamonds, he gave orders to two men who purchased some for him, that as soon as the fathers had completed their purchase they should give notice of it to the master of the customs at Bicholim.[3] Bicholim is a large town on the frontier, which separates the territories of the King of Bījāpur from those of the Portuguese, and there is no other road but by this place, because one cannot elsewhere pass the river which forms the island of Salsette where the town of Goa is built. The Jesuit fathers, believing that the officer of customs knew nothing of the purchase which they had made, embarked in the boat to cross the water, and they

[1] Manucci (ii. 344) tells how M. Raisin presented an emerald to Shāhjahān; for L'Escot, see p. 356 below.

[2] This, with the pardao at 2*s*., would represent a sum of £40,000.

[3] Bicholi in the original, Bicholly in vol. i, p. 146, is now known as Bicholim, and the District bearing the name is included judicially in Bardez in the 'old conquests' (Fonseca, *Goa*, 1).

had no sooner done so, than they were searched, and all the diamonds found on them were confiscated.

I return to the King of Macassar, whom the reverend Jesuit fathers strove to convert, and would possibly have accomplished their design, were it not for a condition which he imposed upon them, which they neglected to fulfil. For at the same time that the Jesuits laboured to attract him to Christianity, the Musalmāns on their part made equal efforts to induce him to embrace their Law; and the Prince, who wished to relinquish idolatry, not knowing which side he should take, told the Musalmāns to summon two or three of their most learned Mullās from Mecca, and the Jesuits to send him an equal number of their ablest men, that he might hear them and instruct himself thoroughly in the two religions; both promised to do so. But the Musalmāns made more haste than the Christians, and eight months afterwards, when they brought two learned Mullās from Mecca, the King, as the Jesuits sent no one, embraced the Law of Muhammad.[1] It is true that three years afterwards two Portuguese Jesuits arrived at Macassar, but it was too late, as the King was then no longer inclined to become a Christian.

The King of Macassar having been made a Musalmān, the Prince, his brother, was so annoyed that he was unable to restrain himself from giving signs of his feeling by a deed which resulted in his disgrace. As he knew that the Musalmāns had a horror of pork, which is one of the common articles of food of the idolaters of Macassar, as soon as the mosque which the King built was finished, he entered it one night, caused ten or twelve pigs to be slaughtered in his presence, and the blood to be sprinkled in all directions, both the walls and the niche[2] where the Mullā places himself to offer up prayers being soiled with it. The King, by the Law of the

[1] This, according to Crawfurd (*Dictionary*, 91), took place in the year 1603; but the people generally did not follow his example till 1616, or a century after the Portuguese had been in occupation of Malacca and the Moluccas.

[2] The Mihrāb, which marks the direction of Mecca. See a drawing of the fine Mihrāb in the Jāmi' or Çathedral Mosque at Fatehpur-Sīkrī (Smith. *Hist. of Fine Art in India and Ceylon*, 429).

religion which he had embraced, was obliged to demolish the mosque and build a new one; the Prince, his brother, withdrew with some other idolatrous nobles, and has never again appeared at Court since that time.

This is all that I have been able to collect of the most singular facts regarding the Kingdoms of the East included in the territories of the Great Mogul and the Empire of China, of which I also have good memoirs; but as I know that several persons have written fully regarding them, I think the reader would prefer that I should give him the result of my own travels and that I should amuse him only with accounts of what I have witnessed with my own eyes.

CHAPTER XX

The Author pursues his journey in the East and embarks at Vengurla for Batavia; the danger which he runs on the sea, and his arrival in the Island of Ceylon.

I LEFT Vengurla, a large town of the Kingdom of Bījāpur, 8 leagues from Goa, on the 14th of April 1648, and embarked on a Dutch vessel which had just brought silks from Persia and was going to Batavia. It had orders to stop at Bakanor[1] *en route*, in order to take in rice, and we arrived there on the 18th of the same month. I landed with the captain, who went to see the King to ask his permission to take the rice; this he gave willingly. It was necessary for us to ascend by the river nearly 3 leagues, and we found the King close to the water, where there were only ten or twelve huts made of palm leaves. He sat in his own hut on a Persian carpet spread beneath him, and there were five or six women, some of whom fanned him with fans made of peacocks' tails, while the others gave him betel and filled his pipe with tobacco. The most important persons of the country were in the other huts, and we counted about 200 men, the majority armed

[1] Bārkūr, an old port on an estuary on the west coast of India, Lat. $13^\circ 28\frac{1}{2}'$. According to the *Imperial Gazetteer* (vii. 22) it was 'the capital of the Jain Kings of Tulava . . . and subsequently a stronghold of the Vijayanagar Rājās. It is often mentioned by the older travellers' (see Yule, *Hobson-Jobson*, 45).

with bows and arrows. They also had with them two elephants. It appeared as if they had some retreat elsewhere, and that they had come to this place merely to enjoy the coolness afforded by the trees and streams. When we left the King and re-embarked on our boat, he sent us, as a present, a dozen fowls and five or six pots of palm wine. We slept the same evening, after a march of a league, in a hamlet where there were but three or four houses, but we had taken with us ample provisions from our vessel. In the morning when we were ready to leave we saw on the river one of our pilots with three or four young men, who came up to us and brought breakfast. When they were landed and we had begun to eat they asked for some tārī [1] or palm wine, and the owner of the hut where we had slept offered to bring us some, which was very good, but he told us that it was strong, and that it might send fumes to the head. Our sailors jeered at that because they drank it often, and sometimes to excess without being inconvenienced. But when you drink it as soon as it is drawn from the tree, and do not allow it to ferment, it is harmless, but if you take too much you feel it ferment in the stomach. The peasant brought us a pot of his palm wine, and each of us drank of it as he felt inclined, one three glasses, another four or five, but I was contented with only one, which contained nearly half a pint. But to tell the truth, we all suffered such severe headaches from it that for two days we were unable to cure ourselves. We asked the natives of the country why this wine had thus troubled us, and they said that it was due to the fact that pepper was planted around the palms, and that it was this which gave so much strength to the wine. We were still somewhat giddy from it when we returned on board, where a governor of the country immediately met us, settled the price of the rice, and asked how much was required. It had to be brought from some distance; this troubled us much, because the wind began to change, and the captain was unwilling to leave, as he had not laden all the cargo he required.

During the night, between the 28th and 29th, the wind began to change, and the pilots told the captain, who had

[1] See vol. i. 128.

never before sailed along the coasts of India, that he ought to hoist the anchor and set sail, although we had not received our full cargo ; but the captain would not consent, replying that we wanted water. The wind having been strong throughout the night, on the following day it calmed a little, and the loading up of the rice was continued. On the day after we strongly urged the captain to leave, and as he saw that we all murmured he sent two boats to get water. But they had scarcely reached the mouth of the river when the wind became so furious that the sailors hastened to return without water ; this they accomplished with much trouble and danger of being lost. When they came on board the two boats were tied astern of the vessel, according to custom, and fourteen men were put in the larger one to watch her and prevent the waves dashing her against the vessel. We wished then to start hoisting the anchor, but the wind became still stronger and more adverse ; of thirty or forty men who were about the winch more than twelve were injured by the bars, the violence of the wind driving them backwards. The captain, wishing also to assist in the work of easing the cable, had his hand badly crushed. At length the sea became so rough that instead of hoisting the anchor it became necessary to put others out, as the wind was driving us on shore. Every one then began to examine his conscience, and prayed thrice in a space of two hours. By midnight we had lost all our anchors, to the number of seven, so that as we had no more and knew not what to do, our pilots called out that every one should try to save himself as soon as the vessel touched the land, and being exhausted they lay down on their beds. A long time before, the captain had gone to rest on account of the great pain in his hand, which was in a dreadful condition. As the moon was shining, I leant against the bulwarks of the vessel watching how the billows urged it towards the shore. While I was in this position the vessel touched land, and everyone believed that she would go to pieces. At this moment two sailors told me that I need fear nothing, and that they would take precautions to ensure our safety, but if God permitted us by His grace to reach the land I must reward them for their trouble. I exhorted them to do their best to save us, and told them there would be 500 écus ready for them as soon as we reached the land. They were two Hamburghers, who had seen me previously at Bandar-'Abbās and Surat, and they well knew that I had all my goods on my person, and needed no camels or mules to carry them. As soon as I promised them this sum they took a spar of wood as thick as a man's thigh and 8 or 10 feet long, and attached to it thick ropes in five or six places, to each of which they allowed a length of only 3 or 4 feet. As they worked at it I kept my eyes constantly fixed in the direction of the land, and I observed that the vessel did not go straight as it had done previously. I feared that it was only the darkness which made me think so, for the moon began to set. I hastened at once to the compass to assure myself, and I saw as a matter of fact that the wind had altogether changed and came from the land. Immediately I cried out to the sailors that the wind had become favourable, and at the same moment the boatswain, who directs the vessel, made a great noise and called all the sailors. He also hailed the fourteen men who were in the large boat, supposing that they were there still; but no one replied, and we saw at daybreak that the cable had parted, and we were never able to ascertain what had become of them. As for the captain, he was unable to rise on account of a severe attack of fever which the pain in his hand had caused. At first everyone took courage, although they were in difficulty how they should steer the vessel, the top of the rudder being broken. To remedy this evil the pilot set a small sail, which was set first on one side and then on the other as he directed, and a rope was tied to the rudder to make it work, for it was only the socket above which was broken, and consequently they could not fix the tiller which comes on board for the steersman. At length the wind blew from the north-east, and the darker the night became, on account of the setting of the moon, the more the wind freshened, and each one gave thanks to God. We were nevertheless not beyond all danger, because it was necessary to pass three great rocks which projected above the water, but the night was so dark we were unable to see them. When ships come to this port where we had taken the rice, they do not generally pass inside these rocks; but our captain, as he had but little time to spare for loading, brought his vessel as close as possible to the mouth of the river for the convenience of those who carried the rice, who were in consequence able to make more frequent trips. At length by God's grace we were, at daybreak, some 3 or 4 leagues from the land. Then we held a consultation in order to settle what direction we should take, because we had no anchors left. Some advised that we should return to Goa to winter [1] there, others that we should go to Pointe de Galle, the first town which the Dutch took from the Portuguese in the Island of Ceylon, for we were about equidistant from both, and the wind was equally favourable for both places. My opinion was that we should not sail for Goa, but for Pointe de Galle; because it was to be feared that at Goa the sailors, who are much addicted to drink, would say or commit some folly which would give an occasion to the Inquisition for arresting them, joined to which there are in that town many facilities for dissipation, so that when time came to put to sea again, the captain would not find, it may be, a single man on board. But in going to Point de Galle there would be no danger, we would meet friends, and we should be able to change to another vessel in order to continue the voyage; this in fact happened. However, we were always in terror lest some tempest might come and throw us on land, as not a single anchor was left to moor the vessel.

Among our sailors there was, by chance, one who had served for many years in this vessel, who assured us that there was a very heavy anchor at the bottom of the hold, but that it had only one arm. Although we desired to get it, we foresaw great difficulty on account of the quantity of goods in the vessel. Nevertheless it was resolved to move the whole cargo, and four or five very skilful carpenters, who had worked at the house at Gombroon for the Company, and were returning to Batavia, said that if they could only get up the anchor they would fix it so as to work as well as if it had two arms. This they did, and in two days both

[1] That is, to remain during the monsoon (Yule, *Hobson-Jobson*, 970 f.).

the anchor and the rudder were in a condition to serve us. To incite the men to work it cost three or four cases of Shīrāz wine, which was distributed to all those who assisted in removing the goods and getting out the anchor.

Eight days afterwards we found that we were off Pointe de Galle, and we took in some of our sails in order to gain the port, one of the worst in all India, on account of the rocks, which are at a level with the water in many places.[1] For this reason as soon as a vessel is sighted at sea the Governor-General sends two pilots to direct and bring her into port. But as both weather and sea were sufficiently favourable, the captain and pilots, who had never been there before, not realizing that we had passed the reefs, which they thought were nearer land, and seeing that no pilot came to bring the vessel into port, put out to sea again ; this caused much surprise to the Governor and the pilots, who did not come out because they saw that we had passed the danger. The wind then beginning to change, drove us 9 or 10 leagues out to sea, and consequently we were two or three days beating about before we could regain the port. If the wind had driven us a little farther to sea we should have been obliged to go to winter at Masulipatam, in the Gulf of Bengal. At length the pilots of Pointe de Galle came out for us, and we entered the port and landed on the 12th of May. I immediately went to visit the Governor Madsuere,[2] who is at present General at Batavia, and he did me the honour to invite me to dine with him during my sojourn there.

I did not find anything remarkable in this town, and scarcely anything remains but the ruins, and mines, and the marks which the cannons made when the Dutch besieged it and drove away the Portuguese.[3] The Company gave land and sites for building to those who wished to dwell there, and had already erected two good bastions, which command the port. If it had accomplished the design which it then formed, it would have made this town a fine place.

[1] 'In addition to being incommodious and small, [it] is obstructed by coral rocks, reefs of which have been upreared to the surface, and render the entrance critical to strange ships' (Tennent, *Ceylon*, i. 52)

[2] In the edition of 1713 he is called Masudere. [Joan Maatsuiker, Governor 1646–50].

[3] In 1640. See Tennent ii. 42 ff.

The Dutch, before they had captured all the settlements which the Portuguese had in the Island of Ceylon, whence they have been entirely driven, persuaded themselves that the trade of the island would yield them enormous sums if they were sole masters of it. This might have happened if they had kept to the agreement they had made with the King of Kandy, who is the King of the country, when they began to make war with the Portuguese. But they broke faith with him, and that gave them a very bad character in these parts.

The treaty with the King of Kandy provided that this King was always to be in charge of the passes, with 18,000 or 20,000 men, to prevent the reinforcements which might come from Colombo, Negombe,[1] Manār, and many other places which the Portuguese held along the coast. And the Dutch were to bring in their large vessels sufficient troops to besiege Pointe de Galle both by sea and land. They agreed, also, with the King of Achīn that he should hold the coast with a sufficient number of small armed frigates, of which he always maintained several.

When the Dutch captured the town, they began to repair some breaches, on which the King of Kandy sent to know when he might come there to receive possession. For it had been agreed in the event of the Dutch taking the town that they would give it back to the King, who by way of recompense was to provide them with a certain quantity of cinnamon every year, and, in case of necessity, to aid them as far as he was able. The Dutch replied that they were willing to hand over the town to him provided he paid them the costs of the war, which they said amounted to many millions; but if he had possessed three kingdoms like his own he could not have paid half the sum. In truth money is scarce in that country, and I do not believe that the King has ever seen a sum equal to 50,000 écus [2] at one time. His whole trade consisted in cinnamon and elephants; but since the Portuguese have been in India he has derived no profit from either. As for the elephants, that is a small matter, for only five or six are captured in a year; but at the same time those

[1] Negombo. [2] £11,250.

of Ceylon are more highly esteemed than the elephants of other countries, because they are more courageous in war; and there is not a King in India who does not desire to have one. I may here state a fact which some may find it difficult to believe, but it is nevertheless quite true; it is that when any king or noble possesses one of these Ceylon elephants, and others are brought into its presence from the places where the merchants obtain them, such as Achīn, Siam, Arakan, Pegu, the Kingdom of Bhutān, the Kingdom of Assam, the territories of Cochin and the coast of Melinde,[1] as soon as these latter elephants see one of Ceylon, by a natural instinct they pay it reverence by placing the ends of their trunks on the ground, and then raising them.[2] It is true that the elephants which the great nobles keep, when brought before them to be examined whether they are in good condition, make a sort of salute thrice with their trunk. This I have often seen; but they are trained to it, and their masters teach them to do it when young.

The King of Achīn, with whom the Dutch failed to keep their promise, had other means for revenging himself than by the aid of the King of Kandy, because the Dutch were not allowed to ship the pepper which comes from his territories; for a long time he refused them permission, and even

[1] This reference to Malinda would seem to imply that the African elephant was domesticated in Tavernier's time (see vol. i. 221): but this is doubtful.

[2] Sir Emerson Tennent, alluding to the common belief that Tavernier had made a statement to this effect, adds that 'a reference to the original shows that Tavernier's observations are not only fanciful in themselves but are restricted to the supposed excellence of the Ceylon animal in war'. This statement is simply incomprehensible, since Tavernier's original passage, which is here translated, is quoted in full in a footnote on the same page (*Ceylon*, ii. 380). Fryer (i. 73) also says that the Ceylon elephants exact homage from all others, which prostrate themselves submissively before them. In reference to the fact that the elephants of Sumatra have points of affinity with the Ceylon variety, it has been suggested that the original stock of the Sumatra elephants was introduced in a domesticated condition from Ceylon. It is on record that some elephants sent as a present to the Sultān of Sulu (or Soolo) by the East India Company, as he was unable to maintain them, were let loose on Cape Unsang in Borneo. (Hornaday, *Two Years in the Jungle*, 220.)

declared war upon them; and without this pepper their trade could not prosper.

This is the kind of pepper which we call 'small', and all Orientals prefer it, because without skinning or crushing they place it whole on their plates of rice, as I have elsewhere said.[1] At length the Dutch were compelled to agree with the King of Achīn, and ambassadors were sent by both sides for this purpose. The envoy who arrived on behalf of the King at Batavia, was treated with much magnificence. When he was about to depart the General and all his Council entertained him splendidly, and the ladies sat at table; this greatly surprised this Musalmān ambassador, who was not accustomed to see women drink and eat with men. But that which astonished him still more was that at the end of the repast, after drinking many healths, they drank that of the Queen of Achīn, who ruled the state during the minority of the King, her son.[2] And in order to honour him still more, the General desired Madame la Générale to kiss the ambassador. The King and Queen of Achīn did not receive the ambassador sent to them from Batavia with less honour. He was M. Croc, who for fifteen years suffered from a languishing sickness; and it was believed that someone had administered to him some kind of slow poison. On the occasion of his third audience with the King, who knew that he had lived for so long a time in languor and without appetite, he asked him if he had ever kept any girl of the country, and how he had left her, if by mutual agreement or whether he had sent her away by force. He admitted that he had left one in order to get married in his own country, and that since that time he had always been languishing and indisposed, upon which the King said to three of his physicians, who were by his side, that having heard the cause of the ambassador's sickness he would give them fifteen days to cure him, and that if they did not

[1] See vol. ii. 11.

[2] 'There were Kings of Achin from 1521 till 1641, when the tyrant King died, and a Queen apparently assumed office, first as regent, and afterwards as absolute monarch. Her reign was not extraordinarily long, only 28 years, but the idea that female rule in Achin had prevailed for many years soon became common belief' (Temple's note on Bowrey, 295 f.; Fryer, i. 121; de la Loubère, 82).

accomplish it in that time he would have them all executed. The physicians replied that they would answer to him for the cure of the ambassador, provided he consented to take the remedies which they would give him, and M. Croc resolved to consent. They gave him in the morning a decoction, and in the evening a small pill, and at the end of nine days a great fit of vomiting seized him. It was thought he would die of the strange efforts which he made; and at length he vomited a bundle of hair as large as a small nut, after which he was at once cured. The King afterwards took him to a rhinoceros hunt, and invited him to give the mortal shot to the animal. As soon as it was killed they cut off the horn, which the King also presented to the ambassador;[1] and at the conclusion of the hunt there was a great feast. At the end of it the King drank to the health of the General of Batavia and his wife, and ordered one of his own wives to kiss the ambassador. On his departure he presented him with a pebble of the size of a goose's egg, in which large veins of gold were to be seen like the tendons in a man's hand, and it is thus that gold is found in this country.

M. Croc, when at Surat as chief of the factory, broke the pebble in two, and gave half to M. Constant, who, under him, held the highest authority there. When he was returning to Holland, I offered him 150 pistoles for it in order to present it to the late Monseigneur le Duc d'Orléans, but he would not consent to part with it.

CHAPTER XXI

Departure of the Author from the Island of Ceylon, and his arrival at Batavia.

On the 25th of July[2] [1648] we left Pointe de Galle on a different vessel from that by which we had arrived, because when it was examined, it was found that it could not make

[1] The horn of the rhinoceros was, and is still in South Africa and Hindostān, valued as an antidote to poison. See the authorities quoted in Fryer, ii. 298.

[2] The July of the original and the June of the edition of 1713 appear to be both wrong, as the month must have been May.

the journey without danger. Accordingly, all the goods were discharged from it and transhipped to that in which we embarked for Batavia.

On the 2nd of June [1] we crossed the line, and on the 6th reached the island called Nazacos.[2] On the 17th we sighted the coast of Sumatra, on the 18th the island of Ingagne,[3] and on the 19th the island of Fortune. On the 20th we saw several other small islands, and the coast of Java, and among these islands there are three which are called Prince's Islands.[4] On the 21st we saw the island of Bantam, and on the 22nd we anchored in the roads at Batavia. On the following day I landed, and went to salute General Vanderlin and M. Caron,[5] the Director-General, who was the second officer in the council.

On the 25th, two days after my arrival, the General sent one of his guards to invite me to dinner, where there were assembled M. Caron, two other councillors, the Avocat Fiscal, the Major, and their wives. Whilst we were at table they conversed about the news from foreign countries, and principally of the court of the King of Persia, and after dinner some began to play backgammon, while waiting till it became cool enough to take exercise outside the town by the river's bank, where there are very fine bathing places. The General went to his office, where he asked me to accompany him. After some conversation on indifferent matters he asked me for what purpose I had come to Batavia. I told him I had principally come to see so renowned a place; and as I had an opportunity of doing service to the Company at the request of the Chief of the factory at Vengurla, I had been

[1] In the 1713 edition this is given, probably incorrectly, as July. June appears to be correct.

[2] Not identified, but it may be remarked that *nusa* is Javanese for a small island, and like *pulo* is used as a prefix to the true name. (Crawfurd, *Dictionary*, 303.)

[3] Ball suggests that it may be Indragiri, a Malay State on the coast of Sumatra: but there is an island named Engano, about 200 miles SSE. of Nassau Island (A. Hamilton, in Pinkerton, viii. 449).

[4] There is a Prince Island in Sunda Strait, between Java and Sumatra.

[5] M. Caron, a renegade Dutchman, founded the first French factory in India, at Surat, in 1668. (*Imperial Gazetteer*, ii. 463, xii. 104.)

led to undertake the voyage, as he might see for himself by the letter which he had received from there. I told him, at the same time, as the Commander of Vengurla had requested me, of the discovery which had been made by a caravel of Portugal, which a storm had driven into a bay situated 30 leagues from the Cape of Good Hope, as I have related at length in the description of the town of Goa.[1] The Commander thought that the General would be able to send a small vessel there from Batavia, and that by conveying the news I would do a service to the Company; and it was also with this in view that he offered me a passage in the vessel which was in the roads at Vengurla. After I had finished my account of the matter the General thanked me somewhat coldly, as if my news was of small importance, although I have since learnt that he sent to seek for the bay, but the vessel was unable to find it. After about half an hour's interview I left him in his office, when three councillors entered at the same moment, and as I left he said that if I would wait for a little we might go together to promenade outside the town. I then joined Madame la Générale, and the other ladies who were keeping her company, and an hour afterwards two trumpets began to sound. The General and Madame, with four of the wives of the councillors, entered a carriage with six horses, and the councillors rode on horseback. I was allotted a horse with Persian saddle and bridle, the furniture of which was very beautiful. There are always forty or fifty saddle-horses in the stables of the General, for there is not a vessel that does not bring him some, either from Arabia or Persia or other places. A squadron of cavalry marched in front of the General's carriage, each dragoon having a collar of buffalo skin and long scarlet hose with silver lace, a hat with a bundle of plumes, a great scarf with a fringe of silver, the sword-guard and spurs of massive silver, and all the horses had very beautiful trappings. Three bodyguards marched at each door carrying halberds, and well clad. Each had a doublet of yellow satin, and the upper part of the hose of scarlet covered with silver lace, and below with yellow silk,

[1] See vol. i. 173, for accounts of this discovery. The details given there are somewhat different.

and very fine linen. Behind the carriage there marched a company of infantry, besides another which went an hour or two in advance to clear the way. When the councillors go abroad, as well as when they are at home, they have each two musketeers for their guard, and when they wish for horses the General's equerry sends them what they require. They have also their small boats to row about on the sea, the river, or on the canals, where each of them has his garden. Our promenade was not long, because when we left the fort two vessels were seen approaching, but no one was able to say what they were. As the General and councillors were impatient to hear the news, they returned to the fort sooner than they had intended; and as soon as we arrived I took leave of the General, the councillors, and the ladies, and withdrew to my lodging.

For three or four days I received numerous visits, which caused me no small expenditure, because custom requires that when any visitor comes you offer him wine. One hundred écus are soon spent; for a pint of wine, of about Paris measure, holds only four glasses. Spanish wine when cheap costs an écu at Batavia, Rhine and French wine cost two, and one must pay 40 sols for a pint of beer, whether English or of Broncevimont.[1]

The people of Batavia are greatly delighted when vessels come from Holland, for they bring all kinds of drinks, which the publicans buy from the Company, and every private person also may buy them. But whether they find more pleasure in drinking at public-houses than in their own houses, or that it is more convenient to them, when they wish to amuse themselves in company, they generally make all their rejoicings in these places. It is a time of great festival when these new drinks arrive, and you meet women and girls in the streets who wager you for a pint or two of wine or beer. Whether one loses or gains, it is a point of honour never to allow the women to pay, and others come also, whose healths you have to drink. This often empties the purses of young people.

[1] These prices in English money were, for Spanish wine, 4*s.* 6*d.*; for Rhine and French wine, 9*s.*; and for a pint of beer, 3*s.* Mr. E. Heawood, Librarian of the Royal Geographical Society, has kindly traced the word 'Broncevimont'. It is Tavernier's way of writing Brunswick Mum, or beer

CHAPTER XXII[1]

Concerning an affair which was raised unseasonably for the Author in the Council at Batavia.

THERE are two Councils in Batavia, the Council of the Fort, at which the General[2] presides, where the affairs of the Company are discussed; and the Council that sits in the Town Hall, and deals with the police and the minor disputes which arise among the citizens. M. Faure, a member of the Town Council, was one of those who came to visit me on my arrival, and during nine or ten days he, with one of his friends, was with me four times. Both of them spoke frequently of M. Constant, who had been Commander at Gombroon, and was for many years the second officer of the factory at Surat, where he had amassed much wealth. He had often trusted me with a part of it, and we had always been good friends. One day, as I was about to leave Surat on my way to the diamond mine, he asked me to purchase diamonds on his account to the extent of 16,000[3] rupees' worth, giving me a letter of credit for that sum on Golkonda, where it was paid me, and I invested it as he desired. I expected on my return to find him at Surat; but during my journey he had received orders to start at once for Batavia, and as soon as he got there he married the widow of General Vandime and went with her to Holland. I was much surprised on my return to Surat to find that he had left without giving orders to any of his friends, Dutch or English, to receive what I had for him, and send it to him by one of the vessels which go to England. I remained at Surat about two months,

[1] This chapter is omitted in the English Translation by John Phillips, but an abstract of its contents is included in ch. xxi.

[2] [Governor-General].

[3] £1,800. (See Index for further references to this traffic carried on by Tavernier on behalf of the Dutch officials.) At a latter period we find English officials engaging in the same trade. (See Colonel Yule's account of the Pitt diamond in Hedges' *Diary*, Hakluyt Society, iii. 91, 161 f.) Thomas Pitt, was Governor of Madras from 1698 to 1709. Another Pitt, Governor from 1730-35, George Morton or Moreton Pitt, appears to have been notable, also, for his private trade in diamonds. (*Kistna Manual*, 106 *n.*; Wheeler, *Madras in the Olden Time*, 505.)

and as I wished to travel, in order not to risk what M. Constant had entrusted to me I placed the whole in the hands of Sr. Francis Breton,[1] the second officer in the English factory at Surat, who, at M. Constant's request, afterwards forwarded it to him in Holland. I had previously asked the Dutch Commander, named Arnebar, to be good enough to take charge of this parcel, as he was a friend of M. Constant; but he excused himself, telling me that if the General or Council at Batavia came to know that he had such goods in his hands they would treat him as a receiver who had not declared them, in other words, he would be deposed from his office and all his property confiscated.

One day, then, while I was at Batavia, M. Faure, whom I have just mentioned, came to see me with three others, bringing a large bottle of Rheims wine and another of English beer. For my part I had contributed a collation, and as we began to drink they asked me if I had not heard the news of M. Constant which had come by land while I was at Surat; to which I replied that I had not received any intelligence, either by sea or land, since he had left Batavia. They expressed surprise at this reply, and told me that they were much astonished, that having been such great friends, and having done such considerable trade together which still lasted, he had not made me acquainted with his movements. I saw from the first that they were come with no other design than to inquire whether I had with me the parcel of diamonds which I had bought at the mine for M. Constant, or whether I had left it with some Dutchman to send to him. I thought it advisable to remove this doubt from their minds, for unless I did so they would be unable to drink the wine they had brought, with comfort. Without keeping them longer in suspense, therefore, I told them that I was astonished that they had not spoken to me of this matter on the first occasion when they had done me the honour to visit me, and I perceived clearly that they wished to know if the last time I had been at the diamond mine M. Constant had not given me a commission to buy for him; that they need not have brought

[1] Francis Breton, President of Surat 1644–9. See the epitaph on his tomb (Rawlinson, *British Beginnings in Western India*, 136). [Cf. p. 62].

wine for that purpose to make me drink, because I differed from most men, who speak much and say more than they know when they have drunk, but, as for myself, it is then I talk least; nevertheless, since I desired to satisfy them, so that they might not have any regret for their good wine, I would tell them the truth frankly. It is true, then, I told them, that M. Constant not only gave me a commission to buy him a parcel of diamonds, but he also gave me money to pay for them, and I purchased them for 16,000 rupees. I had no sooner finished speaking than M. Faure, turning to the three others, 'Gentlemen,' said he, 'you will bear me witness that M. Tavernier has 16,000 rupees' worth of diamonds for M. Constant, which he left me an order to receive when he departed for Holland.' I replied without disturbing myself, that if he wished for them he would have to run after them, but that I did not believe he would overtake them; that it was more than six months since I had dispatched them by land, and that I was much surprised at his having taken this commission, and wondered how M. Constant and he could have known that I would go to Batavia. I saw that it annoyed him to find that he had not got what he expected, and as they did not wish to drink any more they all four departed.

On the following day, early in the morning, an officer of the Company handed me a summons to appear at 11 o'clock before the Town Council, where the Avocat Fiscal was present to take up the case on behalf of the Company. I did not fail to be present at the Town Hall at the hour named, when, immediately, these gentlemen called me in, and with great compliments asked me if it was true that M. Constant had asked me to make an investment in diamonds to the amount of 16,000 rupees, and also where they were. I said that as regards the purchase of the diamonds it was true that I made it, but that I knew not where they were, because more than six months had elapsed since I forwarded them to him from Surat by land. Upon that the gentlemen of the law delivered sentence that it was not for M. Faure to interfere in the matter, but it was the duty of the Avocat Fiscal to follow it up; that at that time M. Constant was in the Company's service, and that, without having defrauded it, he could not out of his wages have amassed so large a sum. At this mention of his having defrauded the Company I was unable to prevent myself from laughing ; this astonished them, and the President of the Council asked me why I laughed. I told him that it was seeing his astonishment at the fact that M. Constant had defrauded the Company of 16,000 rupees, and that if he had only carried off so much, it would have been a small matter, adding that there was scarcely a servant of the Company who had held M. Constant's offices, and had enjoyed the opportunity of trading, as he had, without fear of the Fiscal, who had not made at least 100,000 écus.[1] Two or three members of the Council, then present, were uneasy at hearing me talk in this way, as these remarks particularly affected them For to say the truth, the Commanders and their subordinates in the factories know well how to appropriate large sums for their own benefit, to the great detriment of the Company ; and as they cannot do so without having an understanding with the broker, he does the same on his own account, those below him also taking what they can. I made an estimate once of all the money of which the Company is defrauded on the trade in each factory, and I ascertained that as they annually defraud it in all the factories taken together to the extent of 1,500,000 or 1,600,000 livres,[2] they have abundant opportunity for consoling themselves. For to speak but of Persia alone, I have known Commanders who, both by the sale of spices and on the purchase of silks, have laid apart for themselves in one year more than 100,000 piastres.[3] They practice marvellous artifices which it is difficult for the Company, especially the directors and shareholders of the Company, who are in Holland, to discover. For, as regards the Commanders in India, the scandal must become notorious before the General of Batavia and his council have recourse to law, and most frequently the commanders shut the mouth of the Avocat Fiscal, by a present amounting to more than the third part which would be his share if all were confiscated, another third belongs to the Company, and the other to the Hospital. Thus all passes

18

[1] £22,500. [2] £112,500 to £120,000. [3] £22,500.

in silence, for every one of these Commanders has his patron at Batavia, to whom he sends valuable presents yearly, besides which there is not one of these gentlemen of the Council who has not done the same himself. Moreover, if anyone who is cognizant of a wrong done by a Commander to the Company reports it to the General, he is certain never to be appointed to any factory, and sooner or later an opportunity is found for removing him from the office he holds, and he is sent as a soldier to some island to end his life miserably.

As for the trade which these Commanders do on their own account, there is no one who knows more about it than the poor sailors, who are sometimes very badly treated by the Commanders themselves, or the officers of the vessels who when they go on shore report to the chief of the factory that so and so has so many bales of goods on his private account. Most frequently the chief of the factory, who knows his part, sends to advise the person to whom the goods belong to have them removed, and to arrange to have them carried on shore by night. In order to give him time to discharge all, the informer is so well supplied with drink that he is drunk for a day or two, and when all has been removed the Commander goes to the vessel to make an examination, well assured that he will find nothing. Then the poor sailor or soldier, for the falsehood which they force him to believe he has told, is severely punished, his wages are confiscated, and in most cases he is sent for three or four years to work on the galley dispatched for a cargo of stones. There are, then, some of these Commanders who have defrauded the Company, and have returned to Holland with great booty, 400,000 or 500,000 livres [1] worth of diamonds, pearls, ambergris, and other goods which occupy but small space. For if all is not well concealed, and if the Company is able to discover it, it is lost, and their wages are confiscated. But they have wonderful ways for escaping, even when they have bulky goods, like calicoes and other things which occupy much space, for all cannot go to the places where diamonds are to be purchased, and moreover they more frequently experience

[1] £30,000 to £37,500.

loss than gain by carrying them, while on coarse goods there is always much profit to be made.

As the captain and other officers of the vessel try to do private trade as well as the Commanders, knowing that it will be difficult to take their goods out of the vessels without being discovered, they sometimes discharge them on the coast of Norway, making believe that it is bad weather which has driven them thither. Moreover, when the Dutch are at war with the English, they send vessels of war to meet those coming from India, and into these vessels those who wish to defraud the Company tranship their bales of goods, before arriving at Holland. They also employ, for the same purpose, the fleet of herring fishers when they meet them. In short, there is no kind of artifice of which they do not make use. But when the Company entertains a suspicion that anyone has cheated them, they order the Commanders to undress and put on other clothes, and more than once diamonds have been found in those which were taken off. In conclusion, it has been remarked that the majority of those who have defrauded the Company and have returned to Holland with great wealth have not left their heirs any the richer; all this wealth being, as it were, evaporated in a few years. This proves that wealth ill-acquired does not profit.

Returning to the affair which had been stirred up against me at Batavia. On the order which the members of the Council had given, that the Avocat Fiscal should take the cause in hand on the Company's behalf, three days afterwards he sent me many pages of paper containing written charges, so that I might reply to each. The first demanded that I should declare to what extent M. Constant and I had traded together since we had known one another. The others were mere nonsense, for instance the demand for a reply from me, who was in no wise responsible to the Company, and had only come to Batavia to render it a service; so I had no need to trouble myself about the Fiscal's order. There was a special query that the General and his Council wished to know what M. Constant had done at Bandar 'Abbās, where he had been sent as Commander; that they were aware of the fact that we were together day and night, and that consequently I must be well acquainted with his affairs. They were right in this, but I was not bound to render an account to them. This inquiry lasted fully four or five weeks, during which an officer came to summon me several times to accompany him to the Town Hall to give a reply. I gave always the same answer, that I knew nothing of M. Constant's affairs, and that when he did anything he did not ask my advice. As they saw they could get nothing from me by politeness, they began to threaten me with arrest. I replied boldly that I did not fear them, and that if they arrested me I had the honour to serve a Prince, the late Monseigneur le Duc d'Orléans, who would get me safely out of their hands, and would resent the affront they had done me. At the same time I left their presence without saying another word, and they also said nothing to me. Fifteen days passed without reference to this affair, and during this time I went to take exercise and even to dine with some of these gentlemen. One day the Avocat Fiscal, who had read much and liked to hear about foreign countries, asked me to supper; when we had left the table he took me apart and told me that he had to summon me on the following day, having received an order from the General, who wished to know, absolutely, what I had seen M. Constant do at Gombroon. 'If it is to say what I have seen,' I replied, 'I shall do so willingly, but I desire to speak in the presence of the judges.' Next morning the officer did not fail to summon me. I followed him forthwith, and when I entered the chamber, the President asked me at first if I would tell them something of what I had seen of M. Constant. I said, 'I would satisfy him, and that I desired to give the account at full length,' with which reply the President and Council told me they were quite content. As they had ordered silence for me, and I saw they awaited with impatience what I had to say to them, I spoke in the following terms:—

'The day M. Constant disembarked at Gombroon the Khān or Governor of the town and country made much of him, and kept him to supper, together with those who had accompanied him. The repast was magnificent, and the dishes were much better prepared than usual; I have been at many feasts of Khāns or Governors of Provinces in Persia, where they know of nothing but ragouts, not even understanding how to roast a fowl properly. But at this repast all was well arranged, and it looked as if a Frank cook had a hand in it. All the baladines of Gombroon were present, to dance in their own manner according to custom, and there was much gaiety. The following day M. Constant entertained several Franks at dinner, and at the close of the repast the Khān sent one of his officers to present his compliments to Commander Constant, and to tell him that he would sup with him; this he received very well, as he appreciated the honour the Khān wished to do him. Compliments being finished, the Commander took a large glass and drank to the health of the Khān, and all those who were at table did likewise. As soon as the officer had left, the Commander asked some of those who were dining with him, how a governor should be treated when he did the honour to a commander of coming to see him at home; one told him that the first care he should have would be that as soon as night had come numbers of lamps should be lighted, both outside and in the house. In that country these are little saucers full of oil attached to the walls of the house, and about a foot from each other.[1] But the Commander desiring to do more honour than that to the Khān and to the Company, instead of these lamps ordered white wax candles to be used, so that both within and without the house there was light everywhere. The Khān expressed himself highly pleased with this liberal expenditure, which was done specially to enhance his honour; and all the merchants, both Christians and Musalmāns, were also surprised. It is true', said I to the members of the Council,' that you know that this wax does not cost so much to the Company as it does to private persons, because all the Dutch vessels which come from Mocha carry much of it, as it is very cheap there.'

'The baladines were present in large numbers at this repast, to amuse the company with their dances and graceful attitudes, for there was money to be earned, as they know that the Commanders pay them well, and that it is not the case with

[1] The Chirāgh, used in the same way in India.

them as with the Khān, who generally considers he has paid liberally when he gives them supper.

'Next day those who were in charge of these baladines (for each troupe had an old woman as guardian and directress, whom the baladines call their mother[1]) came to pay their respects to M. Constant, who showed himself so liberal toward them that no one asked for anything from the guests—this is very contrary to their usual custom. Some of those who had slept there, and had passed all the night in making these women dance, were much surprised, on leaving in the morning, at not being compelled to put their hands in their pockets, and took occasion to extol the generosity of the Commander who had so liberally paid for all. Throughout the night the signals which were on the terrace of the lodge were fired, and at each health a dozen were fired to warn the vessels to make a salute.

'Two hours before sunrise the Khān rose from where he had seated himself on his arrival, and where they had drunk and eaten, and his officers bore him away, observing that the wine began to heat him. As soon as he had left, a part of the company returned to eat and drink and the others to see the baladines dance, and the debauch lasted till ten o'clock in the morning. Everyone, when leaving, remarked to another, "It must be admitted that this new Commander is honourable, and does all things with a good grace."

'When M. Constant,' I continued to these gentlemen of the Council, 'arrived at Gombroon, and had to go to the dwelling of the Khān, the finest horses in the Company's stable were brought to him. That for the Commander had rich brocaded trappings, but as the bridle was only of silver he appeared to be surprised, and asked why there was not a golden bridle on his horse, considering that he was not inferior to the other Commanders who had preceded him at Gombroon. They told him that, by order of the Company, the Commander Vanderlin had sent the two golden bridles from Gombroon to Batavia, the gold of one weighing 600, and of the other 450 ducats, and that it had been ordered

[1] Known in Indian Musalmān cities as Sāqan, feminine of Sāqī, 'a cup-bearer', or Nā'ika, 'conductor'.

that, for the future, no Commander should use one of gold on his horse, but must content himself with one of silver. As I saw that this annoyed M. Constant, I told him privately that it would be easy for him to have a golden bridle on his horse without the Company being able to reproach him. That he had only to send to the Khān the present which he had to make him on behalf of the Company on a little more liberal scale than the other Commanders, his predecessors, had done, and he should see that he would soon have a golden bridle. M. Constant believed me, and made a very handsome present to the Khān.

'These presents consist generally of all kinds of spices, porcelain, Japanese cabinets, Dutch cloths, and other things of that kind. But the best part of the present was a ring of diamonds for which he had paid me 1,500 écus [1]; and 1,000 gold ducats of which the King caused a golden bridle to be made, which he sent as a present to the Commander; it weighed but 643 ducats of gold, and the balance remained in the Khān's purse. It is the custom in Persia, when a stranger makes a present to a great person, that he gives another in return, but certainly when one makes one to a King he never receives in return nearly the value of that which he has given.[2] The Khān was altogether amazed at so magnificent a present, and although, according to custom, he should have sent his gift, which is usually a valuable horse, and sometimes two, on the following day, he waited for five or six days, because it required that time to make the bridle. As soon as it was finished the Khān sent two fine horses to the Commander, one with the bridle of gold, and the other with a bridle of silver, the saddles of the Turkish pattern with brocade of gold and silver. Out of politeness it was necessary that the Commander when mounting his horse, should have the golden bridle put on; and thus the Company was not able to say anything.'

This was the account I gave to the Council of Batavia of what I had seen at Gombroon in reference to M. Constant, and it should be remarked, before going further, that all

[1] £337 : 10*s*.

[2] See under Peshkush in Yule, *Hobson-Jobson*, 701.

the presents which the kings and great nobles make to the commanders and the other principal officers of the Company ought to be handed over, when they go to Batavia, to the charge of the General of the Council as property belonging to the Company, but they are sometimes allowed to retain them.[1]

When I spoke in this way to these gentlemen of the Council of Batavia, and told them ingenuously what M. Constant had done during the first days after his arrival at Gombroon, they wished to know what happened afterwards, and they told me that they had already been sufficiently informed of what I had just told them, but wished that I should let them know what trade M. Constant had done. It was then I began to speak to them in a different way, and told them I was not dependent on them and was not their spy; that if they wished to know so much they should have ascertained it when he was at Batavia, or they might write to him in Holland, and would thus be able to satisfy themselves. The President, who saw that I mocked them, rose from his place to talk with some of the councillors, and then told me that they would give me four days to reflect on my reply to the Council, both in reference to the trade which I had done with M. Constant, and that which I knew he had done with other persons. Upon this I retired, without replying, and went to dine with one of the councillors without speaking further of the matter.

The four days having expired, I waited for them to send for me, but they delayed eight days longer, after which they sent an officer to tell me that the President would expect me at the Council at 11 o'clock. When I entered the chamber, the Avocat Fiscal delivered a long discourse, referring to my refusal to reply to the questions which had been given me in writing, and as for himself he required that I should be placed in gesselin, i. e. under arrest, until I had replied. I replied to that 'that I was not the least astonished at what he said, and that I believed the gentlemen of the Council would think more than once before they carried it into execu-

[1] As presents in India are sent to the Government's Toshakhāna, 'wardrobe' or 'store'.

tion; that if he wished me to reply to what he asked, it was necessary to convey it to me in a language which I understood, and not in Dutch.' He replied to this 'that he had often heard me speak Dutch,' to which I answered 'that in truth I did know something of the language, but not enough to enable me to read and understand chicanery.' As I perceived that he was offended by the use of the word 'chicanery' I said to him again in a firmer tone than before, 'that I was not in receipt of wages from the Company, and that I had not been appointed to observe the conduct and actions of M. Constant.' The Council at length ordered the Fiscal to give me his questions in French; this he did, and fixed the period for replying at eight days. I laughed at all these questions, being well assured that I was able to put an end to the proceedings whenever I pleased. I deferred replying for another eight days beyond the eight which they had given me; but seeing that the Council began to be annoyed, I thought that it was time to put an end to the affair.

As soon as the Fiscal had given me his questions in French, I communicated them to M. Potre, the ablest counsel in Batavia, who told me that, not being employed by the Company, I was not obliged to reply to any of these articles; nevertheless, being desirous of putting an end to the affair, I went to the President's house shortly after sunrise, and he came to receive me in his sleeping garment, 'preferring', he said, 'to come to me in that condition rather than make me wait while he dressed.' The reply which I made to this compliment was 'that since he wished me absolutely to tell him all that I knew of M. Constant, I would conceal nothing that had come to my knowledge, even were it to the disadvantage of the General himself and many members of the Council, and of you yourself who urge me to speak,' I added, after he had made his guard withdraw, and he and I remained alone. I told him, then, that 'when leaving Surat to go to the diamond mine, M. Constant entrusted me with 44 000 [1] rupees, asking me to expend it on diamonds, and especially on large stones, that my services would be well rewarded, and that as this sum belonged to the General

[1] £4,950.

he would be glad to have an opportunity of obliging him. Moreover, that the General himself had purchased from M. Constant, when he visited Batavia, all the parcels I had sold him while he was the second officer at the factory of Surat. They were all stones which I had cut, their value being more than 40,000 écus.[1] As for the pearls which M. Constant had bought for the General during the time he was at Hormuz, I did not exactly know the value, but I so far knew that they included two pear-shaped pearls which cost 170 tomāns.[2] That I had also received somewhat considerable sums to invest for M. Carles Renel, M. Cam, and some others, and that he himself could not have forgotten that when M. Constant left Batavia to become Commander in Persia, he entrusted to him 36,000 rupees,[3] asking him to give it to some of his friends to invest it in a parcel of diamonds. That the said M. Constant expected to find me at Surat to place this sum in my hands, but as I had left for Hormuz some days before on an English vessel, he thought to find me there, and place the sum in my hands, supposing that during the same season I should return to India, and to the diamond mine. And in order to make you see,' I further said to the President, 'how M. Constant was devoted to your interest, he purchased with the greater part of your money goods of Sironj and Burhānpur, and as soon as he arrived at Gombroon he was offered 30 per cent. profit on them. It is true', I added, 'that to calculate it at the rate which the other merchants have to pay it would only amount to 5 per cent., but he made all pass as if on the account of the Company, which neither pays the freight of the vessel nor the customs at Gombroon, these two items amounting, in the case of the merchants, to 25 per cent.; that when the vessel which had carried him returned to Batavia, although the goods were not sold, he did not forget to write to you that he had refused 30 per cent. profit in the hope of receiving more; that, however, three vessels arrived at Gombroon laden with the same kinds of goods, so that he had difficulty in getting for them what they had cost in India; this compelled him to

[1] £9,000. [2] £586 : 10s., the tomān being equal to £3 : 9s. [3] £4,050.

give those which he had bought for you at the current price; that, nevertheless, M. Constant had been so generous that he never asked anything from you, but that he had told me in private that he had lost more than 15 per cent. by the transaction.'

Having given all this detail to the President, he appeared to be very much alarmed, and besought me to make no noise about it, in which he did wisely, for I could have named others, all the devices [1] of the chiefs of the Company having come to my knowledge, and the principal part of the large sums which they had invested in diamonds having passed through my hands. Observing then that the President did not wish to hear more, I took leave of him and went to tell my counsel all that had passed. His dwelling being near that of the President, I observed that the latter went to the fort, apparently to see the General. Between 11 o'clock and noon I was about to go to the Town Hall to know what the Avocat Fiscal would say to me, because I knew that the President had gone there when leaving the fort, and that they had conversed together. But I met him half-way, and approaching me with a laughing face he asked me where I was going. I replied that I was going to the Town Hall to reply to some of his questions. 'I beg you,' he replied quickly, 'let us leave that affair to go and have dinner together. I was presented yesterday with two cases, one of French wine and the other of Rhine wine, we shall see which is the best. All I ask from you is a word written with your own hand, that you have nothing belonging to M. Constant.' This I gave very willingly, and in this way the whole case came to an end.

[1] 'Adresses', 'dexterities', or worse. Not 'addresses', as Ball rendered the term.

CHAPTER XXIII

The Author goes to see the King of Bantam,[1] *and describes several adventures in connexion therewith.*

HAVING freed myself of an affair which had been raised so inconveniently for me, I forthwith formed a resolution to visit the King of Bantam, having often heard that he was very fond of men of our nation; this I can confirm on account of the good treatment which I received from him. As soon as one passes beyond the Kingdoms which yield obedience to the Great Mogul, the language which is called Malay is, among Orientals, what the Latin language is in Europe.[2] On the voyage I made to India in the year 1638 I took with me one of my brothers[3] who was my junior, and had a special talent for foreign languages. He required but five or six months in order to learn one, and he spoke eight of them perfectly well. Moreover he was well made in person and was considered brave, of which he gave many proofs. One day he fought a duel at Batavia with an infantry captain, over whom he obtained considerable advantage, and General Vandime, who liked men of spirit, and the principals of the Council, who had much esteem for him, permitted the matter to pass in silence, and as a mark of the affection with which they regarded him they gave him permission to equip a vessel on his own private account and to trade in such goods as he pleased, with the exception of spices. Accordingly my brother bought a vessel of fourteen guns, with which he made many voyages. The first was to Siam, where he made

[1] In the native language, Bantan. It forms the western end of Java and has an area of 2,568 geographical square miles. It is a mountainous country of volcanic formation. An English station was established there as early as 1603, but the Dutch ultimately proved the superior in this region. It is now a Dutch Province, having been taken possession of in 1643. (Crawfurd, *Dictionary*, 38.) *Ency. Brit.*, iii. 355 f. [But see Introd.]. The King of Bantam appears in English literature (Jonson, *The Alchemist*, ii. 1; Congreve, *Love for Love*; Aphra Behn, *The Court of the King of Bantam*).

[2] This is still the case, Malay being the lingua franca in these regions.

[3] This was his brother Daniel (see Introduction, pp. xii and xvi).

a sufficiently large profit, but he lost 5,000 or 6,000 écus of it to the King, who invited him to gamble with him and five of the principal nobles of his court, as he was much pleased at meeting a European who spoke the Malay language so well. It cannot be doubted that the profits are great in this kind of trade, since those who advance the money to traders, on loan, obtain for it cent. per cent. But it is also true that they risk much, because if the vessel is lost the money is lost to them also, and this is called 'the great speculation'. He also made some voyages to the King of Macassar, but they did not yield so much profit as those to the Kingdoms of Siam, Tonquin, and Cochinchina.

Having, then, resolved to go to Bantam, and not knowing the Malayan language, I took with me my brother who was then at Batavia. It was necessary for me to have the permission of the General, according to custom, and he refused because he was not on good terms with the King of Bantam. But two hours afterwards M. Caron, who was at that time Director-General, sent to me to say that I might leave on my voyage for Bantam in all safety, as soon as I wished. Accordingly I set out with my brother in a small barque which we hired to carry us to Bantam, where, on arrival, our first visit was to the English President, who gave us a grand reception, and desired that we should not take other quarters but stay with him. He had still about fifty pots of Mantua wine with which he desired to regale us. This wine is not exported in glass bottles, in which it goes bad, but in earthen pots, in which it always keeps good.

On the following morning my brother went to the King's palace, where he was well known and welcome, in order to ascertain when His Majesty would be able to receive us. But as soon as the King knew that he was there, he would not allow him to return to fetch me, but ordered a messenger to be sent to seek me, and tell me that if I had any rare jewels I should please him by bringing them.

When the King's people came to conduct me to the palace, and I did not see my brother with them, I was on the point of refusing to follow them, and I recalled the manner in which the King of Achīn had treated M. Renaud, who had left Nantes with his brother on the vessels which M. de Montmorency sent to India. I shall record the history of it in a few words, and this short digression will possibly not be displeasing to the reader. A French Company of Commerce established for India sent there four vessels, three large and one small one of eight guns, on board which among others were the two brothers Renaud, who entered the service of the Company. Their journey was the shortest and the most fortunate of any ever heard of, as they arrived off Bantam in less than four months. The King received them with great joy, and in eight or ten days' time he gave them as much pepper as they asked for, and at a very fair price, more than 20 per cent. cheaper than the Dutch do. But as our Frenchmen had not come for pepper only, but wished also to obtain information about the trade in cloves, nutmegs, and mace, they sent the smaller vessel with the greater part of their money to Macassar, where the King's stores are generally full, as I have elsewhere said, because the Dutch, with all their skill, are unable to prevent the people of this island trading with the other islands where the spices grow; [1] this annoys them much, since they desire to compel the trade of all other nations to pass through their hands.

Our Frenchmen having obtained their cargo of pepper so quickly at Bantam, had not patience to await the return of the small vessel which they had sent to Macassar, and, to amuse themselves, decided to go to Batavia, which is not more than 14 leagues distant from Bantam. When the wind is favourable one can go there in a single tide, and they reached the roads at 8 o'clock in the morning. As soon as they had cast anchor the General of the French fleet sent to pay his compliments to the General of Batavia, who did not fail to reply to this civility by asking the General to come on shore that he might entertain him. He sent at the same time to those who remained in the vessel a quantity of refreshments, and especially Spanish and Rhine wine, with instructions to those who carried it to make them drink well and to intoxicate them. This order was so well obeyed that it was easy for the Dutch afterwards to set fire to the

[1] Vol. ii. 13.

vessels according to the orders which they had received, and as, from the saloon of the fort where the General of Batavia receives strangers, all the roads are visible, one of the Indian Councillors who was at the table, seeing the flames, cried out that he believed the French vessels were on fire. The General of Batavia appeared to be much astonished, and the French General, who rightly concluded how it had come about, looked unmoved at the company: 'But that', said he, 'need not prevent us from continuing to drink—those who have lighted the fire shall pay for it.' But he did not remember then that time was worth money, and the Dutch did not pay for a quarter of the damage. The French vessels were all burnt and the crews were saved on the frigates which were dispatched for them in haste. The General of Batavia made the men liberal offers, which they refused, and they returned to Bantam to await their small vessel. When it arrived they could think of no better plan than to sell their goods and the vessel itself to the English, and the money was divided among all according to the rank of each. The English offered them a passage to Europe, but the General and some of the principal officers alone accepted it. The greater part of the French remained in India and took service with the Portuguese, with whom there was some advantage to be gained at that time.

The Dutch did not ill-treat the French alone, after this fashion, as they did a still more serious injury to the English. The English were the first to realize that the voyage to Japan from Surat, Masulipatam, and other places, was too dangerous to attempt in one stretch, without having some place to rest at when the winds were contrary. They found it desirable to build a fort in the island of Formosa;[1] and this has prevented the loss of many vessels, in addition to the great profit which it brought them. The Dutch, jealous that the English had seized so good a position as that, the only

[1] According to W. Milburn (*Oriental Commerce*, 1813, ii. 547) the Dutch had formerly a considerable fort at Tai-wan on the east coast of Formosa, from which they were expelled by the Chinese. 'The English also made some unsuccessful attempts to form an establishment here.'

place in all the island where vessels could lie in safety, as they were unable to take it by force, decided to accomplish their design by treachery. They sent two of their vessels, on board which they put their best soldiers, who feigned to have been very badly injured by a storm, making their vessels appear dismasted and broken in many directions, and all the soldiers pretending sickness. The English, touched by this misery, which was only a sham, invited the chief officers to come on shore to refresh themselves; this invitation they immediately accepted, ordering as many of their people as possible to leave the vessel, under pretext that they were ill, and could be treated better on shore than on board. While the principal officers were at table with the English, who had civilly invited them to dinner, to accomplish their object, they took with them more attendants than politeness permitted, and, to make more come on shore they ordered them to bring from the vessels, from time to time, many kinds of wine, and those who brought it had the word to remain there, of which the English, who were not on their defence, took no notice. The Dutch, seeing that they had drunk well, and that it was time to execute their design, started a quarrel with the English chief; and drawing their arms which they had concealed, threw themselves upon the English garrison, whom they murdered without meeting with much resistance. It was thus they made themselves masters of the fort, which they possessed till they were driven from it by the Chinese. I could tell of many other treacheries by the Dutch,[1] but it is time to return to that which followed the burning of the French vessels in the Batavia roads.

The two brothers Renaud, of whom I have above spoken, received at Bantam a small amount of money from the distribution which was made of the proceeds of the sale of the small vessel, and of the goods which it had brought from Macassar, found means to go to Goa, and knew so well how to gain the good opinion of the Portuguese, that they were permitted to trade in all places where the Portuguese were

[1] Tavernier subsequently resolved to do so, and in his third volume we have his accumulated charges against the Dutch, under the title, *Conduite des Hollandois en Asie.*

in authority. In five or six years they had each earned to the value of 10,000 écus.[1] The elder dealt in cottons and other coarse goods, and the younger in precious stones. The Portuguese had been accustomed to send three or four vessels to Achīn every year to obtain pepper, elephants,[2] and gold, and they took there all kinds of white and coloured calicoes, especially blue and black. They also sent jewels to the King, because he loved and highly valued them. The two brothers Renaud decided to go there, each for his own particular trade, the elder one carrying cottons, and the younger jewels, amongst which he had four rings of the value of about 18,000 écus. On their arrival at Achīn, they went with the other Portuguese to the King's palace, which is 2 leagues from the sea, and showed the King and the nobles who were with him whatever they had brought. As for the jewels, as soon as the King had cast his eyes on the four rings he desired to have them, but refused to pay more than 15,000 écus for them, but the younger Renaud asked 18,000 écus. Not having been able to agree, he took them away, which much displeased the King, who sent for him on the following day. Renaud, who had returned to the vessel, was a long time in doubt whether he should go to the King again or not; but the officers of the vessel advising him to go, he at length resolved to do so, and the King took the four rings for the 18,000 écus, which he paid him forthwith. But after Renaud left the presence of the King no one ever knew what became of him; apparently he was secretly murdered in the palace.

This adventure came to my memory when I saw that the King of Bantam sent to ask for me, and that my brother was not with those who came to summon me. Nevertheless, I resolved to go, and took with me 12,000 or 13,000 rupees' worth of jewels, the largest part consisting of rings with diamonds arranged in roses, some of seven stones, others of nine, and others of eleven, with some bracelets of diamonds

[1] £2,250.

[2] This statement as to the importation of Sumatran elephants is of interest, but requires confirmation. See vol. ii. 248 for suggested origin of the elephants in Sumatra.

and rubies. I found the King with three of his captains and my brother seated in the Oriental fashion, and they had before them five large plates of rice of different colours. For their drink they had Spanish wine and brandy, with many kinds of sherbets. After I saluted the King, and presented to him a diamond ring, another of blue sapphires, and a small bracelet of diamonds, rubies, and blue sapphires, he invited me to be seated, and told the attendants to give me a cup of brandy to excite my appetite. This cup held about half a septier of Paris,[1] but I refused to take it from the officer who presented it to me; this astonished the King. My brother then asked him to excuse me, saying that I never drank brandy; but that I could drink a little Spanish wine, upon which the King ordered some to be given me.

Whether the repast had already lasted a long time, or that the King was impatient to see what I had brought, he did not delay about finishing, and seated himself in a kind of arm-chair, the woodwork of which was gilt with gold and moulded like the frames of our pictures. His feet and legs were uncovered, and beneath him there was a small Persian carpet of gold and silk. His garment was a piece of calico, a part of which covered the body from the waist to the knees, the remainder bound on his back and about his neck like a scarf. He wore as a head-band, a kind of three-cornered handkerchief; and his hair, which was very long, was twisted and tied together on the top of his head. In place of slippers he had placed by the side of his chair sandals with leather straps to go over his feet, like those attached to a spur, which were embroidered with gold and small pearls. Two of his officers stood behind him with large fans, the handles of which were 5 or 6 feet long, and at the ends there were bundles of peacocks' plumes, as large as the bottom of one of our barrels. On his right side there was an old black woman, who held in her hands a small mortar and a pestle of gold, in which she crushed the betel leaves, with which she mixed areca [2] nuts and dissolved seed pearls. When she saw that

[1] Equal to one-fourth of an English pint. It is apparently the one-seventh of a litre, whence the name.

[2] Araque in the original: the nuts of Areca catechu (Watt, *Commercial Products*, 83 ff.).

the whole was well pounded she placed her hand on the King's back, who at once opened his mouth, and she put the betel in with her fingers as women do who give pap to their infants,[1] because the King had no teeth; for he had eaten so much betel, and smoked so much tobacco, that his teeth had fallen out.

The palace of the King of Bantam did not need a very skilful architect. It is a square building surrounded by small lacquered pillars of different colours, 2 feet in height, against which one leans when seated. There are at the four corners large pillars planted in the earth at 40 feet distance from each other, and the floor is covered by a mat woven of the bark of a kind of tree, as if it were a piece of cloth, and neither fleas nor bugs will approach it. The roof is of coco-nut fronds. Close by, under another roof, sustained also by four large pillars, there were sixteen elephants, the most courageous of those which the King keeps—for he has a large number of them—which are destined for war and do not fear fireworks. For his guard he has about 2,000 men, who were seated in squads under the shade of some trees. They are good soldiers both on sea and land, strict Musalmāns who do not fear death. His harem, where his women dwell, must be a small affair, for when he had seen what I had brought he summoned two old black women, to whom he gave some of the jewels to show them to his wives. The two old women entered by a miserable door, and the place was enclosed only by a kind of palisade, with earth mixed with cow-dung between the posts. I observed that nothing which he sent by these women was brought back, this made me conclude that I should stick to the price. Thus I sold him profitably what he took from me, and I was paid at once. After having drunk a cup of sherbet—while my brother drank spirits with the King—we took leave of him, and he made us promise that, on the following day towards evening, we should return to see him, because he wished to show me a dagger which he was having made after the Turkish fashion,

[1] Ball saw the famous hairy woman of Mandalay being supplied with betel by her Burmese attendant in much the same way; being blind, the packet had to be prepared for her and placed in her mouth.

but he did not possess sufficient diamonds to cover the handle, and he desired that I should procure enough to finish it. We then returned with our money to the English House, and our friends were much astonished that the King had spent 20,000 rupees, as they believed it was the most part of his treasure.[1]

Next day my brother and I went to see the King again at the hour which he had fixed, and we found him seated in the same place as on the preceding day. A Mullā read and interpreted to him something from the Korān, which was in Arabic. When the reading was finished the King and the Mullā rose to pray, after which the King sent for the dagger, the handle and sheath of which were of gold. The upper part of the handle was already covered with diamonds, and in the plaque at the end there was a large one cut into facettes, which, as far as I could judge, was worth at least 15,000 or 16,000 écus.[1] The King told me that he had received it as a present from the Queen of Borneo, and that he had sent it to be cut at Goa, but he valued it much higher than what I considered it to be worth. All the handle and the sheath were covered with bezels [1] applied without order, which proved to me that he did not understand design. The King had no other stones, neither diamonds nor rubies, nor anything to place in these bezels, and he wished to induce me to obtain for him some that would fit. I made him understand that this would be impossible, and that he ought not to limit himself to these bezels; that when he had acquired the quantity of stones which were required to cover the dagger, other bezels of the shapes of the stones should be made, and that in Europe when we begin a work of this kind we first arrange all the available stones on wax; this I exemplified to him at the same time, but that was beyond his understanding, and he told me that he did not care to destroy a design which he had himself taken the trouble to arrange, and to have made for his own use. In spite of

[1] As the value of the jewels is stated on page 273 to have been only 12,000 to 13,000 rupees, the transaction was a profitable one for Tavernier.

[2] £3,375 to £3,600.

[3] Bezels (chatons in the original), mountings for individual stones.

any reasons which I could give for the purpose of escaping from a commission which I was not able to execute, the King wished positively that I should take the dagger with me to Batavia. I represented to him then that as I was a stranger he risked much, and that I might go off with the dagger without returning it, but he said to me smiling that he feared nothing on that account, and that he well knew that Frenchmen were incapable of so disgraceful an action. At length, unable to excuse myself further, I took charge of the dagger, and having taken leave of the King, my brother and I went to bid farewell to the English President, and to thank him for the civilities we had received from him.

CHAPTER XXIV

The Author returns to Batavia, and some days afterwards goes again to visit the King of Bantam, giving an account, in connexion therewith, of the dangerous extravagances of some Fakirs, or pilgrims, on their return from Mecca.

My brother and I, after supper this evening with the English President, went on board a barque between 11 o'clock and midnight, for the land-wind that we required generally blows at night, and on the following day between 10 and 11 o'clock in the morning we arrived at Batavia.[1] I remained there twenty days, merely to make the King of Bantam believe that I had not misrepresented the matter, and that during that time I had been looking for what it was impossible to find. As I had nothing to do, these twenty days appeared very long to me; for at Batavia there is scarcely any other amusement but gambling, and all the gain goes in drink; this did not suit me. During the day, on account of the great heat, one cannot even think of taking exercise, which can only be done towards the cool of the evening, and it is moreover necessary to make it very short, because as soon as the sun sets they close the gates, unless the General or Madame or some of the Councillors of India are outside the

[1] See *Voyage of François Leguat*, Hakluyt Society, i. 220 ff.

town in their gardens. During these twenty days M. Cant, one of the Councillors of India, died, and was buried with great honour. A company of infantry attended and bore a large standard, upon which were the arms of the deceased, although when he first came to India he held the lowest office in the vessel. A stick, to the end of which spurs were attached, was borne behind, though, to say the truth, I do not believe he had ever mounted a horse save to go for exercise outside the town. One of the captains carried his sword, another his helmet, and his body was borne by eight military officers. The son-in-law of the deceased followed with the General; after whom walked the gentlemen of the Council; a number of people followed from the fort and town. The four corners of the pall with which the bier was covered were carried by four captains, and all these honours were rendered to him in consideration of the good services which the Company had received from him—as the General and members of the Council proclaimed; but the people used very different language and complained bitterly of the great injustice he had done, both to sailors and soldiers.

Having passed these twenty days at Batavia, I resolved to carry back the dagger to the King of Bantam, without having looked for the diamonds or other stones, for if I had remained years I should not have found any suitable for these bezels. My brother accompanied me again, and I took with me some jewels which the King had not yet seen. On our arrival at Bantam we intended to go first to visit the English President, but, before we had done so, one of the King's officers came to us, and told us that he had been instructed that we should be lodged in one of the King's houses in the town. These houses are made of bamboos, which are, as I have elsewhere said, hollow canes, and though they are as hard as iron, nevertheless split like our osiers, and it is of them that the Indians make nearly everything. We had not spent more than half an hour in this house when the King sent us some pateches,[1] which are very sweet water-melons, and red as scarlet inside. There were also mangoes,

[1] More properly pateca, a water-melon, *Citrullus vulgaris* (Schrader). The name is from the Arabic al-bittīkh. (Yule, *Hobson-Jobson*, 684 f.)

of which I have elsewhere spoken, and another large fruit called pompone,[1] which is also red inside, the flesh being soft like a sponge, and very good. The servant who brought these fruits told us that as soon as we had taken our food we were to go to see the King; this we did, and we found him again in the same place with the old betel pounder, who from time to time made him open his mouth and gave him some with her fingers in the way I have described. There were five or six captains seated round the room, who were looking at some fireworks which the Chinese had brought, such as grenades, fusees, and other things of that kind to run on the water; for the Chinese surpass all the nations of the world in this respect.[2] As soon as I saw the King in a condition to speak to me I presented to him his dagger in the same state as he had given it to me, and told him that Batavia was not a place where one could obtain precious stones, and when I did find some they wanted double their value for them; that this commission could not be fulfilled except by someone who went to Goa, and that I could have accomplished it when at Goa, or at Golkonda, or, better still, at the diamond mine, where parcels of stones of all shapes and sizes are procurable and might be cut with but little loss to suit the bezels. Upon this the old woman took the dagger, carried it into the harem, and the King never spoke to me about it again. Afterwards I showed him the jewels I had brought, and I sold a parcel of them as advantageously as on the first journey. As the sun was setting, which is the time when the Musalmāns say their prayers, the King told us to return on the following day, and said he would arrange for payment being made to us. On arriving at our lodging we found one of the servants of the English President, who came to invite us to have supper with him, and taste some new liquors which had arrived from England on the Company's account. For during the twenty days we spent at Batavia two vessels had arrived, laden with French and Spanish wine,

[1] More properly pommelo, *Citrus decumana* (L.), the shaddock of the West Indies. (*Ibid.*, 721 f.)

[2] On Chinese fireworks see J. D. Ball, *Things Chinese*, 3rd ed., p. 238 ff.

and especially a large quantity of beer. We remained till midnight with the President, who showed much joy at seeing us again.

Next day at 10 o'clock a.m., when going to the palace, with my brother and a Dutch surgeon, who was prescribing for one of the King's wives, we passed along a road with the river on one side and on the other a large garden enclosed by a palisade, and there were intervals between each pair of posts. Behind the palisade a rascal of a Bantamese was concealed who had returned from Mecca and was running a muck,[1] which means in their language, that when someone of the lower class of Musalmāns, who has returned from Mecca, takes it into his head to seize his crease [2] which is a kind of dagger with generally half of the blade poisoned, he runs through the streets and kills all whom he meets who are not of the Musalmān faith, until he is himself killed. These fanatics think they do a service to God and to Muhammad by killing the enemies of his Law, and thus they will be saved. After they are killed the Musalmān mob inter them as though they were saints, and everyone contributes to build them splendid tombs. Often some great mendicant dresses as a Dervish and builds a hut close to the tomb, which he is careful to keep tidy and adorn with flowers. According as donations are given he adds some ornament, because the more beautiful the grave is, so much the more worship and sanctity does it acquire, and by so much the more do the donations increase. I remember in the year 1642 a vessel of the Great Mogul arrived at Suwālī,[3] which is the port of Surat, from Mecca,

[1] À Moqua in the original. The French edition of 1713 has it 'joüoit à Mocca'. This is what is more commonly known as running a muck. See Yule, *Hobson-Jobson*, 18 ff. for etymology and examples of the use of the term.

[2] Cric in the original. The term crease or cris, signifying a dagger, is adopted in the Malay from the Javanese kris or kiris. Ball had seen an ingenious explanation for the waved form of these blades; it is that it is a survival of the outlines of the knives and spears made of obsidian by flaking, and indeed the resemblance is somewhat striking. See Romilly, *West Pacific and New Guinea*; Yule, *Hobson-Jobson*, 274 ff. gives examples of the use of the term. On the magical significance of these marks see W. W. Skeat, *Malay Magic*, 525 ff.

[3] Souali in the original (vol. i. 5).

where there were a number of these Fakīrs or Dervishes. For every year the Great Mogul sends two large vessels there to carry pilgrims, who thus get a free passage. When these vessels are ready to depart the Fakīrs come from all parts of India to embark. The vessels are laden with good articles of trade, which are disposed of at Mecca, and all the profit made is given in charity to the poor pilgrims. The principal only is retained, and it serves for another year, and this principal is, at the least, 600,000 rupees.[1] It is considered a small matter when 30 or 40 per cent. only is made on these goods, for some yield cent. per cent. Besides this all the principal persons of the Great Mogul's harem, and other private persons, send considerable donations to Mecca. I have mentioned at the end of my account of the seraglio of the Grand Seigneur the rich and magnificent present which the Great Mogul sent to Mecca in the year 1644, over and above the ordinary presents which he makes annually.[2]

One of these Fakīrs returned from Mecca in the year 1642, and on landing at Suwālī he forthwith showed signs of diabolical fury. He had no sooner said his prayers than he took his dagger and attacked some Dutch sailors, who were on shore discharging goods from four vessels in the port. Before they saw him and were able to put themselves on their defence, this fanatical Fakīr wounded seventeen, of whom thirteen died. The khanjar[3] which he had was a kind of dagger, the upper part of the blade of which was three fingers wide, and as it is a very dangerous weapon I give a figure of it here. At length the Dutch soldier who was on guard at the entrance to the tent where the Commander and the merchants were seated, shot this madman through the body, and he fell dead. Forthwith all the other Fakīrs in the place, and even the Musalmāns, carried off the body and buried it, and at the end of fifteen days a handsome tomb had been built over it. It is broken each year by the English and Dutch sailors when

[1] £67,500.

[2] On the embassies from the Grand Sharīf of Mecca to Aurangzeb and the gifts sent by the latter see Manucci, ii. 114 f. : Bernier, 133.

[3] Canjare in the original (see vol. i. 82, 246). It is not necessary to reproduce the figure here.

their vessels are in port, because they are then strong; but as soon as they depart the Musalmāns have it rebuilt and place many standards about it. Some also say their prayers there.

To return to the Fakīr of Bantam—This rascal was concealed, as I have said, behind the palisades, and as my brother and I and the Dutch surgeon went along, all three, side by side, and came opposite him, he thrust out his spear, thinking to transfix one of us in the body. By God's grace he was too quick, and the point passed in front of all three. The Dutchman being on my left on the river side, and slightly in advance of my brother and me, the point of the spear cut his high hose and immediately he and I caught hold of the handle, the Fakīr pulling with all his might to recover his spear. My brother, who was on my right on the palisade side, being young and strong, leaped over it, and gave him three sword cuts in the body of which he died on the spot. Immediately a number of Chinese and other idolaters who were close by kissed my brother's hands and thanked him for having slain this fanatic. Thence we went to see the King, who had already heard of what my brother had done, and showed his approval by making him a present of a waistband. For the Kings and Governors, although they are Musalmāns, are well pleased when someone slays these ruffians, knowing well that they are desperadoes of whom it is well to be rid.

The King paid me for what he had purchased on the preceding day; but he was unwilling that my brother should return with me, because he was going to make a great rejoicing, and wished him to be present. It was on the occasion of the launch of four large vessels which he had had built. Never had any King of Bantam built such large ships, and for five or six days there was to be nothing but feasts, dances, and fireworks. Thus I took leave of the King, who presented me with a beautiful embroidered waistband, and we went to sup and sleep at the Dutch surgeon's house.

Next day I went to bid farewell to the English President, who kept me for dinner. While waiting for it to be served, he showed me two strings of diamonds which had come to him from England, and two services of silver, the whole being worth, perhaps, 25,000 écus. He wanted to sell me all, but I bought only one of the strings of diamonds for 2,600 reales, for the stones on the other string were too foul; and as for the vessels of silver, if money had still been coined at Batavia I would certainly have been able to buy them. They coined there formerly, but all their coins contained more than ten per cent. of alloy. This was done on account of the Chinese, who prefer silver to gold, as I have elsewhere remarked,[1] because they have no silver mines in their own country,[2] and they used to carry into China as much of the silver money which was coined at Batavia as they could. These were reales, half reales, and quarter reales, which have no other mark than that of the Company, as is to be seen in the figure which I give here.[3] On one side was a vessel, and on the other a V, an O, and a C, interlaced, these three letters signifying in Dutch 'Vor Oost Indien Compagnie', i. e. for the Company of the East Indies.

This lasted for some years; but in the end all the nations of the East, who had trade with the Dutch, began to be tired of it, especially the people whose sovereigns did not coin silver money; for in fact there are very few who coin after one passes beyond the Empire of the Great Mogul, and it is still bar silver only which comes from Japan. As for gold, there are many Kings who coin it, as the King of Pegu, the King of Achīn, and the King of Macassar; and besides their golden money, they have also copper and tin money. The Chinese—who are careful in all things—in selling their goods calculate according to the standard of the silver; for when they have come home, they reduce all that they received in foreign countries to their own standard, and keep it in ingots.

The principal part of the profit derived from these reales which were coined at Batavia, used to go into the purses of the General, the Councillors, and the Master of the Mint. The

[1] See vol. ii. 122.

[2] There are silver mines in China, in the island of Hainan and elsewhere (*Ency. Brit.*, vi. 178; S. W. Williams, *The Middle Kingdom*, i. 244).

[3] This figure is not reproduced here.

States-General having had notice of it, considered it very singular that the gentlemen of the Company had assumed authority to coin money without permission, and forbade the Company to continue to do so. They condemned them likewise to a large fine, and ordered a careful search to be made for all these reales, in order to give an equal number of good ones to those who had received the bad ones. On this voyage to Batavia, when in the island of Ceylon, I sold some jewels to a lady of Pointe de Galle, who paid me with these reales. When I was leaving, an officer of the Company came on board to ask if I had not received some of these reales, and added that if I had he would give me good ones, piece for piece, without my losing anything; this he did forthwith.

CHAPTER XXV

Concerning the Dutch War with the Emperor of Java.[1]

Before leaving the English President, with whom I dined the day I left Bantam, he discussed with me the reasons why the General of Batavia and his Council had refused me a passage to Surat or the coast of Bengal, where they often send vessels. The President, to compensate me for this refusal, kindly offered me a passage to England; for the season was then past for returning to India. Attracted by his offer, I accepted it without ceremony; and he told me he would be much gratified at having my company, because he himself intended to go home, as the period of his service had expired. But the vessels, English or Dutch, could not leave for Europe for more than three months; and I thought I should do best to pass that time at Batavia, where I might be able to buy something to make my money yield a profit during the voyage. Accordingly, I took leave of the President till the time when the vessels should sail; and he presented me with a large cask of English beer to take with me to Batavia, where he said I should find scarcely any, because the General had made it contraband, knowing that it had come to the English Company. 'But if he does us only this

[1] *La Iave* in the original.

injury,' continued the President, 'the Company will not trouble itself, and will not be the poorer because its beer remains unsold.' It is not really the case that if this prohibition of the Dutch General and his Council had continued it would not have been injurious to the English, for they make a considerable profit on beer, and it yields them a large sum of money annually. I have said above that it is the principal delight of the people of Batavia to see new drinks arrive, especially English beer, and that which they call mom,[1] which comes from Brunswick. It is thought that they contribute to health; and the majority fear that they will not survive till the year's end if they do not receive these supplies. Accordingly all the people murmured loudly against the General and his Council; and even the publicans risked buying beer from the English, the General shutting his eyes, and the wives of the Councillors being very glad to drink it.

As soon as I landed at Batavia one of the guards ran to the entry office to give notice that I had arrived with a cask of beer; however, I landed it from the barque and placed it near the guard. The chief of the office came to me and said that he could not give permission for the cask to be carried to my lodging; that I must be aware of the order of Council; and that it would be best to reship it on the barque, and send it back to Bantam. Seeing that there was no favour to be hoped for, and as there are close to the guard-house cannons, in position, for the defence of the port, and an abundance of cannon balls, I took one of these balls and with it stove in one end of the cask. That done, I cried out to the soldiers and passers-by: 'Children, come and empty this cask, and drink the health of the King of France, my sovereign lord, and that of the Prince of Orange', after which I mentioned the General and the members of the Council. As no one refused to drink, the cask was already half emptied when an officer on the part of the General came to tell me that I might carry my cask of beer to my lodging. Immediately I replaced the end of the cask and had it carried

[1] Mum, German Mumme, Brunswick beer, largely imported into England in the 17th and 18th centuries (*New English Dict. s. v.*)

away, after which I filled a canteen of six bottles, and sent them as a present to the General, knowing well that it would be the first he had to drink that year, and with the rest I regaled my friends.

I had designed, as I have said, to spend at Batavia the three months which remained till the departure of the vessels for Christendom, but the life led in that place being one of idleness is tiresome, and as I had no other amusement than gambling and drinking, I resolved to employ a part of the time in going to see the King of Japara,[1] who is otherwise called the Emperor of Java. He was formerly King of all the island, before the King of Bantam, who was only governor of a province, rebelled against him, the Dutch being maintained in this country by the division of these two powers. For whenever the King of Japara wished to besiege Batavia, the King of Bantam immediately aided the Dutch and when they have been attacked by the King of Bantam, which has happened many times, the King of Japara has come to their aid. In the same way, when these two Kings make war upon one another, the Dutch assist whichever of them is the weaker.

The King of Japara resides in a town of that name, about 30 leagues distance from Batavia, and accessible only by sea along the coast, though nearly 8 leagues inland. From the town you pass down a fine river to the sea, where there is a good port and finer houses than those in the town. The King would prefer to make his ordinary residence at the port, but thinks he would not be safe there.

On the eve of the day I had intended to start, I went to take leave of one of the Councillors of India, and mentioning to him that I was going to the King of Japara, he was much astonished, because the King and the Dutch were then mortal enemies. He explained the matter to me in this way. The

[1] Japar in the original. Japara is the name of a province of Java, comprehending Juwana, situated in the country of the proper Javanese. Its area is 672 square miles, and the population amounts to 671 per square mile, it being the most thickly inhabited region of Java. (Crawfurd, *Dictionary*, 165; Milburn, *Oriental Commerce*, ii. 364; *Ency. Brit.*, xv. 290.)

deceased King, he said, father of the King who reigns at present, ever since the Dutch Company had built the fort at Batavia in his territories, had never been willing to make peace with it : although during the war the King had taken some Dutchmen prisoners, and the Dutch, on their side, had taken twenty times as many of his subjects, offering to give in exchange ten of his for one of theirs, yet he would not give up one, either on that condition, or for money, and on his deathbed he advised his son, who succeeded him, never to give liberty to one of them. This obstinacy troubled the General and all the people of Batavia very much, and obliged them to think of some means to bring him to reason. It is the custom that as soon as a Musalmān King dies, his successor sends some of the principal nobles of his court to Mecca with presents to make the priests pray for the soul of the deceased, and also to give thanks to God and to Muhammad because the new King has come to the throne without any obstruction, and to pray that he may always be victorious over his enemies. The new King and his Council were in much difficulty how they should make this voyage for two reasons, one because the King had only small vessels, and to undertake so long a journey on such vessels was risking much, besides which the native pilots and sailors are able to sail only along the coasts, sighting from point to point, because they do not understand how to take observations. The other difficulty was that the King of Japara could not ignore the fact that the Dutch were always cruising about his harbours to capture his subjects if they went outside. In order, then, to secure that those who went on the pilgrimage should be in safety, he bethought him that it would be best to come to an understanding with the English, believing that the Dutch would not dare to do anything to the pilgrims if they were on board English vessels. With this object, an envoy was dispatched to Bantam to the English President and his Council, who promised to give the King one of the largest and best appointed vessels which the Company sent to India. They stipulated as a recompense that on the trade which the English might do in the future in the Kingdom of the King of Japara, they should not have to pay more than half the custom dues which they had hitherto paid, and that this privilege should be perpetual. This treaty being made, the English equipped a very fine vessel and placed a larger crew and more guns on her than usual. The King of Japara's Envoy and two English merchants embarked on the vessel to ratify the treaty with the King, who at once signed it, being very well satisfied at seeing so fine a vessel, and he concluded that the voyage both ways would be accomplished in safety. Nine of the principal persons of his court, and the majority of his relatives, with eighty or a hundred servants, and some other private persons, delighted to find so good an opportunity of accomplishing their pilgrimage, embarked with much joy on this large vessel. All this was not done without the Dutch being aware of it, as, like the English, they had their spies everywhere. As it was necessary to pass Bantam in order to get out of the Straits, this being the only route, the General of Batavia, who had notice of the time of departure, kept three large war-vessels ready, of which M. Chevres,[1] a Councillor of India, and the Major were placed in command. They met the English vessel off Bantam, and as it was about to enter the Straits sent a cannon-shot as a signal to her to bring to; this the English were unwilling to do, seeing which the Dutch commenced to fire from all three vessels. The English, who well knew that if this continued they would be sent to the bottom, lowered sails and prepared to yield; but all the Javanese nobles, and those who accompanied them, cried out to the English that they were traitors, and that the agreement which had been made was intended to sell them and deliver them over to the mercy of the Dutch. The Javanese at length seeing that no hope of safety was left, and that the Dutch began to board the vessel, seized their creases, or poisoned daggers, and began to run a muck [2] among the English, of whom they killed a large number before the latter had time to place themselves on their defence. It is possible that not one would have escaped if the Dutch had not speedily come on board, when some of the Javanese nobles, twenty or thirty

[1] Cheveres in ed. of 1678.

[2] À Mocca in the original. The French edition of 1713 has it 'to cry *Mocca*' (cf. p. 280 *n.* above).

of their servants, and the passengers refused to accept quarter. The combat was bloody, and seven or eight Dutchmen were killed. When the English vessel was taken to Batavia, the General treated the crew with much civility, and sent them back with their vessel, and afterwards gave notice to the King of Japara that if he consented to make an exchange of the Dutch prisoners, he would give him all satisfaction. But the King would not listen to it, and replied that if the General had taken three times as many of his subjects he would not give up the Dutch prisoners whom he had in his power. Thus the poor Dutch remained in slavery, and the Javanese died of poverty at Batavia, although, through policy, they were sometimes stealthily assisted, so that the King of Japara coming to know of it, through his spies, it might cause him to treat the Dutch prisoners less harshly.

The Javanese are very good soldiers. While Batavia was besieged by the King of Bantam in the year 1659, a Dutch soldier was in ambuscade in a march, and a Javanese advanced to see what the enemy were doing, hot thinking any of them were so close. The Dutchman thrust a pike into him, and the Javanese feeling himself wounded, instead of withdrawing the pike, pushed it into his body up to the hilt, where the Dutchman held it, so as to be able to get near him, and give him two stabs with his dagger in the stomach, of which the Dutchman died.

CHAPTER XXVI

The Author renders the last duties to his brother, who died at Batavia, and has fresh difficulties with the General and his Council.

FINDING myself without hope of being able to visit the King of Japara, I resolved to embark in a small vessel which belonged to one of the citizens of Batavia, and traded along the whole length of the western coast of Sumatra. Here the principal part of the trade of this island, which consists of very poor gold and pepper, is carried on. What induced me to go was the opportunity it afforded of disposing of some diamond rings made according to the fashion of the country. For although these people have for their sole garment only two or three ells of calico, nevertheless, they always like to have some diamond rings or earrings, and they pay well for them. When I was at the port, ready to embark, a small barque arrived from Bantam with my brother, who was very ill with a bloody flux, which arose from the debauches he had indulged in with the King of Bantam. The sight of his condition caused me to give up my voyage and to do what I could for his cure, but all my care and all the remedies which could be applied availed nothing, and at the end of thirty days God took him from this world. For his funeral I was obliged to follow the somewhat strange customs, which the Dutch have invented to cause expenditure of money by the heirs of a deceased [1] person. The first is the fee to those who go to pray at the burial, for the more prayers are said the more honourable is the interment. If only one be engaged he pays him but 2 écus, but if two he must pay 4 écus to each; if three, each ought to receive 6; and if twelve, the payment goes on increasing in the same ratio. As I wished that the thing should be done in an honourable manner, and in ignorance of this pleasant custom, I engaged six of these persons, and when it came to paying them I was astonished to find that each one demanded 12 écus, and that I had to pay 72 for this single item. As for the pall which is placed on the bier, it must be hired at the hospital, and it is a right which the poor enjoy who derive profit therefrom. The commonest is of cloth, and the three others of velvet, one without fringe, another with fringe, and a third with fringe and large tassels at the four corners. This causes an expenditure of from 5 to 30 écus, and I paid 20 for the one which was placed on my brother's bier. A cask of Spanish wine, which was drunk at the interment, cost me 200 piastres.[2] I gave 26 for three hams and some ox tongues, and 22 for

The foregoing lines of this chapter are in the English translation by John Phillips, compressed into the following quaintly expressed sentence :—' While I stay'd at Batavia my brother dy'd; and it was pretty to consider what the Dutch made me pay for his funeral.'

[2] £45.

some pastry. It is also the custom to send on the following day some money to entertain those who have carried the body to the burial ground, and as there were eight of them I paid them 20 écus. It cost 16 for the grave site—100 écus being asked for interment in the church. Thus the whole funeral cost me 1,223 livres[1] of French money, and after I had paid this sum I resolved, for my own part, not to die in a country where it cost so much to be interred. I praised God that notwithstanding the troubles I had experienced in Batavia, and of which I have as yet told only a part, and the small dissipations which one cannot altogether avoid in this country, I have taken such good care of myself that I have never been inconvenienced by the least headache, or by a bloody flux, which is the ailment that carries away many people. That which in my opinion has contributed most to my health is, that I do not think I have ever grieved on account of any misfortune which has happened to me. I have sometimes made great profits, and I have sometimes experienced severe losses; but when in unpleasant circumstances I have never been more than half an hour in deciding what course I should adopt, without thinking more of the past, having always in my mind the thought of Job, that God gives and takes away as it pleases Him, and that one should render thanks for all that happens, whether it be good or evil.

Seeing that the two voyages which I had proposed to myself to make, one to Japara and the other to the coast of Sumatra, in order to dispose of some jewels which remained in my hands, had been prevented, I at length resolved to sell the jewels at Batavia with the least possible loss, and then try to invest the money in something which would yield me a profit in Holland. My jewels having been sold, three or four of my friends told me that as I had ready money I could not invest it better than by buying rekenings from the Company's servants. These rekenings[2] are their accounts of the balance the Company owes them, which are paid when

[1] £91 : 14*s*. 6*d*.

[2] Requenings (for rekenings) in the original, meaning statements of account or pay certificates. (*New English Dict*. *s*. *v*. reckonings.)

they return to Holland. But as there are many of them who, after their term of service is completed, remain at Batavia and become citizens there, or in other places where the Company has settlements, as Malacca, the island of Ceylon, the coast of Coromandel, and other places, each has his account closed with the balance that the Company owes him. In order to obtain this money, since they are domiciled there, and do not think of ever returning to Europe, they sell these statements of account to those who have money and are returning home, and the Company pays them in Holland. Those who buy these vouchers get them as cheaply as they can—thus, for 100 piastres they generally give but 60 or 70, or at the most 80, and they are allowed by the notary to sign a declaration that the seller is content, and had received his payment. Whenever these poor people sold their vouchers in this way to reasonable persons, it was a convenience to them; but most frequently they sold them to hotel keepers and publicans, from whom they did not obtain more than 40 or 50 per cent. at the most. When the latter had thus purchased up to 2,000 or 3,000 écus, they placed the 'statements' in the hands of a notary to resell them to the commanders who were returning to Holland, and who generally gave for them 85 or 90 per cent., contenting themselves with being thus able to conceal what they had taken from the Company, while they were chiefs of the factories.

The Company freely borrows money from those who are willing to lend it, and gives them 25 per cent. interest, but the commanders and other officers take care not to lend the full amount which they have amassed, because they may be asked by what means they have gained so much money, and be obliged to render an account; for some of them, as I have said, on their return to Holland take with them from 400,000 up to 500,000 livres.[1] I dealt then with one of these notaries of Batavia who had about 11,000 guilders'[2] worth

[1] £30,000 to £37,500. (Vol. i. 327).

[2] Guldes in the original. The florin or guilder of Batavia is given by Kelly as being of the intrinsic value of 1*s*. 7·77*d*., and the Dutch coin of the same denomination at 1*s*. 8·49*d*. The currency value was about 1*s*. 8*d*. and 1*s*. 9*d*. respectively in round numbers. Perhaps the true

of these 'statements' at 82 per cent., and on the following day, the transfer was completed, and I paid for them. As I was taking these papers to my lodgings I met the Avocat Fiscal, who asked me what papers my servant carried. I told him they were 'statements' which I had just purchased at a certain price, to which he replied that it was rather dear, and that he knew of some amounting to 6,000 guilders, at a cheaper rate; these I obtained with his assistance at 79 per cent. I sought to buy more, but more were not to be found, for a ship's captain who was returning had bought for himself alone to the amount of upwards of 100,000 guilders; many other persons had also done the same, and the whole amounted in value to more than 400,000 livres.

Five or six days afterwards, while I was still seeking for something in which to invest the remainder of my money, I met the Avocat Fiscal, who asked me if I had bought many of those rekenings. I told him that I had not found any more, and that I had only the two parcels he knew of, amounting to about 17,500 guilders; upon which he told me with many compliments that he was much distressed for those who had bought them, because the General and his Council had ordered him to make them give back all these rekenings, as it had been decided that it was not just that a poor man should lose so much of his wages. I told him that I would willingly give them back into the hands of the parties from whom I had purchased them, provided that I was repaid my money at the same time, and that I would get them over from Bantam, where I had sent them with my baggage, as I intended to return in a few days in order to go to England with the English President, who had civilly offered me a passage. At 6 p.m. one of the General's halberdiers came to tell me that the General wished to speak to me. I immediately went to him and he asked me forthwith why I had not given these rekenings to the Avocat Fiscal when he asked for them in the names of himself and his Council. I replied to him coldly that I was unable to give him that which I had not got, and that they were in Bantam. 'You intend

exchange value of the latter was about 1*s.* 9½*d.* At 1*s.* 9*d.* the 11,000 guilders represented a sum of £9,625.

then,' he said, 'to go to Europe?' 'Yes,' I replied, 'and the President of the English has done me the honour to give me a passage and the use of his table.' I added that it was very true that the long journey which I was about to make to Surat, and thence to the diamond mine, where my usual trade was, would cause me much loss, and that if he had so willed it he might have enabled me to save all this time and avoid the dangers inseparable from these long journeys, by allowing me to embark, as I had asked, on one of the vessels which sailed for Bengal, Surat, or Hormuz; that it would have caused no injury to the Company, and that I believed such courtesy the General and his Council should not have refused me, since I had come to Batavia only in their service. When I had finished speaking all the members of the Council looked at one another, and the General whispering to M. Caron, told me that as I was resolved to go by sea, their vessels were as good as those of the English, and that I should enjoy equally good treatment, and he offered me a passage by one of them. This offer, which I did not expect, amazed me a little, and I did not at first know whether I ought to accept it or not. But at length I accepted, fearing that by refusing it they might detain me for another year without being able to sail in any direction, a friend having told me in confidence that the design of the General and his Council was to so arrange, that, either from Batavia or from Europe, I should not return to India again, and that by this means they hoped to prevent the Commanders or chiefs of the factories, which they have both in India and Persia, from making further use of me to invest for them in diamonds the money of which the Company was defrauded.[1] It was this which led me to accept the passage, for which I thanked the General and his Council. Subsequently the General told me to select the particular vessel I preferred to go by, and that when I informed him he would order a cabin to be prepared for my own special convenience, but if I would take his advice I should go on the Vice-Admiral,[2] because of the good company

[1] The object of the Dutch was in short to deport Tavernier, whom they regarded as a dangerous interloper.

[2] The second ship of the fleet. (Fryer, i. 71.)

which would be on board, and that I should find old friends whom I had known in Persia and in the territories of the Great Mogul. I tendered him my thanks for having placed me in such good company; but after he had made this obliging offer he added that it was absolutely necessary that I should place all the rekenings which I had bought in the hands of the Avocat Fiscal, and that until I did so I should not be permitted to leave Batavia. He received no further reply from me than that I had already given, that the rekenings were at Bantam, and that I should have them sent for, provided he returned my money, on which he told me that for the amount I had disbursed, when I was about to leave, he would give me an order from himself and the Council to be paid in Holland by the Company. Some days passed without the matter being further discussed, save that once or twice I met the Fiscal, who asked me whether I had not yet obtained the rekenings from Bantam. My last reply was that I had written about them to the English President, who had my box in his house, and that I had asked him to send them to me; but that he had replied that I must go for them in person, or at the least send a man with an order in my own hand, and without that he could not send back my box. The truth was that it would have been difficult for him to send them, for the whole were with me, and I wished to see whether the time would not come when I should be asked no more about them. However, all those who had purchased these rekenings, merchants as well as captains and other persons who were returning this year, were put in prison, and the Council took from them, by force, all their papers, dismissed them from their offices, and they were sent to Holland as common soldiers.

Four or five days before the fleet left, the Avocat Fiscal came to tell me that he had the General's command to arrest me if I still refused to place in his hands the rekenings which he had already so often demanded. When I replied I had nothing to give him, he said, 'Be so good then as to follow me'; this I did willingly. He conducted me to a beautiful place on one of the bastions, called 'Sapphire,' where there is a pleasant house devoted to the amusement of the officers, where the majority of the respectable people of the town came to visit me, and sent me presents of the best wines. On the following day two Councillors came to see me, and told me that they knew not what objection I had to place in their hands that which they asked for, especially as they, with good grace, offered me an order for payment on the Company in Holland. I replied that it was not with a sufficiently good grace, and that when I saw the order I should make it my business to get back the rekenings. Two or three days more passed, during which the vessels commenced to set sail. This caused these gentlemen, both those of the Council of India and those of the town to the number of eight or ten, to come to see me. The Major, a very respectable man, was in their company, and he promised me that as soon as I had got the papers and handed them to the members of the Council to calculate the amount, he would so arrange it that the General would give me the order to be paid in Holland on my arrival there. Seeing that the vessels were about to leave and that I could not do otherwise, I told them that they must allow me to go to Bantam; this they were unwilling to agree to, preferring to send someone on my behalf to bring them. Having given my word, they told me that I might go out on parole, and that they were much distressed at what had happened. I replied that they had reason to be distressed, because I had the honour to belong to a great Prince, who was the late M. le Duc d'Orléans, who did me the honour to love me, and he would be able to fully resent the injustice which they had done me, and complain of it to the States. At length, forced by their unjust pressure, and by the necessity of leaving with the fleet, of which I did not wish to lose the opportunity, I gave them my rekenings, and from day to day I went to see if they had counted them, so as to give me the order they had promised. For the Vice-Admiral on which I was to embark remained more than fifteen days after the other vessels, because it was desired to send news by it to Holland, of what had been accomplished by a fleet which the General had sent to take possession of the Philippines by capturing them from the Spanish. On the voyage they met with bad weather so that three or four were lost; and they were obliged to return without accomplishing anything.

It is the custom, when the vessels are about returning to Holland, that the General entertains all the principal officers of the fleet with the Council and the most important personages of the town, and he did me the honour to invite me also. The repast commenced at 2 p.m., and at four tables there were fully sixty persons of both sexes. I was seated between the Major and the Secretary of the Grand Council; they were both men of worth, whose conversation was agreeable. We had been seven or eight hours at table, and they had already asked the General if it pleased him that the comedy should commence, which the youth of the town were to enact; whereupon I reminded the Major that he had promised me that as soon as I had delivered my papers to the Council they would give me an order to be paid on my arrival in Holland. I told him that the Secretary, to whom I had spoken in the morning, had given me reason to hope that I should have it before dinner; but the Secretary then said in my ear that I need not expect it, and when he said this he rose from the table to go to the comedy. I then asked our Vice-Admiral and three or four merchants who were returning to Holland to bear in mind what I should say to the General and his reply to me, and serve me as witnesses before the Directors of the Company when we arrived in Holland. In the *entre actes* of the comedy everyone took a glass and drank healths, and the General, glass in hand, addressed our Vice-Admiral, 'I drink your health,' said he, 'and that of M. Tavernier, whom may God vouchsafe to bless and protect on sea during this journey, as he has done in all the others which he has made by land.' I replied that I thanked him, and that I sincerely hoped that God would bless our journey, but that I should not make it without displeasure and without resentment for their failure to keep their promise—neither he nor his Council having kept the promise which they had made me to give an order on my handing them my rekenings, which amounted to 17,500 guilders; that now, when they had the papers which they asked for, they mocked me; but that I assured them I would publish their proceedings throughout the world. The General replied to this that I need not trouble myself, and that I might be cheerful during the voyage, as the order which he had promised me would be in Holland as soon as myself, and that I should have no cause to complain of them. Though but ill satisfied with the General, I took leave of him, and did not await the remainder of the comedy, being anxious, amongst other things, to prepare for my departure.

CHAPTER XXVII

The Author embarks on a Dutch Vessel in order to return to Europe.

Next day, at a very early hour, I took a small Chinese boat to go on board, where, on my arrival, I found one of the General's bodyguards, who came to convey to me once more his good wishes for my voyage, and to tell me that Madame la Générale begged me to accept a cask of Rhine wine, and some pots of fruits preserved in vinegar, which she sent me. There were cucumbers, mangoes, citrons, and eggs in their shells, which prevents them from becoming salt. I had taken no provisions with me, because some days before our departure the captain of the vessel told me that if I brought any they would not be received on board, as it was forbidden by the General. It is the custom that the General gives 200 écus to each captain of a vessel to furnish himself with all kinds of stores, and as I embarked by his advice on the Vice-Admiral, he caused double the sum to be given to the captain on my account, in order to have the honour to cause no expenditure to a stranger to whom he had offered a passage. Madame la Générale, when sending this present, bethought herself, possibly, of that which I had done some days previously for her daughter. Some friends seeing that I had easy access to the principal ladies of Batavia, begged me to intercede for a young man, a native of Paris, who in consequence of dissipation had come out to India as a soldier, and was in danger of the surgeons cutting off his leg, where he had an ulcer. To accomplish it I made a present to the

General's daughter, in order that she might ask the Major and the Avocat Fiscal not to appear to see this young man when he was leaving.

We were still three days in the roads before setting sail. On the first day the principal merchant of the fort, who kept a record of all the goods which had been embarked, both for Holland and other places, came to the vessel according to custom to examine the bill of lading, and have it read over by the captain of the vessel and the merchants who came with him, whom he made sign it. This bill of lading was placed in the box where they shut up all the account books and records of all that had passed in the factories of India, both concerning trade and as regards civil and criminal justice, and the covering over all the goods was then sealed.

On the second day the Major with the Avocat Fiscal and the chief surgeon also came, according to custom, to examine all those who were in the vessel returning to Holland—the Major to see whether there were any soldiers who were going without leave, for everyone must have his passport with him; the Avocat Fiscal to ascertain if any of the writers were concealed who wished to escape before their term was finished. The Chief Surgeon of the fort comes to see that all the sick persons who are being sent home have ailments which are incurable in the country, because some soldiers may obtain leave from the Major by the influence of friends, as he did, whom as I have said, I carried off; for the surgeon is obliged by oath not to allow anyone to go unless he considers that he cannot be cured but by going to Europe. The Major is bound to give the roll of all the soldiers, both of those who are well and those who are ill, to the Avocat Fiscal, who makes them come on the vessel one after the other; and it is then that the sick men are examined by the surgeon. It was perhaps not impossible that he whom I took might have been healed of his illness in the country; but by the favour of the Fiscal he was not called with the others, and escaped in that way.

On the third day the principal persons of the town and many ladies came to bid adieu to their friends who were leaving, and brought with them wine and food to entertain them, music accompanying the good cheer, and at 6 p.m. all of them returned home.

On the following day at daybreak we set sail, and were clear of the Straits sooner than we expected, because generally the wind is contrary, and besides we were leaving twenty-four days after all the others, the season for going to sea being nearly over. As soon as we had left the Straits we saw Prince's Island.[1] From thence our direction was to make for the Cocos Islands,[2] and when in the latitude of these islands we spent two or three days scouring the sea, expecting to sight them, but we were unable to do so, and this caused us to direct our course straight for the Cape of Good Hope.

On the forty-fifth day after our departure from Batavia—for I do not wish to weary the reader with a journal of our voyage—our Vice-Admiral neglected to order the ship's lantern to be lighted, in the belief that the whole fleet had already arrived at the Cape of Good Hope. It happened that a vessel of the same fleet called the 'Maestricht' also omitted to light its lantern the same night, and as it was very dark and the sea was high, it came into collision with our vessel; this threw everyone on both vessels into great consternation. All began to pray to God, believing that one or other of the vessels would be lost. Ours, which was called 'Les Provinces', was considered to be the largest and the best of the vessels which sailed to India; this was apparent from this collision, when it received so severe a shock. Everyone realizing the danger we were in, laboured to disengage

[1] Prince's Island is at the western end of the Straits of Sunda (p. 251 above).

[2] There are several groups of islands called Cocos: first, there is one in the Bay of Bengal between the Andamans and the mainland; second, a group of four coral-girt islands, in Lat. 3° N., near Hog (or Sinalu) Island on the W. coast of Sumatra; and third, the Cocos or Keeling Islands, from 700 to 800 miles SW. of Sumatra, in Lat. 12° 10′ S. and Long. 97° E. It was probably the last which Tavernier refers to. They produce coco-nuts in abundance, and have for many years been in the possession of an English family, several of whose members and a few Malays reside there. A recent account of this group will be found in A. D. Forbes, *A Naturalist's Wanderings*, and *Ency. Brit.*, xv. 112.

the other vessel from ours, and good fortune willed that the yards of the 'Maestricht', which were entangled in our rigging, broke away, and in order to help matters we cut some of them with an axe. Thus, with great trouble, the 'Maestricht' was disengaged, drifted all along the length of our vessel, and when she was passing the prow she broke off the beak-head.[1]

On the fifty-fifth day of our voyage we came in view of the Cape of Good Hope, and we remained outside five or six days, because the waves were so high that we did not venture to enter the roads to cast anchor. This was not because there was much wind, but because the south wind had blown so long that it had raised a sea on the coast. When the sea calmed down, we cast anchor, and this is what I have been able to observe there.

Of all the races of men I have seen in my travels I have found none so hideous nor so brutal as the Comouks,[2] whom I have mentioned in my account of Persia, and as the inhabitants of the Cape of Good Hope, whom they call Cafres or Hottentots. When the latter speak they make the tongue click (*peter*) in the mouth, and although their voice is scarcely articulate they easily understand one another. They have for their sole garments the skins of wild beasts which they kill in the forests, and when it becomes cold in the winter in this place, which is in 35° and some minutes of latitude, they turn the fur inside, and when it is warm they turn it outside. But it is only the better-to-do among them who are thus clothed, the others having only some miserable scrap of cloth to cover their nakedness. Both men and

[1] 'A small platform at the forepart of the upper deck; the part of a ship in front of the forecastle, fastened to the stem, and supported by the main knee.' (*New English Dictionary. s.v.*)

[2] Comouks in the original, and Comouchs in the *Persian Travels*, Book III, chap. xi, where Tavernier describes them as robbers living at the foot of the mountains of Comanie (i. e. the region between the Caucasus and the north-western shores of the Caspian Sea, bounded on the north by the Terek river). He distinguishes them from another people, the Kalmouchs (Kalmucks), who, he says, inhabit the coast of the Caspian between Moscovie and Great Tartary. For the Kumuk tribe see Keane, *Man Past and Present*, ed. 1920, p. 312

women are of spare habit and small stature, and as soon as a male is born his mother partially castrates him, and gives him sea-water to drink, and tobacco to eat. They perform this partial castration because it makes them swifter in running, so they say. It is true that there are some of them who can capture roebucks by running them down. I have had the curiosity to examine many of these Cafres, and I found they had all been castrated on the right side.[1] They have no knowledge of gold, silver, or any kind of money, and have not, so to speak, any religion.[2]

On our arrival in this place after we had cast anchor, four women came on board bringing with them four young ostriches, which were cooked for some of our sick men. Subsequently they brought many turtles and ostrich eggs, and another kind of eggs as large as the eggs of a goose. The birds which lay these eggs are a kind of goose, and have so much fat that it is impossible to eat them, as they taste rather of fish than of flesh.[3] These women, observing that our cook threw into a wooden bucket the entrails of two fowls and a goose which were for our supper, took them, squeezed them from one end to the other in order to express the contents, of which only half was ejected, and ate them in that condition,[4] being

[1] The object of this mutilation is to prevent the birth of twins (Hastings, *Ency. Religion and Ethics*, v. 580.)

[2] For an account of the religion of the Hottentots see Dr. E. Sidney Hartland's article, *ibid.*, vi. 820 ff., and that on Bantu and South Africa, *ibid.*, ii. 350 ff.

[3] These birds were penguins. (See vol. i, p. 174, *n.*, and ii, p. 307.) They are mentioned by Castanheda as occurring at St. Blaze, 60 leagues to the east of the Cape of Good Hope :—' On the rock also there are great numbers of birds as large as ducks, which do not fly, having no feathers in their wings, and which bray like so many asses.' *Note.*—Lichfield calls them stares, as large as ducks. Osorius says that the natives called them solitario, and that they were as big as geese. (Kerr's *Voyages and Travels*, ii. 309, 393.) Sir T. Roe says, ' They are a strange fowle, or rather a miscelanius creator of beast, bird, and fish, but most of bird, confuting that difinition of man to be *Animall bipes implunæ*, which is nearer to a discription of this Creature.' (*Journal*, ed. Foster, i. 12 : Mundy, ii. 327 f.)

[4] ' They eate the skinns of beasts or fowls, only sindgeing the haire and feathers a little, halfe scortched. Also the intralls, small guts and garbage, excrement and all, only quarter boiled or warmed in the fire ' (Mundy, ii. 322).

much pleased also because our captain gave each of them two cups of spirits to drink. Neither men nor women have the slightest shame about exposing their nudity, and they live almost like beasts.

When they see vessels arriving they drive cattle to the shore and bring what they have to barter for tobacco, spirits, and beads of crystal and agate, which are cheap at Surat, and for some hardware. When they are not content with what is offered them they immediately take to flight, and at the sound of a whistle all their animals follow them, and you see no more of them. Some persons on one occasion, saw them fly, and fired musket-shots in order to slay the cattle, but for some years past, these Cafres have not brought their beasts, and there has been much trouble in inducing them to return. It is a great convenience for the vessels which touch there to obtain supplies, and the Dutch have had good reason for building a fort there. There is now a fine village inhabited by people of all nationalities who live with the Dutch, and all kinds of grains which are imported, both from Europe and Asia, on being sown, grow much better than in the places whence they have been brought. It is a very good country, as I have said, at the 35th degree and some minutes of latitude, and it is neither the air nor the heat which makes these Cafres so black as they are. Desiring to know the explanation of it, and why they smell so strongly, I inquired from a young girl who was taken as soon as her mother had brought her forth, and was nursed and reared in the fort, being as white as one of our European women. She told me that the reason that the Cafres are so black, is that they rub themselves with an ointment which they make of different simples known to them, and that if they do not rub themselves often, and as soon as they are born, they become dropsical like other blacks of Africa, and like the Abyssinians, and the inhabitants of Saba, who have one leg twice the size of the other;[1] few of these people live more than forty years. It is true that these Cafres, brutal as they are, have nevertheless a special knowledge

[1] The disease known as elephantiasis. On the use of grease by Cafres see J. G. Wood, *Natural History of Man*, i. 36 f.

of simples, and know how to apply them to the maladies for which they are specifics; this the Dutch have very often proved.[1] Whether the Cafres are bitten by a venomous animal, or that an ulcer or other disease appears, by means of these simples, which they know how to select, they accomplish the cure in a short time. Of nineteen sick men who were in our vessel, fifteen were placed in the hands of the Cafres, their maladies consisting of ulcers in the legs or wounds received in war, and in less than fifteen days all were perfectly cured. Each sick man had two of these Cafres to attend upon him, and as soon as they saw what the condition of the wound or ulcer was, they sought for the drugs, crushed them between two pebbles and applied them to the sore. As for the four others, they were not given into their hands, being so infected with venereal disease that they could not be cured at Batavia. All four died between the Cape and the Island of Saint Helena.

In the year 1661 there returned from Batavia on a vessel named the 'West Frisland', a young Breton gentleman, who squandered all his money in Holland, and then entered the Company's service. When he arrived at Batavia a multitude of mosquitoes bit him on his leg during the night, and an ulcer appeared on which all the surgeons of Batavia had expended their skill and remedies; if the General had not given him permission to go home it would have been necessary to amputate his leg. When the ship arrived at the Cape, the captain sent the Breton on shore to give him some ease, these Cafres began to examine him, and said that if they were allowed to treat him they would cure him in a short time. The captain placed him in their hands, and in less than fifteen days his leg was rendered as sound as the other which had never had anything the matter with it.

As soon as a vessel has anchored at the Cape, the commander gives some of the soldiers and sailors permission to go on shore to refresh themselves. Those who during the voyage have been most indisposed go first, each in his turn, to the town, where they are fed for 7 or 8 sols a-day, and enjoy good cheer.

[1] Tavernier's statement is repeated by F. Leguat (*Voyage*, ii. 294.)

It is the custom of the Dutch to send parties from time to time to explore the country, and those who go furthest are best rewarded. A number of soldiers went in a party with a sergeant who commanded them, and advanced far into the country, where they made a large fire at midnight, both to protect themselves from lions and for warmth, and lay round it to rest. When they were asleep, a lion seized one of the soldiers by the arm, and immediately the sergeant fired a shot and slew the animal. When it was dead its jaws had to be forced open, with great effort, in order to release the soldier's arm, which was pierced from side to side. It is apparent from this story that it is an error to suppose that lions do not approach a fire.[1] The Cafres healed the soldier's arm in twelve days. There are in the fort several skins of lions and tigers.[2] Among others there is the skin of a horse which the Cafres killed. It is white barred with black stripes pricked out like a leopard, and without a tail.[3] At a distance of two or three leagues from the fort the Dutch found a dead lion with four porcupine's quills in its body, which had penetrated the flesh three-fourths of their length. It was accordingly concluded that the porcupine had killed the lion. The skin is still kept with the spines sticking in the foot.[4]

At one league's distance from the fort there is a fine village which grows from day to day. When the vessels of the Dutch Company arrive, if any soldier or sailor wishes to remain there he is welcomed. He takes as much land as he can manage,[5] and, as I have above said, all kinds of vegetables

[1] Ball notes that some African travellers have been of opinion that a fire attracts lions, and that a substantial fence is requisite for the protection of a camp.

[2] By tigers here we must understand leopards, as tigers do not occur in Africa any more than lions do in the eastern and southern parts of India, where Tavernier has so often referred to their presence in previous pages.

[3] Zebra; it should have had a tail. On the zebra sent from Abyssinia to Aurangzeb, see Bernier, 135, 143.

[4] Numerous cases are recorded of tigers having died in India from this cause, and some have been found, when shot, to have porcupine quills sticking in them.

[5] Here we have an early reference to the first Dutch Boer settlement
21 at the Cape. In 1671 the first purchase of land from the Hottentots,

and pulse, and even grapes grow readily, and rice also is cultivated. These people have young ostriches, beef, and sea and fresh water fish in abundance. When they wish to catch the young ostriches, as soon as the birds are seven or eight days old they go to the nests, drive a stake into the ground and tie the young birds by one of their feet in the nest, so that they cannot escape, leaving them to be fed by their parents till they are of good size, when they are taken to be sold or eaten.

When the Dutch began to inhabit the Cape of Good Hope, they took, as I have said, the daughter of one of these Cafres as soon as she was born. She is white and beautiful, save that she has a slightly depressed nose, and she serves as interpreter to the Dutch. She had a child by a Frenchman, but the Company would not allow him to marry her. On the contrary, they confiscated 800 livres of his wages; this was somewhat hard on him.

In this country there are many lions and tigers, and the Dutch have discovered a contrivance which answers well for killing them. They fasten a gun to a stake driven into the ground, and fix some meat at the end of the gun, which is bound to a cord attached to the trigger. When the animal comes to take this meat the cord draws the trigger, and the balls lodge in its mouth or body. The Cafres eat a root which resembles our root of cherüy,[1] which they roast, and it serves them as bread. Sometimes they make it into flour, and it tastes like chestnuts. As for flesh, they eat it raw, and fish also in the same condition; and as for the entrails of animals,

beyond the fort built by Riebeck, marked the beginning of the colony (*Ency. Brit.*, v. 237), see Ovington, 499, and Du Bois, p. 151.

[1] Dr. E. Sidney Hartland has kindly searched many authorities on South Africa in order to identify this root. F. Leguat (*Voyage*, Hakluyt Society ed., ii. 287) says of the Hottentots: 'They set great store by a Root that resembles our skirrets [a perennial umbelliferous plant, Sium sisarum, *New English Dict. s.v.*]. They roast it, and oftentimes make it into Past, which is their Bread, and somewhat like our Chestnut.' It is apparently a kind of ground-nut, which Junod (*Life of a South African Tribe*, ii. 12) says 'is extensively cultivated, being of every-day use in the Thonga culinary art, which it provides with the fatty principles. . . . Its taste is delicious, either prepared as a sauce to season mealie flour, or roasted'. [In mod. Fr. chervi or -is = skirret.]

as I have already said,[1] they merely squeeze them to exclude the digested matter and then eat them. Most of the women bind these entrails, when dried, round their legs, especially those of wild beasts which their husbands slay in the woods, and they wear them as ornaments. They also eat turtles after they have roasted them for a short time, so that the shells can be removed. They are very skilful in hurling the assegai, a kind of dart, and those who have not got one, use a stick an inch thick, of a very hard wood, and of the same length as the dart. They make a point on it and hurl it to a considerable distance with their hands. They take these sticks with them to the margin of the sea, and as soon as a fish comes to the surface they do not fail to transfix it.

As for those birds which are like our ducks, their eggs contain no yolk; there are a great number in the country, and in a bay which is eighteen miles from the Cape they are killed with blows of a stick.[2]

. . . .

During the time while M. Vandime was General, the Dutch captured a young Cafre boy at the Cape and sent him to Batavia. The General took great pains to have him instructed in languages, so that in seven or eight years he learned Dutch and Portuguese in perfection. He then wished to return to his country, and the General not desiring to constrain him to remain, equipped him with linen and clothes, thinking that when he arrived at the Cape he would live like the Dutchmen, and would aid them in obtaining supplies for their vessels whenever they arrived. But he was no sooner at the Cape than he threw his garments into the sea and fled with the other blacks, eating raw flesh as before, and since then he has remained with them without having any intercourse with the Dutch.[3]

[1] See above p. 302. [2] See i. 174, ii. 302.

[3] Some curious examples of this kind of speedy relapse into savagery, after a long course of education from infancy, have occurred among the inhabitants of the Andaman islands. A good case of a similar reversion to savagery is that of Billy Button, told by Charles Darwin (*Voyage of a Naturalist*, chap. x). Miss Gordon Cumming gives instances of the same kind in Fiji (*At Home in Fiji*). The question forms the subject of a story by Grant Allen, 'The Reverend John Creedy' (*Strange Stories*, 1892).

When these Cafres go to hunt in the forest they collect in large numbers, and cry or shout, so that the beasts are frightened by them, and it is then easy to slaughter large numbers of them. I have even been told that these cries frighten the lion.

CHAPTER XXVIII

The Dutch fleet arrives at St. Helena, and the Author gives a description of that Island.

WHEN we had stayed twenty-two days at the Cape of Good Hope, and found that the wind was very favourable to us, our Vice-Admiral ordered the anchor to be hoisted, and we directed our course for the Island of St. Helena.[1] As soon as the sails were set and prayers had been said, all the sailors and soldiers declared they would go to rest and sleep till they got to St. Helena. For a steady wind always prevails and bears you, generally in sixteen or eighteen days, to the anchorage at that island. During the whole course the sails were not touched, because the wind was always astern, and the only trouble the sailors had was that fourteen days after our departure two of them were sent to the mainmast top to watch, in order to sight the island; for as soon as it is sighted the pilots should take good care to be ready to cast anchor on the side facing northwards, and it is necessary to approach the land in order to cast it, otherwise no bottom can be found. If these precautions are not taken, and if the anchors do not find bottom, the currents in the air and ocean carry the vessel quickly past the anchorage and there is then no hope of returning, because the wind is always contrary and never changes.

As soon as two of our anchors were cast into the sea the soldiers and sailors were summoned, and the crew made the vessel as tight as they could. They also fixed stages outside to scrape the hull and grease it; this was accomplished in two days. Then all on board were divided into two watches, and the Vice-Admiral addressed them from the quarter-deck

[1] Compare Ovington, 89 ff.; *Voyage of F. Leguat*, ii. 298 ff.

as follows: 'Gentlemen, we shall remain here twenty-two days, arrange which of you desire to go first on shore to refresh yourselves and hunt, and let all return here on the eleventh day so that the others may also go in turn.' Each of the men who went on shore was given a pair of shoes, and they carried large cauldrons, and supplies of rice, biscuit, spirits, and salt. On reaching land they ascended the mountain, but three or four remained below to collect sorrel, which grows to two or three feet in height and is very good. When they had collected a load of it they went to find the others, who were in pursuit of wild pigs, which abound in the island. When they had killed some they cooked the flesh with the rice and sorrel, which make a fairly good kind of soup, and purges insensibly without one's knowing it. While on shore they did nothing but sing, drink, and eat, and they had to send some of the pigs to the vessel every day. For each pig an écu and a pair of shoes were given them, because the mountain was high and steep, and this chase gave the men much trouble. I have elsewhere spoken of the Persian greyhounds which are taken to St. Helena for hunting wild pigs, and after having been used they are thrown into the sea, and not carried farther for the reason I have pointed out in the same place.

While those who are on land occupy themselves with this sport, those who remain in the vessel spend their time in fishing; for there is a great abundance of fish around the island, especially mackerel.[1] Each sailor and soldier is given a measure of salt, with which they salt the fish, and then hang them to dry in the wind. They feed themselves upon this dried fish after leaving the island, and generally have sufficient for thirty or forty days, and each receives only a little oil and rice cooked in water; this saves the Company a quantity of food.

All the pigs, sheep, geese, ducks, and hens which were on board were sent on shore, and as soon as these animals had eaten the sorrel, which purges them as well as it does men, in a few days they became so fat that when we approached

[1] Of sixty-five species of sea-fish caught off the island, including mackerel, seventeen are peculiar to St. Helena (*Ency. Brit.*, xxiv. 7).

Holland it was almost impossible to eat them, especially the geese and ducks, on account of the fat.

There are two places off the coast of St. Helena where one can anchor. The best of them is where we were, because the bottom is very good for anchorage, and the drinking water which comes from the top of the mountain is the best on the island. In this part of the island there is no level ground, for the mountain rises from the very shore. There is only a small flat place close to the sea, where formerly there was a chapel where a Portuguese priest of the sect of St. Francis lived for fourteen years; but at present this chapel is half ruined. While this priest lived there he made presents to the vessels which touched there, furnishing them with fish, which he caught and dried, and they gave him in exchange rice, biscuit, and Spanish wine. After he had dwelt there for the time I have said, and had lived a very austere life, he fell ill, and by good fortune it happened that a Portuguese vessel arrived just then. Everything was done to relieve him, but he died five days after the vessel had anchored, and was interred by people of his own nationality.

The anchorage is not so good at the other roads, but on shore there is a beautiful plain where all that is sown arrives at maturity. The orders of the Dutch Company are at present, that, if a vessel takes cabbages, salad, or other vegetables, seeds must be sown for the benefit of those who may come afterwards. There are many lemon and some orange trees, which the Portuguese planted. For this nationality has this to its credit, that wherever it goes it seeks to do something for the benefit of those who afterwards visit the place. The Dutch do the reverse and seek to destroy everything, so that those who come afterwards shall find nothing. It is true that it is not the superior officers who act in this way, but the common sailors and soldiers, who say to one another, 'We shall not return any more', and in order to get fruit from a tree more quickly, they cut it down instead of plucking the fruit.

A serious disturbance was on the point of breaking out. In the fleet although our vessel left Batavia the last of all, since she was a good sailer, she was the second to arrive at

St. Helena. One day the Vice-Admiral, the captain, and other officers of the vessel determined to go in the skiff towards this plain, to obtain some vegetables and lemons. When we arrived there—for I was with the party—we were much surprised to find nothing on the trees, and only some remains of cabbages and radishes on the ground. We did not doubt that the crew of the vessel called the *Encuse,* which had arrived some days before us, had done all this damage, and our Vice-Admiral resolved to go on board to inquire into the matter. When we got there we found quantities of lemons and vegetables in the cabins of the captain and pilot, and all the sailors presented lemons, with which they were well provided, to our men. The captain of the vessel offered a present of some to the Vice-Admiral, which he refused to accept, saying that it was treason to all the fleet, and that all these delicacies must be collected and put together in one place until all the vessels had arrived, so that each poor invalid might have some of them. The sailors and soldiers who had filled their chests with them were very unwilling to consent; but the Vice-Admiral, exerting his authority, said that if they did not bring all the lemons which were still remaining, he would hang a number of the men, when the Admiral and the remainder of the fleet, which consisted of eleven vessels, arrived. The captain, fearing his threat, put so much pressure on his crew that the whole were brought into his cabin and safely shut up until the fleet had arrived, so that each vessel had its share of this small refreshment.

When all the fleet had anchored in the roads of St. Helena, there was nothing but feasting and rejoicing, sometimes on one vessel and sometimes on another; and the English fleet, which consisted of nine vessels, arrived soon afterwards.[1] There arrived, moreover, two Portuguese vessels laden with slaves of both sexes, which came from the Guinea coast, on their way to the mines of Peru. Some Dutchmen in our fleet who had dwelt at Castel de Mine, knew the language of these poor people. They went on board, to see them, and also some Dutch sailors who were in the Portuguese service;

[1] For a summary of the voyages of the early English adventurers see *Imperial Gazetteer,* ii. 453 f.

and on the following night about 250 of these poor blacks threw themselves into the sea. It was believed that the Dutch, who knew their language, had told them that they would be miserably treated when they reached the mines, and this had driven them to despair. It is true that it is a very hard and miserable slavery; for frequently, after having worked for some days, some of the softer strata collapse and suddenly bury 400 or 500 of these poor people. As soon as they are put to mining their faces, eyes, and skin entirely change colour; this is caused by the vapours in the excavations, and slaves are kept alive in these places only by the quantity of spirits which are supplied to both the men and women.

Some of these people are no longer slaves, their masters having given them liberty, but they do not cease to work in the mines and earn large wages. But as they leave the mines on Saturday evening to return on Monday morning, during the interval they drink so much spirit, which is very dear, that they spend all they earn during the week, and thus they are always in a miserable condition of poverty.

While the two fleets were in the roads at St. Helena the English and the Dutch entertained each other in turns, and there was continual festivity. The day our Vice-Admiral entertained our Admiral and some of the chiefs of the English fleet, it was not on board our vessel, for as soon as he told me of his intention, I advised him to give his feast on land; this he did with greater credit and more freedom than the others had done. I offered him for the purpose my tent, and the carpet and cushions which I had still with me, and had used in my journeys by land; and I further promised to open, on his account, my cask of Rhine wine, which Madame la Générale had presented me with, and even to contribute to the collation half a dozen bottles of Mantua wine, and a similar quantity of that of Shīrāz. He was delighted with the offer I made him, and immediately we went on shore to pitch the tent; this gave us some trouble, because we could not find any level spot even of the size of the tent; but our sailors made one near the river, whence, while eating, we might contemplate the high mountains and the pointed rocks, where we saw the male and female goats leaping from one side to the other.

On the following day, between 9 and 10 a.m., he had the pleasure of seeing all the guests in their boats, some with trumpets and drums, others with violins and other musical instruments; this could not have been if the Vice-Admiral had given his entertainment in the vessel, where all these different classes of people could not have come. As the feast, then, was on land, the majority of the ladies, both English and Dutch, who were in the fleet also came, without being invited; and so instead of one table three were required, and those who expected to eat in the tent, under shade, were obliged to yield their places out of politeness to the ladies. During the repast there was a great noise of trumpets and other musical instruments, and at each health all the guns of the vessels fired a discharge. The first health which was drunk was that of the King of England, after which followed those of the States General, of the Prince of Orange, and of the Companies, and then came the healths of the chief officers of the fleet and of some private persons. At the close of the repast, when we were ready to return on board, a disaster happened which somewhat marred the enjoyment of the company. The Admiral's trumpeter, having drunk a little more than he ought to have done, mounted on a high rock in order to blow his trumpet, and from time to time he rolled down large stones. Although ordered to stop, because it was seen that some injury might happen, he did not cease, however, finding some amusement in it; and at length he let go a very large one, which, jumping from rock to rock, went through the tent, where it broke a case of wine and killed a small boy born at Batavia of Dutch parentage. He was being sent to Holland to learn the language properly, and to be taught to read and write. For these children, though born of parents who have come from Holland, never learn Dutch properly while they remain at Batavia, being brought up among servants and slaves, who use the Portuguese language more than Dutch. These children also learn from them a thousand wickednesses, and at the age of nine years they know more lechery than do youths of twenty years in Europe.[1] After burying the child the company returned on board sooner than they would otherwise have done, and they were distressed that a day which had been so joyful had so sad an ending.

On the next two days we had numerous visits, and there was not a lady who did not come to our vessel; I believe it was less on our own account than to ascertain if we had still any Rhine wine, which they had found to be excellent at our Vice-Admiral's feast.

After our vessel had been twenty days at anchor—for the others which arrived later had less time to refresh themselves—the Admiral fired three cannon, and hoisted a large flag on the poop of his vessel, as a signal to all the captains and pilots to come on board; when they arrived, they held council to settle what route should be taken for Holland. The majority maintained that they should go to the west rather than to the south, because the season for navigation was much advanced, and by sailing towards the West Indies we should find the proper winds for Holland. But it happened otherwise; for as soon as we had passed the line we found the winds contrary to what our pilots had expected; this was the reason why we were afterwards obliged to go to the 64th degree in the latitude of Iceland, and return to Holland from the north.

CHAPTER XXIX

The Dutch fleet leaves the Island of St. Helena, and the Author arrives safely with it in Holland.

On the day after the council had been held, the Admiral ordered the three signal shots for parting, to be fired, and at ten o'clock p.m. all the fleet set sail. The English still remained there and we did not know why, unless it was to try to catch one of their sailors, who was ill-treated by his pilot, one day went on shore with him to get water, and slew him with two stabs of his dagger, after which he escaped into the mountain. If he remained there he must have

[1] There is, it is to be feared, some applicability in these remarks to the case of children reared in India at the present time.

passed a bad time, as there is no house in the island. Three days after our departure from St. Helena the crew commenced to pray every morning and evening, but I remarked that they had not done so during the twenty-two days we spent in the roads; this I thought strange, as if one should not pray to God when out of danger as well as while in danger.

On the eleventh day after our departure we crossed the line with a favourable wind. I know that many have written that the heat is insupportable under the line, and that the water and some of the provisions become decomposed, but we experienced nothing of the kind; elsewhere in the voyage we felt much greater heat. I am quite ready to admit that if a calm had caught us under the line, instead of the propitious wind which we experienced, we should have felt the heat more than we did.

After some days' sailing we spent three in passing a bank where the sea is full of a plant, the leaf of which resembles the leaves of the olive.[1] This plant has fruits like large white gooseberries, but they contain nothing inside. At length, after many more days' sailing, we sighted the coasts of Iceland, and afterwards the Island of Ferelle,[2] where the Dutch fleet already awaited us, constantly firing cannon shots to intimate its position to us. As soon as the two fleets sighted one another, each vessel fired all its guns, and took up position by its patron, that of the Admiral by the Admiral, that of the Vice-Admiral by the Vice-Admiral, and so of all the others. We numbered eleven vessels, there came also eleven other vessels to meet us, and after each had recognized its mate, the first thing that was done was to send on board the vessels from India a quantity of supplies, such as casks of beer, smoked meat, butter, cheese, good white biscuit, and for every vessel one cask each of Rhine, French, and Spanish wines. As soon as the supplies were on board our vessel, the soldiers and sailors took three or four of the casks of beer, which they placed on end close to the mainmast, broke them open with a cannon-ball, and they were then

[1] This was the sargossa weed, Fucus natans, or sargassum bucciferum which is found in the Pacific. The so-called fruits are the floats.

[2] Faroe Islands.

free to whoever wished to drink. It was the same with the food, for both drink and food were at the discretion of the crew during the remainder of the voyage. Next day each pilot resigned his charge, giving over the direction to the pilots brought by the convoy. There were three of them for each vessel, and for that purpose pilots of from sixty to eighty years of age, who knew these seas perfectly, and how the sand-banks had changed during the current year, were selected.

Next day the Admiral of the convoy fired three cannon shots, and hoisted his flag on the poop, to give notice to all the officers of both fleets to assemble in council. All the reports and processes which have been made against those who have misbehaved during the voyage are taken to it, and the whole being examined, according as the council adjudicates the accused are brought from each vessel on the following day, and judgement is pronounced. Formerly they took them to Holland, but when it was so, they found friends who obtained their pardon, and they all got off. But at present all are afraid, as there is no longer chance of pardon. This is the reason why the soldiers and sailors are not guilty of insolence and mutiny during the voyage as they were formerly. There were two men of our fleet hanged for having stabbed officers; many were sentenced to the stocks and whipping before the mainmast, and the wages of others were confiscated.

We passed through a fleet of herring fishers, and they did not fail to bring casksful to each vessel. The captains presented them with rice, pepper, and other spices.

As soon as we had sighted the coasts of Holland, all the soldiers of our fleet who had been with those who went to besiege the Manillas, from joy at beholding their country again, fixed a quantity of large and small wax tapers about the poop and bow of the vessel, where the wind, when they were lit, could not extinguish them. The same was done in five or six of the vessels; this gave out such an extraordinary light that the whole fleet was alarmed. On our vessel alone, there were more than 1,700 of these wax tapers, both large and small. The sailors had kept them since they were at the Manillas, from whence they had brought a large quantity, as also from Pointe de Galle in the Island of Ceylon. For when on shore they pillaged and burnt some convents which were in the country, and as wax is cheap in India, and is easily bleached, every religious house always has a large supply of wax tapers for the festivals, when numbers are lighted before the grand altar and in all the chapels. Thus the least of the Dutch sailors had thirty or forty of these tapers for his share, and some of them had some as thick as a man's thigh.

The command was, according to custom, that our vessel, as Vice-Admiral, should go to Zealand. We were on the coast seven whole days without being able to enter Flushing,[1] on account of the sand which frequently changes its position. As soon as we had cast anchor, more than fifty small boats came about our vessel, but kept a short distance off, being forbidden to come alongside. Each then began to call out and ask the names of persons in order to carry the news of their arrival to their relatives and friends.

On the day following that on which we anchored off Flushing, two of the members of the Company came on board to welcome us all, and to tell us to close our chests and place our marks thereon. They were then carried into a hall of the India House, and the day was fixed upon which each should return to claim what belonged to him. It is the custom that before the chests are given up they are opened to be examined, through fear lest they should contain anything contraband.

These two gentlemen summoned the crew on deck between the poop and the mainmast, and taking the captain, whom they placed at their side in front of all, 'Gentlemen,' they said to all on board, 'on behalf of the Directors we order you to tell us whether the captain has ill-treated you during this voyage.' The crew, who wanted to be on shore, where the majority saw father or mother, brothers or sisters, or friends awaiting them, began to cry out that the captain was a good man, that he knew how to act for the interests of the Company and his own also; but that if, when leaving Batavia, God had delivered them from him, they would have

[1] Flessingue in the original.

been much more happy during the voyage. At once, without another word, they all jumped into the boats and went on shore, where they received many kisses and embraces, and immediately all hastened to the public-house. Most of the soldiers and sailors first go there after their debarkation, and generally they do not leave it save to claim their baggage or receive their pay, or to join a party. Some of these soldiers and sailors returning from India have been known to expend, in two months' continual debauch, nearly 1,000 écus, which they had had much trouble in earning in fifteen or twenty years' service to the Company. I have known a sailor at Middelburg, who in a debauch broke glass to the value of 250 livres, when drinking the health of his friends. But the publicans do not receive all the money of these people, as the women of pleasure get their share of it too.

The two Directors of the Company, who came on board as soon as the anchor was cast, to give permission to the crew to go on shore, and appoint persons for the protection of the vessel, did me the honour to salute me at once, and I received many expressions of kindness from them. They ordered a collation to be served at the same time, and, drinking to my health, asked me if I had anything to complain of with regard to any of the officers of the vessel. I replied that on the contrary I had every reason to praise them, that they had all treated me with great civility, and that I gave thanks to the Vice-Admiral, to the captain, and to all the merchants of the vessel for the good friendship they had shown me during the voyage. For it should be stated that besides the Vice-Admiral we had a captain under him. The Directors told me that they were much pleased that I was satisfied with the treatment I had received, telling me that if I had any chests I had only to place my mark on them, and that they would take care to have them carried to the Company's House at Middelburg, where I might come to claim them in four days. It required fully this time for them to discharge a part of what was in the vessel, which could not reach Middelburg with a full cargo. I thanked them for their goodwill, and, having placed my mark on my chests, left the vessel and went by land to Middelburg.

It was the year that the Chamber General was held there, for it is held for four years in succession at Amsterdam, and two years at Middelburg. The reason is, that Amsterdam owns half the Company; Middelburg a quarter; and Rotterdam, Delft, Horne, and Encuse each a sixteenth; and the Company is not bound to hold the Chamber in either of these four last, which only make up one-fourth, and have the right only to have a vessel each year between the four, one year at Rotterdam, one year at Delft, and similarly the others. For the same reason Amsterdam has eight Directors, Middelburg four and the other four towns each its own one; this makes the number sixteen, though they always speak of seventeen Directors, because the President has two votes.

On the fourth day of my arrival at Middelburg I went to the India House, where I found two of the Directors, who were already engaged in delivering the chests to those to whom they belonged, and as soon as they saw me they told me to claim mine; this I did, at the same time handing them the keys of my boxes, so that they might see for themselves whether I carried anything which was contraband. Of these two gentlemen one was from Zealand, and the other from Horne, and the latter took the keys to open my boxes. But the Zealand Director, more civil than he of North Holland, told him I was free, that I was not subject to the Company, and that it had afforded me a free passage. My keys were at once returned to me, and one of the people of the store was ordered to summon some sledges, which are used in Holland instead of waggons, to convey my chests. I may say in passing, that it is not only on this occasion that I have remarked that the more one approaches the north the less civility and honesty we meet among the inhabitants, and that manners follow the harshness and roughness of the climate.

The same evening the Directors did me the honour to send one of their officers to invite me to dine with them on the following day. Many persons interested in the Company were at the repast, and I believe that they were there less for the good cheer than to hear me talk, thinking that I might know many things in regard to the private trade which the representatives of the Company carry on in India. They were not mistaken; and I may say that no one could be better informed than I was of the methods of these agents, who have the management of the factories in Persia and India, to enrich themselves. For they never return to Holland empty-handed, and when they take but 100,000 or 150,000 florins they count it a poor thing. I have known many of them who have amassed up to 600,000 and 700,000 florins; as, for instance, among others the Sieur Nicolas Obrechit,[1] who was chief of the Dutch factories both at Ispahān and Hormuz and other places in Persia, during the years from 1635 to 1640. His friends and those who had done business with him estimated that he carried away more than 15,000 tomāns, which are equal to about 690,000 livres,[2] without estimating what he had expended on the gout with which he was afflicted, and the other ailments which more often arise from relationships with the courtesans of Persia, than from the trouble expended in packing silk, weighing it, examining its quality, and seeing whether it has any bad skeins mixed with the good. The Sieur Obrechit was well able to spend freely, for his profits were large, but such as are rarely permitted or approved of by honest people. All the spices, sugar, and other goods of the Company are sold wholesale, generally at Hormuz or Gombroon, and amount in value, annually, to 15 or 16 tonnes of gold, each tonne being equal to 100,000 guilders, which are equivalent in our money to 120,000 livres, and the 16 tonnes of gold to 1,920,000 livres. The Sieur Obrechit did not sell all these goods without receiving annually for himself, 80,000 or 100,000 guilders,[3] which the Persian merchants presented to him, underhand, through the broker, so that he might allow the goods to be sold at a low price. But he was not the inventor of this fine means of enriching himself, others practised it before him,

[1] The correct name of this official, as Sir W. Foster points out, was Nicolaas Overschie, President der Commissarissen van Huwelykze- en Kleine Zaken in 1741 at Batavia, after which year he disappears.

[2] Equal to £51,750.

[3] Taking the Dutch guilder or florin at 1*s.* 9½*d.* (vol. i, p. 328) the value of the tonne would be about £9,000. Perhaps the guilder ought to be a fraction more, but it is important to have here independent testimony that the livre as understood by Tavernier was about 1*s.* 6*d.*—the proportion being 5 guilders = 6 livres, or 9*s.*

and since his time others have employed it, especially the Sieurs Constant and Van-Wück.

Moreover, there is also the profit that these gentry make on silk. It is true that for some years past the Company has not esteemed Persian silk so highly as it did formerly, because it has not so great a sale in Japan as it would have had if the trade had continued as it was in the years 1636 and 1637.[1] All the chiefs of the factory who succeeded Obrechit could not have made as much as he did; for in the two above-named years silk was dear in Japan, because the people of China and Tonquin were then at war with the Dutch, and the latter prevented them from trading with Japan; so the Chinese and Tonquinese could not obtain silk except through the hands of the Dutch. Whatever it may cost they must have it to clothe themselves with, as they use no other materials for their garments. It was in these two years, 1636 and 1637, that the Sieur Obrechit filled his purse; for instead of 500 or 600 bales of silk, which is the most they receive from the King of Persia, the General of Batavia and his Council wrote to him that at any cost he must send them 2,000 loads. I have alluded, in the first volume of my history, to the agreement made between the King of Persia and the Dutch Company; and I have also made mention, in connexion with this subject, of the small success of the negotiation of the Ambassadors of Holstein, of which the secretary of that embassy has without doubt not boasted in the account which he has given to the public. Therefore, for fear of wearying the reader, I shall not repeat it here, and I shall only ask him to remember that the arrival of these Ambassadors, which caused apprehension and jealousy among the Dutch, caused the latter to raise the price of silk so much that they removed all desire in other nations to outbid them.

Thus Obrechit, having then received an order from Batavia for 2,000 loads of silk, irrespective of cost, and this quantity being all that Persia could supply, as he was shrewd and
22 loved profit beyond all things, succeeded so well in intriguing

[1] For an account of the Persian silk trade see Curzon, *Persia*, i. 366 ff.

with the Armenians and other merchants in Persia that he obtained the 2,000 loads of silk which had been ordered. It is true that beyond the 500 or 600 loads which the Dutch receive from the King, according to the agreement made between his Majesty and the Company, Obrechit was obliged to pay at a high rate for the others; and he bought them from the Armenians, who sold them to him at the same rate as those they had sold to Aleppo and Smyrna. During these two years there was not a single load of silk for which he did not place 4 tomāns in his purse, and he said some loads cost him 60 tomāns. It was represented to him that it would be better not to send so large a quantity of silk, as it was so dear, and that the merchants of the country, both Christians and Musalmāns, were laughing at him; but he only replied that he must obey the Company's order. One day when I was alone with him we were talking together about my travels, and he told me how astonished he was, after my experience of the greater part of the trade of Asia, that I underwent so much trouble in my long journeys; that I should do much better by serving the Company, and that if I wished he would send me to the diamond mines on its account; but I believe it would have been on his own. When I had thanked him for his goodwill, and told him I had no such intention, he replied that I did not know what I was refusing, that I would derive great profit, and that in his factory, with a scratch of the pen, or by changing a figure, he obtained what he wished. I replied to him that on three or four occasions my horoscope had been cast, and on all occasions it had been agreed that I should live to a good age; and so, if I was able to acquire wealth, I desired to acquire it honestly and by my labour, as God had ordained for me, in order to be able to possess it with greater security and comfort to my soul for the remainder of my days, and that my heirs might enjoy it peaceably. If we were not to act in this way, replied he, we should be miserable; for the wages the Company gives us would not suffice to clothe us. On my return from one of my voyages I went to see him at a village bearing his name, situated one league from the Hague. I saw him ill in bed, and suffering from several diseases, and I believe that he often then recalled to mind what I had said to him at Ispahān.

I must now return to the Directors and the members of the Company with whom I dined at Middelburg. Most of them desired that I should inform them of the manner in which the agents of the Company behaved in Persia and India, and the others asked me to speak of my travels. I preferred to satisfy the latter, and avoided all referenec to trade. It is true that if I had not had some suspicion of the deception which they played me subsequently, I would possibly have told them many things from which they might have derived benefit. For in the space of the forty years during which I have often visited Persia and India, most persons in the service of the Company have told me all the tricks they made use of in order to acquire money. In return for this confidence, when they were about to return home, I endeavoured to furnish them with a good parcel of diamonds, which occupy but little space. If then I had declared to these gentlemen what I knew of this matter, they would have gained much in studying the record I should have given, and by discovering the knavery of their servants, and by doing rightly by me, their conscience would not be charged as it is, concerning the 17,500 florins which General Vanderlin and his Council seized from me at Batavia.

What astonishes me most is, as I have elsewhere remarked, that when the General and his Council took from me the value of these 17,500 florins, they made a hundred promises that I should be paid immediately I set foot in Holland, but this was not done in spite of all the steps I could take for recovering the amount. For when leaving the feast that was given at Batavia on the departure of the fleet, I took four witnesses of the fact, namely, our Vice-Admiral and three merchants, to whom, when taking leave of the General and Council, I said aloud in their presence that they would be my witnesses if God permitted us to arrive in Holland or Zealand, and would remember that the General and his Council did not give me on my departure what they had promised, namely, an order which I could show to the Directors of the Company, by which they would see that 17,500 florins were due and payable to me on my arrival. The General's reply was to take a glass of wine and wish me a pleasant journey, assuring me that the order would arrive in Holland before me. The Directors, to justify their refusal to pay me, told me that the General and his Council had written nothing to them concerning the matter, and that when they received an advice of it they would at once pay it. I was at length obliged to bring an action against them which lasted two years, before I was able to find, either at Amsterdam or the Hague, a notary who would serve a summons, every one fearing them, as they were both judges and parties to the suit. During these two years I often entered their assembly, where they always gave me some hope, but in reality they were laughing at me. I have hardly ever been deceived when looking a man in the face, as I know almost exactly what is in his mind. I remarked that many of these men had the appearance of loving their own interests and caring little for those of others, and among others there was a young man who represented Encuse, who gazed earnestly at me. After looking at me for some time he asked why I had been to Batavia, where strangers have no business. I replied that all these gentlemen were sufficiently acquainted with it, and that as he was the only one who did not know, his beard was too young to oblige me to explain to him. As their procedure annoyed me, and I was enraged at seeing myself treated so unjustly, I added in speaking to this young man that he would do better at Encuse selling his butter and cheese than where he was. The President interrupted me gently, and told me that I must offend no one, to which I replied that I had seen too much to render an account of my doings in this manner, and that what I did at Goa and Batavia was at the request of the Chief of the factory at Vengurla, and solely for the purpose of rendering a service to the Company. This discourse being finished, the President asked me to go outside for a short time, which I did. Afterwards, when I returned, he told me that he still knew nothing about the matter, and that all these gentlemen believed that I would not remain there, but would still make another journey to Asia, and as I praised the good treatment I had received on their vessels on my return voyage, they again offered me a passage, and promised to give orders that I should be treated even still better than before; that as soon as I arrived at Batavia I should be paid; that they would send an order to that effect to the General and his Council, and that I might embark on the first vessel which left for Surat or Hormuz. I thanked these gentlemen for all their fine offers, and told them that I preferred to make three journeys by land rather than one voyage by sea. In conclusion, at the end of five years the Directors wrote to my brother—for I had then returned to India—that if he was willing to take 10,000 livres in satisfaction of my claim, he might come to receive them. This my brother did, and he gave them a receipt in full. I leave the reader to judge of the equity and conscience of these gentry. For either they owed me 17,500 florins or they did not. If they did not, why pay me 10,000 livres? And if they did owe me, why not pay me fully? I am not the only person to whom they have done injustice of this kind. I know many other more serious cases, the recital of which would not be to their advantage.[1]

Such was my return from India in the year 1649, the only time I returned by sea, having made, as I have said, all my Asiatic journeys by land, both when going and returning, counting as nothing the short passage in the Mediterranean; and my first journey was wholly by land, from Paris by Germany and Hungary to Constantinople, where I also went on the return from my last journey in the year 1669. From Constantinople I went to Smyrna, where I embarked for Leghorn, and from Leghorn I travelled by land to Genoa, from Genoa to Turin, and from Turin to Paris, where I took the King that beautiful parcel of diamonds of which I have spoken in the discourse on precious stones.[2] His Majesty had the goodness to give me a very favourable reception,

[1] As to the merits of this case, without the other side of the question before us, we cannot venture to decide. But, on the whole, Tavernier got off much easier than did the Dutch subjects, who also bought rekenings at the same time, for they not only had to give them up but were imprisoned and sent to Holland as common soldiers (vol. ii. 295).

[2] See vol. ii. 100.

which was a glorious conclusion to my long journeys, in which I have always had for my primary object to spare nothing in order to make known to the great monarchs of Asia, that there is one grander than them all, in Europe, and that our King infinitely surpasses them both in power and glory.

My first thoughts on finding myself in Paris, on the return from my sixth journey, were to return thanks to God for having preserved me, during the space of forty years, among so many perils which I had run, by sea and land, in regions so far distant.

THE KING'S LICENCE

LOUIS, by the grace of God, King of France and of Navarre, to our beloved and liege Councillors, the Members of our Courts of Parliament, Masters of the Requests ordinary of our House, Bailiffs, Seneschals, or their Lieutenants, and to all others whom it may concern, greeting: our well beloved Jean-Baptiste Tavernier, Esq., Baron of Aubonne, having informed us that he has written a book which has for title, 'Six Voyages made in Turkey, Persia, and India, during the space of forty years, and by all the routes that can be taken,' which he desires to print and sell, if it pleases us to grant our letters, necessary to him who humbly seeks them: for these reasons we have permitted and shall permit the Petitioner to have the said Book printed in such volume, margin, or type, as he may be advised, and to sell and dispose of it throughout our Kingdom and the territories subject to us, during the space of fifteen years, to date from the day on which the said impression may be completed; during which time we expressly inhibit all Booksellers and Printers from printing, selling, or disposing of the said Book, and also reprinting it, except with the consent of the Petitioner or of those who hold the right to do so from him, on pain, to those acting otherwise, of a penalty of three thousand livres fine, one-third to us, one-third to the Hotel Dieu of our City of Paris, and the remaining third to the said Petitioner; also of confiscation of the counterfeit copies, and of all expenditure, damages, and interest; on condition of placing two copies of the said Book in our Public Library, one in that of our Chamber in the Palace of the Louvre, and one in that of our beloved and loyal Chevalier and Chancellor of France, the Sieur Daligre, before offering it for sale, on pain of nullifying these presents, which will be registered in the proper place; and in placing at the beginning and end of them a statement acknowledging that they are bound by the terms agreed upon, and of their willingness to allow the Petitioner to enjoy them quietly and peaceably.

We command in the first place our Usher or Sergeant, on this requisition, to undertake for the execution of these presents all necessary deeds and actions without further permission, notwithstanding 'Clameur de Haro', 'Charte Normande', and all else to the contrary. For such is our pleasure. Given at Versailles the 7th day of October, in the year of Grace one thousand six hundred and seventy-five, and of our reign the thirty-third. By the King in Council.

(Signed) DESVIEUX.

Registered on the Book of the Society of Booksellers and Printers of Paris, the 14th November 1675, according to the resolution of Parliament of the 8th April 1653, and that of the King's Privy Council of the 27th February 1665.

(Signed) THIERRY, Syndic.

And the said Jean-Baptiste Tavernier, Esq., Baron of Aubonne, has ceded and transferred his rights to Gervais Clouzier and Claude Barbin, Merchant Booksellers, in accordance with the agreement made between them.

Printed for the first time the 1st of October 1676.

APPENDICES

[By Dr. V. Ball]

APPENDIX I

1. The Great Mogul's Diamond, and the true history of the Koh-i-Nūr.
2. Summary history of the Koh-i-Nūr.
3. The Grand Duke of Tuscany's Diamond, otherwise known as the Austrian Yellow, or the Florentine; and some further notes on the absolute weights of the carat and rati as they were used by Tavernier.
4. On the Weights of the Diamonds, other precious stones and Pearls, mentioned by Tavernier.

APPENDIX II

List of all the Diamond Mines in India of which there are authentic records; and extracts from an Early Account of the Diamond Mines of Southern India.

APPENDIX III

The Diamond Mines of Bengal.

APPENDIX IV

The Diamond Mines of Borneo.

APPENDIX V

1. The Ruby Mines of Burma.
2. The Sapphire Washings of Ceylon.

APPENDIX VI

A Review in the Philosophical Transactions of Chappuzeau's work entitled 'Histoire des Joyaux' published in 1665 or 1666.

APPENDIX I

1. *The Great Mogul's Diamond and the true History of the Koh-i-Nūr.*

ALTHOUGH the writers on this subject are very numerous, still it is believed that almost everyone of them who has contributed to its elucidation has been consulted in the preparation of this account; and it is certain that many, whose writings have also been consulted, are chiefly noteworthy for the amount of confusion which they have unfortunately introduced into it. The principal authorities are enumerated in the note below.[1] It would only prove puzzling to the reader and cloud the main issue were any considerable space devoted to refuting the errors and correcting the misquotations regarding it, which are so common in works on precious stones. It seems to be a better course to endeavour to secure close attention to the facts of the case supported

[1] It will be convenient to classify the principal authorities according to the theories which they have respectively adopted, as follows:

First, those who maintain the identity of the Koh-i-Nūr with Bābur's Diamond:

Erskine, *Life of Bābur*, 1918, ii, pp. 191–2; Rev. C. W. King, *Natural History of Precious Stones*, Bohn's ed., 1870, p. 70; E. W. Streeter, *The Great Diamonds of the World*, p. 116.

Second, those who maintain the identity of the Koh-i-Nūr with the Great Mogul's Diamond, and who either treat Bābur's Diamond as distinct or make no special reference to it:

James Forbes, *Oriental Memoirs*, 1834, vol. ii, p. 175; Major-General Sleeman, *Rambles and Recollections*, 1918, pp. 288 ff.; James Tennant, *Lecture on Gems and Precious Stones*, 1852, p. 84; V. Ball, *Journ. As. Soc. of Bengal*, 1880, vol. l, pt. ii, p. 31, and *Economic Geology of India*, 1881, p. 19.

Third, those who maintain the identity of the Koh-i-Nūr with both Bābur's and the Great Mogul's Diamonds:

Official Descriptive Catalogue of the Great Exhibition of 1851, pt. iii, p. 695; Kluge, *Handbuch der Edelsteinkunde*, Leipzig, 1860, p. 240; Professor N. S. Maskelyne, Roy. Inst. of Great Britain, March 1860, and *Edin. Rev.*, 1866, pp. 247–8; Gen. Cunningham, *Arch. Reports*, vol. ii, p. 390; Professor Nicol, *Encylopædia Britannica*, 9th ed., Art., 'Diamond'; Dr. H. A. Miers, quoting Ball and N. S. Maskelyne, *Nature*, 1891, p. 44; p. 555, in *Ency. Brit.*, 11th ed.

It would not be difficult to add to the above a score of names of writers who have supported one or other of these theories.

by well-verified references, so that the reader may be in a position to pronounce for himself a verdict on definite evidence alone, and accept or reject the conclusions which are here suggested.

In order, so to speak, to clear the way for the discussion, it will be necessary, as a preliminary, to give short accounts of all the large diamonds with which authors have sought to identify the Koh-i-Nūr.

Firstly, there is the diamond of Sultān Bābur, which his son Humāyūn received in the year A.D. 1526 from the family of Rājā Bikramajit, when he took possession of Agra. It had already then a recorded history, having been acquired from the Rājā of Mālwā by Alā-ud-dīn in the year 1304.[1] Regarding its traditional history, which extends 5,000 years farther back, nothing need be said here; though it has afforded sundry imaginative writers a subject for highly characteristic paragraphs. We have no record of its having been at any time a cut stone.

According to Sultān Bābur the diamond was equal in value to one day's food of all the people in the world. Its estimated weight was about 8 mishkāls, and as he gives a value of 40 ratis to the mishkāl—it weighed, in other words, about 320 ratis. Ferishta [2] states that Bābur accepted the diamond in lieu of any other ransom, for the private property of individuals, and that it weighed 8 mishkāls or 224 ratis. Hence 1 mishkāl = 28 ratis, from which we may deduce that the ratis Ferishta referred to were to those of Bābur, of which 40 went to the mishkāl, as 28 : 40; and this, on the supposition that the smaller rati was equal to 1·842 troy gr., gives a value of 2·63 troy gr. for the larger, which closely approximates to the value of the pearl rati of Tavernier. If on the other hand we deduce the smaller from the larger (at 2·66 gr. for the pearl rati) we obtain for it a value of 1·86. So far as I am aware, this explanation of Ferishta's figures [3] has not been published before. The value of the mishkāl in Bābur's time, as being a more tangible weight than the variable rati, has been investigated by Prof. Maskelyne,[4] and he concludes that it was equal to about 74 gr. troy, and that if taken at 73·69 gr. troy, and multiplied by 8, it would yield a weight exactly corresponding to that of the Koh-i-nūr when brought to England, namely 186·06 carats. Accepting the second estimate for the value of the mishkāl, that of

[1] See Erskine's *Memoirs of Sultan Bābur*, 1918, ii, p. 191; *History of India*, i. 438.

[2] *History of the Rise of the Mahomedan Power in India*, &c., trans. by J. Briggs, London, 1829, Calcutta, 1909, ii. 46.

[3] See also Dow, *History of Hindostan*, 1812, ii. 105.

[4] *Lecture at the Royal Institution*, March 1860.

Bābur's rati would be 1·842 gr. troy, and the value of his diamond in carats might be expressed by the following equation.

$$\frac{320 \times 1{\cdot}842}{3{\cdot}168 \text{ (troy gr. in a carat)}} = 186{\cdot}06 \text{ carats.}$$

In such a calculation it is well to bear in mind that a very slight variation in the rati, as a unit, would, when multiplied, produce a considerable difference in the result. Thus, if 1·86 were put instead of 1·842, the resultant would be enhanced above the desired figure, namely the weight of the Koh-i-Nūr.

Here I must leave Bābur's diamond for the present, without expressing any more decided opinion as to the absolute accuracy of the data which make its weight appear to be actually identical with that of the Koh-i-Nūr, being, however, as will be seen in the sequel, quite content not to dispute their general correctness, though my deduction therefrom does not accord with Professor Maskelyne's.

In the year 1563 Garcia da Orta, in his famous work on the Simples and Drugs of India,[1] mentioned four large diamonds, one of which he was told had been seen at Bisnaguer, i. e. Vijayanagar, and was the size of a small hen's egg. The others weighed respectively—

120	mangelins	= 200	ratis	= 150	carats.[2]
140	,,	= $233\frac{1}{3}$	,,	= 175	,,
250	,,	= $416\frac{2}{3}$	,,	= $312\frac{1}{2}$	,,

None of these three last can be identified with the Great Mogul's diamond, because, even supposing it had been already discovered at so early a date as 1563, it must then, as will be seen hereafter, have been uncut, and had a weight of $787\frac{1}{2}$ carats, or more than double the weight of the largest of them; but it might have been the one spoken of as being of the size of a small hen's egg, as that was probably its form in its early condition when acquired by Mīr Jumla. As to whether any of the stones mentioned by Garcia could have been the same as Bābur's diamond, it is quite useless to speculate; but, as none of them are said to have belonged to the Mogul, it seems to be most improbable.

In the year 1609, De Boot, in his work on gems, &c., referred to all these diamonds mentioned by Garcia, but when doing so, was guilty of three serious blunders, which were, however, detected by his editor, Adrian Toll; they have misled many

[1] *Colloquios dos simples e drogas e cousas medicinaes da India*, p. 159: *Colloquies on the Simples and Drugs of India*, trans. Sir C. Markham, London, 1913, p. 347.

[2] He says the mangelin = 5 gr., the carat 4 gr., and the rati 3 gr. (of wheat). Sir C. Markham gives the weights as 140, 120, 250 carats.

subsequent authors, who have apparently overlooked the editorial comments, including Professor Maskelyne (*Nature*, x. 91). The first was in giving Monardes instead of Garcia as his authority ; the second in treating the mangelin as though it were the equivalent of the carat ; and thirdly, in making, on the supposed authority of Monardes, a statement to the effect that the largest known diamond weighed 187½ carats.[1]

The explanation of De Boot's confusion between the names of Monardes and Garcia is that Écluze (Clusius) published a work in 1574, in which he incorporated in the same volume the writings of these two authors ; and, as pointed out by Adrian Toll, Monardes does not even allude to diamonds, his work being on the drugs of the West Indies.[2]

The question remains—Where did De Boot obtain the figure 187½, which approximates to the weight of the Koh-i-Nūr, when brought to England, and the weight of Bābur's diamond as estimated above ? It has been seized upon by Professor Maskelyne, who quotes it from King, as a link in the chain connecting the two just mentioned diamonds. It is a worthless link, however. It originated in a further manifestation of De Boot's carelessness.[3] What he really quoted from may have been a passage in Monardes's work, as he says, or in that of Garcia this time, as he had already disposed of the diamond mentioned by him; but a commentary or note on the latter's statement about Indian diamonds, by the editor Écluze, and, as will be seen, the note itself, which is of sufficient importance to be given in the original Latin, refers to the largest diamond ever seen in Belgium ![4] its weight being 47½ carats, or 190 gr. There can be no doubt that the statement by De Boot regarding a diamond weighing 187½ carats was, as pointed out by Adrian Toll and De Laet, utterly spurious. It was therefore quite unworthy of the notice it has received from the above-named authors, and is of no value whatever for the purposes of this history.

No attention has hitherto been given by writers to a large diamond which, as pointed out in a footnote,[5] was obtained

[1] *Gemmarum et Lapidum Historia,* 3d ed., by De Laet, 1647, p. 29.

[2] It was first printed at Seville in 1565.

[3] Rosnel, in *Le Mercure Indien*, Paris, 1667, evidently quoting from De Boot, makes the same mistake.

[4] Majorem vero Adamantem in Belgio conspectum haud puto, quam Philippus II. Hispaniarum Rex ducturus Elizabetham, Henr. II. Gall. Regis filiam majorem natu emit, de Carolo Affetato Antwerpia, Anno 1559, Octogies Millenis Cronatis ; pendebat autem Car. xlvii, cum semine (=47½), id est grana 190.—*De Gemmis et Lapidibus*, Lib. II.. J. de Laet, *Lug. Bat.*, 1647, p. 9

[5] See vol. ii. 42.

by a Portuguese who worked the mine at Wajra Karūr in Bellary about the beginning of the seventeenth century. It weighed, apparently, 434·7 carats. Nothing of its subsequent history is known; but it cannot have been the one presented by Mīr Jumla to Shāhjahān. It may, however, have been the Pitt diamond, which, when offered to Pitt in 1701, weighed 426 carats; but if so, it remained uncut for nearly a century, and the generally accepted story of the Pitt diamond is that it was obtained at the mine at Partial.

We may now pass to a brief summary of the facts contained in Tavernier's several independent references to the Great Mogul's diamond—

First, in order of sequence, after describing the Mogul's jewels, he mentions (vol. i. 315) its weight as being 319½ ratis, or 280 carats, the rati being ⅞th of a carat. When first presented to Shāhjahān by Mīr Jumla it weighed, he says, 900 ratis or 787½ carats, and had several flaws, but when he saw it it was round, rose cut, very steep at one side, with a notch on the basal margin, and an internal flaw; its water was beautiful.[1]

Secondly, when describing (vol. ii. 58) the mine of Kollūr (Gāni or Coulour) he says that there was found in it the great diamond which weighed 900 carats (?) before cutting, and was presented to Aurangzeb (?) by Mīr Jumla. This account, as already pointed out, contains several mistakes. Tavernier adds that the mine had been opened 100 years previously.

Thirdly (vol. ii. 75), he states that the Great Mogul's diamond was of perfect water and good form, and weighed $279\frac{9}{16}$ carats. Its value he estimated as amounting to 11,723,278 livres, 14 sols, 3 liards, or £879,245 18*s.* 1½*d.* If it had weighed 279 carats only it would have been worth 11,676,150 livres, and consequently the value of the $\frac{9}{16}$th of a carat, owing to the geometrical method of calculation, amounted to 47,128 livres, 14 sols, 3 liards, or £3,534 13*s.* 1½*d.*

Fourthly (vol. ii. 97), he states that he was permitted to weigh the diamond, and ascertained its weight to be 319½ ratis, or $279\frac{9}{16}$ carats, and adds, 'when in the rough it weighed, as I have elsewhere said, 907 ratis, or 793⅝ carats'. Its form was as of an egg cut in two.

Tavernier's figure of the diamond (see Plate II) has been referred to by Mr. King as being carefully drawn. It is true that very neat representations of it have appeared in works on mineralogy and precious stones, and glass models have been made on the same lines, but the original figure can only

[1] The *Ma'āsir-ul-umarā* ii. 535, gives the weight of this diamond as 216 surkh, or 9 tānk, and values it at Rs. 216,000, or £21,600. Manucci says that it weighed 360 carats (Manucci, i. 237).

be correctly described as a very rude unprojected diagram, in which the facets are bounded by three transverse series of parallel lines which intersect one another irregularly.

The only other early mention of this diamond is by Bernier, who calls it 'matchless', and states that it was presented to Shāhjahān by Mīr Jumla when he advised him to dispatch an army for the conquest of Golkonda.[1]

Let us now endeavour to reduce these statements to a common denomination. First, it must be stated that Tavernier and Bernier, both of whom refer expressly to the famous topaz belonging to Aurangzeb, are not likely to have been mistaken as to the nature of the stone examined; that it was a diamond may be safely accepted, in spite of any suggestions which have been made by authors to the contrary.

With regard to Tavernier's second statement, it is clearly wrong in two particulars, both of which may be attributed to the errors of a copyist, who wrote Aurangzeb for Shāhjahān, and 900 carats in mistake for 900 ratis. This statement, therefore, being put aside from consideration, we have then left for comparison the following:

Original weight 900 ratis = $787\frac{1}{2}$ carats; after cutting, $319\frac{1}{2}$ ratis = 280 carats.

Original weight 907 ratis = $793\frac{5}{8}$ carats; after cutting, $319\frac{1}{2}$ ratis = $279\frac{9}{16}$ carats.

Calculated according to Tavernier's own statement that the rati was equal to $\frac{7}{8}$ of the carat, the equivalents would more correctly be stated as follows:

$$\left.\begin{array}{l} 900 \text{ ratis} = 788\frac{1}{2} \text{ carats}^{2} \\ 907 \quad ,, \quad = 793\frac{5}{8} \quad ,, \end{array}\right\} 319\tfrac{1}{2} \text{ ratis} = 279\tfrac{9}{16} \text{ carats.}$$

We have then, at first sight, the remarkable apparent coincidence in weights between this diamond, when cut, of $319\frac{1}{2}$ ratis, and Bābur's of about 8 mishkāls (i. e. about 320 ratis); but the ratis were of very different values, the former being equal to 2·66[3] troy gr., and the latter to about 1·842 (or 1·86 ?) gr. The respective weights, in carats, as already shown, are $186\frac{9}{16}$ and $279\frac{9}{16}$, the difference in weights of the two stones being therefore, apparently, $93\frac{1}{2}$ carats. But in anticipation of the discussion to be found on page 346 as to the reasons which have led to the conclusion that

[1] *Travels in the Mogul Empire*, 1918, p. 22.

[2] The discrepancy between these two accounts of the original weight of the stone, which Tavernier probably obtained from native reports, one being 900 ratis and the other 907 ratis, does not in the least affect the question here discussed, as it is only the weight of the stone after cutting that we have to do with.

[3] On page 347 Ball explains his reasons for modifying the first conclusion, stated in vol. i, Appendix, as to the value of the pearl rati.

Tavernier used the light Florentine carat, it should be stated here that the weight of the Mogul's diamond, in English carats, was 4 per cent. less than Tavernier's figures, in terms of Florentine carats; hence its weight, in order to be compared with other diamonds given in terms of English carats, should be $268\frac{19}{50}$, from which, if we subtract $186\frac{1}{16}$, the difference would be $82\frac{1}{3}$ carats, nearly. The similarity between the weight of Bābur's diamond at 320 ratis, and the Mogul's at $319\frac{1}{2}$ ratis, is delusive, as in ratis of the same denomination the former figure should be given at about 224 ratis, which is Ferishta's equivalent for 8 mishkāls. So that the real difference amounted to $319\frac{1}{2} - 224 = 95\frac{1}{2}$ ratis, or, expressed in carats, at $\frac{7}{8}$ths of a carat = 1 rati, $83\frac{1}{2}$ carats. This is sufficiently close to the $82\frac{1}{3}$ carats, independently deduced, to justify the conclusion that the weight of Bābur's diamond was about 83 carats less than that of the Mogul's, when cut.

There is, I believe, no direct record of the size and weights of the diamonds carried away from Delhi by Nādir Shāh, but before dealing with that portion of the history, it will be convenient to refer here to an interesting statement by Forbes[1] which has been overlooked by most writers on the subject. He states that a Persian nobleman, who possessed a diamond weighing 117 carats, which was subsequently lost at sea, informed him when at Cambay in the year 1781, long before it had been taken to Kābul, that there had been two diamonds in the Royal Treasury at Ispahān, one of which, called Koo-i-toor (Koh-i-Nūr ?), 'The Hill of Lustre', weighed 264 carats, and its value was estimated at £500,000. The other, called Dorriainoor (Daryā-i-Nūr), 'The Ocean of Lustre,' was of a flat surface. Both formed a portion of the treasure, amounting in value to from 70 to 80 millions sterling, which Nādir Shāh carried away from Delhi in 1739.

Forbes suggests that the first was the Mogul's diamond, described by Tavernier, remarking that the difference between the weights 264 and $279\frac{9}{16}$ carats may easily be allowed between the accounts given by a Persian and a European traveller. (If, as above suggested, the weight of the latter was $268\frac{9}{60}$ English carats, the approximation is still closer.) The Daryā-i-Nūr, as we shall presently see, still belongs to Persia; it weights 186 carats, and there is no known fact which in the slightest degree affects the possibility of its being identical with Bābur's diamond.

Several writers, among them Professor Schrauf of Vienna,[2] have suggested that the Mogul's diamond is to be identified
23 with the similarly shaped Orloff, now belonging to Russia.

[1] *Oriental Memoirs*, 2nd ed., ii. 175.
[2] *Handbuch der Edelsteinkunde*, Vienna, 1869, p. 103.

Apart from the discrepancy in the weights and in the size, as shown by Tavernier's drawing, which was intended to represent the natural size of the former, it is tolerably certain that the Orloff was obtained from the temple of Srīrangam on an island in the Cauvery river, in Mysore. It was therefore a possession of the Hindus, and it is most improbable that it ever belonged to the Moguls.

Reference has been made by some authors to the long historical chain which, they say, connects Bābur's diamond with the Koh-i-Nūr. As to the length of the supposed chain, it would extend over a period of 500 years at the least; but as to the links composing it, there is this to be said—they are all utterly unsound. In making so emphatic a statement I feel the necessity of being very sure of the grounds of my argument, especially as it is opposed to the views of many authorities, who, however, do not agree with one another as to details.

In deference to the opinions of Erskine, Professor Maskelyne, and General Cunningham, it may no doubt with perfect safety be admitted that the weight of Bābur's diamond in 1526 was, as stated above, about 8 mishkāls or 320 ratis, and that these were equivalent to about 186 or 187 modern English carats. But it must be at once plainly stated that there is no direct evidence that any diamond of that weight was in the possession of the Mogul emperors at any subsequent period, up to the time of Nādir Shāh's invasion. We know nothing as to the weight of the Koh-i-Nūr, as such, till about the time it was brought to England, namely, the year 1850; and then, although its weight was $186\frac{1}{6}$ carats, the trustworthy evidence, as to its condition at that time, as will be seen, is to the effect that it was not identical with Bābur's diamond.

In order to put this clearly it is necessary to summarize what has already been stated about other diamonds. Those mentioned by Garcia da Orta were not apparently in the possession of the Mogul, and their weights do not correspond to those of either the Mogul's or Bābur's diamonds. The diamond of $187\frac{1}{2}$ carats referred to by De Boot has been shown to be mythical. Again, Tavernier did not see any stone of the weight above attributed to Bābur's diamond in the possession of the Great Mogul, Aurangzeb, nor can we suppose that he heard of any such diamond being in the possession of Shāhjahān, who was then confined in prison, where he retained a number of jewels in his own possession.[1] If either he or Bernier had heard of such a stone he would surely have mentioned it. It is possible, that Bābur's diamond may have been in Shāhjahān's possession when

[1] See vol. i. 295.

Tavernier saw Aurangzeb's jewels, and that the latter obtained possession of it when Shāhjahān died, and so ultimately it passed to Persia with other jewels taken by Nādir Shāh.[1]

Tavernier's statements, in so far as they relate to this history, are—I. That the Great Mogul's diamond was found in the mine at Kollūr, when, we cannot say, though Murray, Streeter, and other writers have ventured to assign precise dates. II. It was acquired by Mīr Jumla, and presented by him to Shāhjahān about the year 1656. III. It originally weighed 900 ratis or $787\frac{1}{2}$ carats; but having been placed in the hands of Hortensio Borgio, it was so much reduced by grinding, distinctly not by cleavage, that, when seen by Tavernier in 1665, he personally ascertained that it only weighed $319\frac{1}{2}$ ratis or $279\frac{9}{16}$ carats. IV. The figure given by Tavernier, though very rudely drawn, is of a stone which must have weighed more than $279\frac{9}{16}$ carats (Florentine), and it corresponds fairly with his description. V. This description mentions a steepness on one side and certain flaws, &c.

In order to identify the Mogul's diamond with Bābur's, certain authorities, notably Professor Maskelyne, have suggested that Tavernier's description did not really apply to the diamond presented by Mīr Jumla to Shāhjahān; that the stone he describes had therefore not been found at Kollūr; that he was mistaken as to the particular kind of ratis which he mentions, and that consequently his equivalent in carats—calculated on the supposition that they were pearl ratis—was incorrect; finally, Professor Maskelyne maintains that Tavernier's drawing of the stone differs from his description of it, and was wholly incorrect and exaggerated in size.

Thus, in order to establish this supposed link of the chain, we are invited to whittle down Tavernier's account until it amounts to a bare statement that he saw a large diamond, about which all that he records as to its weight and history is incorrect.

If I were not prepared to maintain that a jeweller of Tavernier's large experience could not possibly have made the mistakes which have thus been suggested, I should feel that I had rendered a very ill service in editing these volumes. It is incredible that having actually handled and weighed the stone, at his leisure, he could have made so great a mistake as to believe that it weighed $279\frac{9}{16}$, or in round numbers 280 carats (Florentine), while it was really one of only 186 carats (English).

The custom, which has been followed by many writers, of adopting or rejecting Tavernier's statements according

[1] See vol. i. 275.

as they agree or disagree with their independently conceived hypotheses, is one against which we are bound to protest. It is a kind of treatment which no author should receive. If supposed to be guilty of so many blunders and inaccuracies of statement, the proper course would be to leave all that such a writer states severely alone.

Judging from Tavernier's drawing and description, the stone had been ground by Hortensio Borgio to a fairly symmetrical shape as a round rose, one side being, however, steeper than the other, which feature, though indicated to some extent in the original drawing, is not generally faithfully reproduced in the copies in various works on diamonds, and some of the glass models which have been made are not only defective in this respect, but are altogether too small. This is mentioned here because these models are sometimes referred to as though they afforded authentic evidence of the true form of the stone.

We have now arrived at a stage when we can agree with those authorities who have maintained that Bābur's diamond and the Mogul's were distinct; but with most, if not all of them, we must part company, as they maintain that the Mogul's diamond no longer exists, and that it was upon Bābur's diamond that Nādir Shāh conferred the title Koh-i-Nūr in the year 1739. But the Mogul's diamond has a stronger and more immediate claim to be regarded as *the* diamond, so denominated, which was taken from Muhammad Shāh, Aurangzeb's feeble descendant. The name was an eminently suitable one to apply to the Mogul's stone as it was when seen by Tavernier, though not equally applicable to it in its subsequent mutilated condition, in which it has been so confidently identified by some writers with Bābur's diamond.

The stone which now bears the title Koh-i-Nūr was taken by Nādir to Persia, and from thence we have rumours of its having been cleaved into several pieces, when or by whom is doubtful. Acceptance of these stories has been rendered difficult by some authors having attempted to assign names and weights to these pieces, the sum of the latter being greater than the total weight of the Mogul's stone, as it was when seen by Tavernier. Thus the Orloff, the Great Mogul itself, and the Koh-i-Nūr have been spoken of as having formed parts of the same stone.[1] This hypothesis is in opposition to everything connected with the histories of these stones which can be relied on; but as regards the possibility of the Koh-i-Nūr alone having been carved out of the Great Mogul's diamond, it is not argument—but is simply begging the whole question—to assert that the Koh-i-Nūr existed 120 years before Borgio handled the Mogul's diamond. This

[1] Quenstedt, *Klar und Wahr*, Tübingen, p. 79.

Mr. Streeter has done,[1] and in his accounts of these diamonds he several times repeats that 'all are agreed' that Bābur's diamond and the Koh-i-Nūr are identical, and the Mogul's distinct, which are precisely the points at issue. Indeed, he might be reminded that in his own previously published work [2] he states that 'any doubt as to the Mogul and Koh-i-Nūr being identical is but rarely entertained'; this, I venture to believe, was the sounder opinion than the one more recently advocated by him.

At the meeting of the British Association in 1851 [3] Dr. Beke referred to a diamond found among the jewels of Razā Kuli Khān at the conquest of Khorāsān by 'Abbās Mīrzā in 1832. It weighed 130 carats, and showed marks of cutting on the flat or largest face. It was presented to the Shāh, and the jewellers of Teherān asked £16,000 for recutting it. Dr. Beke suggests that it was a part of the Koh-i-Nūr, meaning thereby the Mogul's diamond. This could not have been the case, because, as we have seen, the Mogul's diamond, if identical with the Koh-i-Nūr, had only a margin of about $82\frac{1}{3}$ carats to lose, while if the latter be identical with Bābur's diamond it could have lost nothing. At the subsequent meeting of the Association [4] Professor Tennant improved on this by suggesting that the Russian diamond, i. e. the Orloff, formed a part of the same. Other suggestions about the Orloff have already been dealt with above.

A host of other writers have taken up this story, and lastly, Professor Nicol in his article on the diamond in the *Encyclopædia Britannica* has unfortunately suggested that these three stones formed portions of the Mogul's stone seen by Tavernier, which amounts to saying that these three, weighing respectively $194\frac{3}{4}$, $186\frac{1}{16}$ and 130 carats,[5] or in all $510\frac{13}{16}$ carats, were portions of one which weighed only between 279 and 280 (Florentine) carats. His statement that 'the three united would have nearly the form and size given by Tavernier' is simply incomprehensible.

If, however, we merely suppose that the Mogul's stone, while in the hands of one or other of its necessitous owners, after it was taken to Persia by Nādir, had pieces removed from it by cleavage, which altogether (there were at least three of them) amounted to the difference between its weight and that of the Koh-i-Nūr as it was when brought from India, namely, $279\frac{9}{16}$ Florentine carats $= 268\frac{19}{50}$ English carats $- 186\frac{1}{16} = 82\frac{1}{3}$ carats, we at once arrive at a simple explana-

[1] *Great Diamonds of the World*, 119. [2] *Precious Stones*, p. 126.
[3] See *Athenæum*, July 5, 1851. [4] *Ibid.*, September 25, 1852.
[5] Professor Nicol gives the weights at $194\frac{3}{4}$, $186\frac{1}{16}$, and 132, the sum being $512\frac{13}{16}$. Compare the article by Dr. H. A. Miers, *Ency. Brit.*, 11th ed., viii. 163.

tion of the cause of the difference in weight between the stones, and are, moreover, thus enabled to show that Tavernier's account requires no whittling down, though the stone itself, after he saw it, appears to have been subjected to that process.

This would be but an hypothesis based on the rumours above referred to, were it not so strongly corroborated by the appearance presented by the Koh-i-Nūr itself when taken by the British from the Treasury at Lahore. Mr. Tennant[1] describes it as exhibiting, when brought to England, two large cleavage planes, *one of which had not even been polished, and had been distinctly produced by fracture.*

No one can examine the authentic sketches and models of the Koh-i-Nūr without feeling a strong presumption that it must have been mutilated, after cutting, and that it cannot have been left in such an incomplete condition by the jeweller who cut and polished it. In addition to its possessing defects similar to some of those described by Tavernier as having been in the Mogul's diamond, Mr. Tennant records that the Koh-i-Nūr had a flaw near the summit which, being on a line of cleavage parallel to the upper surface, may very possibly have been produced when the upper portion was removed—the weight of which, together with that of two portions removed from the sides, and the loss occasioned by the regrinding of four facets on the upper surface, may very easily have represented the difference in the weights of the two stones, namely $82\frac{1}{3}$ carats.

This too, in a measure, explains the discrepancies between Tavernier's description, which, as Professor Maskelyne[2] admits, very fairly characterizes the Koh-i-Nūr (i. e. certain flaws and defects in it, which happened to be in the portion preserved), and the figure, which, as it represents the whole stone, does not, at first sight, seem to resemble the Koh-i-Nūr. The accompanying illustration (Plate VI) and descriptive notes prove not only the possibility of the Koh-i-Nūr having been thus carved out of the Mogul's diamond, but the represent graphically the extreme probability of the truth of that suggestion.

Tavernier's account of the Mogul's diamond has, I think, been fully proved in the preceding pages to be quite inapplicable to Bābur's diamond, while all his facts and the balance of probability favour the view that in the Koh-i-Nūr we are justified in recognizing the mutilated Mogul's diamond. Thus, while this theory, which has been built up on the basis of Tavernier's statements, is consistent with the literal acceptance of all of them, and with the physical condition of the

[1] *Lecture on Gems and Precious Stones*, London 1852, p. 83.
[2] *Proceedings of the Royal Institution of Great Britain*, March 1860.

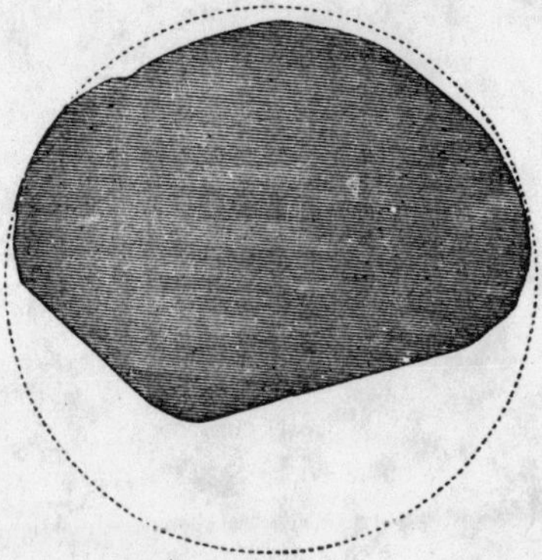

Fig 1.

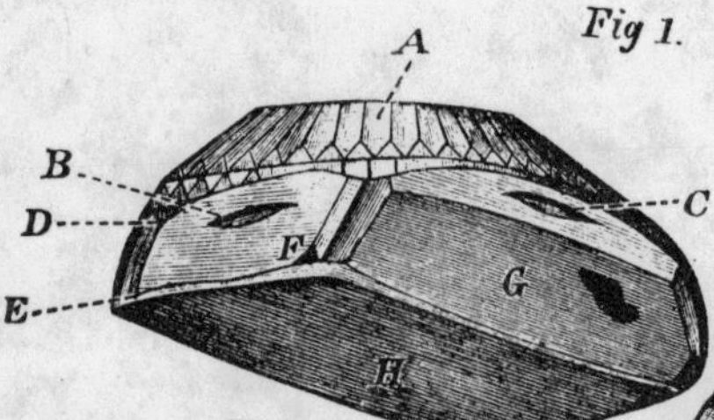

Fig II.

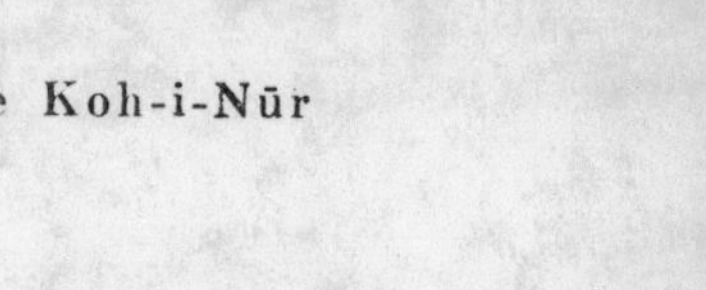

Fig III

Figures of the Koh-i-Nūr

Koh-i-Nūr when it came to Europe, of none of the other theories can the same be said; but, on the contrary, to suit their respective exigencies, they require the total rejection of one or more of the carefully recorded observations on the condition of the Mogul's stone when placed in the hands of this experienced jeweller for examination.[1]

The necessary conclusion is that it is not the Mogul's diamond which, through failure of being historically traced, as some authors assert, has disappeared, but it is Bābur's diamond of the history of which we are really left in doubt. The fixing of the weight of Bābur's diamond at a figure identical, or nearly so, with that of the Koh-i-Nūr when brought to England, though used as a link in the chain, has, as I think I have shown, effectively disposed of its claim to be identified with the Mogul's diamond in the first place, and secondly with the Koh-i-Nūr.

It has already been intimated that the Daryā-i-Nūr, a flat stone which weighs 186 carats, and is now in the Shāh's treasury,[2] may very possibly be Bābur's diamond, with regard to which I can only say that I have in vain sought for any well authenticated fact which in the slightest degree controverts or even throws doubt upon that suggestion.

2. *Summary History of the Koh-i-Nūr.*

This diamond, as related by Tavernier, was obtained in the mine of Kollūr on the Kistnā (see vol. ii, 58). The precise date of its discovery is mere matter of conjecture; but about the year 1656 or 1657 it was presented, while still uncut, to Shāhjahān by Mīr Jumla, who had previously farmed the mines at Kollūr and elsewhere. The stone then weighed 900 ratis or $787\frac{1}{2}$ carats (these, if Florentine carats, were equal to about 756 English carats).

In the year 1665 this diamond was seen by Tavernier in Aurangzeb's treasury, and it then weighed, as ascertained by himself, only $319\frac{1}{2}$ ratis, or $279\frac{9}{16}$ carats (which, if Florentine carats, equalled $268\frac{19}{50}$ English carats). It had been reduced to this size by the wasteful grinding treatment to which it had been subjected by a Venetian named Hortensio Borgio.

In the year 1739 it was taken from Aurangzeb's feeble descendant, Muhammad Shāh, by Nādir Shāh, when he

[1] Among other difficulties introduced into the subject are such as follow from misquotation. Thus Kluge says that Tavernier himself described the stone as weighing $319\frac{1}{2}$ ratis = 186 carats! For this unfortunate and mischievous error there can be no excuse, as he goes on to say quite correctly that the earlier weight was $793\frac{5}{8}$ carats. *Handbuch der Edelsteinkunde*, Leipzig, 1860, p. 341.

[2] See Benjamin, *Persia*, p. 74.

sacked Delhi and carried away to Persia, it is said, £70,000,000 or £80,000,000 worth of treasure.[1] On first beholding it he is reported to have conferred upon it the title Koh-i-Nūr or Mountain of Light, a most suitable name for the stone described by Tavernier.

On the murder of Nādir Shāh at Kelāt, in 1747, it passed with the throne to his grandson Shāh Rukh, who resided at Meshed, where he was made a prisoner and cruelly tortured by Aghā Muhammad (Mīr Alam Khān), who in vain sought to obtain the Koh-i-Nūr from him.[2] In the year 1751 Shāh Rukh gave it, as a reward for his assistance, to Ahmad Shāh, the founder of the Durrānī dynasty at Kābul, and by him it was bequeathed to his son Taimūr, who went to reside at Kābul. From him, in 1793, it passed by descent to his eldest son Shāh Zamān, who, when deposed by his brother Muhammad, and deprived of his eyes, still contrived to keep possession of the diamond in his prison, and two years afterwards it passed into the hands of his third brother Sultān Shujā'. According to Elphinstone,[3] it was found secreted, together with some other jewels, in the walls of the cell which Shāh Zamān had occupied. After Shujā''s accession to the throne of Kābul, on the dethronement and imprisonment of Muhammad, he was visited at Peshāwar by Elphinstone in 1809, who describes how he saw the diamond in a bracelet worn by Shujā', and he refers to it in a foot-note as the diamond figured by Tavernier. Shujā' was subsequently dethroned by his eldest brother Muhammad, who had escaped from the prison where he had been confined.

In 1812 the families of Zamān and Shujā' went to Lahore, and Ranjīt Singh, the ruler of the Punjab, promised the wife of the latter that he would release her husband and confer upon him the kingdom of Kashmīr, for which service he expected to receive the Koh-i-Nūr.[4]

When Shāh Shujā' reached Lahore, soon afterwards, he was detained there by Ranjīt, who wished to secure both his person and the diamond; but the Shāh for a time evaded compliance with his demand for the stone, and refused offers of moderate sums of money for it. At length 'the Mahārājā visited the Shāh in person, mutual friendship was declared, an

[1] According to the *Imperial Gazetteer* 1st ed. (vi. 314) only £30,000,000. In the edition of 1907 (ii. 409) the words used are 'a huge ransom': Smith (*Oxford Hist. of India*, 459) 'incalculable riches': Keene (*Fall of the Moghul Empire*, 25) says the plunder 'has been estimated at eighty millions sterling'.

[2] Sir J. Malcolm, *Hist. of Persia*, 2nd ed. ii. 195 f.

[3] *Account of the Kingdom of Caubul*, ed. 1907, ii. 325 *n*.

[4] Cunningham, *History of the Sikhs*, Oxford, 1918, p. 153.

exchange of turbans took place, the diamond was surrendered, and the Shāh received the assignment of a jāgīr in the Punjab for his maintenance, and a promise of aid in recovering Kābul'.[1] This was in 1813: the Shāh then escaped from Lahore to Rājāurī, in the hills, and from thence to Ludhiāna, after suffering great privations.[2] Here he and his brother Shāh Zamān were well received by the Honourable East India Company, and a liberal pension was assigned by the Government for their maintenance. The above statements, except where other authorities are quoted, are taken from General Sleeman's [3] account, which was founded on a narrative by Shāh Zamān, the blind old king himself, who communicated it to General Smith, he being at the time in command of the troops at Ludhiāna.

In the year 1839 Shāh Shujā', under Lord Auckland's Government, was set up on the throne of Kābul by a British force, which two years later was annihilated during its retreat.

The testimony of all the writers up to this period, and, it is said, the opinions of the jewellers of Delhi and Kābul also, concur in the view that the diamond which Ranjīt thus acquired was the Mogul's, i. e. the one described by Tavernier. It seems probable that the mutilation and diminution in weight by about 83 carats, to which, as we have shown, it was subjected (see p. 342), took place while it was in the possession of Shāh Rukh, Shāh Zamān, or Shāh Shujā', whose necessities may have caused one of them to have pieces removed to furnish him with money.

Ranjīt during his lifetime often wore the diamond on state occasions, and it is referred to by many English visitors to Lahore, who saw it during this period.[4] It is said to have then been dull and deficient in lustre.

In 1839 Ranjīt died, and on his deathbed expressed a wish that the diamond, then valued at one million sterling, should be sent to Jagannāth,[5] but this intention was not carried out,[6] and the stone was placed in the jewel chamber till the infant Rājā Dhalīp Singh was acknowledged as Ranjīt's successor.

[1] Cunningham, *History of the Sikhs*, Oxford, 1918, p. 153. The Shāh's own account (*Autobiography*, chap. xxv) of Ranjīt's methods to get possession of the diamond is more favourable to the latter than Captain Murray's. (See his *Rangeet Singh*, 96.)

[2] Dr. W. L. M'Gregor, *History of the Sikhs*, London, 1847, i. 170.

[3] *Rambles and Recollections of an Indian Official*, 288 ff.

[4] Dr. M'Gregor, *History of the Sikhs*, London, 1847, i. 216; Baron C. von Hügel, *Travels in Kashmir and the Panjab*, 1845, p. 303.

[5] Lieut.-Colonel Steinbach, *The Punjab*, London, 1846, p. 16.

[6] Miss Eden, *Up the Country*, ii. 130, says that the Mahārāja ultimately consented to its not being sent.

When the Punjab was annexed, in the year 1849, the diamond was formally handed to the new Board of Government at one of its earliest meetings—and it was then personally entrusted by his colleagues to the care of John Lawrence, afterwards Lord Lawrence, who, on receiving it, placed the small tin box containing it in his waistcoat pocket, and then forgot all about it till he was called upon to produce it six weeks later, in order that it might be sent to Her Majesty the Queen.

Recalling the circumstances when thus reminded of them, he hurried home and, asked his bearer whether he had got the box which had been in his pocket some time previously. Careful about trifles, like most Indian servants, the bearer had preserved it, though he thought it only contained a useless piece of glass. This strange vicissitude in the history of the stone is related by Bosworth Smith in his life of Lord Lawrence.[1] He adds that he had been told on good authority that it had passed through other dangers, on the way home, before it was safe in the possession of the Queen.

In 1851 the Koh-i-Nūr was exhibited in the first great Exhibition, and in 1852 the recutting of the stone was entrusted by Her Majesty to Messrs. Garrards, who employed Voorsanger, a diamond cutter from M. Coster's atelier at Amsterdam. The actual cutting lasted thirty-eight days, and by it the weight was reduced to $106\frac{1}{16}$ carats. The cost of the cutting amounted to £8,000.

3. *On the Grand Duke of Tuscany's Diamond, otherwise known as the Austrian Yellow or the Florentine; and on the absolute weights of the carat and rati as known to Tavernier.*

When writing of the carat (see vol. i, Appendix, p. 332), and when making the several references to the Grand Duke of Tuscany's diamond, I had not seen Dr. Schrauf's original paper[2] on the weighment of the stone, and, having obtained my information of it indirectly, I was misled as to its precise purport, which does not prove that the absolute weight of the stone is less than Tavernier gave it, but demonstrates that the difference in weight is only apparent. The absolute weight is 27·454 grm. which converted into carats, gives

Florentine (=197·2 milligrams)	. .	$139\frac{1}{5}$ carats.
Paris (=205·5 ,,)	. .	$133\frac{3}{5}$,,
Vienna (=206·13 ,,)	. .	$133\frac{1}{5}$,,

In English carats (= 205·4 milligrams) the weight would

[1] *Life of Lord Lawrence*, i. 327.

[2] *Sitz. der K. Akad. der Wissen.*, Wien, Math.-Nat. Classe, Bd. liv., Abth. i. 479, 1866.

be $133\frac{3}{8}$ carats nearly. The conclusions to be drawn, therefore, are, that, in the first place, the stone has not had any additional facets cut upon it, and that it is, in fact, in the same condition as when Tavernier gave its weight at $139\frac{1}{2}$ carats ; the difference between that weight and the $139\frac{1}{5}$ Florentine carats is so small, amounting to only $\frac{3}{10}$ths of a carat, that it may be fairly attributed to difference in the accuracy of the methods of weighment employed by Tavernier and Schrauf respectively.

Hence we may fairly conclude that in this instance, at least, the carat used by Tavernier was the 'Florentine' ; and that being so, it is hardly conceivable that, when mentioning Indian stones on the very same pages as those where he describes the Grand Duke of Tuscany's diamond, he had other carats in view. Consequently, with greater confidence than I could venture to assume when the Appendix of vol. i. was written, I now suggest the hypothesis that Tavernier's carats were the light Florentine carats, which are exactly 4 per cent. lighter than modern English carats. Thus the English carat of ·2054 grm. less 4 per cent. (·0082) = ·1972 grm. which is the precise value of the Florentine carat.

The conclusion thus arrived at as to the carat of Tavernier having been the light Florentine, involves a reduction in the value of the rati, which has been calculated in the earlier part of his work on the supposition that it was equal to $\frac{7}{8}$ths of the modern French and English carat. It must therefore be reduced by 4 per cent. likewise, so that instead of 2·77 troy gr., it must stand at 2·66 troy gr. This value, it should be added, is identical with that derived from Tavernier's own statement, that 6 melscals or $181\frac{1}{8}$ ratis = 1 French ounce (i. e. 482·312 gr. troy), since $482{\cdot}312 \div 181\frac{1}{8} = 2{\cdot}66$. I am accordingly compelled to accept this value finally as being that of Tavernier's pearl rati ; and I must ask readers to accept this conclusion, which was given as an alternative to 2·77, in the Appendix to vol. i,[1] instead of the latter, which was adopted in the text.

In the following table the weights in carats of the principal stones mentioned by Tavernier are enumerated, and in the last column these weights, reduced by 4 per cent., show the equivalent values in English carats.

4. *On the weights of some of the Diamonds, other Precious Stones, and Pearls, mentioned and figured by Tavernier.*

Assuming that our argument is well founded as to the carats mentioned in the text having been Florentine carats,

[1] See vol. i. 332 ff.

it is necessary in order to reduce them to English carats, to subtract 4 per cent. from them, as in the following table :

DIAMONDS.

		Tavernier's Carats (Florentine).	English Carats.
1*a*.	Great Mogul's (uncut) . .	$787\frac{1}{2}$	756
1*b*.	Great Mogul's (cut) . .	$279\frac{9}{16}$	$268\frac{19}{50}$
2.	Golconda	$242\frac{1}{16}$	$232\frac{43}{50}$
3*a*.	Ahmadabad (uncut) . .	$157\frac{1}{4}$	$150\frac{24}{25}$
3*b*.	Ahmadabad (cut)	$94\frac{1}{5}$	$90\frac{18}{25}$
4.	Grand Duke of Tuscany's ($139\frac{1}{2}$)	$139\frac{1}{5}$	$133\frac{16}{25}$
5.	Blue	$112\frac{3}{16}$	$107\frac{7}{10}$
6.	Bazu	104	$99\frac{21}{25}$
7.	Mascarenha	$67\frac{1}{2}$	$64\frac{4}{5}$
8.	Kollúr	$63\frac{3}{8}$	$60\frac{21}{25}$

RUBIES.

1.	King of Persia's (192 ratis ?)	168	$161\frac{7}{25}$
2.	Banian	$50\frac{3}{4}$	$48\frac{18}{25}$
3.	Bijapur (Visapour)	$17\frac{1}{2}$	$16\frac{4}{5}$

TOPAS.

1.	Aurangzeb's . .	$157\frac{3}{4}$ should be $158\frac{1}{2}$	$152\frac{4}{25}$

PEARL.

1.	American, sold to Shāista Khān [1]	55	$52\frac{4}{5}$

APPENDIX II

List of all the Diamond Mines in India of which there are authentic Records, arranged in Districts.

SINCE this list was first published [2] it has been repeatedly checked, and it contains several additions. Although in various works on precious stones, &c., names are given as being those of diamond mines in India which are not to be found here, they are for the most part either synonyms of names that are, or are spurious. Want of space prevents such synonyms being dealt with, which is to be regretted, as the confusion in the nomenclature cannot be easily described without recourse to details. Names of villages, towns, rivers,

[1] Several other pearls of about this size and smaller were in the Mogul's Treasury. See vol. i. 316.

[2] See *Economic Geology of India*, chap. i. The Madras lists were founded originally on Dr. King's in *Mem. Geol. Surv. India*, vol. iii. but have been considerably amplified.

provinces, &c., are misplaced and jumbled together in almost inextricable confusion. One author gives Pegu as a diamond mine in Southern India; in the Mount Catti of another we trace a reference to the Ghāts of Southern India; and in the Malacca of many authors we must recognize, not as they do, either a place supposed to be in Southern India or the true Malacca, but Borneo, which used to be so called by the Portuguese in the fifteenth century. (See Appendix IX.) For some time I was unable to identify a certain Mr. Cullinger, who was quoted by one writer in connexion with diamonds. Will it be believed that this gentleman ultimately proved on investigation to be the fort of Kālanjar?

MADRAS

Kadapa (or Cuddapah) District

Chennūr on the Penner River: Lat. 14° 34′; Long. 78° 51′ 30″.

Condapetta (or Kanuparti), opposite Chennūr.

Gandikota ?, mentioned by some authors: Lat. 14° 49′; Long. 78° 20′ 30″.

Goorapur ?, close to Chennūr. Not identified: [? *Goulapalli*, *v.* i, 226].

Goulagoonta (close to Jammalamadugu): Lat. 14° 51′; Long. 78° 26′. [? *Gogeron*, *v.* i, 227.]

(Jammalamadugu, close to Goulagoonta which see.)

(Kanuparti, or Condapetta which see.)

Lamdur ? Not identified, mentioned by Heyne.

Ovalumpally (or Woblapully): Lat. 14° 34′; Long. 78° 51′ 35″.

Pinchetgapadu ? Not identified, mentioned by Heyne.

(Woblapully, or Ovalumpally which see.)

Bellary District[1]

Gunjeegoonta, 2 miles south of Wajra Karūr.

Gutidrug ?: Lat. 15° 7′; Long. 77° 42′. (Foote-King, *Annual Report Geol. Survey of India*, 1889.)

Hotoor ?, 6 miles WSW. of Wajrā Karūr.

Wajrā Karūr, Lat. 15° 2′; Long. 77° 27′.

Karnūl (or Kurnool) District

Banganapalle: Lat. 15° 18′; Long. 78° 16′; 37 miles SE. of Karnūl (see A.S. No. 76). Mines.

Bannur, close to Gudipaud; in Nandikotkūr Tāluk.

Baswapur: Lat. 15° 25′; Long. 78° 43′ 30″; in Nallamalai Hills; mines and alluvial washings.

Byanpalle: Lat. 15° 32′; Long. 78° 14′ 15″; 24 miles SSE. of Karnūl.

[1] A locality called Nizam in Bellary is mentioned by M. Chaper. See *Engineering*, 1884, 29th February.

Coomroly (close to Gooramankonda, which see); Nandiāl Tāluk.

Deomurru: Lat. 15° 49′ 30″; Long. 78° 11′. Left bank of Tungabhadra.

Devanur: Lat. 15° 44′; Long. 78° 19′. Diamonds found in banks of Kundur river; in Nandikotkūr Tāluk.

Dhone: Lat. 15° 23′ 30″; Long. 77° 56′.

(Gazerpalle close to Baswapur, which see.)

Gooramankonda: Lat. 15° 32′; Long, 78° 14′ 15″; 24 miles SSE. of Karnūl. Rock workings.

Gudipaud, 2 miles W. of Devanur; in Nandikotkūr Tāluk.

Hassanapur in Doopaud. Not identified.

Jorapur. A diamond of 44 carats found in débris of irrigation works, near Karnūl.

Kannamadakalu: Lat. 15° 42′; Long. 78° 14′ 30″. Alluvial.

Lanjapoleur: Lat. 15° 45′ 30″; Long. 78° 4′; 7 miles SSW. of Karnūl; Rammalakota Tāluk.

Muddavaram: Lat. 78° 9′ 30″; Long. 78° 30′. 9 miles ESE. of Rammalakota; Nandiāl Tāluk.

Munimadagu: Lat. 15° 15′; Long. 78° 2′ 10″; in Pattikonda Tāluk, 16 miles W. by S. of Banaganapalle (formerly included in Bellary District).

Muravakonda: Lat. 16° 1′; Long. 78° 9′; on the Kistnā. Diamonds found below the fòrd, according to Ferishta and Newbold.

Oruvakal (or Woraykal of A.S.): Lat. 15° 41′; Long. 78° 14′; 14 miles SE. of Karnul; Nandiāl Tāluk.

Panchalingala, left bank of Tungabhadra; Rammalakota Tāluk.

Pendekallu, 5 miles SE. of Rammalakota; Rammalakota Tāluk.

Polúr?: Lat. 15° 31′ 30″; Long. 78° 19′; 4 miles NW. of Nandiāl; in Nandiāl Tāluk.

Pyapali; Palikonda Tāluk.

Rammalakota: Lat. 15° 34′; Long. 78° 3′ 15″; 18 miles W. by S. of Karnūl. Rock and alluvial.

Saitankota, right bank of Tungabhadra, ENE. of Karnūl.

Tandrapad: Lat. 15° 51′; Long. 78° 71′; left bank of Tungabhadra, opposite Karnūl. Alluvial.

Timmapuram: Lat. 15° 32′ 30″; Long. 78° 6′ 30″; 6 miles ESE. of Rammalakota. Rock workings.

Yembye: Lat. 15° 32′; Long. 78° 14′ 15″; 24 miles ESE. of Karnūl.

Kistnā and Godāvarī Districts

Ātkur: Lat. 16° 38′; Long. 80° 23′ 30″.

Barthenypadu: Lat. 16° 38′; Long. 80° 23′ 30″.

Bhadrachalum (doubtful; a diamond said by Newbold to have been found there), on the Godāvarī.

Damarapad: Lat. 16° 35′ 3″; Long. 79° 30′.

Golapalle (or Golapilly): Lat. 16° 43′ 30″; Long. 80° 57′.

[1] Kodavatakullu: Lat. 16° 40′; Long. 80° 23′ 30″ (A.S. 75).

Kollūr (the Gāni or Coulour of Tavernier): Lat. 16° 42′ 30″; Long. 80° 5′; right bank of Kistnā.

Madagalu? (in Palnād Tāluk), 8 miles from the Kistnā.

Malawaram: Lat. 16° 35′ 3″; Long. 79° 30′.

Moonaloor (or Moogaloor): Lat. 16° 38′; Long. 80° 23′ 20″.

Muléle (or Mullavilly): Lat. 16° 41′; Long. 80° 56′.

[1] Oostapully (or Ustapalle): Lat. 16° 40′; Long. 80° 23′ 30″.

[1] Partiāl: Lat. 16° 39′; Long. 80° 27′ (A.S. 75).

(Ustapalle, or Oostapully which see.)

CENTRAL PROVINCES

Sambalpur District

Sambalpur, town on the Mahānadī River, and some of the tributaries above the town. (The country of the Sabarai of Ptolemy.)

Chāndā District

Wairāgarh (the Bairagarh of the Āīn-i-Akbarī): Lat. 20° 26′; Long. 80° 10′ (A.S. 73). Probably the Kosala of the Chinese pilgrims. (V. A. Smith, *Early Hist. of India*, 3rd ed., 285.)

WESTERN BENGAL

Lohārdagā District

Sānkh River, a tributary of the Brāhminī.

Sema, on the Koel (the Soumelpour on the Gouel of Tavernier): Lat. 23° 35′; Long. 84° 21′. This was probably the Sambalaka, in the country of the Mandalai, of Ptolemy.

BUNDELKHAND

Pannā

Baghin, Bargari, Brijpur, Etwa, Kamariya, Majgoha, Myra, Pannā, Sakeriya, Saya-Lachmanpur, Udesna, and many others around Pannā town. It is not known when these mines were first discovered. So far as I can ascertain, Tieffenthaler was the earliest European visitor to them who has left any record of them; he appears to have been at Pannā in 1765. He says the diamonds found there could not compare either in hardness or fire with those of Orissa (Soumelpour ?) or of Raoulcound (i. e. Rammalakota). There is no record of any exceptionally large diamonds having been

[1] The three villages, so marked, were reserved by the Nizām on account of their diamond mines when the Kondupelle Circar was ceded to the East India Company in 1766.

found at Pannā. Though it is believed by some that the mines are of very great antiquity, the history of them is defective. However, the *Āīn-i-Akbarī*, by Abū'-l Fazl (1590),[1] refers to small diamonds having been found at 8 coss distance from the fort of Kālanjar. It seems probable that these mines were worked in Tavernier's time, though he was not aware of the fact.

NORTH-WEST PROVINCES

SIMLA ? This is a very doubtful locality, but there are several diamonds in the Calcutta Museum which were said to have been found in a stream near Simla.

NOTE ON THE GOLKONDA AND BĪJĀPUR DIAMOND MINES

There is a very important early description of the diamond mines of these regions, which is of special interest, as it gives a clue to the original source of many names of diamond sites which are to be found in the modern literature of the subject. It was published in the *Philosophical Transactions*, vol. xii. 1677, p. 907, having been presented to the Royal Society by the Earl Marshal of England, who was then Henry Howard, afterwards Duke of Norfolk. His term of office as Earl Marshal lasted from 1672–83. I am inclined to think it may have been written by Mr. Cholmley, who is described by Sir Streynsham Master[2] as having been engaged for several years before 1679 in making the annual purchases of diamonds for the Company, especially at the mines of Gollapalle (or Golapilly) and Malavalle (Mulēli or Mullavilly).

The diamond mines of the Kistnā District belonged to the Kings of Golkonda, Kutb-Shāhī dynasty, from the downfall of the Bāhmanī Kings of the Deccan (*c*, 1500) until their defeat and extinction in 1686. The mines in the Karnūl District also belonged to them after the Rājās of Vijayanagar were driven to the south in 1564. (See *Kistna Manual*, p. 244.)

It is curious to note that while Tavernier only mentions three localities in these regions by name, namely, Rammalakota (his Raolconda), Kōllūr (his Coulour), and Gandikota, together with another unnamed locality (which was Gazerpalle, see p. 371), this paper, published only a year after Tavernier's first edition appeared, enumerates 23 mines in the Kingdom of Golkonda, and 15 in the Kingdom of Bījāpur—in all 38.

As will be seen some of these names correspond with names in the preceding list, others seem to be identical with names of villages in the region, about which there is no independent evidence of their having been diamond producing. The remaining names I have failed to identify. As I hope on

[1] Ed. Jarrett, ii. 159.

[2] *Kistna Manual*, p. 147. Nathaniel Chumley, who lived many years at Golkonda: *Eng. Factories, 1661–1684*, p. 274 *n*.

some future occasion to republish this paper of the Earl Marshal's *in extenso*, with annotations, I shall at present limit myself to a brief enumeration of the localities, their proper modern names being given in brackets.

The Golkonda Mines are—1. Quolure; this is Tavernier's Coulour or Gani [Kollūr]. This is said to have been the first mine worked in Golkonda, but was then, 1677, almost exhausted. 2. Codawillicul [Kodavatakullu]. 3. Malabar [Malawaram]. 4. Buttephalem [Barthenypadu, near Partiāl]. 5. Ramiah [?]. 6. Gurem [?]. 7. Muttampellee [near Karūr ?]. These five (? six) were under the same government as that of Melwillee [Malavalle or Mulēli], see below. 8. Currure [Wajrā- or Vajrā-Karūr, in the Guty Tāluk of the Bellary District]. This identification is confirmed by the statement that it, the most famous and most ancient of all the mines, was taken some years previously, with the Carnatic, by Mīr Jumla from the Hindu Rājās. It is said that diamonds up to 'a seize (? ser) weight, which was equal to about 9 ounces troy, or 81½ pagodas, had been found there; the mine was privately worked by the King, and the stones produced from it were large and well spread', &c. I have elsewhere quoted, see vol. ii, p. 42, the account of this mine having been worked by a Portuguese gentleman. 9. Ganjeeconta [Gunjeegonta]. 10. Lattawar[1] [Lattwārā]. These two last are respectively 1 and 10 miles SW. of Wajrā-Karūr. 11. Jonagerre [?]. 12. Pirai [?]. 13. Dugulle [?]. 14. Purwillee [?]. These four last I cannot identify. 15. Anuntapellee [Anantapur ? is 20 miles from Wajrā-Karūr. Dr. King (*Mem. Geol. Surv. India*, vol. viii, p. 101) alludes to a diamond being found there]. 16. Girregeta [Goulagoonta]. 17. Maarmood [?]. 18. Wazzergerre [Wajirābād ?]. 19. Munnemurg [Munimadagu in Karnūl]. The two last are said to have been the deepest mines; they were carried to depths of 40 to 50 fathoms. Some interesting details are given as to the process of mining. 20. Langumboot [?]; process of mining as in the preceding. 21. Whootoor [Hotoor ?] near Karūr. 22. Muddemurg [Madagula ? in centre of Palnād Tāluk, Kistnā District. This identification is founded on the statement that the locality was about 9 miles from the Kistnā river]. 23. Melwillee, or new mine [Malavalle or Mulēli], worked first from 1670–71, then closed, but reopened in 1673 by the King's licence, owing to the Kollūr mine becoming exhausted.

In Bījāpur there were 15 mines, of which only those yielding the smallest stones were allowed by the King to be worked,

[1] This, as also some of the other localities, are given by Dutens and Castellani as being in Asia !—a rather wide geographical expression; they have long been objects of search to me, till traced by means of this
24 paper.

partly to prevent large stones becoming too common, and partly to avoid exciting Aurangzeb's cupidity. The mines were—1. Ramulconeta [Rammalakota, i. e. Tavernier's Raolconda]; diamonds of a mangelin weight were seldom found there, generally they were much smaller. Broken diamonds, called shemboes, were found there. 2. Banugunnapellee [Banaganapalle, 37 miles SE. of Karnūl]. 3. Pendekull [Pendekallu]. 4. Moodawaram [? Muddāvaram, 7 miles ESE. of Rammalakota]. 5. Cumerwille [Coomroly of A.S. close to Gooramankonda]. 6. Paulkull [?]. 7. Workull [? Oruvakal]. 8. Lungeepoleur [Langapolūr, 5 miles S. of Karnūl]. 9. Pootloor [Polūr]. 10. Punchelingull [Panchalingala, left bank of Tungabhadra]. 11. Shingarrampent [?]. 12. Tondarpaar [Tandrapād, left bank of Tungabhadra]. 13. Gundepelle [?]. 14. Donee [Dhone]. 15. Gazerpellee [this is close to Baswapur].

I would venture to commend the identification of those mines which are unplaced in the above list to someone with local knowledge.[1]

We are told in the Earl Marshal's paper that in Golkonda the miners and merchants were much oppressed, and in a miserable state of poverty, from having to submit to tyrannical squeezing and heavy duties on provisions, tobacco, and betel. With extraordinary inconsistency, although the King of Golkonda, 'Abdulla Kutb Shāh, and the King of Bījāpur, 'Ādil Shāh, had agreements with the miners that all diamonds above a certain weight were to be reserved for them, still they would not only pay highly for large stones conveyed to their capitals secretly by the merchants, but would bestow dresses of honour upon those who brought such stones to them for sale.[2]

APPENDIX III

The Diamond Mines of Bengal.

Although it is possible that many persons in India may be surprised at the statement that there were formerly diamond mines of considerable importance and value in the region of Bengal, which is about to be described; and although it is probably the case that many who have resided for long periods in the very District itself have never heard of the

[1] There is a mountain in the kingdom of Bījāpur 'where they dig out diamonds, which mountain is a league distant from the city, and is surrounded by a wall, and is kept by a strong guard' (Varthema, 118).

[2] Major Leonard Munn has published an interesting paper on 'Ancient Mines and Megaliths in Hyderabad', *Memoirs and Proceedings of the Manchester Literary and Philosophical Society*, vol. lxiv (1921), part ii, No. 5.

A MAP SHEWING THE POSITION OF THE DIAMOND RIVERS OF BENGAL

I Soumelpour on the Gouel i.e. Semah on the Koel in the Palamow Subdivision.

II An intermediate locality on the Sunk river in Burwa, Palkot & Jushpur

III Position of the washings on the Mahanadi near Sambalpur in the Central Provinces.

Diamond rivers

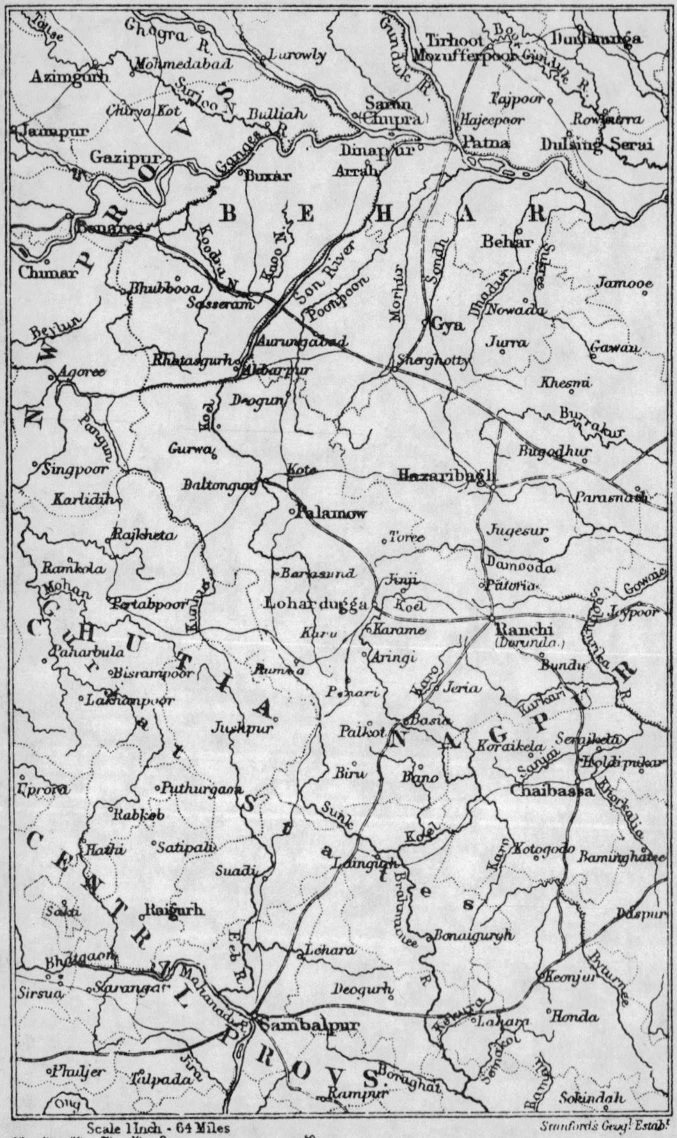

Scale 1 Inch - 64 Miles

50 40 30 20 10 0 50

Stanford's Geog! Estab!

fact, all local traces of the industry being now extinct still the cumulative evidence which can be brought forward is such that I do not anticipate that any serious objections can be urged to the natural conclusions derivable from that evidence.

Gibbon, in the *Decline and Fall of the Roman Empire*, for some reason which he does not give, arrived at the conclusion that it was the mines described by Tavernier at Soumelpour [1] on the Gouel (i. e. Sema or Semulpur on the Koel, in the Sub-Division of Palāmau), rather than any of the localities in Southern India, which supplied Rome with diamonds.

Ptolemy mentions Sambalaka [2] as a city in the country of the Mandalai which produced the finest diamonds in the world. Now, although it is possible that he may have referred to Sambalpur on the Mahanādī, where diamonds are known to occur, I prefer to identify it with Tavernier's Soumelpour, as above, because it was situated in the country generally recognized as that of the Mandali or Mundas, while Sambalpur is beyond its limits.

Further, it may be conveniently remarked here that Ptolemy's Adamas river, although he clearly indicates its origin in Chota Nāgpur (Kokkonage or Kokra), has by some authors been identified with the Mahānadī, while others have with greater probability identified it with one or other of the rivers rising in Chota Nāgpur, namely, the Dāmudā, Subanrikhā or Brāhmanī, with its tributaries the Sānkh and Southern Koel, to which we shall presently again refer. The Mahānadī is probably Ptolemy's Manada,[3] rising in the country of the Sabarae or Savaras, where diamonds were also obtained.

Our next reference to this locality is a very definite and explicit one ; it is separated by a long period of time from Ptolemy. In Professor Blochmann's translation [4] of the Tuzuk-i-Jahāngīrī, we find that 'On the 3d Isfandiármuz of the 10th year of my reign (A.D. 1616) it was reported to me (Jahāngīr) that Ibrāhīm Khān (governor of Bihār) had overrun Kokrah and taken possession of its diamond washings.

[1] By a misprint given as Jumelpur, in Bengal, *Decline and Fall*, ii. 281, *note*.

[2] See *Indian Antiquary*, vol. xiii, 1884, p. 364, where it is identified with Sambalpur. J. W. McCrindle (*Ancient India as described by Ptolemy*, 133) writes : 'Sambalaka is Sambhal, a town in Rohilkhand. Sambalaka or Sambhala is the name of several countries in India, but there is only one town of the name that is met with in the Eastern parts. It is a very ancient town and on the same parallel as Delhi.' (See *Imperial Gazetteer*, xx. 18 f.)

[3] So McCrindle, *op. cit.*, 71.

[4] *Journ. As. Soc. Bengal*, xl. 113 : *Āīn-i-Akbarī*, 480 n.

This District belongs to Sūbah Bihār, and the river which flows through it yields the diamonds.' Then follow accounts of the mines and Ibrāhīm Khān's operations, all of which will be found quoted in the *Economic Geology of India*, p. 25. The account goes on to say, 'The District is now subject to me. All diamonds found in the river are forwarded to court. Only a few days ago a diamond arrived which had a value of Rs.50,000, and I hope many more will be added to my store of jewels.' Among those received from Ibrāhīm Khān was one which was coloured like a sapphire, it weighed several ratis, and the lapidaries valued it at Rs.3,000, though they would have given 20,000 had it been white and stood the test. Professor Blochmann gives a quotation from a MS. history of the Mahārājas of Chota Nāgpur, in which a method of testing diamonds for flaws is described as consisting in fixing them on the horns of fighting rams.

General Dalton recorded that the family of the Rājā of Chota Nāgpur possessed a diamond from these mines valued at Rs.40,000.[1] A large picture, representing the attack on the Palāmau fort in 1660 by Dāūd Khān, contains a figure of the Zamīndār-i-kān-i-almās or Lord of the Diamond Mine. General Dalton was, I believe, rather inclined to think these mines somewhat mythical, while Professor Blochmann[2] identified the river with the Sānkh. As I had conversations with both of them on the subject, I am satisfied that neither of them knew of Tavernier's references to this region, nor did I know of them then, and it was not till some time after I became aware of them that I was able to show that his Soumelpour was quite a different locality from Sambalpur on the Mahānadī, with which most writers had identified it.

In addition to Tavernier's own direct account of this locality, there is another somewhat earlier in date, but which there is reason to believe was derived from information obtained from him. Reference will be found in Appendix VI to a work by Chappuzeau. In it there appears to be reference to the locality in Bengal which produced diamonds under the name Nage (i. e. Kokkonage or Chota Nāgpur). In the year 1657 L'Escot of Orleans (see p. 239) went there to purchase a diamond of 42 carats, but he failed to get it.

Although Tavernier's locality was on the Gouel River—i. e. the Koel, which runs northwards to join the Son, and so reaches the Ganges—the Sānkh and another Koel also take their rise close by, and running southwards they form the Brāhmanī, which joins the delta of the Mahānadī, near the coast of the Bay of Bengal. The Ebe River, a tributary

[1] *Ethnology of Bengal*, 163 n.
[2] *Journ. As. Soc, Bengal*, xliii, pt. i. 240.

of the Mahānadī also, rises in the same neighbourhood, and t is locally called the Hīra or diamond river, and its bed is aid to have yielded diamonds. Hence it is a natural deduction hat the source of the diamonds found in the beds of these ivers, which pursue such different courses, is common to all, nd that the diamond-bearing rocks will be found there. Jnfortunately before leaving India I had no opportunity of putting this theory to the test, and I am not aware that he area has been as yet fully explored.[1]

The accompanying map will convey a clear idea of the relative positions of the three localities, which have hitherto been much confused in the accounts by different authors. In the south there is Sambalpur, on the Mahānadī, of which I have elsewhere [2] published detailed accounts of the geology, and of the records of the yield of diamonds there in former times; farther north is the locality on the Sānkh river, which, as stated above, is one of the tributaries of the Brāhmanī; and lastly, on the other side of the watershed, is the site of the locality, Sema on the Koel, a tributary of the Son, which I identify with the Soumelpour of Tavernier.

As Sambalpur is in the Central Provinces, and is therefore beyond the region of the present discussion, not being included in Bengal, we may now pass to the mention of the other two localities, as they are referred to by various authorities since Tavernier's time.

Sumelpur (Mine de diamans), near a tributary of the Solon (i. e. Sone, called in its upper portion Rivière d'Andi, see *ante*, vol. i, p. 45), is represented on the Carte de l'Indoustan by M. Bellin, which was published in 1752 in the *Histoire générale des Voyages*.

Tieffenthaler,[3] somewhere about the year 1766, wrote of Sommelpour as a place producing an abundance of diamonds of good quality in the river Gouel, 30 *milles* S.E. from Rohtās. He did not visit it himself, and perhaps he quoted from Tavernier.

Pennant,[4] in the year 1798, mentions that a diamond mine was then being worked on the Sānkh river, but he does not name his authority. He also states that Soumelpour on the Gouel was the most noted and most ancient locality for

[1] In connexion with the diamonds of Bihār, it may be noted that in 1585 the King of Chota Nāgpur was reduced to the status of a feudatory, and in the reign of Jahāngīr, up to which time the Musulmān governors had been satisfied with a tribute of two or three diamonds, Ibrāhīm Khān Fath Jang, governor of Bihār, defeated the Rājā and carried off his family diamonds (Sarat Chandra Roy, *The Mundas*, 151).

[2] *Economic Geology of India*, p. 30.

[3] Bernoulli, *Descr. de l'Inde*, Berlin, 1791, i. 433.

[4] *View of Hindoostan*, ii. 140.

diamonds.[1] Here he evidently quotes from Tavernier, as also did Buffon,[2] who calls the locality Soonelpour on the Gouil, which Buchanan Hamilton in 1838 [3] refers to as being probably identical with a diamond mine which he had heard of on the southern Koel. Karl Ritter in 1836 detected the incompatibility of Tavernier's statements as to the position of his Soumelpour with that of Sambalpur on the Mahānadī; but his correction did not serve to mitigate the confusion which is to be found even in the most recent authors upon the subject. I may add that I was pointed out on the map a locality on the Sānkh by a resident in Chota Nāgpur, where local tradition asserts that diamonds used to be found.

Having referred above to Sambalpur in the Central Provinces it may be of interest to add that this Indian Province includes another locality which, though of importance in early times, was so forgotten even a century ago, that Rennell, and after him Karl Ritter, altogether failed to identify it. It was mentioned as being in the country conquered by Ahmad Shāh Walī Bahmanī, both by Garcia de Orta and Ferishta. In the *Āīn-i-Akbarī* the locality is spoken of as at Bairagarh, which is now identified with Wairāgarh in the Chānda District, about 80 miles from Nāgpur. It was probably the Kosala of the Chinese pilgrims and perhaps the Kosa of Ptolemy.[4]

It is just possible that a locality mentioned by Nicolò Conti in the fifteenth century as a diamond mine called Albenigaras may have also been Wairāgarh. He mentions that the diamonds were obtained then by means of pieces of meat, which were flung on to the mountain, where the diamonds could not be collected owing to the number of serpents. The pieces of meat with diamonds sticking to them were then carried to their nests by birds of prey, from whence they were recovered by the diamond seekers.[5] This, with variations, is the story told by Marco Polo, and in the travels of Sindbad the Sailor. Elsewhere I have described the probable origin of this myth. It appears to be founded on the very common practice in India, on the opening of a mine, to offer up cattle to propitiate the evil spirits who are supposed to guard treasures—these being represented by the serpents in the myth. At such sacrifices in India, birds of prey invari-

[1] *View of Hindoostan*, ii. 113.

[2] *Hist. Nat.*, *Minéraux*, Paris, 1786, iv. 280.

[3] Montgomery Martin, *Eastern India*, i. 535.

[4] McCrindle (*op. cit.*, p. 158 f.) fixes Kosa in the neighbourhood of Baital, north of the sources of the Tāptī and Varadā, a tributary of the Tungabhadrā (*op. cit.*, 179).

[5] R. H. Major, *Travels of Nicolò Conti, India in the Fifteenth Century* Hakluyt Society, part ii, 29 f.

ably assemble to pick up what they can, and in that fact we probably have the remainder of the foundation of the story.

It is probable, also, that the story by Pliny and other early writers, of the diamond being softened by the blood of a he-goat, had its origin in such sacrifices.

As to whether these or other diamond mines in India could be profitably worked again I cannot now discuss here; but I may say that I do not believe that they can be truly described as being exhausted.

APPENDIX IV

The Diamond Mines of Borneo.

In the Colloquies of Garcia da Orta, in the Travels of Linschoten, in the works of De Boot[1] and De Laet,[2] and in many treatises on precious stones, up to some of those most recently published, we find, as has already been stated in the note on p. 67, that Malacca is mentioned as a locality where diamonds occur. This was for a long time a sore puzzle to me, especially as among modern writers on Malacca, with the exception of Miss Bird,[3] none claimed that Malacca was known to be a diamond producing country, while some local inquiries which I made through the late Mr. W. Wynne, of the Straits Civil Service, confirmed an opinion, founded on the character of the geological structure, that probably none had ever been found there.

The solution of the difficulty is afforded by the fact that the name Malacca was applied by the early Portuguese writers to Borneo, and that the Taniapura which they mention was Tanjongpura in Borneo.

I am indebted to Mr. D. F. A. Hervey for the information that Tanjong pūra (the Tandjong Poera of the Dutch) is situated about 30 miles up the river Pawān in the northern part of the Mātan District, adjoining Sukadana. The name, he states, is a hybrid, Tanjong being the Malay for a point (of land), and pūra a Malayan version of the Sanskrit pûr, a town.

Such is the true explanation, and not that Malacca was

[1] *De Lapidi. et Gemm.*, 3rd ed., by De Laet, Lug. Bat. 1647, p. 121. When enumerating the localities where the diamond is obtained, he says, 'Alia est rupes ad fretum Tanian in Malacca que etiam profert adamantes qui de rupe veteri vocantur'. De Boot's original work was published in 1609.

[2] *De Gemm. et Lapidi.*, Lug. Bat. 1647, p. 2, 'Juxta fretum Taniapurae haud longe ab Emporio celeberrimo Malacca alia earumdem gemmarum fodina est unde vulgo Malacenses appellantur'.

[3] *The Golden Chersonese*, 261.

a place situated in the Eastern Ghāts ! as stated by Castellani; nor that the idea originated in some jumble about malachite, as has I think been suggested by one writer.

As it was with Pliny, so it has been with a host of other compilers; we find in the literature of precious stones the same places or the same objects called by different names, and treated as though they were distinct. It has been shown on p. 56 that Gāni was a prefix signifying 'mine of' to the name Kollūr, a diamond locality on the Kistnā, though it is commonly treated as though it were a name itself; and when we find Malacca mentioned side by side with Borneo, as a diamond-producing region, we should not suspect that its appearance in the lists is simply due to a survival of an old name for Borneo. It is perhaps needless to add, therefore, that it should be expunged from all future lists.

The following facts with regard to the occurrence of the diamond in Borneo are chiefly extracted from Crawfurd's *Dictionary* and a paper by Dr. Posewitz.[1] The original matrix of the diamonds of Borneo is, as yet, unknown; but, as they are found in alluvial deposits, in the beds of certain rivers, and in older alluvial or diluvial deposits together with gold and platinum, it may be concluded with some probability that all come from the same sources. The platinum is not known to have been met with in the original matrix, but gold has been found *in situ* in Palaeozoic rocks.

The most famous and apparently the earliest known diamond mines were situated in West Borneo, in the Districts of Landak and Sangau, while some diamonds are reported to have been obtained in Sarawak. Dr. Posewitz does not refer to their occurrence at Tanjongpura, on the Pawān river, nor in Sukadana, where earlier writers state they were found.

In Southern Borneo the most abundant mines and washings are in the neighbourhood of the Tanahlaut hills, which form the boundary between Southern and Eastern Borneo, near Martapura and Tjempaka. The produce of these localities is best known in connexion with the name Banjarmasin, a territory and seaport now held by the Dutch. It should be added that there are some minor localities in the region between Banjarmasin and Sukadana. In Eastern Borneo the territory of Kusan, to the east of the Tanahlaut range, also includes some mines. In British North Borneo there are believed to be some diamond-bearing localities, but as

[1] *Das Diamantvorkommen in Borneo, Mitth. a. d. Jahrb. d. K. Geol. Anst.*, Bd. vii, Budapesth, 1885. 'Borneo is amazingly rich in minerals, gold, silver, coal, iron, and even diamonds being won from it, mostly by the industrious Chinese, while in other parts there are rich oil-wells, for which a rich future has been predicted' ('Natural Wealth in British North Borneo,' *The Times*, 24 May, 1921).

yet they have not been proved to be of any very great promise.

In connexion with the subject of Borneo diamonds, mention is frequently made of a supposed diamond in the possession of the Rājā of Mātan. Its great size, 367 carats, and its reputed value, £269,378, as estimated by Crawfurd, have for many years caused it to be an object of Dutch cupidity, and many stories are told of the efforts made by them to induce the Rājā to part with it. It is stated that early in the century the Rājā was offered 150,000 dollars, two large war brigs fully equipped, besides other war material, in exchange for the diamond; but from superstitious or other reasons he refused to part with this emblem of royalty, and it has never been cut. Hugh Low states that the real diamond was not shown to visitors, but that a rock crystal was kept for the purpose. Dr. Posewitz, however, records that in 1868 the so-called diamond was itself definitely proved to be merely a piece of rock crystal, thus proving the accuracy of von Gaffron's previous assertion that it could be scratched by corundum, and had a specific gravity of only 2·63 (namely, that of quartz).

Although diamonds weighing up to 70 and even 80 carats have been found in Borneo, for many years past stones of even 4 or 5 carats have been but rarely met with.

APPENDIX V

The Ruby Mines of Upper Burma and the Sapphire Washings of Ceylon.

Position.—The principal ruby mines of Burma are situated in three valleys, which are known by the names of their chief villages respectively, namely Mogok (or Mogout), Kathé, and Kyatpyen.[1] The elevated tract including these valleys is situated at a distance of about 90 miles NNW. from Mandalay, and is at elevations of from 4,000 to 5,500 feet above the sea. The mountains surrounding the Mogok valley culminate in the peaks of Chenedoung, 7,362 feet, and Toungee, 7,775 feet. The ruby tract, as now defined by the most recent scientific examination, occupies an area of 66 square miles, but mining is at present limited to an area of about 45 square miles. The region is described as being very beautiful, and presenting a thriving appearance; but the climate is somewhat malarious, and Europeans, although the country

[1] For a full account of the Ruby Mines District see Sir J. G. Scott, J. P. Hardiman, *Gazetteer of Upper Burma and the Shan States*, Rangoon, 1901, part i, vol. ii, 213 ff.; part ii, vol. iii, 3 ff.; *Imperial Gazetteer*, xxi. 326 ff.

is so elevated, are subject to attacks of fever on first arrival there.

A totally distinct ruby tract is situated in the marble hills at Sagyin, which is only 16 miles from Mandalay. So far as is known, it is comparatively of little importance, the rubies and other gems which are found there being of inferior qualities. Other localities about 15 miles to the north and north-east of Sagyin are reported to produce rubies, but nothing certain is known about them.

History.—The ruby mines of Burma were first made known by European writers towards the end of the fifteenth century. In the sixteenth century there are more definite references by Portuguese travellers, but they are not of much practical importance. Tavernier,[1] as we have seen, gives an account of the mines and their produce from hearsay; from which it would appear that the reputation they then bore was not very high, or he would probably have made an effort to visit them. The yield, he says, did not exceed 100,000 *écus* (say £22,500) per annum, and he found it profitable to carry rubies from Europe to Asia for sale.

The principal authorities of the present century, previous to the conquest of Upper Burma, are Mr. Crawfurd[2]; the Père Giuseppe d'Amato,[3] who visited the mines about the year 1833; Dr. Oldham,[4] who visited Ava and collected information about the mines in the year 1855, when with Sir Arthur Phayre's mission; Mr. Bredmeyer, who was in the service of the King and visited the mines in the year 1868; and Mr. Spears and Capt. Strover, of the British Burma Commission, both of whom have placed on record their observations. From these authorities we learn that the rubies which were found were generally small, not averaging more than a quarter of a rati, and that the large stones were generally smuggled away, but few of them reaching the King. It was supposed that the Chinese and Tartar merchants who visited Mogok and Kyatpyen conveyed most of them out of Burma. The large rubies were generally flawed, and Mr. Spears states that he never saw one exceeding half a rupee in weight, i.e. about 22 carats.

The King's revenue derivable from the monopoly was variously estimated by these authorities at from £12,500 to £15,000. The more recent information now available confirms these estimates. The figures stated on official authority are 90,000 to 100,000 rupees, the highest sum being 150,000 rupees paid in one year. Besides which, however, was the reserva-

[1] Vol. ii. pp. 77 f. below.
[2] 'Mission to Ava,' *Edin. New Phil. Journ.*, 1827, p. 366.
[3] *Journ. As. Soc. Bengal*, vol. ii, p. 75.
[4] Yule's *Mission to Ava*, p. 347.

tion of stones above a certain size; but it seems to be generally admitted that few large stones were found, and of these a proportion, in spite of severe punishments for concealment, never reached the King; there is no basis then for an estimate of the total revenue which he received from the mines.

If one may judge from the appearance of the rubies forming part of the treasure taken at Mandalay, and which are now exhibited at the South Kensington Museum, valuable stones were rare, as, except a few of the smaller ones, none seem to be perfect.

As is well known, recent accounts by experts have represented the prospects of the mines in a much more favourable light, and the true value will probably be ere long ascertained by the energetic operations of a company conducted on scientific principles.

The different kinds of precious stones found in the mines.—Although the rubies have given their name to the mines, several other varieties of corundum are also found, such as sapphires, oriental emeralds, oriental amethyst, oriental topaz, and white sapphires; and besides these there are to be found spinels of various colours, hyacinth (or zircon), iolite (or dichroite, a stone resembling sapphire), and lastly the semi-precious rubellite, which is a variety of the mineral called tourmaline, of which some exceptionally fine examples have been brought from Ava, one of which has long held an honoured position in the mineral collection of the British Museum.

According to Mr. Spears, the proportion of sapphires to rubies was as 1 to 100, but the former are often of large size and fine quality.

Pegu has been mentioned by some early writers [1] as producing diamonds, but there are no real grounds for supposing that either the diamond or true emerald occur in any part of Burma.

Mode of occurrence and source of the gems.—Although it has for some time been known that the rubies of Sagyin were derived from crystalline limestones or marble, the source of the gems in the principal region at Mogok, Kyatpyen, and Kathé was not actually ascertained till recently, when these localities were visited by Mr. Barrington Brown. It was known that they were for the most part actually obtained in derivative gravels, and it had been inferred that the so-called clefts and lodes, of a report which appeared before his examination, were really fissures in limestones, where the stones had accumulated as the result of the solution of limestone, and by gravitation into these recesses.

[1] See *Description of the Diamond Mines of India, Phil. Trans.*, vol. xii, 1677, p. 907.

Mr. Brown has shown that the geological formation consists of recent deposits of hill wash and alluvium and old crystalline limestones, schists, pegmatite, and other metamorphic rocks. In order to explain the relationship which exists between these formations and the rubies, it will be convenient to describe the various systems of mining, by which the mode of occurrence will be made apparent. The mines, as worked by the natives, may be divided into four classes, as follows :

I. Twinlones, or pits sunk in the alluvium of the valleys.
II. Mewdwins, or open cuttings in the hill-wash over which water is led.
III. Loodwins, or workings in caves and fissures.
IV. Quarries in a bed of coarse calcspar in the limestone, which appears to be the true original matrix of the gems.

The Twinlones are square pits which are sunk in the alluvium of the valleys down to the gem-bearing gravels, which occur at varying depths. These pits have to be timbered to support the sides and, as far as possible, exclude water, which, however, finds access, and the first operation, every day, is to bale out the water which has accumulated during the night. The gravel is hoisted out in baskets by means of balance poles similar to those which are used in India for raising water from wells. The gravel is then washed in shallow baskets made of closely-woven bamboo, and the rubies, as they are picked out, are placed in a bamboo tube full of water and are sorted at the close of the day's work. The larger pits are generally cleared out in about ten days and the smaller in half that time ; when working in one is finished, the timber is removed and another pit is started.

Mewdwins.—These are open cuttings on the slopes of the hills to which water is conducted, often from a considerable distance, and discharged with as great a head as possible on the ruby clay and sand, which is shovelled under it by the miners. The lighter portions are carried down by the stream, the boulders removed by hand, and the residue placed in the sluice and washed, where it is caught by riffles, from whence it is removed and washed in baskets as in the preceding process. The circumstances appear to be such as would suit a more scientific application of hydraulic methods than are known to the natives.

Loodwins.—These are natural caves and fissures in the limestone rock, in the floors and crevices of which the rubies have accumulated in consequence of the solution by water of the limestone matrix. In the ordinary sense of the term these are not mines, i. e. the miners do not excavate the rock, but merely scramble through the natural passages and tunnels to the spots where the loam containing the rubies is found—this they either carry to the surface in baskets or it is hoisted up by means of balance poles—and it is then washed at the surface at the nearest watercourse.

From such caves the finest rubies ever found have been obtained, and from one in the Pingu Hill, near Kyatpyen, Mr. Brown states that, after the detritus had been passed, of every basketful of the ruby clay which was raised half consisted of rubies.

A certain royal mine of this character is said to have produced a ruby as large as a walnut, and in another the rubies were found in association with the bones of some extinct animal of very large size.[1]

This description opens up a somewhat wide vista of speculation, and one can hardly resist the temptation of prophesying as to the wonderful discoveries which *may* be made when adits and shafts are driven to afford access to these natural caves and fissures in the mass of the marble hills. In such safe receptacles it is not unreasonable to suppose that stones which have suffered but little from attrition and fracture may be found, and that there the greatest prizes will be obtained.

Quarries.—To the north of Mogok village, at a distance of about three-quarters of a mile, a bed of calcspar in the limestone, which is 20 feet wide, produces rubies, but in order to obtain them the use of powder has to be employed as well as the hammer, and when chipped out the gems are generally more or less fractured; but good stones have been obtained. Whether any method can be devised of avoiding the injury resulting from the use of explosives is at present doubtful. It is not easy to suggest how a firm rock, such as this calcspar, could be mined without recourse being had to violent methods of some kind.

The rose-pink rubellite (a variety of tourmaline) is obtained on the margin of the Meobychoung river, 15 miles S. of Mogok and 3 miles from Mamlong. The mines in the alluvium are worked by a rude hydraulic system, and the produce is sent to China, large pieces obtaining a good price.

Under the arrangements which have been made with the New Burma Ruby Mine Company, the rights and interests of the miners have apparently been very fully safeguarded, but whether the miners on their part will refrain from smuggling and comply with the regulations, and disclose their more valuable finds and submit them to taxation, remains to be seen. The total production of rubies in 1887, when the

[1] The fossil remains of Mastodons and other large mammalia, allied to those found in the Siwālik hills of India, have long been known to occur in Burma.

country was disturbed, amounted to only 42,486 rupees' worth, but in the first two months of 1888 21,883 rupees' worth had been obtained. Stones of from 5 to 20 carats weight were sold during this period, and the highest price obtained for one was 500 rupees.

The mode of occurrence of the rubies in calcspar is, I believe, somewhat unusual, though spinel is known to be found in calcareous rocks. It is generally the case that the corundum minerals are found in mica schists; such is stated to be the case in Zanskar in the Himalayas, and also in Ceylon; with reference to the latter it may be of interest, in addition to the remarks on p. 102, to add here some particulars as to the sapphire washings of that island.

THE SAPPHIRES OF CEYLON.—Under British rule the monopoly in precious stones, which existed under the Kandyan sovereigns, was early abolished as a source of revenue, and no licence is now required by jewel hunters. Great numbers of people are attracted annually to the washings, to the great detriment of agriculture and the demoralization of the villagers, who are brought into contact with dissolute adventurers. Sir Emerson Tennent, from whom the above facts are quoted, estimated the annual total value of the precious stones which were found as not exceeding £10,000 *per annum*.[1]

According to the *Handbook for Ceylon*, recently published in connexion with the Colonial and Indian Exhibition, the search is conducted in a rude fashion, and, despite the advice and reports by experts, there has been no improvement in the method. It is stated in the same work that, though some returns are attempted by the Government, it is impossible to estimate the annual yield at present, and the mines have never, I believe, been successfully worked by Europeans.

APPENDIX VI

A Review or Abstract in the 'Philosophical Transactions' of Chapuzeau's (sic) work, entitled 'Histoire des Joyaux,' published in 1665; and Note on the English edition of the same work.

THE following is a contemporary abstract published in the *Philosophical Transactions*[2] of a book which seems to be of extraordinary rarity—there being no copy of it, I believe, in any of the great libraries in Great Britain, nor even in the Bibliothèque Nationale—it is therefore of sufficient interest

[1] Tennent, *Ceylon*, i. 37. [2] Vol. ii, 1667, pp. 429-36.

to justify its republication in its original quaint form. But it has in connexion with Tavernier a special interest, because from the glimpse of the contents of the book which it affords, we can see that Chapuzeau (or rather Chappuzeau), by whatever means he acquired them, was in possession of many of the facts recorded in Tavernier's *Travels* at least ten years before the *Travels* were published, and while Tavernier was absent on his last journey. None of the biographies of Chappuzeau mention this work; and although I have not failed to make inquires I have been unable as yet to find any explanation of the mystery.

In Emanuel's bibliography of works on precious stones,[1] the book is mentioned with its full title, and the place and date of publication are given as Geneva 1665.

An Account
Of a small Book in French, entituled
HISTOIRE DES JOYAUX
ET
*Des Principales Richesses de l'*Orient *et de l'*Occident,
par le Sr. Chapuzeau.

This History treats of Diamonds, Rubies, Emeralds, Pearls, Coral, Bezoar, Yellow Amber, Ambergris, Indigo, &c.

Of *Diamonds*, the Author shews:

I. The *Places* whence they are taken; of which he finds but five in all the *East-Indies*, whereof *two* are *Rivers*, vid. *Saccadan* in Borneo and *Nage* in the Kingdom of *Bengala*;[2] at the bottom of both which, *he saith*, the Diamonds are found among the sand, after the waters, that fall as great Torrents from the Mountains, are run off; and the three others are Mines, in the Kingdoms of *Decan*, *Cuncan*, and *Golconda*. In this Relation he observes, that the Diamonds which are found at the bottom of those Rivers, have the best *Water*; but those in Mines have often *Flaws* (which he imputes to the violent knockings of the Rock) and *Blebs*, ascribed to the condition of the Earth or Sand they are found in, *vid.* when that is not pure, but fattish or black. He takes also notice, that Diamonds are the heaviest of precious Stones, as Gold is of Mettals.

II. The *Manner*, how they are found and separated; which is the same in substance with that described in *Num.* 18, p. 328.[3]

[1] *Diamonds and Precious Stones*, second ed., London, 1867, p. 246.
[2] See *ante*, pp. 41 *et seq.* of vol. ii, and Appendix III, p. 356.
[3] This is a reference to another Review, on the *Voyage de l'Évêque de Beryte.* &c.; it is in *Phil. Trans.*, vol. i, pp. 327–8.

III. The *Price* of them, according to the proportion of their weight ; for which he gives this Rule. Take, saith he, a Diamond of 10 *Carats* : this number is to be squared (which makes 100). Then, if the Stone be clean, each Carat, according to its perfection, may be worth 40 to 60 Crowns : if it have no good water, or have a Bleb or Flaw, the Carat will not be worth but from 10 to 30 Crowns. So multiplying the said 100 by the number, which each Carat of such or such a Stone may be worth, the product is the price of the Stone.

For *Rubies*, he discourses also of the *Places* where *they* are found, and of their *Price*.[1] The Places are, the Kingdom of *Pegu*, and the Isle of Ceylon ; whence very few are suffered to be carried away. The Price is, that a good *Rubi* of the weight of 1 *Rati* (which is $\frac{7}{8}$ of a Carat) is esteemed at 20 old *Pagodes* in India, each *Pagode* being about ten shillings *English*.

(A Rubi) of	2	*Ratis*	is valued at	100	*Pagodes*.
,,	3	,,	,,	250	,,
,,	4	,,	,,	500	,,
,,	5	,,	,,	900	,,
,,	6	,,	,,	1,500	,,
,,	7	,,	,,	2,300	,,
,,	12	,,	,,	12,000	,,

Concerning *Turquois*, they are found in *Persia*, in the Province *Chamaquay*, north of *Ispahan*, in two Mines, called the *Old* and the *New* Rock. These of the *New*, are of an ill, whitish Blew ; but those of the *Old* are not suffered to be digged out, but by the King of *Persia* himself.[2]

Emeraulds are affirmed by him, never to be found in the *East-Indies* but in *Perou*,[3] whence they were carried by that trading people to the *Moluccas*, even before *America* was discovered by the Europeans ; and so they come from the Orient ; of much less value than they were formerly, by reason of their commonness. The Author notes, that Emeraulds grow in stones, just as Chrystals, forming a Vein, in which they are by little and little refined and thickened : and that some of them are seen, half white and half green : others, all white : and others all green and perfect.

To Pearls he assigns in the *Orient* four places where they are fished : The Isle of *Baharem*, in the *Persian Gulf* : the Coast of *Arabia Felix*, near the Town of *Catif*, over against *Baharem* : the Isle of Ceylon about Manar : the Isle of Japan. The best at *Ceylon*, but small : the biggest at *Japan*, but uneven. In the *West-Indies* they are fished in the *North-Sea*,

[1] See *ante*, p. 78 of vol. ii.
[2] See *ante*, p. 81 of vol. ii.
[3] See *ante*, p. 82 of vol. ii.

in the Isles of *Marguerite, Cubagua, St. Marthe*: and at *Comana, Comanagote,* near the Continent: and in the *South-Sea,* near *Panama*: which *American* sort, though they are much inferiour to the *Oriental,* in Lustre, yet they far excel them in bigness, amounting sometimes (saith this *Author*) to 42 *Carats.*[1]

In this Relation 'tis mentioned, that sometimes 5 or 6 *Pearls* are found in one Oyster: That *Pearl-fishers* are fed with dry and roasted meat, to give them better breathing: That Pearl-bearing Oysters are not good to eat, being flat and hard of digestion, &c.

As to the *Price* of good *Pearls,* well fashioned, he marketh it, as follows:

Such a Pearl of

Grain	1	*Crowns*	1	*Carats*	4¼	*Crowns*	289
,,	2	,,	4	,,	4½	,,	324
,,	3	,,	9	,,	4¾	,,	361
Carats	1	,,	16	,,	5	,,	400
,,	1¼	,,	25	,,	5¼	,,	441
,,	1½	,,	36	,,	5½	,,	484
,,	1¾	,,	49	,,	5¾	,,	529
,,	2	,,	64	,,	6	,,	576
,,	2¼	,,	81	,,	6¼	,,	625
,,	2½	,,	100	,,	6½	,,	675
,,	2¾	,,	121	,,	6¾	,,	729
,,	3	,,	144	,,	7	,,	784
,,	3¼	,,	160	,,	7¼	,,	841
,,	3½	,,	196	,,	7½	,,	900
,,	3¾	,,	225	,,	7¾	,,	960
,,	4	,,	256	,,	8	,,	1,024

Of Corals, he taketh notice *where* they are fished, and *in what manner.*[2] The *Places, he saith,* to be *Eight*: *Three* upon the Coasts of *Corsica* and *Sardinia, vid.* at *Argueil* (where is the best) *Baza,* and near the *Isle of St. Peter*: one upon the Coast of *Sicily,* near *Drepanum*: *Two* upon the coast of *Africa,* near the *Bastion of France,* and at *Tabarca*: *One* more, upon the Coast of *Catalonia,* at the *Cape* of *Quiers*: And the last, about *Majorca.* Observing, that red Coral is not found, but in the *Mediterranean* alone, where 'tis fished from the beginning of *April* till the end of *July,* employing commonly about 200 Boats. The *manner* of fishing them, is with two big beams of wood, laid crosswise, with a good piece of Lead on the middle, to make it sink, casting about it coarse Hemp, carelessly twisted, and tying this Wood to

[1] See *ante,* pp. 88–9 of vol. ii. [Seemingly '42' here should be 55.]
[2] See *ante,* pp. 104 ff. of vol. ii.

two Ropes, whereof one hangs at the Sterne, the other at the fore-part of the Boat: and so letting this contrivance fall into the Current, along the Rocks, where the Hemp being turned about, and engaged in the Coral, there need sometimes many Boats to draw away the Instrument.

Bezoar, he saith, is not only found in *Golconda*, in the Province of *Renquery*, in the Maw of Goats, whereof some are at times furnisht with a dozen a piece: but also at *Macassar*, in the Isle of *Celebes*, in the body of Apes: bigger than those found in *Golconda*. He mentions, that the people in those parts, to find whether a Goat hath any of those *Bezoar-stones* in its body, do beat his belly with their hands and rub it, till all the stones in the Animal come together, and tell them as you do stones in a bag, &c.[1]

The English Edition of the 'Histoire des Joyaux'.

Since the foregoing pages were printed I have had the good fortune to obtain a copy of a small volume entitled *The History of Jewels, and of the Principal Riches of the East and West, Taken from the Relation of Divers of the most Famous Travellers of our Age; Attended with Fair Discoveries conducing to the Knowledge of the Universe and Trade.*[2] Although not stated to be a translation, the identity of its contents with those of Chappuzeau's *Histoire des Joyaux*, as shown by the above abstract, admits of no doubt that it is the same work in an English dress.

Neither Chappuzeau nor Tavernier are mentioned in it; but the internal evidence conclusively proves that it must have been largely founded on Tavernier's original memoirs. If it be the case that Chappuzeau appropriated these without acknowledgment, it would also appear that the English editor pirated Chappuzeau's book.

A general resemblance of facts alone would not prove Tavernier to have been the original author, but the *History* casually refers to certain dates in connexion with places where we know Tavernier to have been in the same years. Thus on p. 26 reference is made to Mīr Jumla and his occupation at Gandikot in the year 1652, i. e. when Tavernier visited him (see vol. i, p. 227). On p. 23 the depreciated condition of the diamond mines at Kollūr in the year 1660 is referred to, and Tavernier alludes (see *ante*, p. 59) to a falling off in the number of miners since his first visit, and we have otherwise seen that he had visited the mines in 1660 (see vol. i, Introduction, p. xix. On p. 123 the facts stated in reference

[1] For account of Bezoar, see *ante*, pp. 115 ff. of vol. ii.

[2] London, printed by T. N, for Hobart Kemp, &c., 1671, small 8vo, pp. 123.

to bezoar are substantially the same as Tavernier's own personal record (see p. 116 f. *ante*). Tavernier's personal stories about Bohemian rubies (see p. 80 *ante*) and a living worm in dead coral (see p. 106 *ante*) are both in the *History*, pp. 60 and 106.

Short as it is, the *History* contains some facts not given in the *Travels*, but they, for the most part, do not refer to India.

Of facts given in the *History* which are omitted accidentally or are misprinted in the *Travels*, some, as will be seen, confirm corrections and additions already made in the footnotes on preceding pages. On p. 24 of the *History* we find the name of the diamond mine which Tavernier omitted to mention (*ante*, pp. 41 *n*. and 61); it was Gazerpoli (i. e. Gazerpalle or Baswapur, see p. 349 *ante*), two days' journey from Raolconda (i. e. Ramulkota). It is said to have been discovered in 1448, which is not recorded in the *Travels*. On p. 54 Ava is correctly given instead of Siren, where a mistake occurs in the *Travels* (see p. 77 *n*.). On p. 20 there is the same mistake as occurs once in the *Travels* (see p. 57) in reference to the weight of the Mogul's diamond—it being given as 900 carats instead of 900 *ratis*.

The *History* also contains some important facts about the Bengal diamond mines; these have been already noticed (see p. 356).

The value of the rupee is stated in the *History* to be 28 pence, but I venture to think that 27 pence, which has been adopted in the footnotes and in Appendix I, vol. i, is a closer approximation to the value.

The principal discrepancy to be found between the *History* and the *Travels* is in the tables of values of rubies; they are quite discordant.

The concluding paragraph of the *History*—read in the light of this identification of Tavernier as the original author of the work—is of interest. The writer says: 'This is all I have at present collected of what is remarkable in the modern and faithful Relations of our Travellers upon the subject of Jewels, and other rich productions of which I have given a short Account as a platform for a greater work.'

[Owing to administrative changes of recent years, certain tālūks are no longer in the Districts stated above. *E.g.* Palnād tāluk is now in the Guntūr District, and Gutī in that of Anantapur: *v. Imp. Gazetteer of India*, Index, vol. xxv., *svv.*]

INDEX AND GLOSSARY

Words and names in Tavernier's French text are given in italics. D.=Dutch; Fr., French, t., town, and r., river. A few of Ball's identifications of places are retained, though eliminated from the text of his translation by the late Dr. Crooke.

'Abbās (*abas*), a weight for pearls (2·66 troy grs.), i, 332; ii, xxi, 95.
'Abbās II, Shāh of Persia, i, 279.
'Abbāsī (*abassi*), Persian coin (worth 1*s*. 6*d*.) and money of account, i, 20, 330.
Abd-er-Razzāk, quoted, i, 204 *n*.
'Abdullā Khān (Aurangzeb's general), i, 281.
'Abdulla Qutb Shāh (*Abdoul Coutou Cha*), i, 128; ii, 138.
'Abd-ul-Jabbār Beg (the King of Golkonda's general), i, 136, 138.
Āb-i-tāzi (*Betazy*), in Afghanistan, i, 74.
Abū Saīd M'īrzā, Sultān, i, 258.
Abyssinia, ii, 5, 125.
Acerat: see Hazrāhāt.
Achīn or Acheen (for Sumatra), i, 222 *n*.; king of, ii, 147, 234, 247, 248, 273; pepper from, ii, 11; queen of, ii, 249: i, l, li.
Adam, ii, 199.
Adam's fig (the plantain fruit, *Musa sapientum* vel *paradisiaca*) i, 150, 197; ii, 3 *n*., 197, 222.
Addanki (*Adanquige*), i, 212.
'Ādil-Shāhī, dynasty of Bījāpur, i, xliv–v.
Adipati, i, xl.
'Admiral,' for leading ship, i, 250.
'Adoption', of 'Alī 'Ādil Shāh, i, xlv.
Adrican, the *Sieur*, (D.), i, 297.
Adulteration of musk, ii, 113.
Afghāns (*Augans*), i, 75.
Africa, gold in, ii, 123 f.
African Coast, coral from the, ii, 105 *n*.
Aga-sera ? *t*., i, 99.
Agates of Cambay, i, 56.
Agha, Pers., lord or master, i, 68.
Agra from Delhi, i, 85; to Golkonda, i, 121; *maund*, value of, i, 334; palace at, i, 86; to Patna, i, 92 f.; from Surat, i, 54, 72; tombs at, i, 89.
Ahmadābād, i, 59 f.; diamond, the, ii, 98; sale of jewels at, i, 16 *n*., 246, hospital for sick animals at, i, 63; monkeys at, i, 64; indigo from, ii, 7, 9; silks at, ii, 22.
Ahmadnagar, sultanate of, i, xliii.
Aīn-i-Akbarī, the, quoted, i, 7 *n*., 24 *n*., 28 *n*., 31 *n*., 127 *n*., 224 *n*.; ii, 42 *n*.
Ainslie, Dr. (*Materia Medica*), quoted, ii, 17 *n*., 103 *n*., 109 *n*., 122 *n*., 212 *n*.
Ajāib-al-Hind, quoted, i, 61.
Ajītmalt (*Haii-mal*), i, 93.
Ajmīr (*Emir*), i, 278.
Akbar, i, 259; tomb of, i, 91.
'Akbarpur (*Ekberbourg*), i, 99.
Ākil Khān (*Akel Kan*), i, 110, 314.
Akmate, i, 48.
Alacors, sweepers: see Halālkhors.
Ālam Chand (*Alinchan*), i, 94.
Ālampur (*Alpour*), ii, 73.
Albertus (a coin), i, 12.
Alegamma Mudaliyar (*Motiar*), of Ceylon, ii, 148.
Aleppo (*Alep*), i, 7, 161.
Alī (*Haly*), the prophet, i, 298; sect of, i, 130, 139.
'Alībāghān (*Alyboüa*), i, 76.
Aljofar (*aljauhar*, Ar.), seed pearls, ii, 92 *n*., 178 *n*.
Al Katīf (*Catifa*), ii, 85, 88, 94.
Allāhābād (*Halabas*), i, 15, 95.

Almadier (*al ma'dīya*, Ar.), a ferry boat, i, 142 *n*.
Almas, diamond, ii, 76.
Almāsguda ? (*Almaspinde*), ii, 73.
Almonds, bitter, used as money: see *Bādām*.
Aloes, Socotrine, ii, 17.
Aloe-wood (= *lignum aloes*), ii, 17.
Alphabet of the Siamese language, ii, 226.
Alyboüa: see 'Alībāghān.
Amānat Khān (*Menat-kan*), i, 77–8.
Ambād (*Aubar* and ? *Ember*), i, 119, 120.
Ambassadors: see Embassies.
Amber, ii, 108–9, 204, 208.
Ambergris at Mozambique, i, 153; ii, 109 f.
Amboyna Is., in Molucca Sea, i, xliii, 188; ii, 14.
America, cowries sent to, i, 24; early trade with Asia, ii, 82 *n*; pearls found in, ii, 88–9.
Amethyst, oriental, i, 318; ii, 77.
Amīnābād (*Imiabad*), i, 77.
Amsterdam, ii, 319.
A-muck, running, ii, 280, 288.
Ananas, pine-apple, i, 150.
Anantarājupeta (*Ragiapeta*), i, 224.
Andaman Islands, ii, 307 *n*.
Andy (for Chāndia on the Son, which see; also for Handiā, which see).
Animals, wild, at the Cape, ii, 305.
Aniseed (*Fenoüil*), ii, 17.
Ankaī-Tankai (*Enneque-Tenque*, i, 120.
Antelope (*cerfs*), i, 174 *n*.
Antidote to leeches, i, 199 f.
Antivar, for *Dantivar* (see Dāntawarā), i, 31.
Antrī (*Trie*), i, 51.
Ants in Siam, ii, 225.
Anzerūt (= sarcocolla), a gum-resin obtained from *Penaea mucronata*, ii, 17 *n*.
Apes: see Monkeys.
Apples, from Kashmīr, i, 18–19.
Aquera, r., i, 101.
Arabia, Prince of, i, 5; ii, 86; Felix (Yemen, Hyeman), i, 296.
Arakan, King of, i, 105, 292; ii, 147.
Arcalou, cassock, i, 132.
Archbishop of Goa, i, 162–3.
Ardabīl (*Ardeüil*) in Persia, ii, 203.
Ardilière (*Ardilliers*), M. d', ii, 125, 191.
Areca nuts, ii, 274.
Arguerrel (Alghero), coral found at, ii, 104.
Arlet (*harlā* ?) black myrobalan, a drug, ii, 16.
Armenian, an, i, 92; merchants, ii, 204.
Arnebar, the *Sieur*, (D.), ii, 255.
Artemisia maritima, var., ii, 201 *n*.
Artillery drawn by oxen, i, 48.
Arwal on the Son (*Halva-sera*), i, 99.
Asad Khān (*Ast-kan*), i, 116–17.
Āsaf Bin Alī, Arab prince of Norenuaé, ii 86.
Āsaf Khān (brother of Nūr Jahān), i, 266, 270–1; Wazīr, father of Mumtāz Mahall, i, 90.
Ashtā (*Asti*), t., i, 119.
Asia, gold in, ii, 121.
Asiatic troops, Dutch use of, i, xlv.
Asīrgarh (*Asser*), i, 282.
Asoka pillar (*Lāt Bhairon*), i, 98 *n*.
Aspres, ii, 216.
Assam (*Asen* and *Asem*), i, 13; ii, 216.
Assassination by Portuguese, i, 152.
Assayers of gold, ii, 33.
Assegais (*Ageagayes*), ii, 127, 232, 307.
Ast Kan: see Asad Khān.
Asti (Ashtā), i, 119.
Astrologers, Brahman, ii, 192.
Asutinat ? a grain, ii, 17.
Atenara: see Tenara.
Ater-kaira, Hathiyakhera, i, 45–6.
Attock (*Atek*), i, 76–7.
Augans: see Afghāns.
Augustin, Fathers, i, 105, 159, 163–4; church at Goa, i, lvii; de Bordeaux, i, 88.
Aurangābād (Aurenabat), in Deccan, i, 28, 118–19, 120; to Surat, i, 146; old Khajwā,

where Aurangzeb defeated Shujā', i, 94.
Aurangzeb, attacks Golkonda, i, 135 f.; besieges Daman, i, 145; deception practised by, i, 264; defeats Shujā', 286; descent of, i, 258–9; enters Agra, i, 273; embassies to, i, 296–7; discontinues a customary bounty, i, 301 *n.*; Governor of the Deccan, 261; penance by, i, 309; is proclaimed king, i, 284; commencement of reign, i, 295; religion of, ii, 139; seizes Shāh Jahān's jewels, i, 275; seizes Dārā's treasure, i, 274, 317 *n.*; a dervish, i, 264; ii, 139.
Austrian Yellow' diamond, i, 332; ii, 76, 98, 346 f.
Auzerout: see Anzerūt.
Ava, ii, 77, 371.
Avocat Fiscal, the, at Batavia, ii, 251, 256–7, 267, 293, 295, 299.
Azam Khān (*Ast Kan*), i, 116.
Azoo (*Koch Hājo*), ii, 218–19.

Bābur, Sultān, i, 129 *n.*, 259; quoted, 74 *n.*, 333.
Baboo Sarāi (*Bouraky-sera*), i, 96.
Babylone, i, 75.
Bacan (from Pers. *bākand*), a ruby, ii, 77.
Bacha (Pāsha), in Turkey, i, 79.
Bādām (*baden*), nut of almond (*Amygdalus communis*, var. amara), used as money, i, 23 *n.*, 329.
Badelpoura (see Ballabhgarh), i, 85.
Bāftas (cotton cloths), i, 54; (*Bastas*), ii, 5.
Bāghmāra (*Bagamara*), t., i, 104.
Bāglānā? (*Bar–*, *Bergant*, or *Bergam*), i, liv, 31 *n.*, 69 *n.*
Bahādurpur (*Baterpour*), i, 98; battle of, 264.
Bahmani dynasty, i, xliii–iv.
Bahrein (*Bahren*), (pearl fishery), Gulf, i, 154; ii, 84, 94.
Baikunthpur (*Sera Beconcour*), i, 101.
Baker, Aaron, i, lviii.
Baladines (*Baladeira*, Port.), dancing girls, i, 71, 74, 206, 231, 306; ii, 261–2.
Balambour: see Pālanpur.
Balass (*balet*), rubies, i, 303 *n.*, 318; ii, 80, 101; *ballet*, Fr. balais, Diez, *Romance Dy.*, p. 55.
Baldelpoura: see Balledā.
Balkh (*Balch*), in Turkestan, i, 75; ii, 203.
Balki-sera, i, 45.
Ballabhgarh (*Badelpourā*), i, 85.
Balledā (*Baldelpoura*), i, 42.
Ballor (*Balor*), i, 40–1.
Balsara: see Bassora.
Balthasar (a Carmelite monk), ii, 134.
Baltic Sea, amber found in the, ii, 108.
Bamboo (*Bambouc*), stem of *Bambusa arundinacea*, i, 37, 216.
Band (an embankment), i, 121 *n.*
Banda Is., i, xliii; ii, 14.
Bandar Abbās: see Gombroon.
Bandar Sindri (*Bander-Sonnery*), i, 72–3.
Bander, for Shāh Bandar, which see.
Bander-Congo (Kongūn), ii, 85.
Banghy or carrying stick, ii, 180 *n.*
Bangue, Sultān, i, 293–4.
Banian, *Banyan* (*Baniane*), a dealer, in diamonds, i, 5, 48, 49, 60–1, 63, 74, 85, 111; ii, 50; their subtlety, ii, 143.
Baniāna, *v.* Bayānā.
Banjāras (a carrier tribe), i, 33 *n.*
Bankok, in Siam, ii, 226 *n.*
Bantam, in Java, ii, 268 ff., 278–82; pepper from, ii, 11; King of, i, xl, xli, xlii, xliii; English president at, lviii.
Banyan tree (*Ficus Indica*), ii, 154.
Baobhāk Khān: *v.* Budāq Khān.
Baquela: see Waklā.
Baquelpour: see Bhāgalpur.
Bardoli or Panoli (*Barnoly*), t., i, 40, 116.
Barefoot Carmelites, i, 159, 163.
Bargan (? Parthānī), i, 120.
Bargant: see Bāglānā.
Bariabé: see Barikāb.

Barikāb (*Bariabé*), in Afghanistan, i, 76.
Barkī sarāi (*Barqui-sera*), in Gwalior, i, 51.
Bārkūr (*Bakanoor*), on west coast of India, ii, 241.
Barley, i, 226.
Barnā river, near Benares, i, 97 *n.*
Barnoly : see Bardoli.
Baroche : see Broach.
Baroda (*Broudra*), i, 58.
Baroé ? King of, in Africa, ii, 128.
Baroque (an irregularly shaped pearl), ii, 85, 90.
Barundā (*Boronda*), i, 72.
Bassein (*Bassaïn*), i, 142.
Bassora or Basra (*Balsara*), i, 5; ii, 92 ; Dutch at, i, xlvii.
Bastion de France, the, (N. coast of Africa), ii, 104.
Bata (Pate), tin mines, ii, 128.
Batavia, Anglo-Dutch joint Council of Defence at, i, xlii–iii ; siege of, xli ; councils at, ii, 254 ff. ; funeral expenses at, ii, 290 ; Tavernier arrives at, ii, 251.
Baterpour : see Bahādurpur.
Bathing in the Ganges during an eclipse, ii, 192.
Battle of Dharmat between the sons of Shāh Jahān, i, 265.
Baubec Kan ? see Budāq Khān.
Bavarian pearls, ii, 89.
Bayadères : see Baladines.
Bayāna (*Baniana*), in Bhartpur, i, 72–3.
Bazu (a Dutchman), i, xlix ; ii, 99.
Beara (Viārā), i, 116.
Beauce, La, (*Beausse*) in France, i, 47 *n.*
Becchor (? Ranchhor), images placed beside that of Krishna, ii, 189.
Beconcour (Baikunthpur, near Patna), i, 101.
Beer, English, ii, 284.
Begam Sāhib (Jahānārā), i, 15, 261 ; death of, i, 275 ; imprisonment of, i, 274 ; is restored to favour, i, 299 ; saves her father's jewels from destruction, i, 295, 317 *n.* ; present to, i, 113, 115.
Behar or Bihar, prov., i, 264 *n.*, 269 *n.* ; ii, 356.
Bellary District, diamond mines, ii, 349.
Belle Épine : see Vyepu.
Belliporto : see Beypur.
Belloy, M. du, (F.), i, 164–9.
Benares (*Banarou*, *Banarous*, and *Benarez*), i, 96–7 ; ii, 142–3, 179–85.
Bencoolen, i, xliii.
Bengal, diamond mines of, ii, 62, 65, 84, 354–9 ; revenue of, i, 93 ; shellac from, ii, 18.
Berār, i, xliv.
Bergam or *Bargant* : see Bāglānā.
Bernier, M., French physician and author, i, 94, 100, 103, 279 ; quoted, i, 257 *n.*, 265 *n.*, 295 *n.*, 296 *n.*, 305 *n.*, 315 *n.*, 317, 318 *n.*, 329 ; ii, 102 *n.*, 159 *n.*, 175 *n.*, 336 *n.*
Beruzabad : see Firozābād.
Betazy : see Āb-i-tāzī.
Bethico, ? beti-chhot, ii, 196.
Betle (the leaf of *Piper betel*), i, 211, 229 ; ii, 274.
Beypur or Vaipur (*Belli-porto*), i, 187. See Palliport.
Bezoar, ii, 115–19.
Bezwāda (*Bezouar* and *Bezouart*), on the Kistnā river, i, 141, 208–11.
Bhāgnagar or Haidarābād, capital of Golkonda, i, 122–8, 132, 135.
Bhāgalpur (*Baquelpour*), in Behār, i, 102.
Bhāng or Indian hemp, ii, 165.
Bharūndā (*Boronda*), i, 72–3.
Bhutān (*Boutan*), i, 13 ; ii, 201–13 ; King of, i, lvi ; ii, 115.
Bible, Tavernier's, not taken to Goa, i, 163.
Bibliography of the editions of Tavernier's works, i, lx–lxvi.
Bichola (*Bich-ola*), i, 45.
Bicholim (*Bicholly*), i, 46 ; ii, 239.
Bīdar, i, xliii.
Bījāpur (Visapour), properly Vijāyapura, i, 1, 146 ; conquered by

Aurangzeb, i, 130; diamond mines, ii, 352; Kingdom of, i, 129, 146–7; ii, 138, 147; Queen of, i, 148, 171; Sultanate of, i, xliii–iv, xliv–v.
Billiton: see Bordelon.
Bimal (Bhīnmāl), i, 71.
Birds, the, that eat nutmegs, ii, 12.
Birds of Paradise, myth about, ii, 12.
Birgam (Vīrgāon), i, 120.
Bishkhaprā, a lizard, ii, 225 *n*.
Bishop of Beyrout (Beryte), ii, 224, 232; bishops, of Heliopolis (i, lvi), of Megalopolis, ii, 224; of Myra, in Lycia, i, 167.
Bitāra, title of emperors of Majapahit, i, xl.
Bleeding, at Goa, i, 160; a king and queen, i, 242.
Blinding of princes, how caused, i, 268.
Bodies, the burning of dead, ii, 161–2.
Boëte, M., an apothecary, ii, 51, 55.
Bohemian rubies, ii, 80.
Bolāki, *v.* Bulākī.
Bontaing (*Butagne*) Is., ii, 237.
Bonzes (Siamese priests), ii, 230–1.
Borax, ii, 16.
Bordeaux, Augustin de, (F.), i, 88.
Bordelon (P'hattalang) tin mines, ii, 128.
Borgio, Hortensio (a jeweller, I.), i, 315–16; ii, 343.
Borneo, diamond mines in, ii, 67, 359–61; Queen of, ii, 68.
Bouccha (Pers. bughcha, a wallet), ii, 130, 134.
Boullaye le Gouz, M. de La, (F.), i, 168 *n*., 179.
Bouquin-kans (English hats), ii, 207.
Bouraky-sera, i, 96.
Bouro (Buru), ii, 14.
Boutan: see Bhutān.
Boza, coral at, in Sardinia, ii, 104.
Bozan (a Dutch lieutenant), ii, 134.
Brahmans, i, 198; ii, 142–3, 183; the Grand, ii, 177; *pseudo-*, 214.
Bramere, i, 225.
Brampour: see Burhānpur.
Brandenburg, Elector of, ii, 108.
Brazil (*bresil*), wood, ii, 214.
Breton, Sir F., ii, 62, 255.
Bridge over the Jājau, i, 53.
Broach (*Baroche*), i, 54 f., 57.
Broker, *courtier*, ii, 25–6, 30–1; see *Shroff*.
Broncevimont, Brunswick beer, ii, 253.
Broudra: see Baroda.
Budāq Khān (*Baubec Kan*), Persian ambassador to Shāhjahān, i, 298–9.
Buddha (*Baudou*), ii, 200; images of, ii, 227–9.
Buddhism, ii, 200 *n*.
Buffaloes, flesh of, ii, 30.
Bukkur or Bakhar (*Baker*), on the Indus, i, 277.
Bulākī, Prince Dāwar Bakhsh, i, 66, 267–8, 269.
Bundelkhand, diamond mines in, ii, 351.
Burgal (*Parquel*), ii, 73.
Burhānpur (*Brampour*), i, 30, 42–4, 47, 130, 237, 238; Province (? Khāndesh), i, xliii *n*., xliv; ii, 6, 8.
Burial charges at Golkonda, ii, 55.
Burma ruby mines, ii, 361–6.
Burmese amber, ii, 108 *n*.
Burning, the dead, ii, 161–2; of living persons, ii, 162; of widows, ii, 162–9.
Buru: see *Bouro*.

Cabaye: see *Kabā-e-Shāhī*.
Cabouchon, mod. cabochon, a stone polished but uncut. Ball sometimes renders *cabouchon* by 'cut in cabuchon', which is not strictly correct as en cabochon means 'rounded on top and flat on back, without facets;' which is consistent with its derivation: O. E. D., ii, 8.
Caboul: see Kābul.
Cadamtali, r., i, 104.
Cafres, Kaffirs (African), i, 153, 174–5; ii, 124, 126–7, 302–8.
Cairo (*Caïre*), i, 12; ii, 126.
Cakenol, ii, 73.

Calapané, i, 76.
Calico: see Cotton, *Bāftas*, &c.
Calicut, ii, 11.
Callabas: see Kālābāgh.
Calmendar, ii, 4.
Calvetti Bazar (*Calivete*), a quarter of Cochin, i, 190, 194.
Cam, the *Sieur*, (D.), ii, 266: see Cant.
Cambari (Khumbāriā), i, 116.
Cambay (*Cambaya*), i, 56–7; Gulf of, ii, 28.
Cambodia (*Camboya,-e*), ii, 79, 238.
Camels not known in Assam, ii, 220 *n*.
Canapour, Konador, ii, 72–3.
Candahar, Kandahār in Afghanistan, *q. v.*
Candear, Kandahār in Deccan, *q. v.*
Canjare (Khanjar), dagger, i, 82.
Cannanore, i, 193.
Cannon, casting of, i, 231–2. See Guns.
Canol: see Karnūl.
Canol-Candanor (Kandanūl), ii, 72–3.
Cant, the *Sieur*, (D.), death of, ii, 278; Antoni Kaan, i, xlix.
Cantap: see Khandap.
Canton (*Xanton*), ii, 238.
Cape of Good Hope, the, ii, 26–7, 301 ff.; discovery of a bay near the, i, 173; ii, 251.
Cape de Quiers (C. Servère ?), ii, 105.
Capelan: see Kyatpyen, in Burma.
Capuchins, at Goa, i, 159, 186; at Surat, i, 7.
Carabat: see Kārābāgh.
Cararin, Kanarese, i, 152.
Carat (the Florentine, as used by Tavernier, 3·04 troy grs.), i, 332; ii, 346 f.
Caravans of waggons, i, 35.
Caravansarāis, i, 72, 123.
Caravel (Port., a vessel), i, 173; ii, 252.
Cardamom (*Elletaria cardamomum*), i, 149; ii, 10.
Careri, Gemelli, quoted, i, xxxiii.
Carnasarsou, r., Karamnāsā, i, 98.
Carnatic or Karnatik, i, 207, 227.
Caron, the *Sieur*, (D.), i, xlviii *n*., liii; ii, 251, 269, 294.
Carpets made at Surat and Fatehpur Sīkrī, ii, 2.
Carriages in India, i, 36–7.
Carrier tribes, 34.
Casbin: see Kasvīn (in Persia).
Casembrot, the *Sieur*, i, xlix; ii, 129.
Casenbazar: see Kāsimbāzār.
Cassia fistula (*casse*), i, 141 *n*.; ii, 17.
Castes in India, ii, 142–6, 182.
Catalonia (*Catalogne*), in Spain, ii, 105.
Cathay (*Chegathay*), i, 257 *n*.
Catifa: see Al Katīf.
Cattle, draught, i, 35–6.
Caucasus, Mount, i, 3.
Celebes: see Macassar Is.
Ceram (*Seram*), I., ii, 14.
Cesi, M. de, (F.), i, 170.
Ceylon: elephants, i, 221–2; ii, 248; a Portuguese Government, i, 155; King of, ii, 147; precious stones, ii, 77; rubies, ii, 79; sapphires, ii, 366; Tavernier leaves, ii, 250; cinnamon from, ii, 12.
Cha: see Shāh.
Cha Bandar: see Shāh Bandar.
Cha Est Kan: see Shāistā Khān.
Cha Gehan: see Shāh Jahān.
Cha Jenni (Shāh Jahānī) rupees, i, 25.
Chadolki-sera: see Shāhdaura.
Chaez: see *Shāhī*.
Chainpur (*Chenipour*), i, 45.
Chākan (*Choupart*), i, 26, 326.
Chakars, metal quoits, i, 67.
Chakenicouzé (? Shigānu), i, 74.
Chaksū (*Chasou*), i, 72–3.
Chambal river (*Chammel-nadi*), i, 53.
Chanan, r., i, 102.
Chanavas Kan: see Shāh Nawāz Khān.
Chāndā District, diamond mines in, ii, 351.
Chanon, r., i, 101.
Chaour: see Peshāwar.

Chaprā (*Choupar*), near Patna, 100 ; ii, 10.
Charados : see *Sudras*.
Charakhpūjā (swinging festival), ii, 198–9.
Charisafar : see Shahr-i-safā.
Charwā (*Charoüa*), i, 45.
Chasou : see Chaksū.
Château des Bois, M. de, i, 177, 183.
Chativor river, i, 103.
Chaton, 'bezel', ii, 101.
Chaul (*Chaoul*), i, 142.
Chegathay : see Cathay.
Chegos, an arbitrary weight for pearls, ii, 96–7.
Chek : see Shaikh.
Chekaipour : see Shaikhpura.
Chemin, 'way', line of cleavage, ii, 44.
Cheraf : see Shroff.
Cherourabad (Kora Jahānābād), i, 93.
Cheteur, the *Sieur*, Dutch envoy, Steur, i, xlvi–vii ; 231, 241.
Chevres, the *Sieur*, (D.), i, xlvi ; ii, 288.
Chiamay lake (a myth), ii, 217.
Chiidābād (*Sayyidābād*), i, 58.
Children, dealing in diamonds, ii, 48 ; exposure of, ii, 167.
Chilwā, fish, i, 121 *n*.
China, Dutch embassy to, ii, 235–6 ; i, xlv ; gold in, ii, 122 ; King of, ii, 147 ; Russian embassy to, ii, 212–13.
Chinese, at Batavia, ii, 174 ; money, i, 331 ; navigators, i, 204 *n*.
Chintzes (*Chites*), i, 46, 65 ; ii, 4.
Chitpour : see Sidhpur.
Chittagong, i, 106 *n*.
Chōlavaram (*Serravaron*), i, 216.
Chotā Nāgpur, diamonds of, ii, 63 *n*.
Choupart and *Choupar* : see Chākan, Sholāpur, and Chaprā.
Christian converts, a King of Ceylon, ii, 147 ; two sons of Shāh Dāniyāl, i, 270.
Christians in the East, ii, 137 ; Indian, at Madras, i, 216.
Christofle (a French soldier), i, 189.
Cinnamon, bastard (*canelle*), i, 187 ; ii, 12, 15.
Clerc, Walter Clark, captain, (E.) i, 143.
Cloves, ii, 12, 14.
Cobit : see Cubit.
Cobra snake, ii, 121.
Cochin, Dutch Governor of, i, 194 ; King of, i, 193 ; siege of, i, 187–92 ; cinnamon, trade in, ii, 15 ; i, lv.
Cochinchina, King of, ii, 147.
Coco-de-mer, ii, 227 *n*.
Coconut, *coco*, i, 150 ; palm, ii, 65 *n*.
Cocos (or Keeling) Is., ii, 300.
Coetchiel (Kuchhel ?), t., i, 73.
Coffee, ii, 20.
Coins current in India, i, 11–12 ; of Siam, ii, 227 ; value of, i, 327–31.
Cointre (kundur ?), a drug, ii, 17.
Collasar : see Kolāras.
Collision at sea, a, ii, 301.
Coloured stones (precious), ii, 77 ff.
Comets of 1618 and 1665, i, 309 *n*.
Commercial company, establishment of a, in India, ii, 26–8.
Comogote, in West Indies, ii, 89.
Comorin, Cape, storm off, i, 165.
Comouks (a Tartar tribe), i, lvii : ii, 301.
Company for commerce, how to establish a, ii, 26–8.
Condecour (Kandukūr), i, 213.
Condevir (Kondavīdu), i, 212.
Conduite des Hollandois, cited, ii, 107 *n*.
Confession, of crime, i, 234.
Constant, the *Sieur*, (D.), i, xlvii ; ii, 254–67.
Constantinople, i, 167.
Contour, M., a French merchant, ii, 13.
Contraband trading by wives of Dutch officials, ii, 38–9.
Conversion of King of Macassar ii, 240.
Conveyances in India, i, 32 ff.
Copenour (Kopporam ?) t., i, 212.

Copper: coins of India, i, 23; mines (at Singhāna ?), 23 *n.*
Coracles, i, 9, 235; on the Kistnā, 239; ii, 54 *n.*
Coral, red, ii, 104-7, 207.
Cordeliers (monastic order), i, lvii, 159.
Corge (for *korī* = a score), ii, 4.
Coromandel, ii, 168.
Corsa (Khurjā ?) near Agra, ii, 7.
Cosing, for Hassan (see Mīrza Abdul H.) i, 138.
Coss (an Indian measure of distance, about 2 miles), i, 39, 335; short, i, 43, 47.
Costus (*Oupelote*), a drug, ii, 17.
Coteen, t., i, 235.
Cotgia, for *Khoja* (Khwāja), an Armenian's title, i, 92.
Cotki-sera: see Kosi.
Cottapilly (*Cotepali*), i, 235.
Cotton, cloths, ii, 4-6; frauds in, ii, 22-5; spun, ii, 7.
Coulour, a diamond mine: see Kollūr.
Court of Justice, at Golkonda, i, 125; the Mogul's Dīwān, i, 80-2.
Courtesans, i, 58, 127-8.
Courtier, translated 'custodian', i. 314; 'broker', ii, 25-6.
Courua (Kuruvabandalu), a rock near Tripatty, i, 217.
Cousemba, t., i, 45.
Cowries (*cori*), shells, *Cypræa moneta*, used as money, i, 23, 329.
Cows, fines on death of, ii, 169; yielding bezoar, ii, 118.
Cranganore: see Kranganur.
Crapaten: see Kareputtun.
Crease (*cric*), a dagger, ii, 280.
Crime on Dutch fleet, ii, 316.
Criminals tried summarily, i, 232.
Croc, Croke, the *Sieur*, ii, 234, 249-50; ? Paulus Krook, i, xlix-l.
Crocodiles in the Ganges, i, 103.
Croisart (a Genoese coin worth 6*s.* 6*d.*), i, 157 *n.*, 328.
Crore or *karor* = 100 *lakhs*, i, 24.
Crusado (a Portuguese coin), i, 328.
Crystal, rock, vessels of, i, 309.
Cubagua, in the Antilles, ii, 88.
Cubit (a measure of length), i, 335; ii, 1-2.
Culverin, a gun, i, 126.
Cumana, in the Antilles, ii, 88.
Cumbum (*Kaman*), t., i, 236.
Cumin (seed), ii, 16.
Cure, a marvellous, ii, 249.
Custom dues in India, i, 7 ff.
Cutch: see *Kutch*.
Cutch or Kachchh, prov., i, 327 *n.*

Dābhol or Dabul (*Daboul*), t., i, 142, 146.
Dabir-pinta (Debir Lake ?), t., i, 240.
Dacca, i, 105, 107.
Dakijé (Zakkepalli-Gūdūr), t., i, 213.
Dākka (*Taka*), in Afghānistān, i, 76.
Damān, besieged by Aurangzeb, i, 144; Governor of, i, 65; route, i, 142.
Damārapād diamond mine, ii, 61 *n.*
Damascus blades, i, 127 *n.*
Damne (? Dama Archipelago), I., ii, 14; i, lvi.
Dampour, t., i, 103.
Dāntawārā (*Dantiuar* or *Antivar*), i, 31, 58, 69, 71, 88.
Dārā Shikoh, capture of, i, 281; death of, i, 283; defeat of, i, 264-6; flight of, i, 276 ff.; government of, i, 261.
Dārogha (*Deroga*), prefect or superintendent of police, &c., i, 7, 44, 96, 125, 127.
Daryā-i-nūr, the, diamond, ii, 337, 343.
Dāūdnagar (*Daoud-nagar sera*), i, 99.
Daulatābād (*Dulteabat*), Ahmadnagar sultanate, i, xliii; 28; 116-18, 130, 326.
Dauphin (*Daufine*), fort in Madagascar, ii, 27.
Daurāhī (*Sera-dourai*), i, 77-8.
Dāwar Bakhsh, Prince, nicknamed Bulākī, i, 67; see Bulākī.
Dehkhān (*Sera-Dakan*), i, 77-8.
Deity, Idolaters' belief in the, ii, 149 ff.

Delegore (Ligor), tin mines, ii, 128.
Delft, in Holland, ii, 319.
Delhi (*Dehly*), i, 1, 78.
Demi-pique, i, 81.
Denier, a French money of account, i, 327.
Denier, a French weight, i, 333.
Denouserin : see Tenasserim.
Deogan, t., i, 120 ; also Deogāon.
Deogāon (*Disgaon*), i, 116.
Depilatories, i, 77 ; ii, 186.
D'Eriia, *Sera*, Sarāi Daryā, i, 101.
Dervishes (*Dervichs* and *Deruichs*), i, 44, 66–8 ; ii, 280.
Dhanāka of Hiuen Thsiang, i, 209.
Dharmat, battle of, i, 265 *n*.
Dharnā, sitting, ii, 173.
Dholpur (*Dolpoura*), i, 53.
Diamond, Orloff, ii, 337, 341 ; Austrian Yellow, i, 332 ; ii, 98, 346 f. ; Bābur's, ii, 332 ; in Koel river, Bengal, ii, 65 ; 'Blue,' ii, 100 *n*. ; cutting, ii, 44 ; Florentine, ii, 76, 98, 346 f. ; *Koh-i-nūr*, ii, 331–46 ; Mātan, ii, 361 ; merchants, ii, 47 f. ; mines, ii, 41–4 ; in Bengal, ii, 62 f., 354–9 ; in Borneo, ii, 359–61 ; in India, list of, ii, 348 ff. ; in Kadapa (Cuddapah) District, ii, 349 ; of Kollur, ii, 56, 69, 99 ; revisited in 1653, i, 247 ; worked by Mir Jumlā, i, 230 ; miners, pay of, ii, 46 ; mining, ii, 59–61 ; the Great Mogul's, i, 315 ; ii, 75, 97 ff. ; at Kollūr—discovery of, ii, 57, 331–43 ; terms for, ii, 76 ; the Grand Duke of Tuscany's, ii, 75–6, 98, 346–8 ; weights, ii, 69–70 ; i, lviii.
Diamonds, in Borneo, ii, 67, 359–61 ; brittle, ii, 61 ; colours of, ii, 58 ; famous, ii, 97 ff. ; described by Garcia da Orta, ii, 333 ; with green crust, ii, 61 ; Jesuits trade in, ii, 239 ; sold to King of France, ii, 100, Pl. ; to Dom Phil. de Mascarenhas, i, 182 ; Mir Jumlā's, i, 230 ; values of, ii, 73–4 ; private trade in, i, 248 ; swallowing, ii, 46 ; weights of, mentioned by Tavernier, ii, 347–8.
Dilod (*Telor*), i, 46.
Dirauril : see Tarāwarī.
Directors of the Dutch Company, ii 318, 323.
Disease, images offered on cure of, i, 210 ; ii, 178.
Disgaon : see Deogāon.
Distance, measures of, i, 39, 335.
Diu, i, 5, 249 ; ii, 28–30.
Divan (Dīwān), the, i, 80–3 ; a, projecting, i, 88–9.
Diving for pearls, ii, 92 ff.
Dog's flesh eaten in Assam, ii, 221.
Dol-Medan, i, 41.
Dolpoura : see Dholpur.
Dom tribe, ii, 65 *n*.
Dominicans, i, 159, 163.
Donapour, t., i, 103.
Dongri or Dungri (*Dongry*), near Narwar, i, 49.
D'Orléans, M. le Duc, (F.), ii, 260.
Douloudia, i, 103.
Dour-ay (? Duraiba), i, 45.
Drinking at Batavia, ii, 253.
Drugs, African, ii, 127 ; Indian, ii, 16–17.
Ducat (a coin), i, 12, 328.
Dung, grain in cow's, a sacred food, i, 226 ; ii, 164.
Dūpād (*Doupar*), i, 239.
Duraibā (*Dour-ay*), i, 46.
Durgāvatī river (? *Saode-sou*), i, 98.
Durian (*durion*), fruit, ii, 225.
Dutch, the, capture English ship, ii, 288–9 ; at Chaprā, i, 100 ; colonists at the Cape, ii, 305–6 ; commander in Ceylon, i, 206 ; blockade Goa, i, 149 ; at Dacca, i, 105 ; embassy to China, ii, 235 f. ; pay bills, ii, 291–8 ; 323 f. ; perfidy of, ii, 247 f. ; prisoners to Javanese, ii, 289 ; treacheries of, ii, 272 ; vessels of war, i, 249 ; war with Java, ii, 286–9 ; frauds by officials, ii, 257 ff. ; supremacy in Eastern Seas, i, xlv–vi.

Ear-piercing. ii, 223.
Ecclesiastics at Goa, i, 159.
Eclipse in 1666, an, ii, 192.
Écu (or white crown = 4s. 6d.), i, 22, 327.
Élektron (shellac), ii, 18 *n*.
Elephants, African, i, 174, 221–2; ii, 247–8; age of, i, 223; bathing of, i, 243; Ceylon, i, 221–2; ii, 248; hunting of, i, 218–19; iconoclastic, i, 48; mischief done by, i, 72; the Mogul's, i, 223–4, 307; Sumatran, ii, 248 *n*., 273; tusks used for palisades, i, 221; ii, 127; in war, use of, 145, 223–4; where obtained, i, 221; white, ii, 228; as tribute, ii, 206.
Eligada (Lingalla), ii, 73.
El-Katīf (*Catifa*), in Persian Gulf, ii, 85, 88, 94.
Ell (cubit), the, of Agra, i, 32; of Surat, ii, 1–2.
Ellias (Gilolo), I., ii, 14.
Embassies, to Aurangzeb, i, 296–7; from Aurangzeb to Persia, i, 297; from Achīn to Batavia, ii, 249; Dutch to China, ii, 235 ff. (see China); Macassar to Batavia, ii, 237–8.
Ember (Ambād), i, 120.
Emelipata (Vemulakota), i, 236.
Emeralds, Egyptian, ii, 81; 'oriental', 82; Peruvian, ii, 82; Siberian, ii, 82 *n*.
Emir (Ajmer), i, 278.
Encuse (Enkhuizen), in Holland, ii, 319.
English, beer at Batavia, ii, 284–5; at Broach, i, 54; in Ceylon, ii, 253; Dutch naval engagement with, i, 250–3; frauds by the, i, 10–11; injured by the Dutch, ii, 271–2; officials' salaries, ii, 37 *n*.; President at Madras, 1652, i, 215-16; ship captured by the Dutch, ii, 288; in Surat, ii, 129 ff.
Englishman executed in Macassar, ii, 234.
Englishman's revenge, an, i, 9–10.
Éphraïm, Father, Capuchin, i, 132–3, 168, 176–86, 202, 215.
Erengābād (Aurangābād), i, 123.
Ergvga river, i, 101.
Estain, tin, ii, 197.
Estanja, i, 93.
Etāwa (*Estanja*), i, 93.
Eunuchs, tombs of, i, 89, 91.
Examination of passengers from Batavia, ii, 299.
'Exchange' in India, i, 7 ff., 30.

Fakīr, a, running *a-muck*, ii, 281.
Fakirs (devotees and professional beggars), i, 66–8, 312; ii, 139–41, 152–8.
Fanam, *Fano* (an Indian coin), i, 329; ii, 92.
Farah (*Farat*), i, 73.
Fatehpur (*Faty-ābād*), i, 77.
Fatehpur Sīkrī (*Vettapour*), i, 72–3; carpets made at, ii, 2.
Fatwā river i, 101 *n*.
Faty-ābād: see Fatehpur.
Faure, the *Sieur*, (D.), ii, 254–5; i, xlix.
Fāzil Khān, i, 273.
Females, descent through, ii, 69.
Ferdinand, E., (a Jew), ii, 62.
Festival of the Great Mogul, i, 301–3.
Fidalgos of the Cape of Good Hope, i, 151.
Fig: see Adam's fig.
Fines on death of cows, ii, 169, 199.
Fingers, cracking the, ii, 196.
Fire-pots used by pirates, i, 143.
Fīrozābād (*Beruzabad*), i, 93.
Fish diet, i, 61.
Fish's skin, a, valued in Japan, ii, 107.
Florentine, diamond (= Austrian Yellow and Grand Duke of Tuscany's), ii, 76, 98, 346; carat, ii, 347.
Flushing (*Flessingue*), ii, 317.
Fontainebleau, i, 122; ii, 43.
Formalities at departure of ships from Batavia, ii, 299.
Formosa, Dutch capture of, from Spain, i, xlvi, lv; English fort at, ii, 271; gold in, ii, 122.

Franks (*Francs* and *Franguis*, &c.), *i.e.* Europeans, i, 5, 6, 49, 70, 87, 107, 171, 178, 228, 231 ; ii, 42, 49, 52, 134, 234, 261.
Frauds by companies' officers, ii, 35–7 ; on the customs, i, 9 ; by Dutch officials, ii, 257–9, 266 ; in manufactures, ii, 21–6 ; in musk trade, ii, 113–14.
Frederick, Caesar, ii, 42 *n.* ; cited, ii, 76 *n.*
Fremlin (or Frembling), Mr. E., an English President, i, 144 ; ii, 62, 128.
French, company of commerce, a, ii, 270 ; measures of length, i, 334 ; money, i, 327–8 ; traders, ii, 270 ; vessels burnt by the Dutch, ii, 271 ; weights, i, 331 ; adventurers, in Dutch service, i, li.
Fruits, Indian, i, 150.
Funeral ceremonies in Assam, ii, 219 ; expenses at Batavia, ii, 290–1 ; ceremonies in Siam, ii, 230. See Burning of the dead, Suttee, &c.
Furs from Bhutān, ii, 202.

Galata, Franciscans of, i, 167.
Galeass (a kind of galley, an armed boat), i, 154.
Galiote (*galeota*, Port. ; jollyboat, English), i, 156.
Gandak river (*Gandet*), i, 101.
Gandarom (Gandavaram ?), i, 213.
Gandikota, i, 208, 227, 228, 231, 235 ; (*Indecote*), ii, 189.
Ganges canal, ii, 3 ; river, i, 94, 98 ; voyage on the, 102–4 ; water, ii, 180, 198.
Gani for *Kān-i*, used as a name : see Kollūr, i, 139 ; ii, 56.
Gannaur (*Guienaour*), i, 78.
Gansargavī : see *Guisemner*.
Gardens, elevated, at Golkonda, i, 124.
Gargan, i, 120.
Gate (? ghāt), i, 49.
Gau (an Indian measure of distance), i, 330.
Gauges (Gogo or Gogha), ii, 29.
Gāzulamandiyam (*Gazel*), i, 217.
Gemena river : see Jumna.
'General', Tavernier's use of title, i, xlviii.
Gentiles or Idolaters, religion of, ii, 141.
Geroul, i, 120.
Gesselin, for D. *gijzelen*, to arrest, imprison, especially for debt, ii, 264.
Ghāt (*gate*), a pass, i, 49 *n.*
Ghunchi (seed of *Abrus precatorius*), the *rati*, i, 332–3.
Gianabad (Jahānābād ?), west of Kora, i, 93.
Gilolo (*Ellias*), I., ii, 14.
Ginger (the root), ii, 10–11.
Gingi (*Guinchy*) fort, in Madras, i, 201.
Girballi, i, 119.
Goa, the Archbishop of, ii, 120 ; Tavernier's stay at, i, 161 f. ; bar at, i, 149 ; to Bijapur, i, 146; blockades of, by the Dutch, i, 149 ; to Golkonda *via* Bijapur, i, 142 ; Inquisition at, i, 162, 167 ; magnificence at, i, 150–2 ; to Masulipatam, i, 187 ; offices in, i, 155 ; Tavernier's visits to, i, 145–6 ; trade in precious stones, &c., ii, 95.
Goats yielding bezoar, ii, 116–17, 370.
Godāvari District diamond mines, ii, 350.
Godorme : see Kottāyam.
Gogeron (Goriganūr ?), i, 227.
Gogo (*les Gauges*), ii, 29.
Goître, in Tipperah, ii, 215 ; in Assam, ii, 223.
Gold, absorption of, in India, ii, 159 ; in Africa, ii, 123 f. ; in Asia, ii, 121–3 ; in Assam, ii, 216 *n.*, 221, 223 f ; assays of, ii, 33 *n.* ; in China, ii, 122 ; duty on, i, 7 ; ii, 21 ; in Formosa, ii, 122 ; in Japan, ii, 122 ; nugget, ii, 250 ; in Tipperah, ii, 215–16 ; a tree of, ii, 126 ; how weighed, i, 12 f.
Golden rupees (*mohurs*), i, 13 ; value of, i, 15 f. ; virtue of, i, 14.

Golkonda, to Aurangābād, i, 146; a large diamond at, ii, 98; diamond mines, ii, 352 ff.; King of, i, 183, 186, 207; ii, 138, 147; kingdom of, i, ch. x, 121 ff.; to Kollūr, ii, 73; to Masulipatam, i, ch. xi, 139 ff.; siege of, i, 135 f. peace with, celebrated, i, 137; to Ramalakota, ii, 72; revisited in 1653, i, 247; Tavernier's arrival at, i, 204; Sultanate of i, xliii–iv.
Gombroon (*Gomron*), i, 3, 172 *n.*, 187; ii, 128, 260–1; Dutch Commandery at, i, xlvii.
Good Hope: see Cape of Good Hope.
Goraghāt, ii, 217.
Gorakhpur (*Gorrochepour*), ii, 202.
Gos or *gau* = 8 miles, i, 39, 142, 335.
Goudera-sou, r., Kudrā, i, 98.
Goulapali (Gollapalle ?), i, 226.
Grand Mosque at Jahānābād, i, 83.
Grand Seigneur, the (of Turkey), i, 169–70.
Grapes and vines in Assam, ii, 221.
Great Mughal, the, i, 301 ff.: see under special subjects.
Great Mughal's diamond: see Diamonds; elephants: see Elephants; &c., &c.
Grenapuis (Gunongapi), ii, 14.
Gros, French weight = 60.285 grs. troy, i, 21, 331.
Guard of nobles at Golkonda, i, 126.
Gudimitta (*Goremeda*), i, 236.
Guienaour: see Gannaur.
Guilder (a Dutch coin), i, 328; ii, 292, 320.
Guisemner (Gansargavī ?), i, 119.
Gujarāt (*Guzerate*), i, 22, 23.
Gulden (German coins), i, 328.
Gum-lac (*gomme laque*), ii, 16.
Gunners, Frank, i, 117–18, 231; European, 244.
Gunongapi (*Grenapuis*), ii, 14.
Gunpowder, ii, 210; invention of, ii, 217.
Guns, invention of, ii, 217; in Bhutān, ii, 210.
Gwalior, fort and town, i, 51–2; prison, i, 52, 267.

Haidarābād: see Bhāgnagar.
Haii-mal: see Ajītmall.
Halabas: see Allāhābād.
Halālkhors (*Alacors*), outcasts, ii, 146.
Halva-sera: see Arwāl.
Hamadān, in Persia, i, 130.
Handiā (Andy), i, 45.
Hans, Captain, (D.), ii, 129.
Hanumān (the monkey god), ii, 151.
Hartman, the *Sieur*, (D.), ii, 132.
Hasan and Husain, ii, 139.
Hāth or cubit of India, ii, 1 *n.*
Hatiyākherā (*Ater-kaira*), i, 46.
Hayātnagar (Jatenagar), in Golkonda, i, 141.
Hazrāhāt (*Acerat*), t., i, 103, 107.
Heat, greatest in the world, i, 5; at Agra, i, 86.
Herbs, medicinal, i, 240.
Hercules, M., (a Swede), i, 206.
Herring fishers, Dutch, ii, 316.
Highroads in India, i, 233–4.
Hillmen, dress and costume of, ii, 207–8.
Hindaun (*Hindoo*), i, 72–3; (*Indoua*), ii, 7.
Hindustān, extent of, i, 257 *n.*; western frontier of, i, 74; wars in, i, 257 ff.
Hingānī (*Nagouni* ?), i, 121.
Histoire, de la Conduite des Hollandois, &c., quoted, i, xviii; ii, 38 *n.*; *générale des Voyages*, quoted, i, 200 *n.*; ii, 56 *n.*; *des Joyaux*, ii, 366 ff.
Holcora, in Golkonda, i, 240.
Holland, Tavernier's arrival in, ii, 316 f.
Hook-swinging, ii, 198.
Hope diamond, ii, 100 *n.*
Hormuz (*Ormus*), Dutch factory at, ii, 320; Governor of, i, 154; a pearl at, ii, 85–6; occupied by Portuguese, i, 155; to Masulipatam, i, 203; to Surat, i, 3–4, 5.
Horne (Hoorn), in Holland, ii, 319.
Horse, a, presented to Tavernier, i, 17–18, 246–7; the wooden, an

instrument of torture, i, 194; food of, in India, i, 84, i, 226; Hill ponies, ii, 205. 206–7; horses, the Mogul's, i, 79, 306; present of, from Persia, i, 205, 208; prices of, i, 307.
Hospital, at Goa, i, 160; for sick animals, i, 63–4.
Hottentots, ii, 301.
Hugli (*Ogouli*), i, 103, 108–9.
Humāyūn (son of Bābur), i, 259.
Hungary, rubies and opals in, ii, 80.
Hustaart, Jacob, i, xlviii.

Ibn Batuta, cited, ii, 156 *n.*
Ibrāhīm Lodī, i, 86 *n.*
Iceland, ii, 314.
Ichhāwar (*Ichavour*), i, 45–6.
Idols, Indian, ii, 149; made in Bohemia, ii, 204 *n.*; at Jagganāth, ii, 175–6; in Siam, ii, 228–9; of unmeltable metal, i, 232; at Bezwādā, i, 209.
Idolaters, belief as to soul, ii, ch. vii, 158 ff.; customs of the, ii, ch. xiv, 192 ff.
Imenhect ? Prince of Muscat, ii, 86.
Imiabad: see Amīnābād.
Incense, ii, 16.
Indecote (Gandikota), ii, 189.
Indelvai, i, 120; (Yedalvoi), i, 127 *n.*
India House, the, at Middelburg, ii, 319.
Indian coins, i, 329–30; measures of length, i, 334–5; weights, i, 332–4.
Indians, religion of the, ii, 141 ff., 149 ff.
Indigo, i, 56; ii, 7–9.
Indore (? Indūr), i, 127 *n.*
Indoua (Hindaun), ii, 7.
Indūr (*Indove*), i, 120.
Indus river (*Indou*), i, 9, 76 *n.*
Infants, exposure of, ii, 167.
Ingagne Is., ii, 251.
Inquisition at Goa, the, i, 162–3, 164–9, 184.
Inquisitor, the, i, 158, 162–3, 178.
Iri (hīra), diamond, ii, 76.
26 Irish captain, an, i, 180.

Iron, at Haidarābād, i, 127 *n.*, mines in Asam, ii, 220, 222.
Ispahān, i, 171–2; to Agra, i, 3, 73 f.
Italian coins, i, 328.
Ivory from West Indies ? i, 223.

Jacobus (a coin worth 25*s.*), i, 12.
Ja'far Khān (*Giafer Kan*), i, 112, 114–15, 310, 312, 319; ii, 100–1.
Jagannāth, ii, 175–9.
Jagdīs Sarāi (*Yakedil-sera*), i, 96.
Jahānābād, i, 78–9, 114, 275.
Jahānārā, the Grand Begam, i, 113: see Begam Sāhib.
Jahāngir, marriage to Nūr Jahān, i, 89 *n.*; tomb, of, 91.
Jāi Singh, Rājā (*Jesseing*), i, 118, 278; his college at Benares, ii, 183.
Jājau (*Iagou*), on the Utangan river, i, 53.
Jālor (*Chalaour*), i, 71.
Jāmi' Masjid at Golkonda, i, 124.
Jang Bahādur, ii, 205 *n.*, 206 *n.*
Janjirā (*Zangira*), Jahāngirhā, i, 101.
Japan, gold in, ii, 121–2; King of, ii, 147; pearls, ii, 88, 90; Japanese esteem for coral, ii, 106–7; Dutch oust Portuguese from, i, xlvi.
Japara (*Japar*), King of, ii, 286–9.
Jardin, M. Louis du, (F.), i, 206, 215, 245, 269; ii, 90, 125 *n.*
Jask (*Jasque*), Cape, ii, 92.
Jaswant Singh (*Jessomseing*), i, 278, 281, 290–1; ii, 145 *n.*
Jatenagar (Hayātnagar), i, 140.
Jatrapour (Jātrapur), i, 104.
Java, Dutch war with, ii, 284–9; King of, ii, 147; Javanese captured by the Dutch, ii, 288; soldiers, ii, 289.
Jesuit Fathers, i, 91–2, 159; plots against Dutch, ii, 235–6; in Macassar, ii, 236; as fakīrs, 238–9; trade in diamonds, ii, 240.
Jewels, the Great Mogul's purchases, i, 111, 112; shown to Tavernier, 314–19; sale of, to

Shāistā Khān, i, 15 f., 26 f., 106, 245, 326 ; to Ja'far Khān, i, 112.
Jīwan Khān, Malik, (*Gion Kan*), i, 280–2.
Joyaux, Histoire des, quoted, ii, 367.
Jugglers at Broach, i, 54–5.
Jullundur : see Dehkhān.
Jumna river (*Gemna* and *Gemené*), i, 78, 85, 86, 95.

Kabīr, saint the, ii, 179.
Kābul (capital of Afghānistān), i, 73–6 ; ii, 203.
Kachnagana : see Cutch.
Kachnor (*Kasariki-sera*), i, 47.
Kadapa (Cuddapah) District diamond mines, ii, 349.
Kadioue (Khajwā), i, 78, 115 *n*.
Kajāwā (*cajavas*), camel panniers, i, 117.
Kākāni (*Kah Kaly*), i, 141, 212.
Kakeri (Karkhelī ?), i, 120.
Kālābāgh (*Callabas*), i, 47–8.
Kālā ki sarāi (*Calapané*), i, 76.
Kalāt-i-Ghilzāī (*Zelaté*), i, 74.
Kalīndri r. (? *Mart nadi*), i, 102.
Kalyān, t., in Bombay, ii, 160.
Kaman : see Kumban.
Kāmrūp (*Kemmerouf*), ii, 222.
Kanarese (*Canarins*), i, 152.
Kandahār (*Candahar*), in Afghānistān, i, 4 ; to Agra, 73 ; to Kābul, i, 75.
Kandahār or Kandhār (*Candear*), in the Deccan, i, 120–1.
Kandanūl (*Canol-Candanor*), ii, 72–3.
Kandukūr (*Condecour*), i, 213.
Kandy, i, 1 ; King of, ii, 247.
Kaoa river, i, 101.
Kaper, ii, 73.
Kārābāgh (*Carabat*), i, 74.
Karamnāsā river (*Carnasar-sou*), i, 98.
Kareputtun (*Crapaten*), i, 147, 148.
Kariālā or Sarāī Ālamgīr (*Keraly*), i, 77.
Karkhelī (*Kakeri*). i, 119–20.
Karnāl (*Sera-Crindal*), i, 78.
Karnūl or Kurnool (*Canol*), ii, 73 ; diamond mines of, ii, 349.
Karor (*crore*) = 10,000,000, i, 24.
Kārwār, i, lv.
Kasariki-sera : see Kachnor.
Kashmīr (*Kachemir*), i, 19.
Kasiatta (*Qāzīhāt*), t., i, 104.
Kāsimbāzār (*Casenbazar*), i, 103, 106–7, 109 ; ii, 2, 3.
Kasvīn (*Casbin*), in Persia, ii, 218.
Katare (Kosi ?) river, i, 102.
Katīf (for Catifa) : see Al Katīf.
Kāyal, i, lv.
Kāzi (*Cadi*), ii, 202 ; the Grand, i, 284–5 ; -hāt : see Qāzīhāt.
Keraly (Kariālā), i, 76–7.
Kerkoa, or the Begum's *Caravansarāī*, i, 41.
Kerman, ii, 209.
Khaibar ? (*Kiemry*), i, 76.
Khajwā, Khajuhā, (*Kadioue*), i, 78 ; renamed Aurangābād, i, 94 *n*.
Khān, of Gombroon, the, ii, 260 ff. of Hormuz, ii, 87.
Khandap (*Cantap*), i, 71.
Khanjar (*canjare*), a dagger, i, 82, 246 ; ii, 281.
Khicharī (*Quicheri*), rice and spices, i, 225, 311.
Khil'at or *Killut* (*Calaat*), a robe of honour, i, 18, 80, 115, 132, 246.
Khumbaria (*Cambari*), t., i, 116.
Khurjā (*Corsa*), ii, 7.
Khurram, Sultān, i, 116, 259, 268.
Khurramābād ? of A.S. (*Gourmabad*), i, 98.
Khusrū (son of Jahāngīr), i, 259, 267 *n*.
Kiemry : see Khaibar.
King, the, of Bhutān, ii, 210–12 ; of France, ii, 325 ; of Golkonda, i, 128 ff. ; ii, 138 ; Mogul's, the, court, i, 101 ; palace, i, 97 ; throne, i, 99, 381, 387 : see Mogul.
Kings, the idolatrous, of Asia, ii, 147–9.
Kistnā District, diamond mines, ii, 350–1.
Kistnā river, i, 141 *n*., 211 ; ii, 72–3 *n* : see Krishnā.
Koch Hājo (*Azoo*), ii, 218–19.

Koel (*Gouel*) river, in Bengal, ii, 65, 66 *n.*, 355.
Koh-i-Nūr, the, i, lviii ; ii, 46 *n.*, 331–46.
Kolāras (*Collasar*), i, 48.
Kollūr (*Coulour*), diamond mine, i, 139 *n.*, 140–1, 211 ; ii, 56–8, 69–70, 73, 99.
Kondavīdu or Kondavīr (*Condevir*), i, 212.
Kongūn (*Bander-Congo* ?), in Persian Gulf, ii, 85.
Kora Jahānābād (*Cherourabad*), i, 93.
Korān, the, ii, 137, 276.
Kosī (*Çotki-sera*), i, 85.
Kottāyam (*Godorme*), i, 196.
Kotwāl (*Couteval*), Provost, i, 92.
Koyalconda ? (*Cakenol*), ii, 72–3.
Krānganur or Kodangalūr (*Cranganore*), i, 187, 189.
Krishnā (Kistnā), r., i, xliv.
Kuchhel (*Coëtchiel*), i, 72–3.
Kudrā river (*Goudera-sou*), i, 98.
Kumbam (*Kaman*), i, 236.
Kūmūks : see *Comouks*.
Kunwārī river, i, 52–3 ; sarā (*Quariquisera*), *ib.*
Kutab (Qutb) Shāh, King of Golkonda, i, 128 ; ii, 138.
Kutch, resin of *Acacia catechu*, ii, 195.
Kyatpyen (*Capelan*), ii, 77, 361.

Lac : see Shellac.
Lacuaron : see *Lakabaron*.
Ladies, bath at Ispahan, i, 171–2 ; contraband trading by, ii, 38 ; Dutch, entertained by Tavernier, i, 248.
Ladona : see Ludānā.
Lahore, i, 77, 119 (?), 267, 272, 276.
Lakabaron, i, 141.
Lākh or *Lac* (*lekke*) = 100,000 rupees, i, 24, 33.
Lakhya river (*Laquia*), i, 104.
Lakkawurrum (*Lakabaron*), i, 141.
Lama, the Grand, ii, 211 *n.*
Lambert, M., Bishop of Beyrout, ii, 233.
Lan, Pitre de, a Dutch surgeon, i, 241–3.
Lapis Lazuli, in Badakhshān, ii, 123 *n.*
Lasonā (*Lesona*), i, 119.
Lasques (flat diamonds), i, 230.
Lasūr (*Lqzour*), i, 120.
Lāt Bhairon (Asoka's pillar at Benares), i, 98.
Lawali ? (*Nuali*), i, 72.
Lead mines in Assam, ii, 220, 222.
Lead pencils, i, 184.
Leagues (Fr. *lieue*), i, 47, 56, 334–5.
Leaves, used as plates, ii, 60, 177.
Leeches, i, 198–200.
Leper, a, at Goa, i, 163–4.
L'Escot, M., (F.), ii, 239, 359.
Les Provinces (a ship), ii, 300.
Leton, brass, ii, 197.
Letter, from Tavernier to the General at Batavia, ii, 129 : letter-carriers, i, 233 ; letters between Shāistā Khān and Tavernier, i, 320–5.
Ligor (*Delegore*), ii, 128.
Lime (coral or shell), i, 35 *n.*
Lingalla (*Eligada*), ii, 73.
Lions, tame, i, 66 ; in Burma ? ii, 77 ; in Siam ?, ii, 224.
Liquorice, ii, 17.
Livre, French weight, i, 331 ; money of account, i, 327–8.
Lizard, a poisonous, ii, 225.
Lodī, Ibrāhīm, i, 86 *n.*
Lohārdāga diamond mines, ii, 351.
Lohwān (*Nuali*), i, 72–3.
Lonton (*Lontour*), I., ii, 14.
Louis XIV, i, xxx.
Louis d'or, value of the, i, 19, 327.
Louys de Bar-sūr-Seine, Maître, i, 169.
Ludānā (*Ladona*), i, 72–3.

Maatsuiker, Johan, i, xlvii–viii ; lviii.
Macao, a gamblers' resort, i, 166 ; Jesuits' trade with, ii, 236 ; Dutch designs on, ii, 237–8.
Macassar in the Celebes, ii, 13–14, 233 ff. ; King of, ii, 147, 236–7 ; Dutch attack on, i, li.
Mace, ii, 12, 14.
Mācherla (*Macheli*), i, 239.
Madagascar (*St. Laurens*), i, 112.

Madras, i, 176, 180–1, 197, 201–2, 214; diamond mines, ii, 349–51: see also St. Thomé.
Madsuere or Masudere (D.), Governor of Galle,i i, 246: see Maatsuiker.
Madura, i. 198 *n.*
Maestricht, the (a ship), i, 148; ii, 301.
Magalki-sera, Mughal Sarāī, i. 47.
Magic, the Brahmans', ii, 193–4.
Mahmūdī (*mamoudi*), Persian coin, worth from 9*d.* to 1*s.*, i, 21–2, 23, 330.
Mailacheru (*Mellaserou*), ii, 73.
Maillé, M. Claude, of Bourges, i, 95, 96, 228, 231, 241 *n.*
Majorca (*Majorque*), ii, 105.
Makrānā marble quarries, i, 119 *n.*
Malabaris (chiefly pirates), i, 31, 142–4, 156, 161, 165, 179, 188, 197; ii, 93, 200.
Malacca, a Portuguese government of, i, 154; for Borneo, ii, 67–8 *n*; Straits of, i, xlii; Dutch capture, xlvi.
Malāwaram, diamond mines at, ii, 61 *n.*
Malay language, ii, 268.
Malda (*Malde*), in Bengal, i, 110 *n.*; ii, 198.
Maldive Is., i, 23, 204.
Malinda: see *Melinde*.
Mamli: see Murrivemula.
Man who never lied, a, i, 63.
Manār pearl fishery in Ceylon, ii, 88, 91, 93, 94.
Manaris (*Banjārās* ?), an Indian tribe, i, 34 *n.*
Man or *Mand*, a weight: see *Maund*.
Mandāvī river (*Mandoua*), i, 150.
Mandwa (? *Pander*), i, 45.
Mangalia (? Mingrelia), i, 43.
Mangeli or *Mangelin*, a diamond weight, seed of *Adenanthera pavonina*, i, 333; ii, 69–70, 98–9, 101, 333.
Mango fruit (*mengues* or *mangues*), i, 48, 65, 150; ii, 225, 278.
Mango trick, i, 55 *n.*
Mangosteen fruit, ii, 225.
Maniā-kī Sarāī (*Minasqui-sera*), i, 53.
Mansūr (*Mezour*), i, 74.
Mantua wine, ii, 269.
Marble, i, 119 *n.*
Marests, M. des, i, 165, 169–73.
Marguerite I. (in the Antilles), ii, 88–9.
Marriage ceremonies of the Hindus, ii, 197–8.
Marrivēmula (*Mamli*), i, 239.
Marseilles, ii, 106.
Mart-nadi, r. (? Kalīndrī), i, 102.
Martavane (an earthenware vessel) ii, 195.
Marten (*martre*), fur, ii, 209.
Martin, M. St., (F.), i, 191.
Masana: see Mehsānā.
Mascarenhas, Dom Philippe de, i, 161, 164, 165, 173, 182; ii. 127; Governor of Ceylon, i, li.
Massapet (*Masapkipet*), i, 120.
Mastodons, ii, 365 *n.*
Masulipatam (*Maslipatan*), i, 131, 133, 141–2, 206; cottons, ii, 4; to Gandikot, i, 207.
Mātan diamond, the, ii, 361.
Matāram, capital of Java, i, xl, xli–ii.
Mathura or Muttra (*Matura*), i, 85; ii, 175, 186.
Maund, *Mein* (an Indian weight), i, 32, 334; ii, 1, 7, 208.
Mauritius I. (*Maurice*), ii, 112, 236.
Measures and weights in India, i, 7 ff., 332–5.
Mecca, Sharīf (*Cherif*) of, i, 296; a Shaikh (*chek*) of, i, 131.
Mediterranean coral, ii, 105.
Megalithic structures, i, 124 *n.*
Mehsānā (*Masana*), i, 65.
Melinde (Malinda), on east coast of Africa, i, 153, 221; ii, 5, 109, 121.
Melscal: see *Mishkāl*.
Meluari (Shankarpalli), i, 119.
Member, diseased, image of, offered, i, 210; ii, 178.
Menat-kan: see Amānat Khān.
Merchandise yielded by the Mogul's Empire, ii, 1 ff.

Merchants, risks of, i, 31–2; of Tipperah, ii, 214.
Mertā (*Mirda*), i, 71–2.
Mestif (a half-caste), i, 160, 166, 203, 313.
Methold (? Metwold), i, 144 *n.*; ii, 42 *n.*, 56 *n.*, 76 *n.*
Mexico, Gulf of, ii, 88.
Mezour: see Mansūr.
Middelburg, ii, 318–20.
Milmol (Nidumolu), i, 141, 208.
Minasqui sera: see Maniā-kī Sarāī.
Mīngbāshī (*Mimbachi*), i, 100.
Mingrela: see Vengurla.
Mints, the Great Mogul's, i, 8.
Mintmaster, i, 7.
Mīr Jumla (*Mir Gimola, Mirza Mola, Mirgimola, Amir Jemla*, and *Mir Jemla*), conquest of Assam, ii, 217–20; as a man of business, i, 137–8, 233; at Dacca, i, 104; presents great diamond to Shāh Jahān, i, 315, and App. I, vol. ii; his diamond mines, i, 138 *n.*, 230; ii, 67; siege of Gandikota, i, 227–8; dispute with Golkonda, i, 133–4; quits Golkonda, i, 137; life attempted, i, 134; honoured by Shāh Jahān, i, 137; in charge of Sultān Muhammad, i, 287–9; power and influence, i, 285–6, i, 208; -ki-pet (*Mirel-Mola-Kipet*), i, 120–1.
Mirabolan, fruit of *Terminalia chebula*, which see.
Miraculous, distribution of food at Jagannāth, ii, 177; feeding of a multitude, i, 238.
Mīrān Shāh, i, 258.
Mirda: see Merta.
Mīrzā Abdul Hasan (*Cosing*), i, 138.
Mīrzā Arab, i, 324.
Mīrzā Mu'azzam (*Mirza Mouson*), i, 100.
Mīrzā Muhammad (Mīr Ahmad), i, 131 *n.*, 136.
Miscarriages, i, 313.
Mishkāl (a Persian weight), i, 332.
Mocha (*Mocca*), i, 27, 31.
Modrā (*Modra*), i, 71.
Mogor for Mughal, i, 115 *n.*
Mohaniā kī sarāī (*Moniarky-sera*), i, 98.
Mohurs: see Golden rupees.
Moluccas (*Moluques*), i, 152; ii, 12, 14 *n.*
Mom or *Mum* (Brunswick beer), ii, 285.
Money in India, i, 7 ff., 19; spurious, i, 25.
Monghyr (*Monger*), i, 101.
Moniarky-sera: see Mohaniā kī Sarāī.
Monkeys, yielding bezoar, ii, 118–19; combats of, i, 217; veneration for, i, 63–4, 65; worship of, i, 158.
Monomotapa? ii, 158, 160.
Monsoons, i, 4 *n.*
Montani (Prince Virakerala), i, 193.
Montecour: see Munugudu.
Morality, Indian, ii, 196–7.
Morimol (Poraimāmilla), i, 236.
Moscovites, ii, 213.
Mosque, at Ahmadābād, i, 59; at Aurangābād, i, 119; at Benares, i, 97 *n.*; defiled, ii, 240.
Mosul (*Moussul*), i, 75.
Moukaran (? Karanga), in Africa, ii, 126.
Mozambique, Governor of, i, 153; ii, 5, 109, 124.
Mufti (*Moufti*), i, 90 and *n.*
Mughal, the Great, diamond, ii, 75, 97, App. i; elephants, i, 307; festival, i, 301–3; horses, i, 306; jewels, i, 314–19; mints, i, 8; presents to, i, 301–2; throne, i, 80–1, 303–6, 308; weighing of, i, 301. See also under respective subjects.
Mughal Emperors, the, i, 258–9.
Mughals, the, i, 257 ff.
Mughal Sarāī (*Sera Mogoul*), in Punjab, i, 78; (*Magalki-sera*), in Tonk State, i, 47.
Muhammad Amīn, Mīr Jumla's son, i, 133 *n.*, 285 *n.*
Muhammad, Sultān, son of Mīrān

Shāh, i, 258 ; son of Aurangzeb, i, 133, 137, 285–9.
Muhammadan, the, travellers, cited, ii, 82 *n.* ; Muhammadans, i, 10 ; their religion, ii, 137–9.
Mullā (*Mollahs*), i, 91 *n.*
Multān, on the Chenab river, i, 73–4.
Mumtāz Mahāll (Arjumand Begam), i, 90 *n.*
Mungīr ; *v.* Monghyr.
Munugudu (*Montecour*), ii, 73.
Murād Bakhsh (*Morat Bakche*), Prince, i, 52, 262–7.
Muralīdhara (*Morli*), ii, 182, 184 *n.*
Murder at Burhānpur, i, 43–4 ; by a Persian physician, i, 95–6 ; in Mughal's presence, ii, 170–1 *n.* ; murders by Portuguese, i, 152.
Murrhine vases, ii, 160 *n.*
Murshidābād (*Madesou Bazarki*), i, 108.
Muscat or Maskat (*Mascaté*), i, 4, 151 ; ii, 85.
Music in the palace, i, 81.
Mūsi river, at Haidarābād, i, 122 *n.*, 141 *n.*
Musk, ii, 112–15, 201–2 ; deer, ii, 113.
Muslins, i, 46–7 ; ii, 6.
Mussuck (*Mashak*, Hind.), the inflated skin of a goat, i, 60.
Mutilation, punishment by, i, 234.
Muttra : see Mathura.
Myra, in Lycia, Bishop of, i, 167.
Myrrh (*Mirrha-gilet*, and *M.-Bolti*, ? *wilāyatī*), ii, 16–17.

Nabir : see Raver.
Nadiād (*Neriade*), i, 59.
Nādir Shāh, ii, 340, 343–4.
Nadiyā (*Nandi*), i, 108.
Nadour (Nander), i, 119.
Nāga (snake), i, 35 *n.*
Nagarkot (*Naugrocot*), Kangra, ii, 200, 206.
Nagis (for *Najis*), i, 299.
Nagouni (? Logāon), i, 120–1.
Nagulpad (*Naglepar*, *Nazelpar*), i, 141 ; ii, 73.
Naif (Pl. *Naives*) : see *Point-naive*.
Nails, grown long, i, 144 ; ii, 200.
Naktī Rānī, Rājā of Srinagar, i, 277, 289–92.
Nali Kan : see Nihāl Chand.
Nāmpur (*Nimpour*), i, 116.
Nānder (*Nadour*), on Godavari river, i, 119.
Nandi : see Nadiyā.
Nandurbār (*Nasarbar*), i, 41.
Naqqār-, Naubat-khāna, at Delhi, i, 80 *n.*
Nārāyanavana (*Naraveron*), i, 217.
Narbadā river, i, 45 *n.*, 129 *n.*
Narsinghā (*Narsingue*), Vijayanagar, i, xliii–iv ; Rājā, i, 129, 130.
Narwar (*Nader*), i, 50.
Naushahra (*Novéchaar*), i, 76.
Naval engagement, a, i, 249–53.
Navigation in the Indian Seas, i, 4–5.
Navsari (*Renonsari*), ii, 5 *n.*
Nawāb (*Nabab*), a title, Prime Minister, i, 81.
Nawapura ? Nārāyanpura (*Navapoura*), i, 41, 116.
Nazacos I., i, lvi ; ii, 251.
Negombo, in Ceylon, i, liii ; 164–5 *n.*, 173.
Nellore (*Nelour*), i, 213.
Nepāl (*Nupal*), ii, 202, 206.
Neriade : see Nadiād.
Nernūrupād (*Nosdrepar*), i, 213.
Nero (Pulo Neīrā), I., ii, 14.
Nevelki-sera, i, 45.
Nihāl Chand (*Nali Kan*), i, 110.
Nīl (= 100,000 *padams*, *q.v.*), i, 214.
Nilimor (Pāmarru ?), i, 141.
Nilmol : see Milmol.
Nimlabāgh (*Niméla*), i, 76.
Nimpour : see Nāmpur.
Nishapur (*Nichabourg*), turquoise mines, ii, 81.
Noākhālī, Portuguese at, i, 102.
Norenuaé, a petty province of Arabia, ii, 88.
Nosdrepar : see Nernūrupād.
Nova-sera (Nau Sarāī), i, 45.
Novéchaar : see Naushahra.

Noviciate, the Jesuit, at Goa, i, 159.
Nuali : see Lohwān.
Nūrjahān, marriage of, i, 89 *n*.
Nutmeg, ii, 12–13, 14.

Obrechit, Overschie, the *Sieur* Nicolaas, ii, 320–1.
Officers of the Company, frauds by the, ii, 34 ff., 37.
Ogouli : see Hugli.
Omberat (Umapurānā), i, 120.
Omrahs, Omerahs, properly *Umara*, i, 79, 87, 302–3, 308 ; ii, 171.
Once, Fr., ounce, i, 331.
Onquenas, i, 45.
Opals in Hungary, ii, 81.
Opium, ii, 19.
Or, Persian (?), = 5 'abbāsīs, i, 330.
Orhni (*ormis, ornis*), a woman's mantle, i, 43 ; ii, 4, 35.
Orloff diamond, the, ii, 338, 340.
Ormus : see Hormuz.
Ostriches, ii, 302, 306, 307.
Oudecot : see Uttukkōttai.
Oudecour : see Utukūr.
Oudemeda (Voutimitta), i, 225.
Oupelote (Costus), root, ii, 17.

Pack cattle, i, 32–3.
Padam (*Padan*) = 100,000 *crores* or *karors, q.v.*, i, 24.
Pagla river (*Pagalu*), i, 104.
Pagoda (an Indian coin), i, 130, 329, 330 ; ii, 70–1, 101.
Pagoda at Benares, ii, 179–85 ; at Bezwada, i, 209 f. ; (mosque) at Bhāgnagar, i, 124, 132 ; courtesans', i, 58 ; girls', ii, 185–6 ; at Jagannāth, ii, 175 f. ; at Kākānī, i, 212 ; at Muttra, ii, 186 f. ; in Siam, ii, 227–9 ; pagodas, of the idolaters, the principal, ii, 175 ff.
Pain (loaf of gold), i, 331 ; ii, 111, 238. Cf. also Foster's *Eng. Factories in India, 1634–6*, p. 33 ; and *Travels of Peter Mundy* (Hakluyt Soc.), iii, pt. i, p. 311.
Paisa (*pecha*) = 0·54*d*., i, 22–4, 29, 329.
Palace, at Agra, i, 86–9 ; at Bhāgnagar, i, 123–4 ; at Delhi, i, 79–84.
Palam, i, 120 ; see Polliam.
Pālanpur (*Balambour*), i, 69.
Palāsnī (*Palavaseny*), i, 71–2.
Palão or *pulão*, a dish of rice, meat and spices, &c., i, 125, 187, 218, 246 ; ii, 11.
Pālkī Sarāī (*Paulki-sera*), i, 47.
Pallankeen, i, 37, 142, 310, 312.
Palliport (*Belli-porto*), i, liv.
Palm wine : see *Tāri* and *Suri*.
Palwal (*Peluel-ki-sera*), i, 85.
Pander : see Mandwa.
Pangal (*Pengeul*), i, 141.
Panjāb (*Penjab*), i, 77.
Panna diamond mines, ii, 351.
Pansār (*Panser*), i, 65.
Pantangi (*Patengy*), i, 140–1.
Paposhes (*papouches*), Pers. pāposh, 'foot-garment', slippers, i, 117.
Paraida ? (*Peridera*), i, 240.
Pardao (Portuguese pardo), an Indian coin, worth 2*s*. to 2*s*. 6*d*., i, 155, 329–30 ; ii, 109.
Paris, Tavernier's return to, in 1649, ii, 326.
Parquel (Burgal), ii, 72–3.
Parsimony of the shroffs, i, 29–30.
Parthānī (*Bargan*), i, 120.
Passports, i, 319–20.
Patamata (*Patemet*), i, 208.
Patane : see Patnā.
Pate (*Bata*), ii, 128.
Patecas (*pateches*), water melons, ii, 278.
Patengy : see Pantangi.
Paterki-sera, i, 52–3.
Pathāns (*Patane*), i, 279.
Patnā, in Bengal, i, 99–101 ; ii, 172–3, 192, 205, 214 ; (*Patane*), in the Deccan, i, 116.
Patoles (*pattuda*), silken fabrics, ii, 3 *n*.
Pathri (*Patris*), i, 120.
Patonta (Patantā), i, 119–20.
Patronage, Dutch, in appointments, ii, 40 ; of offices in Goa, i, 153, 155.
Paulists, the, at Goa, i, 159.
Paulki-sera : see Pālkī Sarāī.

Pauzecour (Pānchgaur or Panchama), ii, 145 *n.*

Pay-bills at Batavia, ii, 291 ff.

Pea-fowl, i, 57–8.

Peacock throne, i, 303–5.

Pearl, fisheries, ii, 84 ff.; a matchless, ii, 86–7; the Mughal's, ii, 103; a perfect, ii, 103–4; King of Persia's, ii, 103; *rati*, value of, i, 333; ii, 348; sold to Shāista Khān, i, 17, 112–13; ii, 103; Mosque, i, 86 *n.*

Pearls, figures of, ii, 103; large, i, 112, 229; in Mughal's treasury, i, 316–17; offered to King of Golkonda, i, 242–4; origin of, ii, 91–2; season for fishing, ii, 92–6; where obtained, ii, 84 ff.

Peasants, oppression of the, i, 311–12.

Pegu, ii, 18; deficient in the arts, ii, 19; King of, ii, 147; precious stones of, ii, 77.

Peluel-kī-sera: see Palwal.

Penances, ii, 199–200; Aurangzeb's, i, 296, 309; by widows, ii, 168.

Pengeul: see Pangal.

Penguins, i, 174 *n.*; ii, 302 *n.*, 307.

Penner river, in Madras, i, 227 *n.*, 228 *n.*, 230 *n.*

Peon (*pion*), a foot-soldier, i, 69–70.

Pepper, two kinds, ii, 11–12; small, ii, 248–9.

Pepper-House, the, at Cochin, i, 190.

Persia, Aurangzeb's embassy to, i, 297–9; the Shah of, *ib.*; i, 6.

Persian, adventurers in India, i, 139; ii, 138–9; coins, i, 330–1; greyhounds, ii, 309; jewellers, at Court, i, 110.

Peshāwar (*Chaour*), i, 76.

P'hattalang (*Bordelon*), ii, 128.

Philip IV, K. of Spain, ii, 112.

Philippine Is., ii, 82–3.

Physicians, Persian, i, 95–6; Indian, i, 240, 242.

Piastre, or Seville piece of eight = 4*s.* 6*d.*, i, 22, 144, 328.

Pigeons (*Carpophaga*), fruit-eating, ii, 12.

Pigs, wild, on St. Helena, ii, 309; pigs' blood used to defile a mosque, ii, 240.

Pilgrimages of the idolaters, i, 237–8; ii, 190–2, 281.

Pillāu: see Palāo.

Pimpalner (*Pipelnar*), i, 116.

Piombi sera, i, 45.

Pion: see Peon.

Pipal tree (*Ficus religiosa*, Linn.), ii, 155 *n.*

Pīpār (*Pipars*), i, 71–2.

Pipri (*Pipeli* and ? *Pipelgan*), i, 119, 120.

Pirates: see *Malabaris.*

Pistoles, i, 19, 328.

Pite or Pitre, a German, i, 214.

Place Royale, in Paris, i, 88, 140.

Plantain fruit: see Adam's fig.

Pointe de Galle, i, 206; ii, 245–6, 284.

Pointe naïve (a diamond crystal), ii, 57, 67.

Poison, Portuguese use of, i, 182; in Macassar, ii, 233; poisonous reptiles in Siam, ii, 225.

Police, of Golkonda, i, 125; in Shāh Jahān's time, i, 260.

Polish Princes, prisoners in Turkey, i, lvii, 169.

Polleron (Pulo Run or Rung), I., ii, 14.

Polliam (*Palam* ?), i, 121 *n.*

Pompon-sou: see Pūnpūn.

Pongangel (? Sikrīgali), i, 102.

Ponocour (Vellutar ?), ii, 73.

Pont Neuf, at Paris, i, 123.

Ponter: see Pūdēru.

Pope, the, i, 183.

Poraimāmilla ? (*Morimol*), i, 236.

Porakād (*Porca*), i, lv. 192, 195.

Porcupine stone, the, ii, 119.

Portuguese, bandits, i, 102, 105; character of, i, 151–2; at Goa, wealth of, i, 155–6; money, i, 328; possess best port in India, i, 150; priest, a, ii, 310; slavers, ii, 311.

Postal runners, i, 233.

Potre, M., (D.), ii, 265.

Pouleay (Pulo Ai or Wai), I., ii, 14.
Pratt (Prat), Mr., at Dacca, i, 107.
Precious stones, Begam Sāhib's, i, 275; of Ceylon, ii, 79, 366; Shāh Jahān's, i, 275, 295.
Presents made by Tavernier, i, 113–14.
Prester John (*Preste Jan*), ii, 125.
Priapender, the Emperor, ii, 147.
Prices, of diamonds, ii, 73–6; of rubies, ii, 78.
Prince's Island, ii, 300.
Princesses, the Imperial, i, 312–13.
Private trade of the Dutch, ii, 319 ff.
Processions of gods, i, 237; ii, 109.
Ptolemy, quoted, ii, 355.
Pūdēru (*Ponter*), i, 213.
Pulicat (*Palicat*), i, xlvi; 213–14.
Pulo (island) Ai or Wai (*Pouleay*) ii, 14; Neīrā (*Nero*), *ibid.*; Run (*Polleron*), *ibid.*
Pūnpūn (*Pompon sou*) river, i, 101 *n.*
Pythons, ii, 121.

Qabā-i-Shāhī (royal robe), i, 132.
Qāzī-hāt (*Kasiata*), t., i, 104.
Quarinadi, Kunwārī nadī, i, 53.
Quariqui-sera, Kunwārī-kī Sarāī, i, 52.
Queen, of Bījāpur, i, 148, 171; of Borneo, ii, 68; of Golkonda's house, i, 140; of Achīn, ii, 249.
Qutb Shāh Muhammad Kuli, i, 122 *n.*

Rachepot, a French soldier, i, 95, 194–203.
Ragiapeta (? Anantarājupeta), i, 224.
Rāībāgh (*Rabaque*), i, 147.
Raisin, M., (F.), ii, 239.
Rājāpur (*Rejapour*), in the Ratnāgirī District, i, 142, 146 *n.*, 147; ii, 11.
Rājmahāl (*Ragemehale*), i, 102.
Rājputs (*Ragipous*), i, 50; ii, 196.
Rakshasagudda (*Rasigar*), i, 147.
Rāmā, ii, 150–2.
Rāma Rāja, i, xliii.
Rāmāyana, ii, 150–3.
Ram-kam, ii, 184.
Ram-Marion, ii, 185.
Rammalakota or Ramulkota (*Raolconda*), diamond mine, ii, 41, 43, 69, 70, 73.
Ranchhōrdās (*Richourdas*), ii, 185, 189 *n.*
Raout (Arāvad), ii, 7; i, lv.
Ratī, an Indian weight (Tavernier's = 2·66 grs. troy), i, 332–3; ii, 69, 78, 336–7. See Pearl.
Raushanārā Begum, i, 261, 299–300.
Rāvana, ii, 151–3.
Raver (*Nabir*), i, 41–2.
Rawāt (*Roupaté*), i, 76–7.
Reale or *real*, a Spanish coin, worth 4*s.* to 4*s.* 10*d.*, i, 19–21, 328; of Batavia, ii, 283.
Rebellion of Shāh Jahān's sons, i, 262 ff.
Recollects (an order of monks), i, lvii, 159.
Recüeil of Tavernier, cited, ii, 26, 36, 39.
Red coral, ii, 104–7.
Reḍḍypullay (? *Regivali*), i, 120: see Yellaredipētta.
Refiners of gold and silver, ii, 33.
Regivali, i, 120.
Réglisse (liquorice), ii, 17.
Rekenings (pay bills), ii, 291.
Religion, of the idolaters of India, ii, 141 ff.; of the Muhammadans of India, ii, 137–9.
Renal, the *Sieur* C., (D.), ii, 266.
Renaud (Fr.), the two brothers, ii, 110, 269–70, 272–3.
Renonsari (Navasārī), ii, 5.
Revenue of Bengal, i, 93.
Rhinoceros, a tame, i, 93; a, hunt at Achīn, ii, 250.
Rhubarb, ii, 80, 209.
Rice, scented, i, 41, 116.
Rinkula, i, 116.
Rio de la Hacha, in Columbia, ii, 89.
Rivers in Siam, ii, 226.
Rixdollars (*Richedales*), worth about 4*s.* 7*d.*; i, 19, 328.
Roboli (a French merchant), i, 181.

Rock crystal, vessels of, i, 309.
Rockets, i, 311 ; ii, 218.
Rohtāsgarh (*Rodas*), fort of, i, 99 ; ii, 64–5.
Ronova river, i, 102.
Rose, M. Jean de, (F.), i, 165–6.
Rose noble (a coin worth 6*s*. 8*d*.), i, 11 ; diamond, ii, 74.
Roseguin (Rosingen), I., ii, 14.
Rotterdam, ii, 319.
Roupaté : see Rawāt.
Roux, Rev. Father, i, 76.
Rubellite (a mineral), ii, 363, 365.
Rubies, in Ceylon and Cambodia, ii, 79–80 ; in Europe, ii, 80 ; finest seen by Tavernier, ii, 100–2 ; of King of France, ii, 102 ; the Mughal's, i, 318 ; value of, i, 304 *n*. ; ii, 368 ; weights of, ii, 348.
Ruby, the Banian's, ii, 102 ; King of Bījāpur's, ii, 101 ; mines of Burma, ii, 77–9, 361–6 ; Ja'far Khān's false, ii, 100–1.
Rūp Singh (*Roup*), Rājā, of Lahore, i, 276, 289.
Rupee (= 2*s*. 3*d*.), i, 22, 329–30 ; ii, 71.
Russian embassy to China, ii, 212 ; leather, i, 205 ; woman bearing child in old age, ii, 213.

Sa'adu-llā kī Sarāī (*Saudoul serail*), i, 96.
Saba, in Arabia, ii, 5.
Sābarmatī river, i, 59.
Sabia, basin of upper Sabi, in Africa, ii, 127.
Saffron, ii, 16.
Saidupur : see *Setapore*.
Saif Khān (*Seif Kan*), i, 282–3.
Saingour : see Sengar.
St. Amant, M., (F.), i, 161, 164, 165, 166, 167, 175 ; ii, 28.
St. André (a church at Cochin), i, 188.
St. George, fort at Madras, i, 214–16.
St. Helena, annexed by English, i, lii ; ii, 27 ; description of, ii, 308 ff.
St. Jean (a church at Cochin), i, 188, 190, 194 ; Point (*Sajān*, &c.), i, 5.
St. John, Christians of, i, 200–1.
St. Laurens (in Madagascar), ii, 112.
St. Martin, (F.), i, 191.
St. Paul (a church at Cochin), i, 194 ; St. Paul's College at Goa, i, 159.
St. Pierre, coral at, ii, 104.
St. Thomas (a church at Cochin), i, 190 ; the apostle, i, 215.
St. Thomé (near Madras), i, 177, 180, 181–2, 183, 215 ; ii, 239.
St. Vincent, coral at, ii, 105 *n*.
Sakorā (*Secoura*), i, 116.
Sālagrām, the, ii, 149 *n*.
Sal ammoniac, ii, 16.
Salaries of English officials, ii, 37 *n*.
Sale of jewels to Shāista Khān, i, 15 ff., 26 ff., 106, 246.
Salīm Khān or Islām Shāh, Nawāb, tomb of, at Sāsarām, i, 98–9.
Salli, Sala (*Salé*), in East Africa, i, 12.
Salsette, near Goa, i, 158 ; ii, 120.
Salt in Assam, ii, 221–2.
Saltpetre at Chaprā, i, 100.
Sambalpur District, diamond mines, ii, 351 : see Soulmelpour.
Samorin : see Zamorin.
Samūgarh (*Samonguir*), near Agra, i, 272 *n*.
Sanctissima Casa, la, i, 186.
San Dominique (in the Antilles), ii, 88.
Sandstones at Agra, ii, 187.
San Jago, coral, ii, 105 *n*.
Sangore : see Senggora.
Sank (*Sanike*) river, in Gwalior, i, 52.
San-kaira, i, 46.
Sānkh river, in Bengal, ii, 66 *n*., 357–8.
Sānklī (*Senquelis*), i, 41–2.
Sanqual (Sanklā), i, 93.
Sanselc : see Sipri.
Sāntāpur (*Satapour*), i, 119–20.
Santesela (Sancherla), i, 236.
Santis, Dominíco de (Venetian), ii, 119.

Saode-sou, river, i, 98.
Sapphire washings of Ceylon, ii, 79, 366.
Sarāī Sīrsī (*Satragy-sera* ?), i, 98; Murlīdās, i, 93; Shāhzāda (*Serrail Chageada*), i, 94.
Sarawaram (*Sarvaron*), ii, 73.
Sardinia coral fisheries, ii, 104.
Sargossa weed (*Fucus natans*), ii, 315 *n*.
Sārkhej (*Suarkej*), i, 59; (*Sarquesse*), i, 56; ii, 7.
Sarquet (Sarkār ?), i, 25.
Sarūrnagar (*Tenara*), i, 141.
Sarvēpale ? (*Serepelé*), i, 213.
Sāsarām (*Saseron*), i, 98–9; ii, 64.
Satanaga (Satulanagar), i, 119.
Satapour (Sāntāpur), i, 119.
Satins, ii, 3.
Satragy-sera (? Sarāī Sīrsī), i, 98.
Satulanagar (*Satanagar*), i, 120.
Saudoul Serail, i, 96.
Savagery, a relapse into, ii, 307.
Scimdi: see Sind.
Scotch pearls, ii, 89–90.
Secoura: see Sakorā.
Secret, purchase, a, ii, 50–1; signs, sales by, ii, 53; trade by officials, ii, 38.
Sects, Muhammadan, ii, 137–8.
Sere, ser (a weight), i, 334; ii, 1, 208.
Semencine (worm powder), ii, 203, 209.
Sena river (in Africa), ii, 126, 127.
Senepgond (Sunnapagunta), i, 213.
Sengar river (*Saingour*), i, 93.
Senggora, Singora (*Sangore*) tin, ii, 128.
Sequin (a Venetian coin), i, 328.
Sera-balour: see Phillaur.
Sera-Chabas: see Shāhābād.
Sera-Crindal: see Karnāl.
Sera-dakan (? Dehkhān); an old sarāī at Jullundur, i, liv, 77.
Sera-dourai: see Daurāhī (Dorāhā).
Sera-Mogoul: see Mughal Sarāī.
Serail Morlides (Sarāī Murlidās), i, 93; *Atakan* (Hatgāon), i, 94.
Seram (Ceram), I., ii, 14.
Seronge: see Sironj.
Serpent worship, i, 35; ii, 194.
Serravaron (Cholavaram), i, 216.
Seruer, i, 119.
Setapour (Saidupur), ii, 72–3.
Setlana: see Sītalwānā.
Shāhābād (*Sera Chabas*, ? Shāhbāzpur), i, 78.
Shah 'Abbās II, i, 279.
Shāh-Bandar (*Cha-Bander*), i, 6, 10.
Shāhbāz Khān (*Chabas Kan*), i, 262, 266.
Shāh Dāniyāl, i, 259.
Shāhdaurā (*Chadolki-sera*), i, 47.
Shāhī (*Chaez*), a Persian coin worth 4*d*. to 4½*d*., i, 20, 330.
Shāhjahān (*Cha Gehan*), bribery of, i, 15; his children, i, 261; death of, i, 274; descent of, i, 259; his jewels, i, 295, 299; life endangered, i, 220; his prison, i, 274; his rebellion, i, 269; a refugee at Golkonda, i, 136; seizes the throne, i, 271; his sickness, i, 260–1; his tomb, i, 91; his treasure, i, 265.
Shāh Jahāngīr, i, 259, 267–9, 271.
Shāh Jahānī (*Cha Jenni*), rupees, i, 25.
Shāhjī (a Marātha chief), i, 147 *n*.
Shāh of Persia, the, i, 297–9.
Shāh Nawāz Khān, father-in-law of Aurangzeb, i, 279.
Shāh Safī II of Persia, i, 271; ii, 6.
Shahr-i-safā (*Charisafar*), i, 74.
Shāhzādā Sarāī (*Serrail Chageada*), i, 94.
Shaikh-kī-Sarāī (*Cheki-sera*), i, 85.
Shaikh Mīrzā, Umr, i, 258.
Shaikh of Mecca, a, i, 131.
Shaikhpurā (*Chekaipour*), i, 46.
Shāista Khān (*Cha Est Kan*), i, 15–18, 26–8, 105–7, 113, 245–7, 266; his wife, 313; correspondence with, i, 319 ff., 319–26; ii, 89.
Shāmiyānā (*simiane*), an awning, i, lviii; 204.
Shankarpalli, i, 119.
Sharkej (*Sarquesse*), i, 56, 59; ii, 7.
Shellac, ii, 18–19; in Assam, ii, 221.

Shell bracelets, ii, 214, 223.
Sher Shāh, the Afghān, tomb of, i, 98 *n.*
Shi'ās (*Chias*), ii, 137–8.
Shigānū (*Chakenicouze*), i, 74.
Shipwreck, escape from, ii, 242–5.
Shīrāz, wine of, i, 229.
Shoe question, the, i, 157 *n.*
Sholāpur ? (*Choupart*), i, 26, 326 : see Chākan.
Shroff (*cheraf*), a broker, i, 24, 28, 29; ii, 71, 144, 159.
Shupanga (*Chepongoura*), ii, 124, 127.
Shushbur, i, 114.
Siam, ii, 79 *n.*, 224–33, 269; King of, ii, 147.
Sidhpur (*Chitpour*), i, 65–6.
Sight, of Father Ephraim, improved by imprisonment, i, 185.
Sīhor (*Signor*), i, 46.
Sikandrā (*Sekandera*), i, 91 *n.*, 93.
Sikrīgalī ? (*Pongangel*), i, 102.
Silent trade, ii, 53.
Silk, in Assam, ii, 220–1, 222; Persian, ii, 321; silks, ii, 2, 3; frauds in, ii, 21–2.
Silver, duty on, i, 7–8; ii, 21; mines in Asia, ii, 128; Assam, ii, 220; Bhutan, ii, 212; Japan, ii, 128; standards of, i, 28–9; coin in Assam, ii, 221.
Simiane, a kind of sail, i, 204.
Simla diamonds, ii, 352.
Sind, Sindi (*Scimdi*), i, 9, 14, 249, 253.
Singalese (*Chinglas*), i, 188.
Singatoria ? (*San-kaira*), i, 46.
Singhānā copper mines, i, 23 *n.*
Singora (*Sangore*), ii, 128.
Sinkheda (*Senquera*), i, 41.
Sipihr Shikoh, i, 280, 282, 283.
Sipri (*Sansele*), i, 49.
Sirhind (*Serinde*), i, 77–8.
Siriam (*Siren*), ii, 77.
Sironj (*Seronge*), i, 30, 46, 53,
Sītā, the goddess, ii, 150–2.
Sītalwānā (*Setlana*), i, 71–2.
Sitanaga, i, 119.
Sivajī, Rājā, i, 107, 118, 147.
Skirrets (Fr. cherüy), at Cape of Good Hope, ii, 306
Skulls, towers of, i, 104.
Snake, -bite, i, 49; with two heads, ii, 225; -stone, ii, 120–1; worship, i, 35; ii, 194.
Sofāla (Africa), ii, 124, 126.
Sol (Fr. coin = ·99*d.*), i, 29 *n.*, 328.
Soldiers, Dutch, desert, i, 191; ii, 318; at Golkonda, i, 127; Indian, i, 311.
Sonde, la : see Sunda.
Son-sou, river Son, i, 99 *n.*
Sorrel at St. Helena, ii, 309.
Soulmelpour (for Sou-) (Sambalpur), a diamond mine, i, 99; ii, 62, 65, 66, 351, 355.
Soutiqui : see Sūtī.
Spanish money, i, 328; wine, i, 229.
Sperm whale, ii, 109 *n.*
Spices, ii, 10 ff.
Spinel rubies, ii, 77, 123 *n.*, 363.
Spirits, palm, ii, 194–5.
Spurious coins, i, 25; ii, 284.
Srīnagar, in Garhwāl, i, 277.
Stables, the Imperial, i, 84.
Steel mines in Assam, ii, 220, 222.
Steur : see Cheteur.
Story, a strange, of a child, i, 60–2.
Su (*sou*), 'river', i, lvii.
Sudras, ii, 144 *n.*
Sufra, a table-cloth (*sofra*), i, 218; ii, 4.
Sugar-candy, ii, 17; becoming poison, ii, 19.
Sukadana or Soekadana, in Borneo, ii, 360.
Sulaimān Shikoh, Sultān, i, 264, 276–7, 289, 290–2.
Sultān Parwez, third son of Jahāngīr, i, 259.
Sultān Salīm, afterwards Jahāngīr, i, 259.
Sultān Shujá', i, 134–5, 261, 264; 285–6; in Arakān, i, 292–4.
Sumatra, west coast of, ii, 289.
Sumbaco, i, li.
Sumpitan (*sarbatane*), a blow tube, ii, 234.
Sunda (*Sonde*), Strait, i, xlii, 154; Archipelago, ii, 7.
Sunnapagunta : see *Senepgond.*
Sunnīs (*Sounnis*), ii, 137–8.

Surat (*Surate*), i, 3, 5; to Agra, i, 40, 72; to Broach, i, 54; to Goa, i, 142 ff.; to Golkonda, i, 115, 119, 120, 121; to Hormuz, i, 4; captured by Murād, i, 262–4; Tavernier's return to, i, 247; English captives at, i, xliv; Governor's assassination at, i, lii, 196.
Suri (palm wine), i, 243: see *Tārī*.
Sūti (*Soutiqui*), i, 103.
Suttee, a, i, 175–6; ii, 162–8.
Suwālī (*Souali*), a port in Gujarāt, i, 5; ii, 29, 30, 280.

Tabarka (*Tabarque*), ii, 104.
Tabrīz, ii, 203, 213.
Taè river, i, 102.
Taffetas, ii, 3.
Tāj-makān (*tasimacan*), -mahall, -muqām, i, 90–1.
Taka: see Dakka.
Tālikota, battle of, i, xliii.
Tamerlane (*Temur-leng*), i, 129, 258.
Tanahkeke (or Island of Sorcerers), off Celebes, ii, 237.
Tankai (*Tenque*), i, 120.
Tapis (Fr.), carpets and table covers, ii, 22. Miss L. M. Anstey feels convinced that 'these were not carpets but silk and cotton piece-goods. The term appears frequently in the seventeenth century at the Company's sales, and the goods were always spoken of as containing pieces, whereas carpets were always sold separately'.
Taptī river, i, 41, 43.
Tarāī, the, ii, 205.
Tarāwarī (*Dirauril*), i, 77.
Tārī (toddy), the sap of *Phoenix sylvestris*, i, 128; ii, 242: see *Suri*.
Tartary, i, 13, 75.
Tartīpur (*Toutipour*), i, 103.
Tasimacan (Tājmakān), i, 90.
Tasman, Abel, a Dutch commander, ii, 14.
Tasū (*tassot*), an Indian inch, i, 335; ii, 1.
Tāt or *tānt* (*toti*), fibre of *Corchorus capsularis*, i, 149.
Tatta (*Tata*), in Sind, i, 9, 14; ii, 191.
Tattooing, among Banjārās, i, 35; in Siam, ii, 232.
Taurus, Mount, i, 3.
Tavernier, Daniel, ii, 234, 277–8, 290–1.
Tavernier, Life of J.-B., i, xi–xxxvii; his claim against the Dutch, ii, 323 ff.; visits Bantam, ii, 268 ff.; arrives at Batavia, ii, 250 ff.; leaves Batavia, ii, 298; leaves Ceylon, ii, 250; leaves Dacca, i, 107; leaves Gandikota, i, 234–5; visits Goa, i, 145–6; visits Golkonda in 1652, i, 240–4; his honesty, ii, 52; his journeys by land to the east, ii, 325; his ignorance of Eastern languages, ii, 50 *n.*; his letters to and from Shāista Khān, i, 319 ff.; voyage to Hormuz, i, 247 ff.; life threatened, ii, 131; &c.
Temple explored by Tavernier, i, 211.
Tenara or *Atenara* (Surūrnagar), i, 139–40, 240.
Tenasserim (*Denouserin*), ii, 224.
Terate (a fishing boat), ii, 85.
Terminalia chebula (*mirabolans*), i, 59.
Thālner (*Tallener*), i, 41.
Thomas, Father, in Siam, ii 232.
Thrones of the Mughal, i, 80–1, 303–6, 308.
Thunderbolts, i, 205; -stones, ii, 66.
Tibet gold, &c., ii, 122.
Tin mines in Siam, ii, 227; in the Malay Peninsula, ii, 128; trade, English, injury to, ii, 128.
Tipperah, the Kingdom of, ii, 214–16.
Tiquery (? Tumrī), i, 45.
Tirupati (*Tripeti*), pagoda, ii, 175, 189.
Tobacco, ii, 19–20.
Tokens, the Mughal's, i. 259.

Tola (an Indian weight), i, 12, 333-4.
Tomān (Persian money of account = £3 : 9*s*.), i, 20, 172, 331 ; ii, 130.
Tomb, of Akbar, i, 91 ; of Aurangzeb's concubine at Aurangābād, i, 118 ; of Jahāngir, i, 91.
Tombs, at Agra, i, 89 ; Tāj-mahall, i, 90 ; of Golkonda Kings, i, 125.
Tongue, cleansing the, i, 75-6.
Tonne (of gold), i, 331 ; ii, 320.
Toolmeden, i, 45.
Topaz, the Mughal's, i, 318 ; ii, 100, 348.
Tortoiseshell bracelets, ii, 214, 223.
Touan (Taiwan), i, liv.
Touchstones, i, 29.
Toulapéca (Tulpurī), i, 76-7.
Toutipour (Tartipur), i, 103.
Transmigration of souls, ii, 158-61.
Travelling in India, i, 32-9.
Treasure, buried, ii, 159, 219.
Trepani (*Trapano*), ii, 104.
Trichinopoli, i, 198 *n*.
Trie : see Antrī.
Tripatty : see Tirupati.
Tripurāntakham (*Tripanté*) pagoda, i, 239.
Tuban (*Touan*), ? in Java, i, 191 ; see *Touan*.
Tulpuri (*Toulapeca*), i, 94.
Tungabhadra river, ii, 73 *n*.
Tun of gold : see *Tonne*.
Turquoise, Persian, ii, 81.
Tuscany diamond, ii, 76, 98, 346 f.
Tuticorin, ii, 11.

Umapurānā (*Omberat*), i, 120.
Umarā : see *Omrahs*.
'Umr Shaikh Mīrzā, i, 258.
Usbeg or Usbek Tartars, i, 75, 84, 296.
Utangan river, i, 53 *n*.
Ūttukkōttai (*Oudecot*), i, 216.
Ūtukūr (*Oudecour*), i, 224.
Uyyuru (*Vouchir*, *Wouhir*), i, 141, 208.

Vaipur (Beypur, Belli-porto), i, 187.
Vāl (an Indian weight), i, 21, 333.
Vanderlin or Vanderling, General, (D.), Cornelius van der Lyn, i, xlvii ; ii, 251, 262, 323.
Vandime, General, (D.), ii, 68, 254, 268, 307 ; Antoni van Diemen, i, xlvii.
Van Goens, Rijklof, i, xlviii.
Van Rez (Dutch soldier), i, 189.
Van Wück, the *Sieur* H., (D.), ii, 129-33 ; i, lii.
Velant, the *Sieur*, (D.), i, 87.
Vellore (*Velou*), Rājā of, i, 130 ; ii, 170.
Vellutar, on the Kistnā, ii, 73 *n*.
Vemulakota (*Emelipata*), i, 236.
Vengurla (*Mingrela*), i, 142, 148-9, 161, 168, 175.
Vessels, Indian, i, 5 ; Dutch, of war, i, 249.
Vettapour : see Fatehpur Sīkrī.
Vez Cábouli (*Aconite* ?), ii, 17.
Vice Admiral (second ship of fleet), ii, 296.
Viceroyalty of Goa, i, 153.
Vijayanagara (*Narsingue*), i, xliii-iv, 129.
Virakerala, King of Cochin, i, 193.
Vīrgāon (*Birgam*), i, 120.
Visapour : see Bījāpur.
Volcano in Banda, ii, 14.
Vontimitta (*Outemeda*), i, 225.
Voubebaran, ii, 124.
Vouchir : see Uyyuru.
Vyepu (*Belle Épine*), i, 188, 191.

Wachttendonk, the *Sieur* Arnoul van, (D.), i, 107-8 ; ii, 33.
Waggons, i, 32, 35.
Waikenton, ii, 33 : see Wachttendonk.
Wairāgarh (*Beiragurh*), ii, 351, 358.
Wajrā Karūr (*Currure*) diamond mine, ii, 42 *n*., 57 *n*., 335, 349.
Waklā (*Baquela*), i, 116.
Wars, of Golkonda, i, 129 f. ; Macassar, ii, 235.
Water, fresh, from under the sea, i, 214 ; ii, 84 ; of the Ganges, i, 94-5 ; ii, 179-80, 198.
Wax, candles, ii, 316-17 ; tapers made from cinnamon, ii, 15.
Wazīrābād (*Zerabad*), i, 76-7

Weighing of the Emperor, i, 301–2.
Weights, of diamonds, &c., ii, 69, 347–8 ; in India, i, 12 f., 332–4.
West Indies, ii, 82–3.
White, Cafre, ii, 306 ; elephant, ii, 228.
Whiteness, Orientals' preference for, ii, 91.
Widow burning, ii, 162–8.
Wine, at Lahore, i, 77 ; from Persia, i, 229.
'Winter' (*hiver*) in India, i, 6.
Woman, a courageous, ii, 172 ; an aged, becomes a mother, ii, 213.
Women, of Goa, i, 151 ; hairless, i, 77 ; a pagoda for, ii, 185–6 ; porters in the Himalayas, ii, 206–7 ; in Siam, ii, 230.
Woodecotah, Ūttukkōttai (*Oudecot*), i, 216.
Worm powder : see *Semencine*.
Wuddagaon (*Bargan*), i, 120–1.
Wungaon (*Bergant*), i, 31 *n*., 69 *n*. : but see Bāglānā.
Wuntimitta, Vontimitta (*Outemeda*) pagoda, i, 225.

Yakedil-sera (? Jagdīs kī Sarāī), i, 96.
Yams (?) at the Cape of Good Hope, ii, 306.
Yawning, ii, 196.
Yellaredipetta (*Indelvai* or *Regivali*), i, 120.
Yellow amber, ii, 108.
Yellow, the Austrian, diamond, ii, 346–8.
Yuthia, ancient capital of Siam, ii, 226 *n*.

Zamorin (*Samarin*), the, i, 189, 192.
Zangira : see Janjirā.
Zealand, ii, 317.
Zebra, skin of a, ii, 305 *n*.
Zeb-un-Nissa, i, 110 *n*.
Zelaté : see Kalat-i-Ghilzāī.
Zénon, Father, i, 168, 178–81, 202, 215.
Zerabad : see Wazīrābād, i, 76–7.

THE END

57